DATE DUE			
16 SEP. 1994	9 SEP 1995	OCT 0 8 2013	
04 OCT. 1994	SEP 2 3 1995		
27 OCT. 1994	JAN 0 3 1996		
19 NOV. 1994	MAY 2 4 1996		
29 NOV. 1994	AG 26	OCT 2 5 2013	
15 DEC.	JUL 1 2 2005		
18 JAN 1995	JUL 2 3 2008		
28 JAN 1995	AUG 2 5 2010		
28 MARS 1995	MAY 2 3 2011		
18 AVR 1995	DEC 0 4 2014		
29 AVRIL 1995	JUN 2 3 2016		
SEP 0 8 1995			

B. Frank   *50/26*

HASKELL FREE LIBRARY

Derby Line, Vt.   Rock Island, P.Q.

Any resident of Derby Line, Rock Island or Stanstead may take out books, free of charge, for 14 days. A fine of 2c per day will be charged on late books. Charges will also be made for damaged or lost volumes.

The librarian shall deliver no books to persons delinquent in the above regulations.

GAYLORD M2

A Passage to Egypt

BOOKS BY KATHERINE FRANK

A Voyager Out: The Life of Mary Kingsley

A Chainless Soul: A Life of Emily Brontë

A Passage to Egypt: The Life of Lucie Duff Gordon

KATHERINE FRANK

A PASSAGE
TO EGYPT

The Life of
Lucie Duff Gordon

HOUGHTON MIFFLIN COMPANY
BOSTON   NEW YORK   1994

50126

For information about permission to reproduce selections from
this book, write to Permissions, Houghton Mifflin Company,
215 Park Avenue South, New York, New York 10003.

Library of Congress Cataloging-in-Publication Data
Frank, Katherine.
A passage to Egypt : the life of Lucie Duff Gordon / Katherine Frank.
p.   cm.
Originally published: London : Hamish Hamilton, 1994.
Includes bibliographical references (p.   ) and index.
ISBN 0-395-54688-5
1. Duff Gordon, Lucie, Lady, 1821–1869. 2. Women — England —
Biography. 3. Women — Egypt — Biography. 4. England — Biography.
5. Egypt — Biography. 6. Upper class — England — History —
19th century. 7. England — Social life and customs — 19th century.
I. Title.
CT788.D846F73   1994
962'.03'092 — dc20   94-12343
[B]   CIP

Printed in the United States of America

MP 10 9 8 7 6 5 4 3 2 1

To the Memory of Saeed-ul-Islam
1952–1988

Contents

Acknowledgements

The seed for this book was sown when Penelope Lively urged me to read Lucie Duff Gordon's *Letters from Egypt* and over the years she, as well as Lucie, has been a source of inspiration. In the beginning Dorothy Middleton also opened doors and, as always, provided encouragement and advice.

It would have been impossible to write the biography without the assistance of Lucie Duff Gordon's descendants who hold the majority of the manuscript papers. They have not only provided access and help, but also given freely of their inherited Duff Gordon gifts of friendship, hospitality and generosity of spirit. I doubt if any biographer has been as fortunate or as happy while writing a book as I have been these past four years. I am greatly indebted to the late Gordon and Kitty Waterfield, to Michael Waterfield, Harriet Leppan and the late Jeffrey Leppan, to Antony Beevor and Artemis Cooper. Sir Andrew Duff Gordon let me borrow his great-great-grandmother's diaries, brought to light important documents, and cheerfully answered a barrage of queries relating to his family's history. Above all, my deepest thanks to Lucie Duff Gordon's great-granddaughter, Kinta Beevor, who has sheltered me, fed me, deciphered with me, cheered me, consoled me, loaned me precious family photographs and papers, and, at the end of it all, read the manuscript of the book with great tact, sympathy and intelligence. This is not, however, an authorized biography and its vision of Lucie Duff Gordon is my own. I alone must also be held responsible for any errors of fact.

Lotte and Joseph Hamburger, the biographers of Sarah and John Austin, shared valuable information about Lucie's parents with me. I am grateful to Dr John Moore-Gillon for discussing Lucie Duff Gordon's tuberculosis with me and also treatment of

ix

the disease in the nineteenth century. Phillip Mind, Librarian at HM Treasury, and F. A. Higginson of the Inland Revenue gave me information about Alexander Duff Gordon's professional career. Michael Page of the Surrey County Council provided details of Maurice Duff Gordon's time at Holloway Sanatorium. Professor Jack Lively discussed the Utilitarians with me. Professor Rosemary Ashton solved the mystery of the location of the correspondence between Sarah Austin and Prince Pückler-Muskau, and introduced me to Jeremy Bentham's remains at University College London. Ann Monsarrat provided information about the Brookfield papers, and Andrew Ward was helpful with regard to Azimullah Khan and Nana Sahib. Naseem Nathoo expertly word-processed all of the handwritten, transcribed copies of Lucie Duff Gordon's letters.

I am grateful to the Earl of Shelburne for allowing me to read and quote from the letters that Sarah Austin and Lucie Duff Gordon wrote to Henry Petty-Fitzmaurice, third Marquis of Lansdowne. My thanks as well to Virginia Murray of John Murray Ltd for making available to me correspondence between John Murray and Sarah Austin, Lucie Duff Gordon, and Alexander Duff Gordon, and for giving me information about the publication history and sales of Lucie Duff Gordon's books published by the firm. John Handford of Macmillan provided me with similar information regarding the two Macmillan editions of *Letters from Egypt*.

I am also indebted to the staffs of the Bodleian Library, the British Library, the London Library and the National Library of Wales. My special thanks to Dr Marian Zwiercan of the Jagiellonian University Library in Cracow, Poland, for sending me a microfilm copy of Sarah Austin's and Pückler-Muskau's letters. I am also grateful to Peter Dorman and Sue Lezon of the University of Chicago's 'Chicago House' in Luxor for making available to me a fascinating archive of nineteenth-century photographs of Luxor and for reproducing several for my use, including one of Lucie Duff Gordon's house.

In Egypt I was able to explore and delight in Lucie's 'golden world' of kindness and poetry because of the friendship and generosity of numerous people: Sahar Sobi, Mervat Nasser, Margot Badran, Faiek Al Rezaky and family, Ida and Mustafa and family, Khalid Soroor and Wafaa Soroor, the families of Mohammed Kamel and Ahmed Mohammed, Saleh Shaalan Mahmoud, Madame Nagwa and, above all, Nura Mohammed and the whole team in Karnak.

My thanks to Bruce Hunter of David Higham Associates in London and to Virginia Barber in New York for looking out for both my and Lucie Duff Gordon's best interests. Andrew Franklin of Hamish Hamilton and Janet Silver of Houghton Mifflin have been astute and inspiring editors.

For seeing me through – once again – my thanks to Rosemary Grave, Laura Kalpakian and Anthony Mann. I am especially grateful to my father, Arthur Voss, who went to Egypt with me in 1989 and turned what I feared would be a journey of sorrow into a healing time that enabled me to return to Egypt in the years that followed. My thanks, as well, to my mother, Isabel Voss, for moral support from afar and a sensitive early reading of the manuscript. And finally, love and thanks to Stephen Riley for the gift of happiness at Dampier House and abroad.

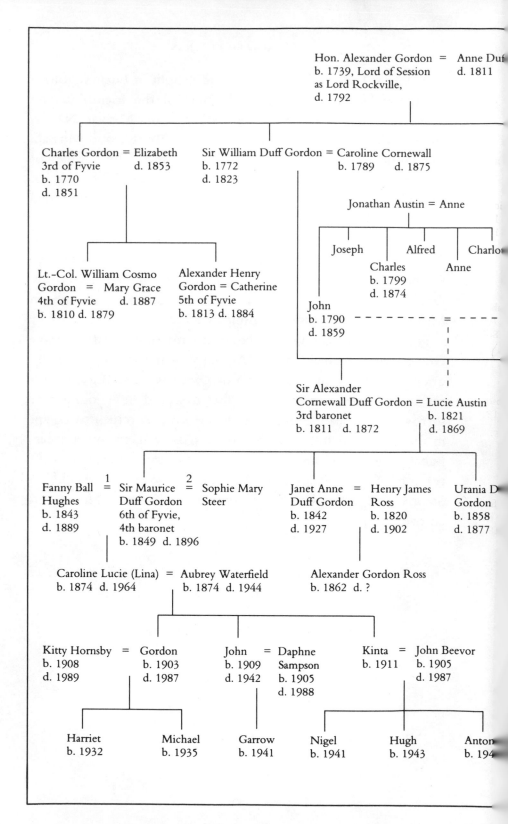

Hon. Alexander Gordon = Anne Duf
b. 1739, Lord of Session   d. 1811
as Lord Rockville,
d. 1792

Charles Gordon = Elizabeth   Sir William Duff Gordon = Caroline Cornewall
3rd of Fyvie   d. 1853   b. 1772   b. 1789   d. 1875
b. 1770   d. 1823
d. 1851

Jonathan Austin = Anne

Joseph   Alfred   Charlo
              Charles   Anne
              b. 1799
              d. 1874
John
b. 1790 - - - - - - - - = - - - -
d. 1859

Lt.-Col. William Cosmo   Alexander Henry
Gordon = Mary Grace   Gordon = Catherine
4th of Fyvie   d. 1887   5th of Fyvie
b. 1810 d. 1879   b. 1813 d. 1884

Sir Alexander
Cornewall Duff Gordon = Lucie Austin
3rd baronet   b. 1821
b. 1811   d. 1872   d. 1869

                    1   2
Fanny Ball = Sir Maurice = Sophie Mary   Janet Anne = Henry James   Urania D
Hughes   Duff Gordon   Steer   Duff Gordon   Ross   Gordon
b. 1843   6th of Fyvie,   b. 1842   b. 1820   b. 1858
d. 1889   4th baronet   d. 1927   d. 1902   d. 1877
               b. 1849 d. 1896

Caroline Lucie (Lina) = Aubrey Waterfield   Alexander Gordon Ross
b. 1874 d. 1964   b. 1874 d. 1944   b. 1862 d. ?

Kitty Hornsby = Gordon   John = Daphne   Kinta = John Beevor
b. 1908   b. 1903   b. 1909 Sampson   b. 1911   b. 1905
d. 1989   d. 1987   d. 1942 b. 1905   d. 1987
                                        d. 1988

Harriet   Michael   Garrow   Nigel   Hugh   Anton
b. 1932   b. 1935   b. 1941   b. 1941   b. 1943   b. 194

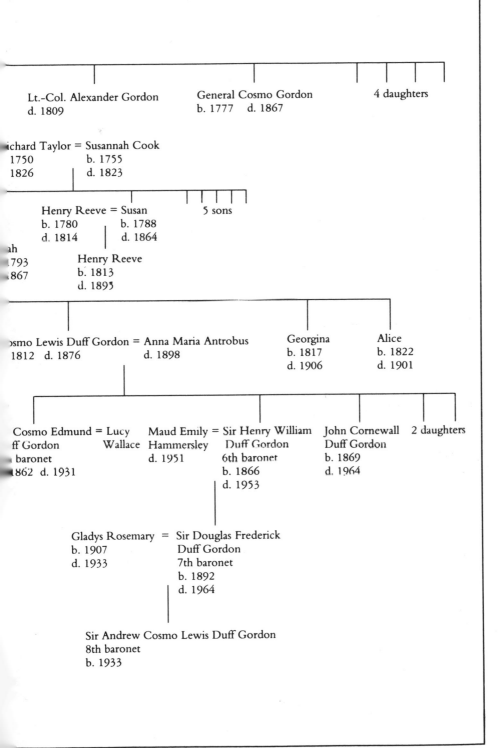

Lt.-Col. Alexander Gordon
d. 1809

General Cosmo Gordon
b. 1777   d. 1867

4 daughters

ichard Taylor = Susannah Cook
1750   b. 1755
1826   d. 1823

Henry Reeve = Susan   5 sons
b. 1780   b. 1788
d. 1814   d. 1864

ah
1793
867

Henry Reeve
b. 1813
d. 1895

osmo Lewis Duff Gordon = Anna Maria Antrobus
1812   d. 1876   d. 1898

Georgina
b. 1817
d. 1906

Alice
b. 1822
d. 1901

Cosmo Edmund = Lucy
ff Gordon   Wallace
baronet
862   d. 1931

Maud Emily = Sir Henry William
Hammersley   Duff Gordon
d. 1951   6th baronet
              b. 1866
              d. 1953

John Cornewall
Duff Gordon
b. 1869
d. 1964

2 daughters

Gladys Rosemary = Sir Douglas Frederick
b. 1907   Duff Gordon
d. 1933   7th baronet
                  b. 1892
                  d. 1964

Sir Andrew Cosmo Lewis Duff Gordon
8th baronet
b. 1933

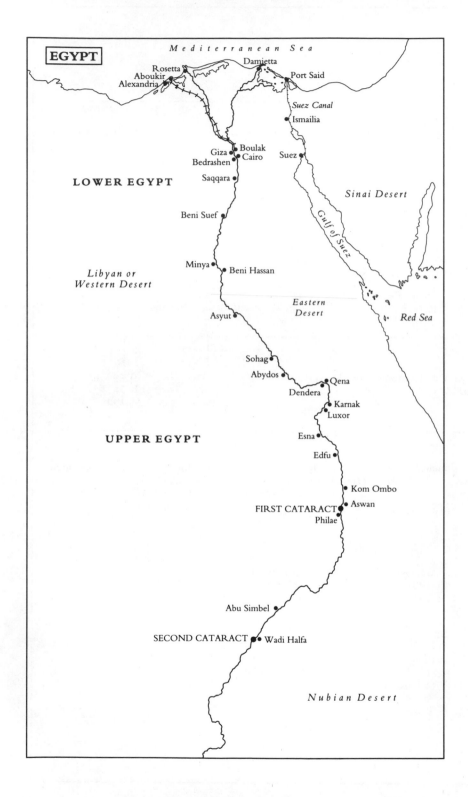

EGYPT

Mediterranean Sea

Damietta

Rosetta
Aboukir
Alexandria

Port Said

Suez Canal

Ismailia

LOWER EGYPT

Giza
Bedrashen

Boulak
Cairo

Suez

Saqqara

Sinai Desert

Beni Suef

Gulf of Suez

*Libyan or
Western Desert*

Minya

Beni Hassan

Asyut

*Eastern
Desert*

Red Sea

Sohag

Abydos

Qena

Dendera

Karnak
Luxor

UPPER EGYPT

Esna

Edfu

Kom Ombo

FIRST CATARACT

Aswan

Philae

Abu Simbel

SECOND CATARACT

Wadi Halfa

Nubian Desert

I recognize I am among the lakes in the
Fields of Offering.
Here I am strong, I am full of glory,
Here I exist.
I plough the fields, I reap the fields,
I am fruitful.
Here I remember.
I do not forget.
I am alive.

From *The Egyptian Book of the Dead*. Engraved in the sandstone north wall of the mortuary temple of Ramesses III at Medinet Habu, Thebes.

Prologue

THE CITY OF THE DEAD

In the Muqattam Hills south-east of Cairo, just beyond the strip of emerald lushness which borders the Nile, lies the City of the Dead: graveyard after graveyard – sandy expanses the size of playing fields – filled with the jerry-built shelters of the homeless squatters who take refuge here from the squalor of Cairo's slums. Better to dwell without water or electricity among the dead than in the filth and congestion and uproar of the living. The permanent inhabitants of the City of the Dead, those who slowly and silently slough off their bodies like chrysalises underground, make no noise, need no food or water. Yet they are the hosts and benefactors of the living.

At first glance the graveyards all appear identical – barren wastes, a congeries of leaning, crumbling tombs with partially effaced inscriptions, a surrounding ironwork fence with a gate which is locked at sunset, after the *mahgrib* prayer. And the squatters who enjoy a chaotic, deprived peace here look alike too: men in torn, soiled *galabiyas*, women swathed in black gowns and veils, children in parti-coloured rags. But these cemeteries aren't all the same. Some are very old, others are new. Some are for the rich, many more are for the poor. Most are for Muslims, but there are also graveyards for Copts, Protestants and Catholics in the City of the Dead. And there are special plots for foreigners – Turks, Lebanese, Syrians, Iranians, Indians, Pakistanis, Europeans, Americans and British – strangers who have died far from home.

Beyond the dusty miles of the City of the Dead stretches the desert – infinitely it seems, to the uttermost ends of the world. Only twice a day are its distant horizons clearly demarcated: when the glowing globe of the Egyptian sun rises in the east, and when it sets in the west in a pool of fiery orange and crimson splashed over the cloudless blue sky. The voice of the muezzin echoes in the silence of dawn or brings a hush of peace to the city at dusk – calling out to the faithful that prayer is sweeter than sleep.

★

Like so many before me, I came to Egypt in search of the dead. It was the grave of Lucie Duff Gordon, who died in 1869 in Cairo, which I sought in the cemeteries of Cairo and the City of the Dead in the Muqattam Hills. She had been born forty-eight years earlier, in 1821, to John and Sarah Austin, and had passed a somewhat troubled childhood in London, Bonn and Boulogne. John Austin was a renowned jurist and a chronic invalid – a difficult husband to Sarah, who was nevertheless devoted to him. She, like her daughter after her, was a gifted translator and a highly industrious one too, for throughout Lucie's childhood and for many years after, Sarah was the principal wage-earner in the Austin household because John Austin's 'delicate' health made for long periods of unemployment.

A month before her nineteenth birthday, Lucie married Sir Alexander Duff Gordon – ten years her senior, intelligent, charming, handsome as a Greek god, but not, unfortunately, affluent for his only means of support was a junior clerkship at the Treasury. But despite a shortage of money, the marriage was a profoundly happy one, and in time blessed with three children. Lucie and Alexander, with their good looks, wit, and literary interests, were one of the most glamorous and popular couples in London in the 1840s and 1850s. Lucie, especially, was admired for her beauty, her intellect, her delicious sense of humour, her radical political views and her unpredictable but always striking choice of dress. The children kept snakes and mice for pets, as Lucie had as a child. And when you called on the Duff Gordons in Queen Square, Westminster, the door was opened by a diminutive Sudanese boy named Hassan. 'Lady

Buff', as Lucie was known, dressed the salad herself before dinner, presided over a long table of guests, smoked a cigar and drank port with the men afterwards. Tennyson was mesmerized by her and said she inspired *The Princess*, while George Meredith modelled at least two of his heroines on her.

But Lucie's fate was not merely to be a muse. She had grown up among writers and philosophers in her parents' home and then held a regular salon for them herself as a London hostess. She was clever, original and also, rarer still, deeply empathetic and wise. People, including Thackeray and Meredith, said she should write her own books. And shortly after the birth of her first child, she did embark on a literary career as a translator and editor, producing over the next eighteen years ten books translated from German and French: books that were well received and earned her money, and a growing of circle of friends.

And thus things might have remained. It certainly didn't seem that she lacked anything (except perhaps a bit more money) to make a completely fulfilled life. Had Lucie, however, kept up her settled, happy, domestic, social and literary life in London, we would scarcely have heard of her, unless, while looking for something in the British Library catalogue, we were distracted by an entry for an obscure compilation of French criminal trials or a book on witchcraft in seventeenth-century Germany or some other book she translated. Or unless we came across her name in a critical introduction to one of Meredith's novels, or paused at a footnote in John Stuart Mill's or Carlyle's letters.

What rescued Lucie from historical and literary obscurity – and what sent her to Egypt – was illness. In the 1850s she contracted tuberculosis. She tried to cure herself, without success, by going to South Africa for a year, and then, in 1862, when she was forty-one, she sailed for Egypt in search of recovery. This she didn't find, but she fell in love with Egypt and stayed on until her death seven years later. But although health eluded her, her quest for it resulted in the extraordinary book she had always had it within her to write: *Letters from Egypt*. A book about herself, about her discovery of 'the real Arabian Nights' of Egypt, as she put it, with all its poetry, kindness and beauty. By going to Egypt Lucie was exiled from everything she held dear, and yet what she found there was not loss but undreamt-of gain, not recovery but a species of rebirth. A new world and a new life, and these wrought, in time, the great achievement of her *Letters*. They are her legacy to us and her monument to the 'golden existence' she found both in Egypt and within herself. For Lucie was a true traveller, and for such as her, to voyage out is to journey within.

★

In early October 1988, a hundred and twenty-six years after Lucie Duff Gordon reached Cairo, I went to Egypt to find her. I was confident that I would, if only I could summon the necessary stamina, sympathy and words. What I didn't consider was how this quest for Lucie Duff Gordon's life might unalter-ably affect my own. Because I planned to live in the past – that other country which we think of as fixed and over and therefore safe – I had no intimations of sea changes, no fears of loss, only hopes of gain. Not even as I made my way through the heat, dust, smells and noise of the maze of Cairo's dark-alleyed streets to the City of the Dead on the edge of the desert.

A photograph taken many years after her death shows the Christian cemetery where Lucie Duff Gordon was buried: an oasis of trees and granite and marble tombs, a replica – thanks to imported shrubs, masonry and artificial irrigation – of a village churchyard back in England. No penniless beggars with their families perch here. The dead are in complete possession. In the photograph Lucie's grave is a large, stone, coffin-shaped affair, mounted on a raised, rectangular platform. The epitaph carved across one side was written by Lucie's cousin, Henry Reeve, and reads:

4

In this spot is laid Lucie, wife of Alexander Duff Gordon, Bart., only child of John and Sarah Austin. Drawn by illness from the home she loved and the society she adorned, she dwelt for seven years on the banks of the Nile, where her energy and benevolence drew to her the hearts of the people. And here, trusting in the Mercy of God the Father of all races of men, she died on the 14th of July 1869, aged 48 years.

Does Lucie Duff Gordon really lie 'in this spot' of European landscape and decorum? Despite my search for her grave, I had my doubts, doubts planted by Lucie herself. In a letter written to her husband she had said that her Egyptian friends in Luxor had assured her that wherever she happened to die she would 'be buried as a daughter of the Arabs'. An old man had told her that she would 'assuredly lie in a Muslim grave' because 'when a bad Muslim dies the angels take him out of his tomb and put one of the good from among the Christians in his place'. After seven years in Egypt, Lucie was *bint el-beled* – 'daughter of the country' – and when her time had come, the people of the country promised she would rest with them.

What I planned to do during this first trip to Egypt was to find Lucie Duff Gordon's grave – to begin with her end – and then, moving back through space and time, recover and record her life. Lucie once said of Egypt that it was a palimpsest with the Bible written over Herodotus and the Koran over the Bible. She was never quite sure when she was living one or two or four or ten thousand years in the past. For me, a nineteenth-century layer of rediscovery, excavation and imperial encroachment overlaid the Koran, and Lucie's story was embedded in this layer that I wanted to explore.

★

Lucie lived in Luxor, in Upper Egypt or 'the Saeed' as it is called there. Luxor Temple was literally her home because she inhabited a large, ramshackle house with few windows and even fewer doors built on top of the ruins of the temple. But

5

much as she loved Luxor, Lucie's 'paradise' in the Saeed was the island temple of Philae near Aswan. Philae was one of the many Egyptian temples dedicated to the goddess Isis, the wife of Osiris, the god of the dead. When Osiris was brutally murdered and dismembered by his brother Seth, the god of mortality, Isis travelled the length of Egypt, collecting the pieces of her husband's body. It was at Philae that she found his heart. When she had gathered all the fragments, she 're-membered' Osiris. As the goddess of memory, magic and mourning, she merged together the pieces of her dead husband and made him whole and alive again. Memory, Isis' story shows, is active and creative. To 're-member' is to recall imaginatively the fragments of our past, to imbue them with new life, to make them live once again in the present – and the future. Isis' pilgrimage and her re-membering were born of anguish and completed with love.

I was faced with a multitude of fragments of Lucie Duff Gordon's life scattered about the globe. I went in quest of her to Egypt – where she lived most fully and died – but her letters and papers, an Indian silk gown shot through with gold thread, and a necklace of emeralds, rubies and pearls survived in London and Kent, as did drawings and photographs, a bust of Lucie's husband, Alexander, and copies of her books. In Lucie's letters to Lord Lansdowne at Bowood House in Wiltshire, I discovered how a much-wanted first son had died in infancy. After protracted negotiation, one day I finally received a small brown parcel tied up in coarse string sent from a Polish university in Cracow. It contained a microfilm of passionate love-letters written by Lucie's mother to a rakish German prince when Lucie was a child. And there, in the midst of her mother's outpourings, were four letters, in painstakingly correct German, from eleven-year-old Lucie to the prince – her earliest extant writings. At Downton House in Wales, Sir Andrew Duff Gordon produced a drawing of Lucie at eighteen, her marriage settlement and twenty-one stout volumes of her mother-in-law's diaries. These journals shed light, along with a great deal else, on Lucie's friendship with an Indian prince named Nana Sahib who was later implicated in the 1857 Indian Mutiny – and the source of the Indian silk gown and necklace of emeralds, rubies and pearls. Lucie wore vaguely oriental dress, too, when she sat for Henry Phillips's 1851 oil portrait. Today it hangs next to the reclusive Brontës in the National Portrait Gallery off Trafalgar Square in London.

All these bits and pieces of Lucie's life – the yellowed letters, faded photographs and forgotten documents – had to be sought out and gathered together before I set off for Egypt. With hindsight, everything in Lucie's life seems to lead to Egypt, but I had to find my way there through a maze of inconveniently dispersed materials. When I had located and collected them, I was ready to re-member them in the 'amber light' of Egypt that Lucie loved. I booked my flight. I departed. I touched down in Cairo.

★

But my quest for Lucie Duff Gordon in the autumn of 1988 was cut short before I even left Cairo for Upper Egypt. My brief stay began with my search for her grave, but before I found it, I was in another cemetery in the City of the Dead, not far from where Lucie is said to rest.

My husband, who came to Egypt with me, died suddenly four days after we arrived in Cairo. The day after his death he was buried in the Muqattam Hills. I could not face continuing our journey alone. I left Egypt and retreated to England.

A long, dark London winter followed. I spent most of it reading and taking notes with a kind of feverish intensity in the round, domed Reading Room of the British Library. I found refuge there as others might in a church. When I walked through the heavy swing doors of the Reading Room it felt as if I had checked my personal identity and grief as did the tourists their coats and umbrellas and cameras in the large entrance lobby. Or at least some days, for some hours, it felt so. It was really only in the Reading Room – surrounded by ascending tiers of books and sheltered by the glass dome overhead – that I felt safe. The Reading Room was full of the presence of the dead. And they were alive. For what were we all doing, bent over our books, but reading, writing about, re-membering the dead?

As the weeks and months passed, I became more and more haunted by the idea of time – that great, seemingly unalterable force which severed me from my husband and, of course, from Lucie as well. I wanted, above all, to understand time's relation to memory and death. Is it memory alone that stems time's flow? And is time inexorably destructive? We usually think of time as a river, a river like the Nile, with a strong, swift current bearing us further and further away from what we have been towards the time when we will not be at all – birth, death and the brief transit of life in between. But perhaps we should think of time as a deep, still pool rather than a fast-flowing river. If time were a pool, we could kneel at its edge and gaze at our reflections and then beyond them to what lay deeper still. Instead of looking back at time, we could look down into it – just as we could peel back the layers of the palimpsest – and now and again different features of the past – different sights and sounds and voices and dreams – would rise to the surface: rise and subside, and the deep pool would hold them all, so that nothing was lost and nothing ever went away.

★

Eventually I returned to Egypt, to Cairo, to the cemetery in the City of the Dead. And then, after that pilgrimage, I went on to Upper Egypt and Lucie's home in Luxor. I found a home of my own there and settled in. I learned that in fundamental ways Luxor and the Saeed hadn't changed greatly since Lucie's day. By now I'd collected all the surviving fragments of her life in England and Egypt. It was time to begin writing.

Nothing is ever lost. Nothing ever goes away. This was Isis' belief when she scavenged Egypt for the fragments of her dead husband. It was the belief, too, of the ancient Egyptians with their obsession with embalming and preserving. And, of course, it is the creed of biographers.

What follows is a re-membering: Lucie Duff Gordon's life from her birth on a glorious June morning in Westminster, London in 1821 to her death in the early hours of 14 July 1869, just as the sun rose in all its midsummer splendour from the Eastern Desert. A biography of Lucie Duff Gordon, the record of my quest for her, the life I wrote while I struggled to re-member my own. But I hope, too, that it is a book about time and the power of human memory, imagination and desire – about life in the City of the Dead.

Part I

LUCIE AUSTIN

Chapter One

London, 24 June 1821: a brilliant early summer's day. In Queen Square, Westminster, Big Ben can be heard tolling the hour. Then, when the the echoing chimes cease, silence. The little square of tall, red-brick houses is a quiet oasis, sandwiched between Birdcage Walk and the green expanses of St James's Park on one side, and on the other the majesty of Whitehall and Westminster Abbey. Rows of grinning, grimacing gargoyles decorate the otherwise plain façades of the Queen Square houses. In Number One, a stone's throw from the statue of Queen Anne which presides over the square, the curtains are drawn and the brass knocker is muffled in cloths.* The fine summer weather – kept at bay by latched windows and heavy velvet curtains – doesn't penetrate the house. Inside, though it is nearly midday, John Austin and his wife Sarah are both in bed. In separate beds – at opposite ends of the first-floor corridor.

For John Austin, occupying the master bedroom with a table of phials and tonics and pastilles beside him, this bedridden state is not unusual. Though he is only thirty-one, his hair is already grey, and his health - both physical and mental – 'delicate'. He is often indisposed: with migraine, dyspepsia, 'bilious fever', rheumatic aches and pains, numbness of the limbs, nervous tremors and palpitations. He is also a martyr to that scourge, melancholia. This particular morning, while the birds sing outside his bedroom window, Austin is so submerged in his own gloomy ruminations that he is scarcely aware of his wife's ordeal down the hall in the small spare-room at the back of the house.

---

* In the 1880s, part of Queen Square was torn down and what survived renamed Queen Anne's Gate. Number one is now gone, but the statue of Queen Anne remains, as do the grimacing gargoyles.

Three years younger than her husband, Sarah Austin is in the throes of labour, attempting to give birth to their first and (as it will turn out) only child. The baby seems reluctant to be born into the world of this darkened house whose inhabitants languish in bed while the summer world runs riot outdoors. Fortunately, however, the celebrated physician, Maudsley, is on hand to assist the delivery. It is characteristic of the Austins that they have summoned the most eminent doctor in London for the occasion.

Maudsley presides with brisk competence, ordering basins of hot water and towels, brandishing a new-fangled pair of gleaming forceps. Sarah pushes and strains and stifles her groans. She is the most practical, conscientious young woman imaginable; she shirks no duty, recoils from no necessary task. And yet despite all her efforts, the baby refuses to make an exit from her heaving body.

Finally, with Maudsley's encouragement and adroit assistance, the 'puny infant' emerges from Sarah's womb. But it lies strangely inert and silent in his large hands. Maudsley swiftly tips the slippery bundle of flesh upside-down, lays it face down on his knee, and whacks its back until the baby lets out a magnificent howl that fills the room and echoes all the way down the hallway to John Austin's chamber. Lucie Austin is launched in the world.

★

From whence had she come? John Austin had not always been a semi-invalid, nor had Sarah always stoically borne whatever cards fate dealt to her. Their marriage was every bit as eccentric and intermittently tortured as Thomas and Jane Carlyle's, and just as earnest and intellectual as the partnership the Austins' neighbour, John Stuart Mill, would later make with Harriet Taylor. But things had not always been thus with them.

John Austin was born in 1790 to a well-to-do miller and corn merchant in Ipswich. He was the eldest of a large family nurtured by a mother who was as deeply religious and charitable as her husband was practical and prosperous. But Mrs Austin's health was precarious and she was also prey to 'fits of nervous depression' which sent her to bed and left the running of the household to servants and John's younger sisters. The boy inherited both his mother's religious feeling and her melancholy. At the age of three he was able to read the Bible out loud to her. At seven, he was found on his knees in the garden one day, fervently praying for a bow and arrow.

With his dreamy temperament and religious inclinations, young John Austin might have been destined for the Church or some sort of literary profession. Perhaps the least appropriate career for this gentle, bookish boy was the military. Yet in 1807, just three weeks before his seventeenth birthday, he joined the army, 'apparently in a fit of anti-Napoleonic enthusiasm'. He was first commissioned an Ensign in the 44th Regiment. A year later he was promoted to Lieutenant and sent to serve in Sicily and Malta under Lord William Bentinck.

During an extended stay in Malta in 1811 and 1812, Austin, now twenty-one, kept a diary which recorded in considerable detail his dissatisfaction not only with army life, but even more with his own conduct and distressing state of mind. On New Year's Eve 1811, for example, he confided to his diary that 'the retrospect' of the year just closing 'has hardly given rise to one single feeling of self-satisfaction. During that period, the waste of money, of time and of health has been enormous; and indolence – always the prominent vice of my character – has within the last nine months assumed over me an empire I almost despair of shaking.'

Melancholy gripped him. Early in 1812, he jotted down the following cryptic diary entry: 'Reading. Fears of never emerging from obscurity. Height 5 feet $9\frac{1}{2}$ inches in boots.' In his diary Austin berated himself for laziness, ennui, lethargy and indecisiveness – all rather passive sins. Sometimes, however, he was more actively at fault. When the garrison officers were presented to a visiting General, Austin recorded that he 'was guilty of an unseasonable affectation of wit which might, without much injustice, have been termed an impertinence'. More seriously, he became embroiled in a row with a Colonel Hamerton: 'my own arrogance and want of caution,' Austin wrote, 'will enable him to injure me'.

As his granddaughter was to observe many years later, the tone of John Austin's youthful army diary was 'grey, austere and inelastic'. In order to counteract dour thoughts and feelings of worthlessness, Austin set himself a course of edifying reading: Locke's *Essay Concerning Human Understanding*, Dugald Stewart's *Essay on the Beautiful*, Mitford's *History of Greece*. Such were the companions of his late-night hours of insomnia. By day he was, among other scrapes, hounded for an unpaid tailor's bill and confined to quarters for an unnamed offence.

Austin was in the army for five years. It was an uncongenial forcing house for such a delicate plant, but in 1812 he was released from the military by the sudden death of his younger brother Joseph, who had served in the navy and died of yellow fever on board a warship off Java. Mrs Austin was beside herself with grief and begged her husband to make John resign his commission so that the family might never suffer another such loss. Thus at the age of twenty-two John Austin found himself back in England: the slate was wiped clean and he was in need of a new profession. In a surprisingly short period of time, given Austin's congenital indecisiveness, he began to read for the Bar in London and he fell in love with a friend of his younger sister: Sarah Taylor, the youngest child of the prominent Unitarian Taylor family of Norwich.

*

Nineteen-year-old Sarah Taylor, with her abundant dark hair and large eyes, was a beautiful, high-spirited, even passionate young woman, but what attracted John Austin was her intellectual curiosity and unusual degree of learning. While her friends were busy playing the pianoforte, drawing and embroidering, Sarah received the same masculine education as her brothers. She studied Latin, mathematics, philosophy, political economy, French, German and Italian. This was the doing of Susannah Taylor, Sarah's remarkable mother, who insisted that her daughters grow up capable of thinking for and taking care of themselves. 'The character of girls,' Mrs Taylor wrote to Sarah when her daughter was staying with relations in London, depends 'upon their reading as much as upon the company they keep. Besides the intrinsic pleasure to be derived from solid knowledge, a woman ought to consider it her best resource against poverty. A well-educated young woman may always provide for herself.'

Susannah Taylor instilled in her daughter the necessity for female independence and self-sufficiency, a lesson Sarah never lost sight of and bequeathed to her own daughter, Lucie. Not, however, that the Taylor and Austin women ever shared the radical, feminist views of Sarah's cousin, Harriet Martineau. They didn't question women's secondary position as wives and mothers. But within this limited female sphere, there was still opportunity to exercise their intelligence and, if need be, to make a financial contribution or even to support themselves.

Almost from their very first meeting, Austin recognized in Sarah the fruits of Mrs Taylor's advanced ideas on female education. But he found Sarah's lively, witty, flirtatious behaviour – which he knew made her attractive to other men – distressing. Austin tried, however, to overlook what he called Sarah's 'volatility' because he valued her keen intelligence and sound judgement. They embarked, then, on a curious courtship enacted in various Norwich parlours. Jane Austen would have relished this little drama: John Austin as cool and constrained a suitor as Fitzwilliam Darcy and Sarah as clever and vivacious as Elizabeth Bennet.

But John Austin was not Sarah's only admirer. She could, in fact, have had her pick of any number of handsome, well-off young men who paid court to her. Why, then, was she drawn to the silent, humourless, financially insecure Austin? Sarah had inchoate but compelling aspirations. She yearned for a mission, some transcendent purpose or aim to focus her talents and desires. But she was scrupulously honest with herself and knew her own limitations. In addition, she didn't question women's ancillary role in the scheme of things. Recognizing, then, that she could not achieve greatness on her own, she sought it in others and only John Austin came up to the mark. In him she perceived genius – but genius latent, troubled and too easily baffled. What higher calling could she hope for than to be the companion, the helpmeet, even the midwife to Austin's brilliance?

It took some time, however, for Sarah's dreams to take shape. Austin was the most cautious and dilatory of suitors. For months at a time he did not visit Norwich at all. While she spurned others' declarations of love, Sarah began to despair of ever receiving one from Austin. She wondered if perhaps she had merely imagined his admittedly restrained gestures of affection and admiration.

Months and then years passed and Sarah reached the advanced age of twenty-one still unbetrothed. And then, at long last, like a bolt out of the blue, one morning she received a thick envelope addressed to her in Austin's hand. In length and appearance it resembled a complicated legal document, but as soon as she began to read it, Sarah realized that it was the long-awaited proposal of marriage.

Never, perhaps, has a woman been so strangely wooed. Austin's letter, dated 12 November 1814, opened with his declaration that he would indulge in no fine sentiments or flowery expressions, but rather proceed to the business at hand: namely, whether or not they should marry given all the difficulties, hazards and obstacles to their union which he was about to set forth.

Assuming that we feel a mutual inclination to each other, our great object should be to enquire as calmly as we can, whether it is or is not likely that we should promote our well-being by *yielding* to that inclination. I shall sincerely endeavour to lay before you those harsh but useful truths relating to myself, without a due consideration of which you would be mad to decide in my favour, and I feel confident that you would with equal sincerity intimate to me whatever might render it expedient for me to withdraw these merely conditional proposals.

As I shall accordingly proceed to enumerate the greatest and most comprehensive of those evils which you must or may undergo from an attachment to me; and having thus fairly and steadily presented to your view the facts most unfavourable to my suit, I shall then require you to submit to a self-examination which may perhaps severely wound your vanity, but which you must triumphantly encounter before I can dare to hang the fate of my feelings upon the chance of your consistency.

Here, perhaps, Sarah paused for breath and steeled herself for the catalogue of 'evils', as Austin called them, which would attend first their engagement and then their marriage.

'*Primo*', according to Austin, was the length of their engagement period. It would be three or so years until he was called to the Bar and there was no way to calculate how long it would be before he established himself. Taking, as always, the least sanguine view of things, Austin estimated that it would be at least five more years and possibly as much as ten before he would be in a position to marry Sarah.

'*Secundo*', and more seriously, they had to face very real financial uncertainty. Austin bluntly stated that it was 'very probable that my profession may never bring me one shilling'. They might spend the long, weary years of their engagement in vain and be unable, in the end, to marry because of sheer poverty.

'*Tertio*', Austin boldly confessed that he might 'play the fool and scoundrel' and abandon Sarah in order to marry more profitably elsewhere. Or, as he put it, 'at the moment you are expecting from fortune the completion of your long deferred hopes, I may forget your love and your faith in the wane of your beauty . . . and damn myself to wealth . . . in the arms of age and ugliness and folly'. Austin conceded, however, that his third point was the least likely of all the possible 'evils' he was summoning up for Sarah's consideration, especially, as he told her, 'if *you* will but lend your efforts to prop and secure my constancy'.

At this point Sarah may have ruffled through the remaining densely written pages and realized that she was only half-way through. Resuming her reading, however, she would have seen that Austin had ended his catalogue of obstacles. Now he turned to Sarah's 'defects' and outlined the noble and worthy life she would have as Austin's wife could she but reform herself to his specifications.

He exhorted her 'to restrain the wanderings of your coquetry and your vanity . . . by cultivating that quick and subtle perception of propriety, that anxious and vigilant prudence which would surround you with an atmosphere of purity and safety'. Only thus could Sarah hope 'to enter into . . . [Austin's] comprehensive views and soften my technical asperities; to brace . . . up that fortitude or playfully tease my sinking spirits into alacrity'. If Sarah could but assure him of her 'unviolated integrity', neither of them need fear 'those slight stains upon your reputation, which a more guarded deportment combined with my respectful and . . . protecting attachment will gradually wear away'.

But despite this reassurance, Austin himself was far from certain of Sarah's 'unviolated integrity'. On the last page of his letter he suddenly dropped his portentous, adjudicatory tone and burst out: 'I am tortured by an interest too vehement and too painful . . . and my happiness, my peace, nay my safety, loudly command me to ascertain whether you are in truth that volatile, vain and flirting thing, hackneyed in the ways of coquetry and submitting its light and worthless affections to the tampering of every specious coxcomb.' Austin was consumed with anxiety that Sarah's 'tarnished' reputation was deserved, and that she would drive him to ruin rather than be the means of his salvation.

And yet the letter finally closed with a vision of Sarah as the ministering angel of his lonely, arduous path in life. He called upon her to 'strengthen and sustain the weakness of a spirit that must cling to sympathy for support . . . and urge me on to heroic industry [with] that best and dearest of all rewards – the full and exclusive and proud possession of a thinking, feeling, high-minded woman, "loving, lovely and beloved"'. Only here, at the very end of his long letter, did Austin bring up the subject of love in the borrowed poet's phrase, enclosed in inverted commas. He was incapable of making vows – as distinct from premises, propositions or conditions – in his own words.

One wonders whether Sarah felt more insulted or uplifted by Austin's treatise of a proposal, or whether it filled her more with doubt or relief. Though he enjoined her to submit herself to an 'ordeal of self-examination' and to make him 'acquainted with the issue of [her] . . . scrutiny', Sarah's reply to him has been lost. But a letter to her cousin, Mary, written soon after she had received Austin's proposal, shows that if Sarah did have doubts they were swiftly allayed. 'After some weeks of suspense and anxiety,' Sarah wrote breathlessly to Mary, 'I am enabled, thank God! to tell you that my doom is most happily sealed.' She then went on to rhapsodize that Austin was all she had ever dreamed of, that they were madly in love, that he had a brilliant future before him, and that, finally, Sarah was 'the happiest girl in the world'. But she was not so carried away as to be blind to how her fiancé might appear to others. She was afraid Mary would find Austin stern and haughty and mistake 'his lofty and delicate feelings of honour towards our sex' for indifference and neglect. 'At any rate,' Sarah begged Mary, 'if you don't like him, never tell me so . . . it would give me pain. So . . . let him be all perfection.'

Whether John Austin remained 'all perfection' during the five long years of his engagement to Sarah Taylor is doubtful. But if he changed in any way, it paled in comparison with Sarah's transformation. When she accepted his condition-laden proposal Sarah was committing herself to an intellectual and moral education at the hands of her future husband. Far-seeing as Mrs Taylor's educational views had been, Austin felt that Sarah needed further schooling. She now must read the same books he read, study the same thinkers and writers he most admired, understand and adopt his religious, philosophical and political views.

While Austin continued to prepare himself for the Bar, Sarah embarked on an arduous course of study under her fiancé's close supervision. Austin set Sarah a formidable reading list that included Tacitus, Cicero, Machiavelli, Bacon, Hume, Malthus, Jeremy Bentham and James Mill. When she finished a text Sarah recorded its title and the date in a notebook she kept for this purpose, and then wrote an essay-letter to Austin which he duly corrected, both in terms of expression and content, and returned to her. It was scarcely a romantic correspondence – those long, dry letters which flew back and forth between Norwich and London. Sarah curbed all her high feeling and warmth when writing to Austin, while he complained that his legal training had already given him so 'exclusive and intolerant a taste . . . for perspicuity and precision that I . . . [can] hardly venture on sending a letter of much purpose, even to you, unless it be laboured with accuracy and circumspection'.

It was a question of the sapling bending to the wind. One Norwich friend wrote to another, 'I have just seen Sally Taylor, but alas! How changed . . . from all that was dazzling, attractive and imposing, she has become the most demure, reserved and decorous creature in existence. Mr Austin has wrought miracles for which he is blessed by the ladies and cursed by the gentlemen and wondered at by all.'

Through her reading and their long letters, Sarah soon

imbibed Austin's ideas, prejudices and convictions. In the course of his legal studies he had shed his early religious beliefs and become a Utilitarian and disciple of Jeremy Bentham (an old friend, as it happened, of the Taylor family) and James Mill. And like most Utilitarians, he was now a radical Whig in politics and a free-thinker or agnostic in religious matters. He subscribed to the Utilitarian view of an orderly, rational, quantifiable universe where human problems could be solved by recourse to the Utilitarian formula of the greatest happiness of the greatest number. Founded though it was on a humanistic and hopeful vision of progress, Utilitarianism was still a highly intellectual and mechanistic philosophy. When Sarah dutifully embraced it, her passion, wilfulness, romanticism, even her sense of humour were all severely curbed.

The years passed with both John and Sarah bent over their books, writing each other long, earnest letters late at night. They were seldom together and Austin was periodically unwell, but still they were, in their own rather high-minded way, happy. Sarah, at least, was full of hope. She was betrothed to a man whom she felt possessed genius, and she felt sure she could aid its fullest and finest expression.

At last, in 1818, when Austin was twenty-eight and Sarah nearly twenty-six, Austin was called to the Bar. Though his prospects and income remained uncertain, they set a wedding date. This was made possible by the marriage settlement arranged by the two families: Austin's father, Jonathan Austin, was to provide £300 per annum and Sarah's father, John Taylor, £100 to the newly-weds. On £400 a year, with an eye to economy, they could manage until Austin's practice was secure.

On 24 August 1819, a bright, warm late summer's day, Sarah Taylor and John Austin were married in the parish church of St George's, Colegate. Everything went according to plan until they departed from Norwich on the London coach. One of Sarah's disappointed suitors waited alongside the coach road and, when they passed, he tossed a beautiful, ornate gold watch through the open window into Sarah's lap.★ Austin, no doubt, turned as red with anger as Sarah did with painful embarrassment at this gesture of unrequited love. They rode on in strained silence to their new life in London.

★

By a stroke of good fortune, the newly-weds found a house to let in the very same area − Queen Square, Westminster − where Austin's Utilitarian heroes, Jeremy Bentham and James Mill, both lived. Still indefatigable and 'codifying like a dragon' at the age of seventy-one, Bentham had a house called The Hermitage across the square from the Austins. Though he was something of a recluse and hated idle intruders, for his new neighbours Bentham broke his rule of never having more than one guest for dinner. He was impressed by Austin and 'cheerfulised' (one of Bentham's many neologisms) by Sarah's wit and beauty. To his earnest young disciple, Bentham expounded on his great *idée fixe* − his plans for a panopticon prison which was the basis of his work on penal reform. Another enthusiasm was physical exercise. Bentham was a firm believer in housing a sound mind in a sound body, and had had his coach-house transformed into a gymnasium where neophyte Utilitarians such as Austin gathered to balance on bars and swing from trapezes while carrying on philosophical discussions with their host and mentor.

Bentham's closest follower, James Mill, lived next door to the Austins. The year before the Austins moved to Queen Square, Mill had completed his exhaustive *History of British India*, which had occupied him for more than a decade, and in 1819 he was just beginning his long career with the East India Company. Later he would be remembered chiefly as the father − and a

---

★ This watch was later inherited by Lucie, who in turn left it to her daughter, Janet Ross. Today it is displayed in one of the glass cases in the Victoria and Albert Museum in London.

highly overbearing and unsympathetic father at that — of his more sensitive and gifted son, John Stuart Mill. But when the Austins first met the elder Mill he was one of the leading Utilitarian reformers of the day.

Temperamentally, Austin probably felt more at ease with Mill, who was as cool and cerebral as himself, than with Bentham, who despite all his lofty ideas and aims was a jovial, affectionate man. Bentham and Mill, in fact, made a rather odd duo, and their personal circumstances were also very different. Bentham was a confirmed bachelor with childlike eccentricities: his indifference, for example, to his clothes and appearance. Mill, on the other hand, was unhappily married to a woman he felt in every way his inferior, though marital incompatibility did not hinder him from fathering nine children.

Because Bentham had no wife and Mill's was too preoccupied with caring for her continuously expanding family, Sarah was left on her own a good deal in the early days of the Austins' marriage when John crossed the square or dropped in next door to sit at the feet of his masters. Not that Sarah greatly minded her husband's absences; she was filled with vicarious pleasure that he should be admired by their eminent neighbours, whose good opinion only strengthened her belief in Austin's brilliance.

In addition, she had all the countless domestic chores of setting up house to see to — curtains to be hung, carpets laid, walls papered, grates cleaned, and chimneys swept. And then there was Austin's study to arrange — the inner sanctum of the house behind the parlour where he would harvest the fruits of his teeming and exacting brain. Sarah had his desk placed so that the light from the French windows poured in throughout the day; his chair was put at just the right distance from the fire; shelves were constructed all along one wall to hold his books, and the windows fitted with thick curtains to muffle distracting noises from outside.

One afternoon, when he returned from visiting the Mills next door, Austin told Sarah that he had met another youthful

Utilitarian follower named George Grote, a banker by profession but an historian by vocation. It was the beginning of a lifelong friendship not only between Austin and Grote, but also between their wives. George and Harriet Grote were, like the Austins, newly-weds and still in their twenties. Their courtship had been protracted because of family disapproval and while it went forward by fits and starts, Harriet had undertaken a regimen of study directed by her future husband. She was now assisting him to write the monumental history of Greece which he had decided was to be his life's work. But Grote, like Austin, was subject to bouts of depression, and even at the best of times he was a quiet, retiring man. Harriet, resolute and energetic despite her own precarious health, was always able to rouse and cheer him.

When Sarah met Harriet Grote she immediately recognized a kindred spirit, and the two women quickly became intimate friends. Harriet's, however, was the more forceful personality. While pushing her husband to achieve great things, she didn't in the least obscure or conceal her own talents. Brilliant, opinionated and witty, she became in time one of the foremost hostesses in London. One admiring wag described her as 'the only man in the Radical party'. Sydney Smith said that he liked George Grote because he was so ladylike and Harriet Grote because she was such a gentleman. The Grotes' was an unconventional but highly successful marriage. For Sarah it must have seemed an ideal to aspire to.

Soon Sarah was presiding over her own parties at 1 Queen Square, where young intellectuals such as the historian Thomas Babington Macaulay and the writer and editor John Sterling joined Bentham, Mill and the Grotes round the Austins' dining table. From Norwich, Susannah Taylor wrote to her daughter that economy need not be 'an insuperable barrier to good society'. The roast joints and milk puddings served at the Austins' table might be plain fare, but the conversation carried on in the front parlour was always animated, even heated, as

Sarah's guests debated parliamentary reform, Catholic emancipation, the immoralities of George IV or the misdeeds of Tory aristocrats. Sarah began to emerge from under the shadow that had descended on her and quenched her 'volatility' when she became engaged to John Austin. Safely married now, she could give some latitude to her high spirits, her charm and her sharp tongue. She was finding her feet as a hostess, and literary figures such as Samuel Rogers and Anna Jameson began to join young radicals and Utilitarian reformers in Sarah's budding salon.

For it was all Sarah's doing – the teas and dinners which were attracting some of the leading men in London to Queen Square. Austin at times joined in; more often, he refused to see his guests until dinner was served. Sometimes he never appeared at all. Preoccupied with weighty philosophical problems, at the mercy of some physical complaint, or sunk in gloom, he observed the assembled guests gathered round his table and felt a stranger in his own house. Sarah tried to anchor him in these social waters.

Austin needed anchoring in other ways as well, because by the time he and Sarah celebrated their first anniversary it was becoming clear that he was a man adrift. In the two years since he had been called to the Bar, he had done little or nothing to establish himself professionally. He had discovered, in fact, that he was as ill-suited for the law as he had been for the military. On the few occasions when he appeared in court, he felt faint and nervous and was scarcely able to stammer out a few words. The bewigged judge, the other black-robed barristers, the noise and close air of the courtroom, all overwhelmed him. He beat a hasty retreat home and went to bed.

To Sarah, he explained that quite apart from the fact that the atmosphere of the courts made him ill, he had no taste or aptitude for the practical, active side of the law. He preferred intense discussions from the perch of Bentham's trapeze to arguing cases before the judge's bench. What Austin wanted to pursue now were the intricacies of political theory and legal philosophy. These were lofty areas of study and he hoped, like his mentors Bentham and Mill, to make weighty contributions to them.

It was necessary for both Austin and Sarah to transform his failure at the Bar – a failure thrown into relief by the success of his younger brother, Charles Austin, as a barrister – into a stepping stone to higher things. Unfortunately, this change in direction in Austin's career meant continued financial dependence and uncertainty. But Sarah knew this was almost always the case with great thinkers. She was confident that somehow they would manage.

Austin's health, his future and their finances, the running of the household and entertainment of a growing circle of friends were all more than enough to consume Sarah's energies as a young wife. But young wives almost invariably become young mothers. Sarah and Austin, of course, knew this, but they still may have been surprised when Sarah discovered that she was pregnant in November 1820. After their initial, perhaps ambivalent, reaction to Sarah's pregnancy, she tried to calculate all the changes, large and small, that would have to be made at 1 Queen Square when the baby arrived the following summer. It would need a nursery as distant as possible from the sanctuary of Austin's study, and a nanny to feed and bathe it and take it for walks in the square. Someone would have to sew and knit gowns, blankets, caps and little sheets and pillow cases since Sarah possessed no needlework skills. Luckily, Harriet Grote was also pregnant for the first time, and the two high-minded mothers-to-be were able to discuss all the rather bewildering practical arrangements to be made.

But did they confide their deeper anxieties about the revolution in their private lives – their marriages – they knew motherhood would bring? Sarah, especially, had cause for alarm, for after the baby arrived her loyalties would be divided, and her energies and sympathies too. What would happen when the baby cried in the middle of the night while Austin, always a prey to insomnia, tossed and turned beside her in bed? What would Sarah do if he had dyspepsia when the baby developed colic, or toothache while the baby was teething? Austin, in fact, was so dependent upon her and so demanding that it was difficult to imagine him as a father or even sharing her attention and affection with someone else – even a someone else who was an infant.

Sarah's anxieties about motherhood were made worse when Harriet Grote gave birth to a premature son who died before he was a week old and nearly carried off his mother with him. Up until now Sarah's worries had focused on the effect the baby would have on her marriage, on Austin's health – physical and mental – and on his work. Now she realized that there were more immediate, graver things to fear, including childbirth itself.

★

Hence her lonely ordeal in the upstairs back bedroom that June morning in 1821 when Lucie Austin – who would always in later life take a rather cavalier view of punctuality and do things in her own sweet time – made her desultory way into the world. Maudsley coaxed her forth and started her breathing: Lucie howled and Sarah sank back into the pillows, overcome with exhaustion and relief. Maudsley then hastened down the hall to congratulate Austin, who had already been roused by the baby's cry.

An hour or so later, Maudsley left the house – dark and silent now, for the curtains were still drawn and both mother and child slept. Perhaps John Austin slept too, but then again perhaps the sight of his tiny, dark-haired daughter acted on him like a tonic, and he dressed and went downstairs to his study to wrestle with abstruse ideas and make his own gestures towards futurity.

All this while, outside in the deserted square, pigeons perched on the statue of Queen Anne and atop the fantastic gargoyles, and the sun poured down from a cloudless blue sky – just as it did in other latitudes undreamt of as yet.

Chapter Two

As soon as Sarah recovered from childbirth, the Austins fled hot, dusty, midsummer London and went to Norfolk, where they rented an old, rambling farmhouse not far from the Taylors in Norwich. Here they passed the remainder of the summer and the autumn, surrounded by fields of golden wheat and mustard and corn. The vast East Anglian sky stretched from horizon to horizon. Brooks and streams cut dark ribbons in the fields where tawny cattle grazed. Here and there a white-paddled windmill beat the clear country air.

Idyllic surroundings, but not perhaps an idyllic time for the young family. Despite the experienced presence of Lucie's nurse, the Austins were nervous, as well as highly serious, parents. John Austin probably dealt with the noise, discomfort and anxiety created by the baby in characteristic fashion, by retreat: taking long walks in the fields and in the evening closeting himself in his makeshift study in the farmhouse. Sarah, meanwhile, would have hovered and responded to Lucie's every cry. Motherhood may not have been exhilarating, but it must have been absorbing and demanding, and then, too, the baby's needs were so uncomplicated and so easily met compared with those of her husband.

They returned to London and Queen Square in November when Lucie was nearly six months old. Sarah's mother, Susannah Taylor, had fallen in love with her tiny granddaughter over the summer and now wrote in response to Sarah's latest bulletin, 'It is a great comfort to hear of your animated little being. If she should keep to her present measure of health and activity, she will begin to walk by the time you visit Norwich [again] . . . Enjoy your precious child, dear Sally.'

There was another addition to the Austin household this same winter of 1821 and 1822. While Sarah was preoccupied with Lucie, John Austin set aside an hour or two each day to tutor James Mill's eldest child, fifteen-year-old John Stuart Mill, in Roman law and Benthamite Utilitarian thought. Soon serious, handsome young Mill became a sort of adopted son in the family. One of the first phrases Lucie learned to stammer out was 'Bun Don' for 'brother John', and later, when John began to study German with Sarah, he took to calling her *Mütterlein* or 'little mother'. Austin's role, however, remained that of mentor and tutor rather than father to John. No one could have supplanted the overbearing patriarch, James Mill. Yet the Austin home became a refuge for John; it was so different in every way from his own household next door, where his parents kept their distance (except at night in their bedroom) and eight younger brothers and sisters produced a continual din that disturbed his studies.

The younger Mill, as Austin soon discovered, was a prodigy: the successful product of James Mill's bold and unconventional experiment in childhood education. When John was only three, James Mill had started his instruction with lessons in Greek. By the time he was eight, the boy was well versed in Latin, history, mathematics and philosophy. He had read all the major classics before he was eleven, and at twelve he began to write a history of the Roman government in imitation of Hooke. In his teens, logic, chemistry, political economy and general literature were added to the programme. When he was fifteen, in 1821, his father decided that John should read for the Bar; hence his study of Roman law with Austin. And even after the law was rejected as a suitable profession and John followed in his father's footsteps with a clerkship in the East India Company, he continued his lessons with John Austin. By this time, young Mill was practically one of the family. As Sarah wrote to her mother, 'John Mill is ever my dearest child and friend and he really doats [*sic*] on Lucie and can do anything with her.'

Thus when the Austins went to Norwich again for the

summer of 1822, they took young Mill with them. The Taylors found him charming and young Mill became particularly close to Sarah Austin's widowed sister, Susan Reeve, and her nine-year-old son, Henry. John Mill and Henry Reeve, in fact, were almost Lucie's only childhood playmates for some years to come, and she saw Henry only when the Austins visited Norfolk. During this happy summer with the large Taylor clan and far removed from his father's stern influence, John Mill belatedly tasted the freedom and simple happiness of childhood. Playing one day with one-year-old Lucie, who was just learning to totter across the garden, he sufficiently forgot himself to lose his pocket-watch – a gift from James Mill – in the tall grass. Though he wrote to his father with great remorse over this misadventure, it was perhaps a telling one. There was no need to keep track of the time during those lazy summer days in Norwich.

★

Lucie's early childhood was undoubtedly strange – because she had no friends of her own age, because her father was so gloomy and remote, because there were no little brothers or sisters to join her in the nursery – yet it was not unhappy. Almost as soon as she could talk and understand the stories that her nurse and Sarah told her, she created a whole imaginary world of elves and fairies to keep her company. She saw companions everywhere and one day asked Sarah why the sunflowers in Regent's Park didn't speak to her. Animals, too, became a passion, and Lucie collected a menagerie of pet mice, canaries, newts and turtles.

When she was old enough to cross the square on her own, Lucie played in Bentham's garden at the Hermitage, where she could eat her fill of mulberries. But she had to be careful not to disturb the tapes laid out on the flowerbeds which marked the ground plan of Bentham's panopticon prison. If from his study window the old Utilitarian glimpsed 'Toodie', as she called herself and was called by others, he would sometimes join her:

as fantastical a figure as any that populated Lucie's pretend world of elves and fairies. For fifty years Bentham had scarcely bothered to alter his style of clothing: he wore an antiquated grey tail-coat, white woollen stockings which sunk down in folds about his ankles, ornately buckled shoes and a broad-brimmed straw hat, under which his white hair hung down to his shoulders. With Lucie in tow, he would lope about the garden at a pace somewhere between a brisk walk and a trot, making, as he explained to her, either an 'ante-prandial circumgyration' or a 'post-prandial perambulation'. Their exercise completed, Bentham might invite Lucie into his study, where she was transfixed by the numerous small bits of paper pinned to the heavy curtains. These, Bentham explained, were memoranda for improving the world. 'Many a constitution for the continent was born on that curtain.'

Meanwhile, John Austin's own particular contribution to the betterment of the world remained stubbornly inchoate. Though for some years he had scarcely set foot in a courtroom, it was only in 1825 that he formally gave up his practice at the Bar. His legal career now ended, Austin, in his interludes of relatively good health, tried to redouble his scholarly labours. But here, as in the lawcourts, he was stymied: not by his mental foes – anxiety and depression – but by his exacting intellectual habits of application. He could do nothing by halves, and had the sort of mind incapable of seeing the wood for the trees. So finely attuned and receptive was his intelligence that he was scrupulous not to neglect secondary or minor points even at the risk of distracting from the major issue. As Sarah later put it, 'he could do nothing rapidly or imperfectly; he could not prevail upon himself to regard any portion of his work as insignificant; he employed a degree of thought and care out of all proportion to the nature and importance of the occasion'. Things which should have been consigned to footnotes or omitted altogether consumed pages – and hours – of fastidious analysis. Arguments were engulfed by tangential observations. Bent over his writing desk, Austin foundered in nuance, suggestion, and obscure sequelae.

The result of this excessive intellectual thoroughness was that what Austin did manage to write was rendered virtually unreadable because of its lack of focus and bewildering maze of digressions. And more seriously still, almost nothing was ever completed. Closeted in his study, Austin was like a man in a bad dream who strenuously runs towards some goal only to have it continuously recede before him as he struggles to reach it. His study grate filled up with the products of this doomed chase: countless false starts, isolated asides, detached transitions and inconclusive perorations fuelled Austin's fire.

But not his career. He had failed in the army and at the Bar and now it looked as if he were bound to fail, too, as a legal theorist and Utilitarian philosopher. Sarah began to worry about money. In the five years since they had married, prices had sharply risen while their marriage settlement remained static. And of course now there were three of them, plus the additional expense of Lucie's nurse. Financial constraints as well as Austin's ill health also contributed to their decision not to have more children. As a close family friend observed, 'So straitened were they in their circumstances that they . . . looked upon the advent of another child as . . . a serious calamity.'

At a time when large families were still the norm and when contraception was uncommon and unreliable, it is not only the Austins' decision to have just one child – and a girl at that – which is striking. They were also surrounded by childless couples: the Grotes (no children followed the baby boy who died the same year that Lucie was born), the Carlyles, and – in time – John Stuart and Harriet Mill. In all these marriages, intellectual creativity – books produced by the men rather than babies by the wives – took precedence. The same was true of the Austins, but John, to Sarah's mounting anxiety, remained stubbornly barren.

Such was their state of affairs in 1826, the year Lucie was five, when a new, secular university in London was conceived and planned by Austin's Utilitarian and Whig friends, James Mill, Thomas Campbell, George Grote and Henry Brougham. From the beginning, London University offered a breadth of curriculum unknown at Oxford or Cambridge, and one of its new disciplines was jurisprudence. Mill and Grote, who knew that Austin's learning was vast despite his small written output, agreed that there was no one more able to hold the Chair of Jurisprudence, and Austin's was one of the first appointments made by the new university council.

Nothing could have been more opportune or timely. Here, at last, was a profession – that of university professor – which seemed both worthy of and congenial to Austin's talents and peculiarities. True, he would be called upon to lecture, but (John and Sarah agreed) the intellectually rarefied atmosphere of the lecture hall was far removed from the noise and congestion of the courtroom which had made him so ill. In every respect, he seemed ideally suited to an academic life.

The mere prospect of his professorship served to rouse and animate Austin. The university was not scheduled to open its doors until the autumn of 1828, and in the interim he decided to go to Germany to study comparative jurisprudence and prepare his lectures. Sarah, already fluent in German, was keen to go, and Lucie was eager for adventures that would take her beyond the familiar boundaries of St James's and Regent's Parks and summer holidays in Norwich.

★

John and Sarah closed up the Queen Square house in October 1827, and travelled first to Heidelberg and then settled in Bonn – the home of such scholars and thinkers as Schlegel, Niebuhr, Brandis and Heffer. They took lodgings close to the university and lived in an area of narrow, cobbled streets, cloistered halls and college greens. In the distance loomed the spires of the Gothic Münster; further afield, beyond the city gates, were the orchard-bordered banks of the Rhine where Lucie fed ducks and swans on Sunday afternoons.

The whole family thrived, but the most dramatic transformation was in John Austin. He found the heady, intellectual atmosphere of Bonn bracing and stimulating, attended Saturday night lectures at Schlegel's home, took tea at Niebuhr's and studied German and German law with a young Doctor of Law recommended to him by Schlegel.

But most important of all, he made progress with his own work. In early December Austin wrote to George Grote, 'I have been busily engaged with my lectures and in consequence of a great improvement in the state of my health, I have of late pursued and am now pursuing the work with hope and ardour, as well as with my wonted assiduity.' Instead of staying in bed until noon or for the whole day if his head ached or his digestion was awry, Austin now rose early and kept to a strict schedule. 'The following is the manner in which I pass my day,' he wrote to Grote: 'from eight to twelve, work; from twelve to two, exercise; from two to four (or half past) dinner, rest and reading some light book; from thence to ten or eleven, work. Consequently I have already made considerable progress.'

Sarah, too, was happy and for her the full days also passed quickly. 'Life here glides along,' she wrote to Harriet Grote. The people 'smoke and eat, work and dance; the studious men pore over researches . . . the women cook and knit and higgle for pfennigs'. Above all, she was buoyed by her husband's new industry and sanguine spirits. Tentatively, Sarah began to hope that their years of worry and illness were over. 'My glorious man,' she told Harriet Grote, 'goes on with the utmost steadiness and with unvarying cheerfulness and satisfaction. I believe with all my heart, my dear and most valued friend, that you will rejoice to see his excellencies come to view and my anxieties cease. If his health does but stand I fear nothing.'

Lucie must have thrived in this new atmosphere of her parents' contentment. She was now sent to school for the first time, where she learned writing, arithmetic, geography and, of course, German. And at last, Lucie had friends of her own age.

She invited her schoolmates to the Austins' lodgings for tea-parties, taught them English games and told them English stories.

'Our dear child is a great joy to us,' Sarah wrote to Harriet Grote when they had been in Bonn for four months. 'Her German is very pretty – she interprets for her father with great joy and naiveté.' On Christmas Eve, the Austins dined with the Schlegels and Lucie was entranced with the tall Christmas tree illuminated with scores of tiny white candles. Outside carollers sang on the cobbled streets and at midnight a bearded St Nicholas appeared with a bag full of toys over his shoulder. It was a night of enchantment and perhaps we can attribute to it Lucie's lifelong love of Germany and all things German.

By April 1828, John Austin had completed his study of German jurisprudence and outlined his first term's lectures. In the course of his studies, he had decided that he wanted to teach extemporaneously. So while in Bonn, he did not laboriously write out his lectures, but instead made extensive notes of their major points under various headings. He imagined himself at London University discoursing fluently on the intricacies of legal theory, pausing for effect when explaining particularly difficult points, and then at the end of the hour fielding his listeners' questions and delivering clever ripostes as well as further elucidation. He was eager now to return to London and begin delivering these engaging lectures.

In early May, Sarah packed up all the German books they had acquired – literature, philosophy, history, biography – and they prepared for the journey home. For Lucie, leaving Germany, where she first went to school and had friends her own age, and where her parents ceased being so preoccupied, gloomy and unwell, must have been a terrible wrench. Their idyll now was over, and so, too, was Lucie's fleeting taste of a conventional, secure, happy childhood.

But something else within her had also happened during this year in Bonn, and this she did not leave behind when the

Austins departed for England. Henceforward travel, for Lucie, would always be associated with well-being and wholeness. It was in Germany, among a different people, speaking a strange tongue, that she first fell under the spell of foreign lands.

★

Despite John Austin's eagerness to begin his academic career, almost as soon as the Austins crossed the threshold of Queen Square in June, his health broke down. Once again the curtains were pulled shut and Austin languished in bed with migraine, dyspepsia or merely paralysing lassitude. His lecture notes and books remained corded up in boxes in his study. Sarah reverted to her role of sick-nurse and her habitual state of anxiety. Lucie had to be careful not to make any noise that might disturb her father or distract her mother.

Except for Latin and German lessons with Sarah, she was now left largely to her own devices, and she soon resurrected her fantasy world and collected a new menagerie of toads, newts, goldfish and canaries. But most of all, now and in the years to come, Lucie read – voraciously: the *Odyssey*, *Don Quixote* and *Robinson Crusoe*, *The Rime of the Ancient Mariner*, Grimm's fairy tales (in German), Hakluyt's and Cook's *Voyages* and the *Arabian Nights*. Poring over these heavy, gilt-bound volumes, Lucie dreamt of strange and dangerous voyages, of icebergs and hurricanes and shipwrecks, of magic carpets and enchanted lamps. The books themselves became a magic carpet which transported her away from the hushed, morbid atmosphere of her parents' house.

By the time Lucie was eight, Sarah had begun to worry about her gifted, wayward daughter, though she didn't seem to realize that Lucie's precocity and self-sufficiency were partially the result of being left so much to herself. Writing to her sister, Susan Reeve, Sarah described Lucie as 'a monstrous, great girl, but though she has admirable qualities, I am not satisfied with her. She is too wild, undisciplined, and independent; and though she knows a great deal it is in a strange, wild way. She reads everything; composes German verses, has imagined and put together a fairy world, dress, language, music, everything, and talks to them in the garden; but she is sadly negligent of her own appearance.'

But Sarah had a great deal more to worry about in the autumn of 1828 than Lucie. By the time London University opened in October, John Austin had lost all his confidence and he now recoiled from the prospect of delivering extemporaneous lectures. Pleading ill health, he delayed taking up his professorship from one term to the next, insisting privately to Sarah that he must now write out his lectures in full before he could begin teaching. Months passed with Austin alternating days in bed with laborious stints at his desk, drafting and redrafting his inaugural lecture.

Finally, in November 1829, several weeks after the term had begun, Austin mustered his courage and, gripping the pages of his carefully written-out lecture, ascended the platform in the university lecture-hall. The class was larger than he expected – some thirty-two students, including Austin's old disciple, John Stuart Mill. Austin should have felt himself among like-minded friends, but the sea of masculine faces gazing up at him left him panic-stricken. His mouth went dry and he gulped for air; his hands shook convulsively as he shuffled the pages of his manuscript to find his place. When he finally cleared his throat and began to speak he was virtually inaudible.

Austin's discomfort was so acute that even if he had been able to make himself heard, it would have been difficult to follow what he was saying. One of his students, Henry Crabb Robinson, later explained that Austin was 'in so great a terror that the hearers could not attend to the matter of his lecture from anxiety for the lecturer'. Another student came away with the impression that this introductory lecture had consisted of a statement and restatement, many times over, of the impossibility of formulating an introduction to such a vast and complex subject as the theory of jurisprudence. Hesitant, mumbling, shaking, Austin spoke for a whole anguished hour on the futility of attempting to do what he, in fact, at that very moment was trying to do: introduce his students to the study of legal theory. He proved uniquely adept at pulling the rug out from under his own feet.

During subsequent lectures Austin was better able to control his stage-fright, but his performance was still an ordeal for both him and his listeners. He wrote and rewrote the lectures – sometimes postponing classes so that he had more time to revise – and then clung tenaciously to his dry, convoluted, repetitive text, which he read out in a whispery monotone. Not surprisingly, the number of students diminished with each lecture until, by the end of the session, there was only a handful left. And these hardy souls were a disgruntled lot. Austin had cancelled lectures so often because he was ill or unprepared, and he had got himself so lost in a maze of digressions, that he covered only a fraction of the stipulated material by the close of the academic year in June. In the end, Sarah had to intervene with the university authorities and arrange for Austin to give supplementary lectures, at no additional expense to the students, in the autumn.

By the summer of 1830, following his first session as a professor, Austin was so exhausted that he went on a short holiday to Sussex, without Sarah or Lucie, to try to recover from the great strain of writing and delivering his lectures. From here he wrote home to Sarah, 'My dear heart, pray tell me of your health. I am sorry to say that I am still in a state of incessant malaise, stomach deranged and a most distressing languor. This morning, however, I have begun with the cold bath; and that, I have little doubt, will set me up.'

Sarah, meanwhile, was greatly worried about how to keep the whole family 'set up' financially if Austin's academic career kept to its disheartening, downward course. His salary was dependent upon the number of students he attracted and the fees they paid. If he continued to drive them away he would swiftly make himself redundant. Horrified at this prospect, Sarah nevertheless steeled herself to prepare for it. Shortly after Austin returned from Sussex – not appreciably better in health or spirits – the family moved to a cheaper, smaller house that Sarah had found at 26 Park Road, close to Lucie's favourite haunt, Regent's Park.

★

It was not long before the Austins met their new next-door neighbours at Park Road. The Taylor family consisted of John Taylor, a wholesale druggist, his beautiful, intellectual wife, Harriet, and their two boys, the eldest of whom, Herbert, became Lucie's playmate. The two children soon discovered a hole in the hedge separating their houses which they crawled through when they wanted to meet secretly. Lucie led Herbert on clandestine expeditions to Regent's Canal, where they removed their shoes and stockings and paddled in the muddy water.

Sarah was much impressed with Herbert's mother, twenty-three-year-old Harriet Taylor, though perplexed that such a gifted woman had married a man like John Taylor who was a devoted and amiable enough husband and father, but without any imaginative spark or intellectual interests. Harriet, indeed, had come to feel increasingly restless and unfulfilled in her marriage, and shortly before the Austins moved to Park Road she had turned to her minister, the liberal-thinking Unitarian William Johnson Fox, for counsel. Fox was an enlightened man and said nothing of Harriet's marital duties or her husband's conjugal rights.* Instead, he took her desire for intellectual companionship – a partnership of minds based on shared interests

---

* Fox's liberal views were also reflected in his own domestic situation. When a member of His congregation died, he informally adopted the man's two daughters, Eliza and Sarah Flower, and in time became the lover of Eliza. In 1835 Mrs Fox publicly denounced her husband, whereupon he left her, taking Eliza Flower with him. Despite the ensuing scandal Fox remained a popular and influential preacher and also a prolific journalist.

and values – seriously, and suggested she befriend one of the most intelligent and able men of his acquaintance: none other than the Austins' 'adopted son' and former neighbour at Queen Square, John Stuart Mill.

Mill and Harriet Taylor first met at a dinner party at the Taylors to which Harriet had invited, among others, Fox and Sarah Austin's cousin, Harriet Martineau. John Taylor sat at the head of the table, genial but rather out of his element, while at the opposite end Mill and Harriet quickly became absorbed in an intimate conversation. At this time Mill was emerging from a four-year 'mental crisis' – a protracted breakdown, during which he had sunk into a depression as deep and black as any sounded by John Austin. Utilitarian precepts of happiness and social progress had been powerless to alleviate his melancholy. But Mill had found relief in Wordsworth's poetry, and now he discovered further solace in Harriet Taylor's intense sympathy. By the time the port was served, they had already reached an understanding.

But it remained for some time a difficult and delicate alliance. Harriet had no intention of leaving her husband and children, nor did Mill ever wish her to do so. Instead, a curious *ménage à trois* gradually evolved; its success depended not only on John Taylor's remarkable tolerance, but also – after Harriet bore Taylor a third child, a girl, in 1831 – on Harriet's abstaining from sexual relations with both her husband and Mill.★ Such abstinence also rescued Harriet from further childbearing which would have interfered with her desire to write, especially on the subject of the oppression of women.

Hence it came about that after moving to Park Road in 1830, Lucie and her parents still saw a great deal of 'Bun Don' Mill because of his almost daily visits to Harriet Taylor. On

★ The celibacy of Mill and Harriet's relationship, even after they married in 1851, has been the subject of a good deal of speculation and debate. One of the best discussions of their strange alliance is Phyllis Rose's in her irreverent study of Victorian marriage, *Parallel Lives* (1984).

Wednesdays, when the Taylors were 'at home', Mill didn't stir from his parents' home in Queen Square where he still lived. But on other weekday evenings, which John Taylor conveniently spent at his club, Mill invariably made his way to Park Road. The Austins' move was a great boon to him, for it made Harriet more accessible. Eyebrows might have been raised had Mill paid court four or five evenings a week to the Taylors. But no one would have commented on frequent visits to the Austins. And what could be more natural than to cross the garden and drop in on Harriet Taylor before making his way home to Queen Square?

John Austin was probably oblivious or indifferent to the developing 'affair' between Mill and Harriet Taylor, but Sarah must have been intrigued, perhaps even slightly jealous, for Mill and Harriet were in the process of creating precisely the sort of elevated union of minds and souls that Sarah had dreamt of during her long engagement to Austin. Lucie, if she wondered at all about the friendship between her old ally and Herbert Taylor's beautiful mother, wouldn't have thought it unusual. Her own mother was visited and admired by any number of men who stayed for tea or supper even when Austin was too ill or depressed to make an appearance. Lucie, indeed, grew up almost entirely ignorant of conventional ideas about the relations between men and women.

★

In November 1830, at the beginning of his second session of lectures, Austin arrived at the lecture hall one dark, wet evening to find it completely empty. The next morning he wrote to the university authorities, 'I waited last night in my Lecture Room from 6¾ to 7 o'clock but no pupil appeared . . . If I shall have no class during the present session, I shall be somewhat surprised as well as discouraged.' He postponed the course until January 1831, by which time eight students had been mustered, but his tenure with the university remained precarious and James Mill and George Grote had to organize a special subscription to subsidize Austin's professorship. The move to a cheaper house had relieved Sarah's immediate financial anxieties, as did the emergency subscription, but now she worried about the long haul and how they would manage if, as seemed increasingly likely, Austin lost his university post. As Sarah wrote to her sister, 'we cannot live on air'.

For years she had tried to inspire, cajole and finally goad Austin into industry. Now Sarah realized that her best hope lay in self-reliance. She decided to earn money herself as a translator and teacher. At the end of 1830, she published *A Report on the State of Public Education in Prussia* by the French philosopher and educationalist, Victor Cousin. It didn't earn her much money, but it was the first of many translations, the beginning of an independent career. Private tuition was a much humbler vocation, but not one Sarah felt beneath her. 'I have now ... undertaken another trade,' she informed her sister, 'namely giving lessons in Latin ... Lucie and I trot down to Bentinck Street with our bag of books, and quite enjoy it. I do not fancy myself at all degraded by thus agreeably earning a guinea a week.'

Nor did Lucie think it degrading. On the contrary, her mother was a potent example. The guineas in Sarah's pocketbook and, as time passed, the row of her translations ranged on a shelf next to her writing-table in the parlour proved her industry and self-sufficiency. During the years of Lucie's childhood the foundation of her parents' marriage was gradually shifting as Sarah came to displace Austin as the principal wage-earner. Given the times, though Lucie didn't realize it, her parents' marriage reversed the conventional roles of husband and wife: as Austin became increasingly passive and dependent, Sarah, of necessity, became more and more capable and energetic. 'I have to act,' she wrote to a friend, 'for if I sink, he falls.' To another she later confided, 'I am the man of business in our firm.'

She was also, as she said in another letter, 'the busiest woman in the world ... I have an immense deal to do – Lucie's education, nursing John, needlework, writing, etc.'. Something had to be delegated, and it couldn't be nursing John or writing. Hence in 1831, when Lucie was ten, she was sent to school again, to her delight, but to a very different establishment from the one she had attended in Bonn. Influenced by Cousin, Sarah selected for Lucie an advanced boys' school in Hampstead run by a learned German named Dr Biber. Like Sarah herself, Lucie was to have a masculine education, for Dr Biber made no concessions to his sole female student. 'Accomplishments' such as music, drawing and needlework – the staples of young ladies' education at the time – obviously were not offered. Instead, Lucie applied herself to a regimen of classics, mathematics, philosophy and ancient history. Lessons were demanding and challenging and competition with the other students keen. But Lucie thrived at Dr Biber's and Sarah was vindicated in her unusual choice. To her sister, Sarah wrote: 'the being relieved from the constant wear and fret of seeing my dear child not half educated is an immense thing. She seems chiefly to take to Greek with which her father is very anxious to have her thoroughly imbued ... I am quite willing to forego all the feminine parts of her education for the present.* The main thing is to secure her independence; both with relation to her own mind and outward circumstances. She is handsome, striking and full of vigour and animation.'

Dr Biber tamed Lucie's wildness and she soon outgrew her mischievousness and untidiness. She read the *Odyssey* in the original now, discovered Herodotus and immersed herself in the ancient worlds and wonders and travels of her classical studies. A new caller at the Austins' was much intrigued and impressed by Lucie at this time. He found her both 'really remarkable' and

---

* As it turned out, 'the feminine parts' of Lucie's education were permanently dispensed with. She never learnt how to play a musical instrument, do needlework or draw. Years later, in Egypt, she much regretted being unable to repair or sew clothes and, even more, to sketch, draw or paint.

'excessively odd': 'a very curious and interesting dark, pale . . .
young lady, solid, independent and self-possessed'. He was also
struck by her dreamy 'air of inspiration and abstraction . . . she
gazed up from her Latin lesson . . . as if she might be exclaiming
within herself, "Say, Heavenly Muse!" and when she spoke it
was, "Mother, what is the genitive case of *felix*?" '

★

Lucie and Sarah spent hours working together in the small Park
Road parlour – Lucie construing Latin and Greek verbs, Sarah
translating German, French and sometimes Italian books for
various London publishers. Most of these books were serious,
often scholarly works, but early in 1831 the publisher John
Murray sent something quite extraordinary to Sarah: an eccentric, intermittently ribald travelogue of England with the
bizarre title *Briefe eines Verstorbenen* ('Letters from a Dead Man').
The book was already a bestseller in Germany and had made its
author a celebrity, but his name – Prince Hermann von
Pückler-Muskau – was quite unknown to Sarah.

When she read the book Sarah was both captivated and
shocked by Pückler-Muskau's adventures in Britain in the late
1820s. Though his 'letters' were addressed to his wife back in Germany, they recounted various flirtations and worse with married
English ladies of the upper class. Pückler, in fact, was divorced
from his wife (with whom, however, he remained on amiable
terms while she continued to live in his castle in Muskau). He
had gone to England in search of an heiress to marry, and
though he failed in his quest, he cut a broad swathe through the
upper reaches of fashionable society, whose habits, customs and
institutions he described in great detail in his racy narrative.

Murray decided that the book was too risqué for him to publish, but Sarah was so intrigued by it that she persuaded another
publisher to commission a translation, with the understanding that
objectionable passages be cut or bowdlerized. This necessitated
correspondence with the author, and by the time a half-dozen
letters had been exchanged, Sarah had embarked on a 'postal

46

affair' with Pückler – the great romantic adventure of her life.

Yet she went into it with her eyes open. Even before she began work on the translation, Sarah made inquiries regarding Pückler's reputation in London, and what she learned was hardly reassuring. Rumour informed her that he was a middle-aged dandy, Don Juan and fortune-hunter, mocked by his detractors as 'Prince Pickling Mustard'. He was said to dye his hair and wear rouge, but like his hero, Byron, he had an extraordinary capacity to attract women, unmarried and married alike. Indeed, one of the darker stories Sarah heard of Pückler was that he had extorted £2,000 from the husband of a hopelessly infatuated woman with whom he had had an affair. No one could have been less like John Austin.

Very soon Sarah's letters to Pückler, with their lists of translation and editorial queries, began to shade into something quite different. Pückler was an adept at seduction and he spared none of his amorous talents to woo Sarah. He was by turns solicitous and kind, amusing and entertaining, concerned and appreciative. Soon Sarah found herself pouring out her heart to him, confiding all the difficulties of her situation: John Austin's ill health, coldness and indifference, their financial problems and uncertain future, and her only solace – her beautiful, intelligent young daughter, Lucie. Pückler announced that he was falling in love with his translator-in-distress, that he wanted to lighten her load and bring sunlight into her dark life. By the time Sarah published his expurgated book under the English title, *The Tour of a German Prince in England, Ireland and France*, in 1832, she was hopelessly enthralled and, in her biographers' phrase, 'contemplating adultery'.*

---

* Lotte and Joseph Hamburger have written two aptly titled books about Sarah and John Austin: *Troubled Lives* (1985), a biographical study of the Austins' marriage, and *Contemplating Adultery: The Secret Life of a Victorian Woman* (1991), based on Sarah's recently rediscovered correspondence with Pückler, which had been reported as war losses by German libraries. The letters are now in the Jagiellonian University Library in Cracow, Poland.

Sarah now spent her evenings in the parlour with Lucie writing Pückler passionate love-letters. He was her 'dear Original', her *'coeur de mon coeur'*, *'mon âme'*, her 'sweetest and dearest'. At first Sarah dwelt on their spiritual union: 'I love you ... I want to be yours ... [we] should pass blessed hours together [and] live together in a sort of oneness ... such as is not to be found twice.'

But Pückler had a more carnal vision of their relationship, and Sarah – in her loneliness and depression – proved equal to his sexual fantasies. Her sexual relationship with John Austin, she told Pückler, had 'been dead for years – *he would have it so*'. After such a long period of 'inhuman neglect and unkindness', she professed herself now both sexually eager and inventive: 'darling, I think were I with you in your embrace in your bed, I should be more glorious if I could invent a new pleasure for you.' To further kindle Pückler's desire, Sarah graphically enumerated all her physical charms, adding at the end of her catalogue, 'in truth, my love, all that is beneath the petticoat is worth one thousand times the rest'.

Not only did Sarah strive to present herself as sexually attractive to Pückler. At the same time, she downplayed her intellectual pursuits, denied that she was a 'blue stocking', and emphasized her unorthodox views and beliefs. Having heard that Pückler had taken male as well as female lovers, Sarah boldly stated that she saw nothing wrong with such 'Greek loves'. She was equally unconventional when it came to marital fidelity: 'chastity' to her seemed 'as little conducive to the good of the human race' as did fasting; 'if I were free ... to live with you ... be assured my conscience would never give me a single twinge'. Together thus, she told Pückler, they would experience 'the delight of giving and receiving equal rapture'. She promised him, 'I would humour you in your wildest vagaries and desires.'

Despite her avowals, Sarah was less sexually frustrated than starved of love, but it was the uninhibited sexual dimension of her correspondence with Pückler that made it so dangerous. Terrified that Austin might happen upon a letter, she used her publisher as a mail drop. Pückler had friends at the German embassy in London so their letters travelled to and fro between London and Muskau in the diplomatic bag rather than the more hazardous post. Sarah also told Pückler to write always in German (she herself used English), in archaic German script rather than his normal handwriting. The love-tokens they exchanged – portraits, locks of hair, handkerchiefs, jewellery – had to be hidden and closely guarded. When, for example, Pückler sent Sarah a locket containing some of his greying hair, Sarah wrote back, 'a thousand thanks for the lock of hair and for having it enclosed in such a manner that my lips can touch it. I am however afraid to wear the medallion. My child and I have . . . no separate existence. She has always been with me and sees all I do and all I wear. I would neither conceal it from her nor lie to her . . . I must have the hair put into some concealed place where I may wear it invisible to all eyes but mine.'

Yet despite Sarah's precautions with the locket, Lucie was not ignorant of Pückler's existence. On the contrary, from the beginning of the 'postal affair', Sarah took pains to involve Lucie in her strange new alliance. Pückler himself reassured Sarah 'that I always include your child in my fantasy picture of yourself'. Sarah responded with her wonted passion, focused now not on her epistolary lover but on Lucie happily reading Cicero beside her in the parlour as Sarah wrote: 'Oh, if you could see [my] . . . darling child – the sun of a gloomy life – the hope of a heart in which hope for itself was nearly extinct. She is a *herrliches kind* [wonderful child] – ten years old, tall and vigorous, with a rather pale face, a noble, thoughtful brow, from which her hair is parted and braided like that of a German child. She is perfectly natural . . . full of imagination and tenderness for every living thing. She loves you for your liaison with a mouse, for she has two tame ones in a cage. She speaks and reads German as a second *Muttersprache* [mother tongue] and has learned Latin from me since infancy. She has just begun Greek ... How she would delight to run about the fields and woods with you ... She has invented a *feen welt* [fairy world] ... of her own and tells me how the fairies are dressed, what they do and say and what sort of garden they live in ... "They ride," she said to me one day, quite earnestly, "on white staggs [*sic*] as light and small as antelopes, and while they gallop along their long hair floats in the wind." She is more Deutsch than English.'

By emphasizing Lucie's proficiency in German, imagining her playing outdoors with Pückler and sharing his love of animals, and finally by asserting that Lucie 'was more Deutsch than English', Sarah was, in effect, claiming Pückler as her daughter's spiritual (and therefore 'real') father. Occasionally, when they let their imaginations soar, Sarah and Pückler indulged in a fantasy love-child of their own: 'little Hermann'. (Though at other times, they discussed the necessity of using contraceptives should they ever be able to consummate their affair.) But it was much more realistic and rewarding to draw Lucie in as a participant in their relationship.

Not, of course, that Lucie at this time (or perhaps ever) understood its romantic nature. What fascinated Lucie about Pückler was that he was a prince who lived in a magnificent castle in Germany, a country of which Lucie still harboured fond memories. And his existence became even more vivid to her when Sarah undertook a great deal of shopping for Pückler in London. Very soon after they declared themselves to each other, in fact, Pückler's letters were as full of lists of goods he needed as of endearments. Sarah and Lucie went on long shopping expeditions during which they purchased for him sets of china, vases, rugs, mats, curtains, soap, sponges, curry powder, fish sauce, pickles, mustard, perfumes, fire-screens, replicas of the Elgin Marbles, and a bust of Byron (they failed to find the other requested one of Gibbon). Sarah was particularly pleased with the curtains she bought for Pückler's bedroom, but anxious about their care. 'If you can't get them properly cleaned,' she told Pückler, 'send them to me when they are dirty.'

Lucie, too, soon had her own little parcels to send to Pückler, accompanied by letters written in scrupulously correct German. Her earliest surviving letter is one to Pückler. Translated into English it reads:

DEAR PRINCE,

I am sending you a box of tapers to light lights and pipes. Send me back the box when it is convenient and I will fill it up again for you. Muskau must be very beautiful if it is like the picture which you sent to Mother. I want very much to come there and go around with you.

YOURS,
LUCIE AUSTIN

P. S. I made the tapers myself.

In subsequent letters Lucie sent Pückler some garden seeds, scented bags, and bookmarks, thanked him for a book of verse he had given to her, and then told him how she had adopted a pet dove: 'A cat killed its mother when it was only a few hours old and I have raised it. Now it sits on my shoulder and shouts his love for me in my ear for he loves me very much and I love him.' Even when Lucie didn't write to Pückler herself, she still communicated with him through her mother. In an early 1832 letter, for example, Sarah wrote, 'my child is well. She sends her love to you. Sweet and innocent creature, how you would love her. She bids me tell you she has a quite tame white mouse.'

Why did Sarah make Lucie a party to her affair with Pückler? Most obviously because it would have been difficult, if not impossible, to carry on with it without Lucie's knowledge. John Austin was usually in bed, closeted in his study or out, so that

Sarah could write her long letters to Pückler and pore for 'delicious hours' over his to her without Austin being any the wiser. Lucie, however, was almost constantly in Sarah's presence and aware of what or to whom her mother was writing.

But beyond this strategic consideration was another, more important reason. Sarah was playing with fire and doing so with a man not known for his discretion or moral fastidiousness. To protect herself from him, to invest their affair with a much-needed element of wholesomeness and simplicity, she drew in her 'sweet and innocent' daughter. Pückler, Sarah believed, would certainly think twice before compromising her child. And then Lucie, to some extent, must have also assuaged Sarah's own growing sense of guilt. Sarah was not as liberated as she boasted to Pückler, and it felt less like deception when Lucie accompanied her on her shopping trips for Pückler or to her publisher to collect or drop off letters, or when Lucie wrote her pretty little German notes to enclose with Sarah's own letters.

★

Throughout the early months of 1832 Sarah was obsessed with her correspondence with Pückler, but she also had to attend to the demands of daily life. Lucie rose to the top of the final class at Dr Biber's school and reluctantly left it. Sarah was too preoccupied and too busy to teach her now and hired a Swiss tutor to come three times a week to give her Greek lessons. A French governess named Madame Cauer was also employed for a time – 'a sweet, noble-minded and noble-looking woman', as Sarah described her to Pückler, 'not profound or accomplished but truly good and sensible'.

Meanwhile, in June 1832, John Austin gave his last lecture of the session at London University to a mere handful of students. Rather than confront such a meagre class again the following autumn – or, even worse, an empty lecture-hall – he decided to resign from his professorship. Thus the long, drawn-out débâcle of Austin's academic career drew to an end. Sarah later saw Austin's resignation as the tragic climax of her husband's life: 'the hope, the animation, the ardour with which he had entered upon his career as a teacher of Jurisprudence had been blighted by indifference and neglect; and in a temper so little sanguine as his, they could have no second spring ... This was the real and irremediable calamity of his life ... from which he never recovered.'

In the midst of calamity, Sarah was determined that something be salvaged from Austin's labours of the past three years. Phoenix-like, a greater, more enduring good must rise from the ashes of his failure. She urged him to publish the London University lectures which had been so inaudible and tedious on delivery, but would, she hoped, gain a comprehending and appreciative audience in print. When Sarah broached the idea to Austin he was, as usual, indifferent: he told her he wouldn't oppose publication, but neither would he exert himself in any way to bring it about. It was left to Sarah to negotiate with John Murray, who had turned down Pückler's book but was willing, if not eager, to publish Austin's. Sarah meticulously prepared the manuscript and corrected the proofs, even though she herself was in the midst of translating no less than three books from the German. *The Province of Jurisprudence Determined*, as the collection of Austin's lectures was entitled, was published at the end of 1832. Thus, within months of each other, Sarah brought out both her husband's and her 'lover's' books.

Unlike Pückler's extravagant travelogue, Austin's was a slender volume which, despite Sarah's hopes, provoked little attention and even less admiration. While the *Tour* became a bestseller, *The Province of Jurisprudence* withered on the vine. No reviews appeared in the popular press and the notices it eventually received in learned journals were wary and lukewarm. It is questionable whether reviewers even bothered to plough through a whole book of Austin's turgid prose. Lord Melbourne judged it 'the dullest book he had ever read . . . full of truisms elaborately set forth'.* None of this, of course, buoyed Austin's already low spirits after resigning his professorship or alleviated Sarah's worries.

Foremost among these was money, or rather the lack of it now that Austin was once again unemployed. They still had their marriage settlement allowance and Sarah calculated that she could earn £100 a year with her translating and reviewing, but even so it would be difficult to make ends meet even if they moved to a still cheaper house and Lucie's Swiss tutor and French governess were dismissed. Not surprisingly, Sarah's thoughts turned to Germany, where they would be able to live much more economically, where Lucie could receive the best instruction for a fraction of the cost of her education in England, and Austin could happily pursue his scholarly activities as he had in Bonn four years earlier. But Sarah now proposed Berlin – only about fifty miles away from Muskau – rather than Bonn as their prospective continental home.

Lucie was delighted at the prospect of returning to Germany and of visiting Prince Pückler at his beautiful castle in Muskau. Austin was not enthusiastic, but neither was he opposed to the idea of another period of exile. Sarah was elated at how fate now seemed to be playing into her dream of meeting Pückler, and she went so far as to ask him if he could find some dignified and appropriate employment for Austin in Berlin. Pückler, himself, was far less eager to have the Austin family almost on his castle doorstep, and from the time that Sarah first broached

* Posthumously, however, Austin has had his day. In *Troubled Lives*, Lotte and Joseph Hamburger assess his position as 'a major figure in legal philosophy. [After his death, Austin's] theory of law acquired . . . great influence, and it continues to provoke interest and controversy among scholars – the very word "Austinian" has become part of the language. Austin's work established the study of jurisprudence in Britain; he was the catalyst that set others on the path of examining fundamental legal notions.' While it is difficult to imagine Austin as a catalyst, it is true that his ideas still possess currency today in academic circles, and thus Sarah's determination to publish *The Province of Jurisprudence Determined* is vindicated.

the plan in her letters, Pückler's own letters became distinctly cooler and less frequent.

For more than a year the possibility of a season of retrenchment in Berlin remained up in the air. In June 1832, Lucie celebrated her eleventh birthday. She was now slender, and almost as tall as her mother. She stopped plaiting her hair and let it hang in a dark, heavy mass down her back. Her eyes were large and dreamy under straight brows, and she had a pale, translucent complexion that suffused with colour when she became excited.

Soon Lucie would develop into a striking young woman, but the whole process was to be a rather lonely ordeal. Sarah was preoccupied with Pückler and busy with translations, and Lucie had no sisters, nor even friends who were girls to initiate her into the mysteries of all these changes. Her childhood had been spent almost exclusively in the company of boys and men — 'Bun Don' Mill, her cousin Henry Reeve in Norwich, old Bentham in Queen Square, Herbert Taylor on Park Road and her classmates at Dr Biber's school in Hampstead.

Though she lacked female friends of her own age, Lucie had a great deal of adult companionship in her parents' parlour in the evenings. For despite their reduced circumstances, Sarah kept up her salon at Park Road and Lucie was allowed to stay up later now and mix with the various Utilitarians, radicals, editors, scholars and writers who congregated at the Austins' on their evenings 'at home'. These included old friends such as Bentham, the Mills, and the Grotes. But there were also a number of newcomers. Sarah's various writing and translating projects had, in fact, considerably enlarged the Austins' social net, and among the new fish who swam into it was a queer Scottish specimen named Thomas Carlyle.

When the Austins first met him, Carlyle was an unknown, largely unpublished, impoverished, dyspeptic writer of thirty-six: a tall, gangling man with copious side-whiskers and piercing eyes. He had come to London to seek a publisher for his book,

Sartor Resartus, an eccentric philosophical treatise-cum-autobiography strongly influenced by German Romanticism. Given their shared enthusiasm for German literature, it is not surprising that Sarah and Carlyle got on well. And Lucie's fluency in German and tales of German life in Bonn utterly charmed him.

After his first evening at the Austins', Carlyle wrote to his wife, Jane, back in their remote Scottish village, Craigenputtock, that Sarah was 'the most enthusiastic of German mystics ... a true Germanized spiritual screamkin', and then he added, 'but I must give you some notion ... of her visual aspect: ... a symmetrical length (the middle size) with a pair of clearest, warm blue eyes (almost hectically intense), considerable mouth, and moustache on the upper lip'.* Carlyle was equally vivid but considerably less enthusiastic about John Austin, whom he described as 'a lean, greyheaded, painful looking man, with large, earnest, timid eyes and a clanging, metallic voice that at great length set forth Utilitarianism *steeped* in German metaphysics, not dissolved therein: a very worthy sort of limited man'.

Despite his reservations about John, Carlyle's friendship with the Austins prospered. Lucie became his 'Lucykin', while Sarah was elevated to 'Dear Heroine' and 'Sunlight through waste-weltering chaos'. Certainly Sarah tried to shed some light on Carlyle's literary prospects. She introduced him to writers and editors, and encouraged him in the daunting task of finding a publisher for *Sartor Resartus* (unsuccessfully at first, but eventually it was serialized in *Fraser's Magazine*). And it was Sarah who introduced Carlyle to John Stuart Mill, thereby initiating one of the most celebrated friendships of the era. When Jane

---

* Carlyle wasn't the only contemporary of Sarah who remarked on her moustache. Like some dark-haired women, she had visible facial hair, and though she resorted to other cosmetic measures such as dyeing her hair when it turned grey, she doesn't seem to have done anything about her moustache. It was one of her physical defects that she had to concede to Pückler, who not only shaved but also wore rouge.

Carlyle came and joined her husband in London she was equally impressed by his new friends. Sarah Austin, she wrote to her niece, was 'the best woman I have . . . found here', while young Mill, she said, 'I like best of all the literary people'. By the time the Carlyles returned to Scotland they had become fast friends of the Austins.

Another new addition to the Austins' Park Road drawing-room was a young lawyer and budding writer named Charles Buller, soon to distinguish himself as a radical MP in the House of Commons. Buller was one of the few people to persevere to the end of *The Province of Jurisprudence Determined* and admire it, and he was also familiar with Sarah's translations. In the summer of 1832, when Sarah was still trying to smooth the way for going to Germany, Buller invited the Austins to his country home in Cornwall and the Berlin plan was deferred indefinitely. Sarah wrote disconsolately to Pückler, 'this summer it is decreed that we all go to Polvellan in Cornwall . . . so no hope of [Germany] . . . for this year'. The Cornwall holiday also disrupted Sarah's correspondence with Pückler – a severe but necessary deprivation, as she wrote to him before they left: 'I think it safest . . . for you not to write me . . . while I am away . . . The letters arrive at Polvellan at breakfast time and are laid on the table before a score of people . . . I know my treacherous face and the rush of blood from my heart to it, that will follow the sight of your hand . . . I will write to you and bear the privation [of no letters from Pückler] as I may.'

Lucie, too, was disappointed that they weren't going to Germany, but cheered when Sarah asked John Stuart Mill to join them in Cornwall. Lucie, indeed, was the only one who seemed to enjoy the holiday. From Polvellan, Sarah wrote of her to Pückler, 'Lucie . . . is the happiest being in the world, fishing, riding and picking up shells on the shore.' While Lucie thrived outdoors in the bracing Cornish air, Sarah sat inside working on her translations and writing furtive letters to Pückler. Austin, meanwhile, got a severe cold which developed into a fever and bronchitis. Both Lucie and Sarah nursed him and when the worst of his symptoms passed, they all went on an outing to Land's End which, Mill wrote to Carlyle, 'set [them] up in health and spirits'.

For Lucie the holiday in Cornwall was an idyll – catching butterflies with Mill, riding one of Buller's horses through woods full of summer wildflowers. But it may well have been a bittersweet time for Sarah and Austin and 'Bun Don' Mill: reminding them of their visit to Norwich ten years earlier, when Lucie was scarcely more than a baby, and the future beckoned with hope and promise. Now the intervening decade cast a long shadow: Mill was scarred by his protracted 'mental crisis' and the Austins by years of false starts, worry and failure.

Lucie had no memories of that golden summer in Norwich and how young Mill had lost his pocket-watch playing with her in the tall grass. And she had, too, nothing to mourn or regret. She didn't realize how strange her childhood had been nor how odd her parents were: a father with overwrought nerves and a deranged stomach who spent days in bed while her mother laboured at abstruse translations, wrote voluminous letters to and went on endless shopping trips for a German prince she had never met. Lucie was far more her mother's than her father's child: independent, resourceful and brave, but without Sarah's burden of anxiety and overwork. And Lucie possessed a capacity for joy and a delight in beauty that her parents had long since left behind, but which never in the years ahead would desert her.

Chapter Three

During those long summer days of 1832, back in London, in Queen Square, Lucie's old playmate Jeremy Bentham lay dying. He was eighty-four, but still, as John Stuart Mill put it, 'a boy to the last'. And a romantic boy at that. Shortly before the Austins went to Cornwall, Bentham wrote to Sarah, 'odd as it is, I am still alive', and enclosed with his letter a lock of his long white hair and a ring, the only ring, he told her, that he had ever given to a woman.

Now his life was ebbing away and his books and papers and blueprints for a better world were gathering dust in his library. Scarcely half a mile distant from Bentham's silent house, one of his great causes, the first Reform Bill, was being debated in Parliament. The Austins and their radical friends, of course, all supported the bill, which was designed to bring about electoral reform by abolishing 'rotten' and 'pocket' boroughs and extending the franchise to the moneyed middle classes. Another Austin friend, Sydney Smith, only slightly exaggerated the high hopes in Whig circles for the bill when he quipped: 'All young ladies expect that as soon as the Bill is carried they will be instantly married; schoolboys believe that gerunds and supines will be abolished, and that currant tarts must ultimately come down in price; bad poets expect a demand for epics, and fools will be disappointed as they always are.'

Two days after the bill was passed in June, Bentham departed from a world he had always found wanting, but never ceased trying to improve. Even in death he was an inveterate Utilitarian. To the horror of his friends, he left his body to University College London, to be dissected in accordance with his idea of the 'Auto-icon or the Use of the Dead to the Living'. Once he thus proved himself scientifically useful, his remains were clothed in his usual eccentric attire (including his straw hat), and stored in a cupboard at the College.*

Bentham's death left a hole in the fabric of the Austins' social and intellectual life, but it was soon partially filled by a man who was in many respects Bentham's opposite: a wealthy, Irish aristocrat named Thomas Spring-Rice, who was Secretary to the Treasury. Spring-Rice, who had also been a warm supporter of the Reform Bill, may have been introduced to the Austins by Mill. His wife was an invalid and seldom seen in society, but one or more of their eight children often came with their father when he called on the Austins.

Lucie, long accustomed to the staid company of adults, was fascinated by the lively Spring-Rices, and the youngest daughter, Alice, who was fifteen and called 'Dofo', became Lucie's intimate friend and confidante. Lucie, in fact, quickly lost her heart to Alice, who was three years her senior and the first girl-friend she had ever had. Now, at last, she had someone to help her negotiate the difficult passage of adolescence. And also – perhaps inevitably – to fall in love with. Lucie and Alice embarked on a feverish correspondence; soon Lucie was calling Alice 'my own darling wife', and closing her long letters with love from 'your faithful husband, Roger Austin'.

It is in her ardent letters to Alice Spring-Rice – so different from the simple, correct schoolgirl notes she had written to Pückler a year or so earlier – that we first see Lucie from within. She bared her soul to Alice as she had to no one else, not even to her mother; she wrote poems to her, loaned her German books, urged her to read Shakespeare's sonnets. Above all, Lucie was transported by their emotionally charged friendship. 'Dofo, my dearest friend,' she wrote to Alice, 'how is it, how can it be that you love me so much? When I think of it I

* And there, in all his grotesque splendour, Bentham remains to this day at University College in Bloomsbury. Now, however, he is on permanent display – the cupboard having been fitted with a glass front – an enduring monument to his belief in 'the use of the dead to the living'.

feel bewildered and wonder whether I am really that Lucy★ [*sic*] Austin whom the Spring-Rices are fond of . . . No one else loves me or ever did love me, how is it, what is it in me that you above all others see to love? There are people better, more wise, more clever, more amiable, more beautiful, of higher rank, of greater fortune and interest, who move in better society, who are amusing and yet you choose to love and to take for a friend Lucy Austin, and what can possibly recommend her? I can think of but one thing, look round the world and find one who will love you more and then cast off Lucy.'

Lucie adored Alice, but she did not feel entirely sure of Alice's devotion to her. The Spring-Rices moved in élite, titled circles, and in a few years time Alice's father would be elevated to the peerage as Lord Monteagle. There was, then, an aristocratic, social dimension of Alice's life that Lucie could scarcely hope to share. While she construed Latin verbs and read Herodotus and Virgil in the small Park Road parlour, Alice was caught up in a social whirl of balls and dinner parties and nights at the theatre. As her diary shows, there was no time for Alice to moon over her relationship with Lucie: 'I go to a party [at the Duke of Kent's] on Wednesday; on Thursday . . . a ball in the evening; on Friday I go to a ball; on Saturday we have a large party; on Sunday we have [another] large party, to which Mrs and Miss Austin are coming.' What to Lucie must have been the high-point of the week – going to the Spring-Rices' and seeing her 'beloved Dofo' – was for Alice merely one more party in a week full of such occasions.

It is striking, however, that in their fantasy 'marriage', Lucie assumed the dominant role of the husband, 'Roger Austin',

★ As a child Lucie often spelled her Christian name with a final 'y' rather than 'ie' and Sarah Austin and Lucie's husband Alexander always spelled it this way. On her marriage certificate and even in an 1867 legal document, Lucie also used the more conventional 'Lucy' spelling. But after her marriage in 1840 she invariably signed letters with 'Lucie', perhaps because it was more distinctive and unusual; it was also the German spelling of her name.

while Alice, who was older, more socially aware and experienced, played the part of Lucie's 'darling wife'. Despite Alice's age, social position and wealth, she was the passive partner. Lucie had been raised and educated with boys; in her own family her mother was 'the man of business in our firm'. Alice Spring-Rice was a most conventional young lady; Lucie was her mother's daughter – strong and independent – even in love.

★

While Lucie alternated between ecstasy and anxiety over Alice, Sarah kept doggedly at her translations, and almost as doggedly she still clung to her dream of going to live for a spell in Germany, ostensibly to economize, but even more to be near Pückler. But then suddenly in the summer of 1833, everything was turned upside-down in the Austin household, and for the first time in years Sarah found herself contemplating a future that didn't threaten financial disaster.

In July, John Austin's father came to London and, seeing how hard-pressed his son's family was, Austin senior provided immediate financial assistance and then made out a generous will. Sarah related the details of this windfall to Pückler, and also how her father-in-law negotiated with her rather than his son: 'Austin père . . . had a tête à tête with me at night, made known his intentions of giving us whatever was necessary to our living here – and of instantly making his will with such provision for my husband, self and child as will place us beyond the reach of anxiety and secure to the dear girl [Lucie] a very good fortune at our death.'

Fast on the heels of Jonathan Austin's largesse came two additional, unexpected strokes of good fortune. John Austin was appointed by his friend, Henry Brougham the Lord Chancellor, to the Criminal Law Commission, at a salary of £500 a year (more than double his professorial salary at London University), and he was invited by the Society of the Inner Temple to deliver a course of lectures on jurisprudence which would also bring in a handsome remuneration.

Across the English channel, in Muskau, Pückler must have heaved a sigh of relief when he got Sarah's letters reporting all their good news. Reduced circumstances would not now propel the Austins to his castle gates. But Sarah herself, and perhaps also Lucie, who longed to meet her mother's German prince and visit his castle, felt ambivalent about their improved fortunes. 'Whether to rejoice or not,' Sarah wrote to Pückler, 'I in my secret life know not, but *to all appearance* this is a matter of great congratulation.' She went on to confess, however, 'if you think I am very violently happy, you are mistaken'.

John Austin's immediate reaction to the promising future which now confronted him was, characteristically, to fall ill. Except for his father's gift, Austin was going to have to *earn* his generous salary and stipend from the Criminal Law Commission and the Inner Temple. Any change for Austin – large or small, good or ill – was registered on the delicate barometer of his physical and mental health. Favourable prospects could be as daunting as collapse and failure. Austin went to bed. It was a sultry, hot summer and he didn't improve. In August, Sarah decided they should go abroad for Austin to regain his health and fortify himself for all the work which lay ahead. Germany – Muskau – beckoned again, of course, but she closed her eyes to their claims. She knew that Austin would need and demand every last ounce of her energy, as a nurse, secretary, and self-sacrificing wife. This was no time to consummate her 'postal affair'. And so Sarah settled on Boulogne, just across the channel from Dover, where the climate was mild in summer, and where, too, they could live cheaply until Austin was well enough to return to London and his great expectations.

★

Sarah and Lucie set off for France early in August 1833, leaving Austin to follow with Sarah's maid (an excellent nurse) when he felt strong enough to travel. After a rough crossing, they reached Calais at one in the morning. It was a pitch-dark night, but Sarah managed to find the Hôtel de Bourbon and woke up the housekeeper, who was amazed to see a respectable English-woman and her pretty daughter at that hour, without a husband or even a maid. She gave them a room for what remained of the night, and the next day Sarah and Lucie took the coach to Boulogne and found rooms at the Marina Hotel, overlooking the harbour. A week or so later, in his own good time, John Austin arrived with Sarah's maid.

Boulogne in the 1830s was still a quiet fishing village with narrow, cobbled streets and clapboard cottages bordering the sea front. It was also something of a haven for financially beleaguered English families. The Austins, however, shunned their compatriots: Sarah was busy preparing a volume of selections from the Old Testament, and John Austin, who remained enervated and off colour, rarely stirred from the inn. Lucie, however, flourished in the clear, salt sea air. She quickly became as fluent in French as she was in German, and was a great favourite with the French fishermen and their wives and children: helping to mend their nets, learning their ballads and sea tales. A sailor named Pierre Henin taught Lucie how to swim, but her closest friends were a family named Fleuret. Monsieur Fleuret, she wrote to Alice Spring-Rice, was 'the handsomest *matelot* and the best bred and most gentlemanly man in Boulogne . . . I must pay him a visit of congratulation tomorrow for his wife *a fait un enfant aujourd'hui* at which he is much pleased. I can't think why,' Lucie added, 'for he has five already and only one room to put himself and his family in . . . [but] it is the neatest and cleanest [room] I ever saw.'

Lucie was intrigued by the lives of the French fishermen and struck by the power exercised over them by their wives. 'The men are null except at sea,' she explained to Alice. 'They bring home their fish, the wives go down to the boat, each takes her husband's share on her back in a basket, trots off to market and sells it, never giving her husband any account of the money: the wife furnishes the house, clothes her husband, children and self, so the husband has nothing to spend at the alehouse and is entirely under the dominion of his . . . wife, and a very excellent thing for him too.' The responsibility which Sarah Austin assumed by default was, according to Lucie, the natural order of things in France: 'it is the women . . . [who] do the hard labour which requires great strength and patience, not the men'.

Lucie spent her days at Boulogne out on the wharves or in the Fleurets' one-room cottage, but at sunset she returned to the inn and dined with her parents and the other guests. One evening, waiting in the drawing-room for dinner to be served, she noticed a short, fat man scowling in the corner, a book open on his lap. Close by, two Englishwomen chattered shrilly, oblivious to the dark glances the reader cast in their direction. Finally he snatched off his spectacles and interrupted them: caustically observing in a pronounced German accent that if his reading disturbed their conversation he would be very glad to leave. At this the silly women fell silent, just as the dinner gong sounded.

Seated in the dining room, Lucie found the volatile man gulping down his soup beside her. As was their habit, Lucie and Sarah conversed in German over dinner. No sooner had they begun discussing the day's events than the man at Lucie's elbow announced in German that he was none other than Heinrich Heine. Lucie was struck dumb for a moment and then, before Sarah could speak, she asked, 'And who is Heinrich Heine?'

Fortunately Heine was amused by Lucie's ignorance, and Sarah hastily made up for it with her admiration of his poetry and political writing. In the coming days, in fact, Sarah and Heine had lengthy discussions about his work-in-progress: a learned attack on contemporary German thought and literature that was a departure from Heine's earlier romantic poetry and topical satire.

Lucie leavened the drudgery of Heine's labour on this *magnum opus*, and she also lightened a heavy heart. Part of Heine's spleen was due to the fact that, like Sarah, he was in the grip of an impossible love affair — in Heine's case with a much younger, beautiful Parisian shopgirl. Lucie sang him English ballads and the French songs she had learned from her *matelot* friends. She took long walks with Heine by the sea, and he, in turn, fabricated strange tales for her in which 'fishes, mermaids, water sprites and a very old French fiddler with a poodle . . . were mixed up in the most fanciful way'. As Lucie said much later, she 'always remembered with great tenderness the poet who told me the beautiful stories and . . . [was] so kind to me and so sarcastic to everyone else'.

One stormy night at the end of August, just as Lucie and Sarah were preparing for bed, they heard a commotion out on the beach below their windows: shouts of men mingled with the moaning gusts of wind; beams of light cast by lanterns danced along the shore. Despite the high tide and crashing white breakers, fishermen dragged their boats down to the water from high ground. Then, when a full moon emerged from a passing cloud, Lucie and Sarah saw what was wrong: etched against the indistinct line dividing the ink-black sea from the purple-blue of the sky, they could make out the shape of a sinking ship.

Leaving Austin sound asleep, Sarah and Lucie hurried down to the main hall of the inn just as the first bodies of the victims were being carried in. They saw to their horror that these were all of young women, several of which had the corpses of babies strapped to them. Then one of the sailors explained: the doomed vessel was the *Amphitrite*, a transport ship full of women convicts bound for Botany Bay, New South Wales. For most of these unhappy passengers the ocean, as Heine later observed, 'was as pitiless as the laws of England; it showed them no mercy and interred them icily'.

Efforts were made, however, to save them. Despite the storm and towering waves, Lucie's friend Pierre Henin swam out to the remains of the ship in the vain hope of trying to rescue any surviving passengers clinging to the wreck. Back at the inn, Sarah ordered a ground-floor room to be cleared for use as a first-aid station, and with Lucie at her side, she tried to resuscitate a number of the women who were washed up on the beach. But the room where she and Lucie laboured became a morgue rather than a hospital as body after body was carried in. Out of the 131 passengers on board the *Amphitrite*, only four of the crew were saved. All of the women and children perished, and it was of little consolation to Sarah that she was later awarded a medal for her bravery by the Royal Humane Society.

The whole gruesome episode haunted her for weeks afterwards, even after they returned to London. She came to feel that the real horror of the *Amphitrite* disaster had not occurred off the coast of Boulogne, but rather in England, where these women had been driven to theft and prostitution and then condemned and exiled for their 'crimes'. Sarah finally vented her outrage in a letter to *The Times*: 'These 120 women and children [who drowned] . . . were more kindly treated by the raging elements than by the Society that corrupted and then cast them forth. My poor offending sisters! It is not your death I weep for, terrible as it was, it is the bitter hours of shame and guilt that preceded it – the cruelty and injustice of man to you.'

After the *Amphitrite* wreck, the weather abruptly changed; it became too cold for Lucie to swim or spend her days outdoors. It was time to go home. Austin's health remained uncertain, but the work of the Criminal Law Commission and the students at the Inner Temple were awaiting him whether he was ready or not.

★

It was autumn when they returned to London, and in a matter of weeks all of Austin's good prospects withered as surely as the last green leaves of summer. He braved fog and rain to attend the opening meetings of the Criminal Law Commission, but returned 'disheartened and agitated'. To Sarah he tersely conceded that he had argued with the other commissioners, but he refused further explanation. Instead, he retreated to his study to work on the Inner Temple lectures. These, however, soon threatened to be a distressing reprise of Austin's London University career. He cancelled the opening lectures because he was unable to prepare them in time. When he finally did appear at the Inner Temple, gripping his inaugural lecture, he could neither control nor conceal his stage-fright. He stammered out the opening sentences and then lapsed into a tedious and for the most part inaudible monotone. Not surprisingly, only a handful of students turned up for his second lecture. Before he finished writing the third, Austin was informed that the series was cancelled.

In the face of Austin's double failure in the winter of 1833 – for he soon resigned from the Criminal Law Commission as well – Sarah did what she had done in the past under such circumstances: she worked and moved house. She laboured on a translation of Falk von Müller's three-volume *Characteristics of Goethe*, and in November they left Park Road and Regent's Park and moved to a cheaper, nondescript, three-storey house at 5 Orme Square: a cul-de-sac facing a small patch of garden that hardly qualified as a square, just off the decidedly *déclassé* Bayswater Road.

By the time they had moved down in the world to Bayswater, Sarah had become something of an expert at house-hunting on a budget in London. Hence when the Carlyles decided in early 1834 to emigrate from remote Craigenputtock to London they appealed to Sarah to find them a suitable and economical house. Though she was hard-pressed by publishers and editors, and the weather was dreary and cold, Sarah and Lucie took to spending their afternoons combing the streets and squares and mews of Bayswater, Kensington, Knightsbridge and Chelsea for just the right home for the Carlyles. The ideal home, Sarah explained to Lucie, required above all a comfortable, warm and *quiet* study for Carlyle, whose powers of concentration were prodigious, but who was, like John Austin, plagued with physical and mental ailments, including chronic dyspepsia.

Though Lucie and Sarah did all the legwork, up north in

Craigenputtock Carlyle soon wearied of the whole endeavour of finding a house. 'My . . . soul grows sick in the business of house-seeking,' he wrote to Sarah in March. 'I get to think, with a kind of comfort, of the grim house six feet by three which will need no seeking.' Nonetheless, Carlyle went on to specify his simple needs: 'I must have air to breathe; I must have sleep also, for which latter object' – and here he burst into Latin – '*procul, o procul este* [away, away with you] ye cursed tribes of bugs, ye loud bawling watchmen that awaken the world every half hour only to say what o'clock it is!'

After a month or so of searching, Sarah and Lucie found a detached house with a 'little bed-quilt of a garden' in Kensington for the very reasonable rent of £32 a year. Carlyle was delighted and wrote back to Sarah by return post that 'the house which Lucykin and you describe so hopefully seems as if it had been expressly built for us'. But Sarah and Lucie's labours were not finished. Jane Carlyle, 'full of cares, tumults and headaches', did not write to Sarah directly, but her husband's letters now were taken over with her housewifely queries and worries. 'What are the fixtures, beyond grates,' Carlyle wrote to Sarah. 'We have window curtains, venetian blinds, etc., etc. . . . which might chance to fit . . . The measured dimensions of all the rooms and windows (if you can procure them) will bring the whole matter before us.' There was also the problem of carpets: again, Carlyle said, 'nothing can be decided till we know the sizes'.

Sarah and Lucie took tape-measures to Kensington and carefully ascertained the exact dimensions of all the windows and floors. But then, very late in the day, Carlyle and Jane abruptly withdrew from the negotiations for the Kensington house and decided instead to take another at 5 Cheyne Row, Chelsea, found for them by their friend Leigh Hunt, who lived nearby.

They moved to London in June, with Jane's canary, Chico, and a maid named Bessie Barnet. Sarah and Lucie were among their first callers. Lucie was captivated by Chico and Sarah sympathized with Jane's difficulties hiring servants and silencing a rooster next door – both matters not easily remedied. The Carlyles also called on the Austins in Bayswater. John Austin's gloom, however, made it a trying visit. Three years earlier, Carlyle had found Austin 'limited' but 'worthy'. Now his verdict was 'so acidified a man has he grown; and produces nothing but acid'.

If Carlyle – who was renowned for his own acerbity – found Austin's acidity oppressive, the atmosphere at the Orme Square house for Lucie and Sarah must have been at times nearly insupportable. To escape it, Sarah decided that they should go to visit her brother in Hastings for a month or so and then spend the rest of the summer again in Boulogne.

In late June, shortly after Lucie's thirteenth birthday, they decamped from Bayswater and took the coach south to Hastings, the history of which Lucie well knew. Like Boulogne, almost directly across the channel, Hastings was a seaport and fishing village. It was also a popular watering place, and on fine days, along its three-mile promenade bordering the sea front, men and women of means and fashion strolled or pushed or reclined in cumbersome Bath chairs.

Soon after arriving in Hastings, the Austins made the acquaintance of one of the town's most prominent citizens: Frederick North, MP for Hastings, and a Whig like the Austins who had voted for the Reform Bill. North was married to the widow of Robert Shuttleworth of Gawthorpe Hall, Lancashire, and by her first husband Mrs North had a daughter named Janet who was about the same age as Lucie. The two girls immediately became fast friends and soon Lucie was spending almost as much time in the Norths' house as in her uncle's. She fascinated Janet's younger half-sister, Marianne North, who later recalled how Lucie's 'grand eyes and deep-toned voice, her entire fearlessness and contempt for what people thought of her' impressed the whole family. On rainy days when they couldn't search the beach for shells or walk the promenade, Lucie 'would sit for hours . . . in a rocking chair' at the Norths', reading Shakespeare out loud to Janet and Marianne, 'acting and declaiming her favourite parts', and entrancing her audience.

But Lucie's dramatic flair could be alarming as well as entertaining. Shortly after the Austins moved to Bayswater Lucie had acquired a pet snake which she liked to carry about coiled up in her sleeve, or – if she really wanted to create a sensation – twisted up into her plaited hair. This creature travelled with her down to Hastings in a hamper on her lap, and she often took it along with her – concealed in her sleeve – to the Norths. Seated at the tea-table, Lucie would then lure the snake out with milk which it lapped out of the palm of her hand with a forked tongue. Her audience was even more amazed when Lucie removed the many rings she always wore and distributed them on different parts of the table. The snake would then collect them, stringing the gold and silver loops on its lithe body, and finally tie itself into a knot, keeping the gleaming rings hostage until it chose to uncoil. This last trick never failed to horrify the ladies present. The only thing which distressed Mrs North more was Lucie's promise to wear the snake braided into her hair the next time she was invited to dinner.

All this, of course – the desire to startle and shock – was scarcely ladylike behaviour. Lucie now had a restless streak, a need to impress, to subvert polite gatherings and challenge empty social forms. As Sarah told Pückler, she had become 'un peu unmanageable'. Anxiety and a sort of nameless unhappiness probably lay behind her rebelliousness. It would have been impossible for Lucie to remain unaffected by her parents' worries and illnesses. The important thing was not to be swamped by their misery.

The impressions of another visitor to Hastings that summer are revealing. They come from a young man named Henry Taylor,* who was, as it happened, in love with Lucie's treasured

* Henry Taylor was a popular dramatist, essayist and man of letters in the nineteenth century. Among his papers now at the Bodleian Library in Oxford are Lucie's passionate and revealing letters to Alice Spring-Rice, who married

friend Alice Spring-Rice. Henry Taylor found Lucie both fascinating and formidable. She was, he wrote to his sister, 'handsome and very striking, with a stern, determined expression of countenance which might qualify her to sit for the picture of Cassandra or Clytemnestra ... She speaks German and French like a native, and knows as much of Greek and Latin ... as most boys ... She is pleasant when she is pleased; but I cannot help thinking that if anyone were to inconvenience her and there were to be a dagger, a pair of scissors, or any other sharp, pointed instrument, she would be hasty and inconsiderate; ... in other words ... I regard her as a potential homicide.' Henry Taylor obviously exaggerated but he seized on Lucie's essential characteristics: her intelligence, courage and determination. And perhaps he realized, too, that these were often laced with a warm sense of humour and a capacity for deep and lasting affection.

In early August, the Austins crossed the channel to Boulogne and took rooms in the same inn, overlooking the harbour, in which they had stayed the previous summer. Lucie was delighted to see the Fleuret family (enlarged by a sixth child) and Pierre Henin and her other *matelot* friends. But the warm, sun-filled days failed to restore her father's health or her mother's flagging spirits. To Pückler, Sarah wrote, 'I am half-killed with expense, anxiety, sorrow and physical fatigue. Courage! I shall go through with it and remain what the Lord Advocate★ calls me, "the Heroine of Domestic Life". I must.'

★

When they returned to London in October 1834, Sarah had ample opportunity to display – and try to the utmost – her

---

Taylor in 1839. He was not related to Sarah Austin's family in Norwich nor to the Taylor family of Park Road. Later we shall encounter Tom Taylor, with whom Alexander Duff Gordon lived for a time after Lucie went to Egypt. Altogether, then, there were four distinct and unrelated Taylors in Lucie's life.
★ The Austins' friend Francis Jeffrey, who was also a man of letters, and one of the founders and editor of the *Edinburgh Review*.

domestic heroism. A winter of discontent settled on the Bayswater house and froze all hope and energy and the will to work within. For years, John Austin had been subject to incapacitating panic attacks. Now these 'severe feverish attacks . . . became more and more frequent and violent'. First he refused to leave the house, then to come down to dinner or to meet guests. He dwelt in a kind of twilit world upstairs, in retreat from all excitement and stimulation, neither, as Pückler put it, 'fully alive nor dead'.

Pückler, himself, meanwhile, was about to embark on a very different kind of retreat. While Sarah was digging in her heels in Bayswater, Pückler escaped from his own financial cares in Muskau on a six-month tour of Europe. Then he decided to make an even more extensive trip through North Africa and the Middle East during which he would be gone for months, even years. Not only would Pückler then be beyond the reach of his creditors. He would also, as Sarah immediately realized, be out of touch with her for long, desert-like periods.

The 'postal affair' with Pückler had been Sarah's prop and stay for nearly three years and had sustained her at times of bitter disappointment and worry. Now that her crutch was about to be withdrawn, her domestic heroism began to falter. Throughout the winter she hovered on the brink of collapse. 'I am oppressed and dejected beyond description,' she wrote to Henry Brougham, 'my courage is breaking down.' To Pückler himself she said, 'I am well nigh worn down to the earth with care and sorrow, with ceaseless fears and inquietudes and fatigues.' And to Jane Carlyle she confessed, 'Oh, my dear, I feel as if I could clasp my hands over my eyes and die. But *that* I must not, and yet I am frightened at myself.'

In the lulls of her depression Sarah was wracked with guilt and acute anxiety. She now looked upon her correspondence with Pückler with horror and destroyed all his letters. But she was tortured by the knowledge that he still had hers and also copies of many of those he had written to her. In her mind's eye, those onion-thin sheets of paper crossed and criss-crossed with her spidery handwriting rose 'like demons . . . to torment me'. And the act of writing to Pückler – even to implore him to destroy the letters – left her with 'nerves so taut that I can hardly hold the pen . . . so much I tremble in doing something secret'.

Sarah became terrified that somehow her letters would fall into others' hands, that, deliberately or not, Pückler might betray – and ruin – her, destroy her marriage and drag her family's name through the mud. 'You must realize,' she told him, 'how entirely and absolutely my life is in your hands, and that an indiscretion on your part – the vanity of shewing [*sic*] a letter, of quoting a fond sentence – might as effectively kill me, as if you poured down my throat the poison I should swallow . . . I must [have been] mad or stupid not to see the risks I run . . . If you can trust yourself with the sacred keeping of the lives and happiness of three persons . . . then I will trust you. But in the name of God, Hermann, as you are a man and a gentleman – if you doubt your discretion, your self-command, your earnest sense of the solemnity of what I say to you, in the name of God, be frank and candid and save me, save us all from danger. Imagine me on my knees before you, my eyes full of tears.'

Sarah tried to shield Lucie from all this misery and anxiety. As she wrote to Jane Carlyle, 'I cannot consent to lay any part of my burthen on my young and light-hearted child. Let her go free, as long as she can, poor thing.' Brave words, but Lucie would have to have been deaf, dumb and blind not to be aware of the desperate straits her parents were in: Austin immured up in the darkened bedroom and Sarah burning masses of letters in the sitting-room fire below. Lucie could hardly have been 'light-hearted' and 'free' in such circumstances.

Though she saw Alice Spring-Rice occasionally and wrote to Janet Shuttleworth in Hastings, for the most part Lucie was left alone again, to her own devices. Her education, for the time being, was suspended. There was no money with which to reinstate the Swiss tutor and French governess. At the same time, the Austins' social life – because of Austin's illness and reclusiveness and Sarah's deepening depression – had nearly ground to a halt. So, too, of course, had the shopping trips for Pückler and the house-hunting and other domestic chores for the Carlyles.

At last, in the spring of 1835, things came to a head. The Austins' finances were in such an alarming state that they could no longer afford even the Bayswater house. Their only recourse was to go abroad to live for an indefinite period – until Austin was well enough to work again, or their fortunes improved in some other unforeseen way – but now, of course, it was too late to consider Germany and Muskau. Pückler himself was abroad and, in any case, he had become for Sarah much more a source of anxiety and pain than of pleasure. She settled instead on Boulogne, knowing that they could just manage to survive there on their slender means.

As the first step of their exile, in June they went to Hastings again, this time to stay with the Norths, and here Sarah broke down completely. Banishment to France, the loss of her home and friends and work in London, her husband's ill health, and above all, perhaps, the realization that her love affair with Pückler was drawing to a close – all these things combined were too much to bear. From Hastings, Sarah wrote to a friend, 'the clouds which have long hung heavily over me seem now to have closed around me, and I can see no ray of light, at least on earth. My husband's health is worse and worse. We have left London – we have given up our house – I have left home, friends, everything that helped to cheer me, and we shall soon leave England. The packing up of books, papers and all lesser moveables – then coming down to settle my husband [and] child . . . then returning . . . to sell my furniture & wind up all our affairs – (all of which I did myself) – then hurrying back to my husband, who was worse – need I say these things have . . . exhausted my strength and spirits. Indeed . . . my heart is . . .

overloaded and I write with effort and difficulty.' To John Murray, who had published so many of her translations, Sarah tried to strike a lighter note. 'I am now subject for the Vagrant Act,' she wrote and then added, without irony, 'having neither house nor home.'

While Sarah down in Hastings wrote mournful accounts of their homelessness and imminent banishment, back in London Sydney Smith★ got wind of the Austins' departure and sat down to write a characteristically avuncular farewell letter to Lucie:

> Lucie, Lucie, my dear child, don't tear your frocks: tearing frocks is not of itself a proof of genius. But write as your mother writes, act as your mother acts: be frank, loyal, affectionate, simple, honest, and then integrity or laceration of frocks is of little import. And Lucie, dear child, mind your arithmetic. You know in the first sum of yours I ever saw there was a mistake. You carried two (as a cab is licensed to do), and you ought, dear Lucie, to have carried but one. Is this a trifle? What would life be without arithmetic but a scene of horrors? You are going to Boulogne, the city of debts, peopled by men who have never understood arithmetic. By the time you return, I shall probably have received my first paralytic stroke, and shall have lost all recollection of you. Therefore, I now give you my parting advice – don't marry anyone who has not a tolerable understanding and a thousand a year. And God bless you, my dear child.

Kind-hearted and well-meaning, the now quite elderly Smith didn't realize to whom he was writing. His letter was addressed to a child who no longer existed – a much younger Lucie who carelessly tore her dresses and just as carelessly made mistakes in her sums. Nevertheless, Sydney Smith's advice was sound for the fourteen-year-old young woman Lucie had become: emulate

---

★ Sydney Smith, Anglican clergyman and canon of St Paul's, is remembered today for his witty, humane letters, and as one of the founders, along with Francis Jeffrey, of the *Edinburgh Review*. Alan Bell has written the most recent biography and also edited *The Sayings of Sydney Smith*.

your mother and marry someone intelligent and solvent. Lucie carefully folded up Smith's letter and took it with her to Boulogne.

★

When the Austins arrived in Boulogne in July 1835, they did not go to the Marina Hotel where they had stayed the previous two summers. They were expatriate inhabitants of an indefinite duration now, rather than short-term visitors, and so they rented rather drab furnished rooms in a boarding house on the Quai de la Flotille. The Fleurets and Pierre Henin and Lucie's other friends were delighted to see her, and especially pleased when she told them that her stay was likely to be a long one. The other English in Boulogne kept their distance from the locals; though in flight from their creditors at home, they cultivated a haughty dignity when it came to mixing with French fishermen and their families. But Lucie had a kind of genius for befriending and inspiring devotion in them. And they, in turn, knew that her affection was genuine, without a hint of condescension in it.

As the summer waned, however, the carefree, happy existence Lucie enjoyed out on the beach and in the neat little cottages of her friends gave way to an unsettled, vaguely discontented and lonely period. In late September she wrote to Alice Spring-Rice, 'I am in a most unsatisfactory state of existence. I am not absolutely idle, and yet I do nothing . . . I am not absolutely miserable and yet I am far from being happy.' She tried to keep up with her Latin and Greek and to pursue a systematic course of reading, but kept lapsing into 'a lazy, melancholic fit'. Nothing changed, of course, with her parents: Austin was unwell and Sarah overworked with translations and preoccupied with financial worries. 'You cannot conceive what a desperately humdrum life we lead here,' Lucie wrote again to Alice, adding even that it was at times 'perfectly wretched'.

There were diversions, however. Henry Reeve came to visit and so, too, did Sydney Smith (not yet felled by a stroke) on his way to Paris. Then John Austin's unmarried sister, Charlotte, arrived with a cousin named Frances Staff for a longer stay. Charlotte Austin was a shy, reclusive, somewhat eccentric spinster. But she was devoted to Lucie and, unlike Sarah, gave her niece her undivided attention. They spent hours walking the beach with Frances in all weathers, all three carelessly dressed, as Lucie described, 'in the shabbiest old gowns and straw bonnets and most vile blanket shawls'.

After Charlotte and Frances departed, Sarah invited John Stuart Mill to Boulogne, as company for Lucie and also, perhaps, in the hope that he might be able to rouse Austin. But Mill was in no mood to take a holiday. His maid had recently used the manuscript of the first volume of Carlyle's *French Revolution* (mistaking it for scrap paper) to kindle a fire. Nothing of it remained but a heap of cold ashes. When Mill discovered the catastrophe he immediately went to the Carlyles with Harriet Taylor, who, for some reason, remained in the carriage in Cheyne Row while Mill went in to explain. Carlyle and Jane caught a glimpse of Mrs Taylor when they opened the door to Mill, who stood pale as a ghost and shaking on the threshold. They assumed, given the evidence before their eyes, that Mill had come to announce his elopement with Mrs Taylor. When he finally stammered out that the manuscript had been destroyed, the Carlyles had to comfort and reassure Mill – 'the very picture of despair' – rather than he them. Only after Mill left at well past midnight did the magnitude of the loss sink in. Carlyle had kept no copy of the manuscript, nor even his notes. But, as even the Austins in far-off Boulogne learned, in a remarkably short time and with uncharacteristic resilience Carlyle embarked on the first volume all over again.

When Mill failed to come to Boulogne, there was nothing to look forward to in the long winter months which stretched before them. One by one the summer visitors departed, and life was even more lonely, uneventful and humdrum than before. In her solitude, Lucie became almost morbidly introspective and reported, in detail, the results of her sustained self-analysis in letters to Alice Spring-Rice. She indulged in a great deal of religious soul-searching, and tried to justify her admittedly unconventional beliefs to Alice, a staunch Anglican. She told Alice that she had received no religious instruction, that her mother was a Unitarian and that her father, though not an atheist, took a strictly Utilitarian view of religion as a source of sound morality. Lucie described, too, how 'our house [in London] was much frequented by a certain set of young men, Sir William Molesworth, Charles Buller, Cornewall Lewis and a good many others . . . all downright and avowed infidels, and I heard all their discussions with my father and among themselves'. But despite her lack of religious instruction and the heretical views of those who surrounded her, Lucie had discovered her own spiritual beliefs and these she tried now to explain and defend to Alice.

'When very young,' she told her, 'my religion was that of the birds and flowers, gratitude . . . that there was some being that gave existence and happiness for both of which I was very grateful . . . I grew older and I found out that people were unhappy as well as happy and wicked as well as good . . . I believed that there were two principles, good and evil, both equally powerful and constantly striving against each other . . . I got an intense love for Jesus Christ whom I considered as the best man ever born and a great philosopher who had constructed the highest code of morality which I had determined to follow to the best of my power. I can *prie Dieu* just as well in one church or chapel as in another, and I cannot say I belong to any particular sect which indeed is not necessary to true religious feeling; if it were necessary for me to choose a particular sect, I should hesitate between the Catholics and the Unitarians, for I am loth [*sic*] to part with our Lady, it is so delightful to pray to a woman, but I cannot believe in the trinity [as] you do, dear Dofo, but you wish me to tell you the truth and you will be too tolerant to think worse of me, besides which one person worships God under one form, one under another, each choosing the form or image most congenial to his or her imagination, but it is the same Creator and Preserver everywhere.'

Lucie was only fourteen when she wrote this careful, well thought-out, and deeply felt account of her religious convictions, but her insistence on toleration and the essential unanimity of all faiths is something she henceforth always held fast to. It is unlikely, however, that she found a very sympathetic audience in Alice. Lucie's description of Christ 'as the best man ever born and a great philosopher' and her confession that she couldn't believe in the trinity must have shocked Alice.

And yet despite her unorthodox views, Lucie attended mass from time to time in Boulogne – because it was 'delightful to pray to a woman', and perhaps, too, out of loneliness and even boredom. She became a great friend of the young local priest and even gave him some money for an engraving for his church. But she drew back sharply when he tried to convert her to Roman Catholicism. As she reported in a letter to Janet Shuttleworth, Lucie parried his arguments with 'one or two unanswerable reasonings of my father which silenced him'. They remained friends, however, and spent hours discussing their beliefs together. Lucie found the young curé 'very tolerant and gentle', and he was intrigued by a young woman who had thought so deeply about spiritual things.

Apart from conversations with this young priest, Lucie had little to say of herself in letters to Alice and Janet. Life in Boulogne in the winter and early spring of 1836 was dreary and uneventful. They seemed to be existing in a state of suspended animation, like the frozen reaches of ocean that stretched out from the sea front and deserted promenade. John and Sarah and Lucie waited, passively, for something to recall them from exile.

And – amazingly – something did. In the late spring, they received word that John Austin had been appointed head of a two-person commission charged with inquiring into various colonial grievances in Malta, where Austin had served so many years before as a young army officer. The appointment was the work of several of Sarah and John Austin's well-placed friends in the Colonial Office and Parliament, and it had the effect of a *deus ex machina*: in a stroke they were rescued from their obscure, monotonous, eked-out existence in Boulogne, and in his capacity as a colonial commissioner Austin was to earn the undreamt-of salary of £1,500 a year.

★

Austin wasn't expected in Malta until November so they stayed on in Boulogne for the summer, to economize and to fortify his health for the task ahead. Though the year abroad had been a mixed cup for Lucie – a time of loneliness and discontent as well as happiness – she was distraught to leave. On the morning she sailed with her parents in late September, Pierre Henin and the Fleurets all wept. The last thing Lucie saw from the deck of the boat as it headed for England was Pierre's red cap which he waved as he stood at the end of the pier until the boat was lost to sight.

Rain and high winds made for a miserable and protracted crossing. Though they left Boulogne at nine in the morning, the boat didn't reach London Bridge until past midnight. Lucie, who had always been a hardy sailor before, was ill the whole way: 'drenched literally to the skin by the waves', she told Janet Shuttleworth, and 'fainting every half hour . . . never in my life did I suffer so dreadfully at sea'.

They were back on English soil, but their return was scarcely a homecoming. They had, in fact, no home to come back to and, in any event, Sarah and Austin were merely in transit: pausing in London only long enough to arrange their affairs and prepare to sail to Malta. They rented furnished lodgings in Doughty Street, near St Pancras, and from here Lucie wrote to Janet the mournful news that she would not go with her parents to Malta, but instead go to a boarding school run by a Miss Shepherd in Bromley Common. Sarah had decided on this step, hateful though the thought of being separated from Lucie was to her. She feared the hot climate and tropical diseases of Malta, and she felt, too, that it was time for Lucie's education to be completed. She made various inquiries about female academies and finishing schools, visited several with Lucie, and decided – perhaps because it was recommended by Mrs North – on Miss Shepherd's.

Lucie, for her part, was full of doubts and misgivings. She had never been separated from her parents, and nearly everything she had seen at Bromley Common filled her with dismay. 'I am to be prodigiously dragooned at Miss Shepherd's,' she wrote to Janet. 'I am neither to receive or write any letters whatever, except from Mama, and all that I write or receive from her must be read first by Miss Shepherd. Neither may I speak to any of my [visitors] . . . except in her presence. Now all this is annoying; but still more so is that I shall have to sleep and dress in the same room with several other girls which I think excessively improper . . . and do not like . . . at all. However, I think that my imperturbable insouciance will carry me through anything, and whomsoever I offend, I shall quarrel with no one.'

Lucie was an only child who had always slept alone, and indeed spent many of her waking hours alone as well, and so the prospect of losing her privacy was even more distressing than Miss Shepherd's vigilance. But her great resource, as she put it in her own brave phrase, would be her 'imperturbable insouciance'.

Insouciance, however, would serve her less well when it came to the religious atmosphere at Bromley Common. Because Janet's mother, Mrs North, knew Miss Shepherd, Lucie rather anxiously asked Janet to 'tell me whether Miss Shepherd is evangelical, whether I shall have to learn a catechism, whether there are prayers there, whether she will persecute me about my religion . . . and so forth'. The thought of having to participate in compulsory devotional activities was even more alarming than sleeping and dressing in the presence of other girls.

Anxieties about Miss Shepherd's and the coming separation from her parents preyed on Lucie's mind as the early autumn days passed. And as if these weren't enough to bear, there was additional cause for disquiet. On her return from Boulogne, Lucie found Alice Spring-Rice – her beloved 'Dofo' – cool and distant. Lucie wondered if she had offended Alice in her letters from Boulogne describing her religious views. Whatever the reason, when Lucie called on the Spring-Rices, she couldn't rekindle their old intimacy. She reported to Janet that Alice intended 'to drop' her. Mr Spring-Rice told Sarah that they would be happy to see Lucie while the Austins were abroad, but this open invitation Lucie dismissed as 'nothing beyond civility'. Losing Alice, she told Janet, was 'a severe blow', but she viewed it as almost inevitable given their difference in rank: 'one cannot have friendship with people in such a different station of life . . . it is in the nature of things or of aristocrats'.

And so the first great love of Lucie's life receded, leaving her confused and saddened at a time of much upheaval and unwelcome change. But she kept the pain of losing Alice to herself. Her parents, in any event, were preoccupied. They moved from their lodgings near St Pancras to furnished rooms in Bury Street, close to St James's Square and Piccadilly. Sarah was busy with packing and Austin with Colonial Office affairs so Lucie was again left a great deal on her own. Some afternoons she walked south through St James's Park, strewn with brown and copper autumn leaves, to Birdcage Walk and on to Queen Square. The statue of Queen Anne, grasping ball and sceptre, still presided over the little square and the rows of gargoyles grinned and grimaced as ever. But Bentham was dead and the Mills had moved, and strangers now inhabited 1 Queen Square.

In early October, the Austins booked their passage to Malta for the end of the month, and it was decided that Lucie should enter Miss Shepherd's on the 21st. On the 20th, Janet Shuttleworth came up to London from Hastings with her stepfather, Frederick North, expressly to see Lucie. The furnished rooms in

Bury Street were crowded with half-filled trunks and piles of books and papers – an uncomfortable, cramped and melancholy atmosphere in which to say goodbye.

The Austins had been exiles and vagabonds for more than a year, but because Lucie had always been with her parents, she had never really felt homeless until the evening before she was sent to school. Janet could offer little in the way of consolation, though it was arranged that Lucie would spend most of her holidays with the Norths in Hastings or Lancashire. The Austins expected to be gone at least two years – perhaps even longer – during which it was unlikely they would be able to return to England. The separation which stretched ahead of Lucie, then, promised to be a long and bitter one.

Early the next morning, Lucie and Sarah travelled the eight miles south-west from Piccadilly to Bromley Common. They rode in a hired cab, Lucie's trunk strapped to the roof. Miss Shepherd, erect in black, greeted her new pupil with a manner somewhere between a mother superior and a gaoler. After this frosty welcome, when Lucie's things had been carried up to the dormitory and they had drunk tea and talked about the weather and the post and the climate in Malta, mother and daughter said their farewells and embraced. Then Sarah was gone and Miss Shepherd's fortress-like door swung shut, and a secret door within Lucie must have closed, echoingly, too.

Chapter Four

Years after she left Miss Shepherd's – when, in fact, Miss Shepherd and her school at Bromley Common had both ceased to exist – Lucie was reading a novel one winter evening, her feet propped up on the fender, as was her habit. The book, by a complete unknown with the curious name of Currer Bell, had been lent to Lucie with the highest praise by her friend William Makepeace Thackeray. Despite the mystery of its authorship, *Jane Eyre* (as it was entitled) was creating a sensation in London literary circles. But what Lucie found riveting as she read late into the night was not so much the passionate love of Jane and Rochester, nor the madwoman incarcerated like an active volcano up in the attic. It was the orphan Jane's misery at Lowood School that absorbed Lucie and carried her back twelve years to the autumn of 1836 and her early weeks and months at Miss Shepherd's.

No environment could have come as a greater shock, nor contrasted more with Lucie's carefree, independent existence in Boulogne the year before. At Miss Shepherd's, every moment of the day was accounted for, beginning with the jarring clang of the bell which woke the girls shortly after dawn. The rest of the day then stretched out like a prison sentence: morning prayers, breakfast, lessons until midday, dinner, study period, more lessons, recreation outdoors (whatever the weather), tea, Bible reading, study period, evening prayers. And then at last, at nine, the girls went up to bed, doused their candles and sank into a reprieve of darkness and silence and – after a time, and no doubt a long time for the homesick Lucie – sleep. From which they were harshly roused eight hours later by the early morning bell, and then the whole dismal cycle began all over again.

Each day was exactly like the previous one, with the exception of Sunday, which soon became the most trying time of the week for Lucie. Miss Shepherd kept a strict sabbath. Immediately after breakfast the girls donned their woollen capes and bonnets and walked in a long crocodile across the common to the parish church, where they spent the entire day, attending both the morning and afternoon services. In the long interval between the two, they had a cold 'picnic' lunch under grey November and December skies out among the graves in the churchyard. Then as dusk closed in after the second service, Lucie and the others trooped back to school and yet more prayers and finally to bed.

In the course of these dreary Sundays, as well as during the hours devoted to prayers and Bible reading at school, it became apparent that Lucie had received no religious instruction – cause enough, in itself, for her to feel uneasy and inadequate. But she was even more mortified when she was found wanting in nearly all the academic subjects offered at Miss Shepherd's. These, of course, did not include Greek or Latin or German – at all of which Lucie would have excelled. Instead of Homer or Herodotus or Virgil, Lucie now studied Mrs Chapone's *Letters on the Improvement of the Mind* and Miss Mangnall's *Historical and Miscellaneous Questions for the Use of Young People*. She could scarcely recognize her favourite characters and passages in Bowdler's expurgated *Family Shakespeare*. And no one at Miss Shepherd's had ever heard of Schlegel and Niebuhr or Lucie's friend Heinrich Heine. Lucie also performed woefully at geography – or rather the simplified lists of capitals of countries, rivers, and mountain ranges that passed for geography in the education of girls in the nineteenth century. Even after poring over Butler's *Exercises on the Globes*, she found herself unable to answer questions on such subjects as 'the difference in latitude between the places where Burns was born and Lazarus was raised'. It is even doubtful that she knew of the existence of the equator.*

At Miss Shepherd's, education was reduced to mastering a collection of historical, literary and geographical facts and the acquisition of 'accomplishments' (at an additional cost per lesson) such as piano playing, drawing, needlework and Italian and French.† Lucie's problem, of course, was that she knew how to think rather than memorize: her mind was original, agile and wide-ranging. A young girl who had grown up with John Stuart Mill and Jeremy Bentham and sat up late in her mother's drawing-room while Carlyle and other members of the intelligentsia held forth was out of her element at Bromley Common. Miss Shepherd and the other girls failed to recognize how gifted and well, if strangely, educated Lucie really was.

A month after Lucie went to Miss Shepherd's, Janet Shuttleworth and her mother, Mrs North, visited her and were shocked by her miserable state. Janet wrote in her diary that 'we found [Lucie] . . . looking ill and wretched and Miss Shepherd cross and not amiable about her. Harriet Stone [another student] . . . said Lucie had been crying violently. I, who know her pride, know full well how very miserable she must have been to have cried. When she embraced me at parting, her eyes filled and her voice faltered. Dearest Lucie, she has much misery in store, with her strong feelings, philosophical pride and lack of religion. Insouciance is nonsense . . . By nature, Lucie's disposition is perfectly good; she is a splendid creature, full of genius, of talent and honesty, simplicity and confidence in others and herself. I suspect Lucie may have shocked Miss Shepherd's conventionalism.'

* Many years later, when Lucie's daughter, Janet Ross, was an adult, she startled a friend by asking what the equator was. He told her with some amusement that it was an imaginary line encircling the earth, to which Janet replied: 'Imaginary line . . . I never heard of anything so ridiculous' (Lina Waterfield, Castle in Italy, p.51).
† Lucie didn't take French or Italian lessons at Miss Shepherd's, but she became fast friends with the Italian master, a refugee named Signor Prandi.

Writing to Harriet Grote in November, Lucie tried to put a brave face on things. 'I like my *convent* very much,' she said, but by underlining 'convent' she emphasized the constraints of school life. All incoming and outgoing letters were, of course, inspected and thus Lucie explained, 'I cannot give my opinion of Miss Shepherd for I won't praise her to her face, and I dare not abuse her if I would.' Such ingenuous honesty did little to warm Miss Shepherd – who did all the inspecting of mail – to her new pupil. Not surprisingly, Lucie was quite desperate for letters and visitors. She told Harriet Grote, 'I am dying to see you or hear from you.' With Sarah so far away, Lucie increasingly turned to her mother's oldest and closest woman friend. And the childless Grotes did all they could to comfort her.

So, too, did Sarah's widowed sister, Susan Reeve, who had moved from Norwich and was now settled in Hampstead, in a little house on Well Walk not far from Hampstead Heath. After several days with the Grotes over Christmas, Lucie went to the Reeves for the rest of the holiday. She was happy and at ease with her aunt and cousin, though she found Henry puffed up with self-importance. 'Lord Reeve', as Lucie mockingly called him in letters to Janet, was now a handsome young man of twenty-four who had already made a name for himself by translating de Tocqueville's *Democracy in America*.* But the shadow cast by Bromley Common stretched all the way across London to Hampstead and darkened the final days Lucie spent with the Reeves. She dreaded returning to the restrictions of school life and even more the possibility of conflict with her headmistress. Thus, while still at her aunt's house, Lucie wrote to Harriet Grote in early January 1837, 'I would ask you to write to me [at Bromley Common], but perhaps it is better not to, as it might cause some disagreements between Miss Shepherd and me, which it must be my study to avoid as much as possible. On this account do not tell anyone that I find any fault

* Some years later, when Henry Reeve was writing on foreign policy for *The Times*, his colleagues called him 'Il Pomposo'.

with anything, as every word is sure to be reported to Miss Shepherd and will get me into trouble more than you can imagine; as nothing makes her so angry as one's not being happier with her than anywhere else.'

By the end of January, Lucie was back at school for the long spring term. Gradually and painfully, she resigned herself to school life. She adapted because she really had no choice but to do so: she memorized, she 'improved' her mind along Mrs Chapone's lines, she read the Bible. Susan and Henry Reeve visited Lucie one afternoon and marvelled at the effects of Miss Shepherd's 'salutary influence', as Henry described it. To them Lucie's manners and whole demeanour seemed 'softened and improved', and they also praised her 'improved appearance' in the neat school uniform.

Despite these signs of outward 'improvement' and conformity, Lucie was still far from happy. A constant source of pain and anxiety was her separation from her parents, especially Sarah. Letters from Malta were infrequent and subject to long delays, and when they finally arrived – sometimes months after they had been written – were disappointingly short and uninformative. In April, Lucie wrote to Mrs Grote, 'I . . . have had dispatches from Malta, but not very voluminous, so there is not much to say about father and mother, and she does not mention her return at all.' Sometimes, indeed, Sarah herself didn't even write the letters, but rather had her maid scribble Lucie a note on the eve of a packet's departure, saying they were well, but busy and hard worked.

★

The truth was that far away in the Mediterranean under tropical skies, the Austins were, for the first time in years, flourishing. After their impoverished purgatory in Boulogne, they were suddenly catapulted into a position of prominence and even acclaim – for the Maltese had great hopes that Austin's commission would speedily ameliorate all their ills under colonial rule. The Austins, indeed, enjoyed a rather unusual position in Malta and were looked up to by the resident English as well as the Maltese. Along with the other commissioner, George Cornewall Lewis, they found themselves at the summit of the island's colonial society, with only the Archbishop and Governor-General above them. The latter was unmarried, which meant that Sarah was the colony's most prominent woman and the official hostess to admirals, diplomats and other notables.

She revelled in this role and its duties – presiding over banquets and receptions and other official functions. But at the same time – and this is what endeared her to the Maltese and alienated the resident English – Sarah became deeply involved in the social problems on the island. While John Austin considered petitions and set about restructuring the constitution and legal system, Sarah threw herself into improvement schemes. She established village schools, raised revenue by arranging for Maltese crafts to be sold in England, and when a fierce cholera epidemic broke out, she nursed the sick and dying, without a thought for her own safety. All the other British residents shut themselves up in their houses and thought her quite mad.

But Sarah was, in fact, in top form. And though she scarcely found time to dash off a note to Lucie, she did write at some length of her aversion to colonial society and the sorry plight of the Maltese to John Stuart Mill and Sydney Smith. The latter congratulated Sarah on her great success, but then urged her not to damage her health with all her exertions: 'don't ruin your own constitution in order to give a Constitution to Malta – the Maltese can live without liberty – but how can I live without you? So come or I positively will book myself for Malta and perspire with you.' Then, chiding her for not answering his queries in earlier letters about Lucie, he added, 'you will not tell me where you have deposited your young Lady, so I suppose you intend she should be hermetically sealed'.

★

Certainly Lucie, herself, felt hermetically sealed at Miss Shepherd's. Outside – in Malta, even in London – life went forward. Her parents were too busy to write. John Stuart Mill and the Carlyles, as well as Sydney Smith, had no idea where she was. Immured in her 'convent', Lucie ticked off the monotonous days in her almanac.

But at Easter she broke free when she went to stay with her father's old friend Nassau Senior* and his family in their large house in Kensington Gore, just opposite Hyde Park. With the two Senior children, Lucie recovered some of her old aplomb. They thought her 'tall, handsome, precocious, and self-confident, but so good-natured and amusing that we submitted willingly to her temporary rule'. Lucie organized spirited games of charades after dinner, and one evening 'the word was "romantic" and the last scene was to end in an elopement. The lover was bashful, so Lucy [sic] donned cloak and hat and showed him how to act his part with the most passionate emphasis.'

When she returned to Bromley Common in late April, however, Lucie had to subdue all this reawakened passion and originality. Her self-confidence began to ebb away too, and she began for the first time to be deeply troubled by religious uncertainty. After daily doses of Miss Shepherd's evangelical Anglicanism and the daunting weekly sabbaths, Lucie's grip on her own idiosyncratic and rather mystical beliefs was slipping. Separated from her parents and their enlightened, intellectual milieu, surrounded by conventional young girls so different from herself, labouring at lessons that held no meaning or pleasure for her, Lucie badly needed something or someone to guide and solace her. And there was really no one at hand other than God.

But He was no longer the accessible, benevolent presence

* Nassau Senior, an economist, lawyer and Professor of Political Economy at Oxford, had been instrumental in formulating the 1834 Poor Law. In 1855 he went to Egypt with Ferdinand de Lesseps to determine the line of the projected Suez Canal. In Cairo he became friends with Hekekyan Bey, and it was through Senior that Lucie, too, became a devoted friend of Hekekyan when she went to Egypt in 1862.

Lucie had relied on in the past and described so movingly in her letters to Alice Spring-Rice. To make matters worse, Janet Shuttleworth was at this time going through a particularly enthusiastic religious phase, and she urged Lucie to be more devout and orthodox. Janet's exhortations, of course, only undermined Lucie further. She was dismayed when Janet told her that Unitarians couldn't be considered Christians because they didn't believe in the Trinity (a sensitive point for Lucie). Responding to Janet's persistent questions, Lucie wrote, 'do not ask or expect me to speak of my present opinions. I have been lately disgusted with a great deal of illiberality, and am not therefore in an unprejudiced state of mind; be sure, however, that I admire the doctrines and sentiments of Christianity above all others, whatever my own feelings may be with regard to the truth of your belief.'

Janet's religious fervour made Lucie anxious about visiting the Norths during the summer. Before going down to Hastings, Lucie wrote apprehensively to Janet, 'I hope you will think Miss Shepherd has improved me. I think so myself, and wish my friends should [too].' But as it turned out, the North house was full of guests, and Lucie was in great demand to organize charades, perform scenes from Shakespeare and lead shell- and butterfly-collecting expeditions, with the result that Janet had scant opportunity to pry further into Lucie's spiritual state.

After several weeks in Hastings, Lucie went to the Reeves in Hampstead for a few days and then in early September on to North Wales, where Sarah Austin's brother John Taylor lived at Coed-dhu near Mold in Flintshire. In the midst of the rugged beauty of the Dee valley and the Clwyd Hills, Lucie regained her pantheistic faith, or at least experienced a reprieve from doubt. She wrote to Janet that she had developed a passion for Wales and all things Welsh, and even adopted a Welsh name, 'Thonys'. 'You remember my Londonmania? . . . I [now] hate London most cordially and will live in Wales . . . You must expect to be bitten Wales-mad by me.' This love-affair with

Wales recalled Lucie's spells in Bonn and Boulogne: when she travelled to a foreign land – and Wales with its breathtaking scenery and strange, lyrical language *was* a foreign country to her – she adopted it as her own, assimilated, and even acquired an indigenous name.

'I wish you could come and ramble over the beautiful Welsh hills,' she wrote to Janet. Lucie went out hunting with her uncle and cousins and confessed a new 'passion for field sports', even though she described as 'laughable' the 'torn, wet, scratched figure I came home after a day's shooting'. And it wasn't only her Taylor cousins who adopted her. One Sunday Lucie was invited to the home of 'the vicar of a queer little village in the mountains . . . I stayed some days with them and was never so kindly treated in my life; they took a most unaccountable liking to me, and kept me there till Wednesday, when I only went to spend Sunday with them.'

In late October, Lucie reluctantly left Wales and returned to Miss Shepherd's for the autumn term. She found a letter from Sarah waiting for her with the good news that the Austins hoped to come home in the spring – but whether for good or merely for a visit wasn't clear from Sarah's hasty account. Other than this news, little else cheered Lucie on her return. And, inevitably, as the late autumn days grew darker and shorter, Lucie fell prey once more to the religious doubts which had only been deferred, not resolved, during her Welsh holiday. The oppressive evangelical atmosphere at Miss Shepherd's soon reduced her to what she described in one letter as a 'painfully unsatisfied state of mind'. Nothing in her life now seemed certain or stable, and Lucie was experiencing all the disturbing emotional and physical changes of adolescence very much on her own.

During this season of unhappiness and confusion in the winter of 1837, Lucie sat as a model on several occasions for the drawing master and his pupils. Two portraits have survived and are the earliest likenesses of her. A certain straightness (and largeness) of nose and Lucie's high, smooth brow are common to both, but in every other respect they reflect two very different versions – and visions – of Lucie at the age of nearly seventeen. In the less flattering drawing Lucie holds several sheets of a letter, but she isn't reading it. Her face is averted and she gazes into the distance with a sombre, even melancholy, expression. Her thick hair is tucked behind her ears and wound into a tight knot at the back. Everything in the picture conspires to give the impression of a quite proper and serious, but also rather sad young lady.

In the other drawing Lucie's long dark hair cascades down her back and over one shoulder. And herein lies all the difference. Again she is in profile, but this is a beautiful, luminous Lucie, unscathed by her confined existence at Miss Shepherd's. And instead of gazing blankly and morosely ahead, her eyes are cast down on a book she holds in her lap, a book which absorbs her and liberates her from the schoolroom and the drawing master and his charges.

★

When it came to planning how and where she would spend Christmas during this second year of separation from her parents, Lucie was torn between the two invitations and claims of Susan Reeve and the Norths in Hastings. Only in early December was a compromise arranged whereby she would spend the first part of the holiday in Hastings and then after Christmas come back to London and see in the new year with Susan and Henry Reeve in Hampstead.

Arriving in Hastings the week before Christmas, Lucie learned that the youngest North child, a baby girl named Catherine, was to be baptized over the holidays. Impulsively, Lucie told Janet and Mrs North that she wished to be baptized and received into the Established Church along with the baby. Janet was overjoyed, but her mother was understandably hesitant when Lucie told them that she had discussed her decision with no one, nor yet written to her parents. If she had gone to Susan

Reeve in Hampstead first and then on to Hastings after the baby's christening things might have turned out differently, and Lucie might have remained outside the fold. But what in fact transpired was that Miss Shepherd travelled down from Bromley to sponsor Lucie along with Stephen Spring-Rice (Alice's oldest brother, who had been asked to be godfather to the North baby).

On the last Sunday of the year Lucie, the Norths, Miss Shepherd, Stephen Spring-Rice and numerous North relatives and friends gathered together in the old Hastings parish church. The baby, in her long, ivory-coloured lace christening gown, howled when anointed. Lucie, also in white and very pale, was flanked by Miss Shepherd and Stephen Spring-Rice. She leaned forward at the font and received the benediction with closed eyes and almost certainly with relief. After being alone for so long, she finally belonged to a larger community of souls, and, she hoped, to God.

Lucie's conversion was, perhaps, more an act of hope than faith. Certainly it wasn't the product of long and careful deliberation. Voices hadn't spoken to her in the wilderness. But she had become weary and even fearful of continuing to dwell out there alone. She wanted to silence all the doubting voices within her, and she also longed for support and direction as she left childhood behind. Sarah and John Austin were far away and even if they had been accessible, Lucie would have found their example too unorthodox now. Instead, she looked to Janet and the Norths and, most of all, to Miss Shepherd, who gave to Lucie as a baptism gift the writings of the eminent eighteenth-century prelate Samuel Horsley: eight stout volumes of Horsley's sermons, Biblical criticism and commentaries on the Psalms.

Considerably weighed down by Horsley's collected works, Lucie travelled up to London to stay with Susan Reeve early in the new year. She also brought a small leather-bound Bible given to her by Janet which was fastened, like a diary, with a lock, the key to which Lucie wore on a ribbon around her neck. Lucie's aunt, of course, was a Unitarian, and once Lucie crossed the Reeve threshold in Hampstead, she could not bring herself to speak of what she had done in Hastings. It was not so much Susan Reeve's disapproval she feared as her scepticism and even mockery. And then, too, her aunt might be incensed that Lucie had taken such a step without consulting her. In the end, Lucie remained silent and wrote her aunt a long letter of explanation similar to the one she had written in Hastings to her parents. When Lucie left Hampstead in late January for Miss Shepherd's, she left the letter to her aunt behind.

Her reunion with her headmistress was, of course, now a warm and happy one, and the other students rejoiced, too, over Lucie's new spiritual state. Insouciance was now a thing of the past, and Lucie no longer hovered on the periphery of the school community. But peace of mind still eluded her. All might be well at Bromley Common, but Lucie was very anxious about the reaction to her conversion in three other quarters. The post hour became a dreadful time for her as she alternately hoped for and feared letters in response to those she had written to her aunt, Mrs Grote and, most of all, her parents.

Susan Reeve replied first. She was not greatly disturbed by the news that Lucie had become an Anglican, but she did criticize her niece's 'want of confidence in never talking of religious subjects to her before'. She told Lucie, however, that she would be glad to inform the rest of the family as Lucie had requested. On the whole, Lucie found her aunt's letter 'truly liberal' and heaved a sigh of relief.

The next day a letter arrived from Malta which Lucie opened with trembling hands and a beating heart – and disappointment once she'd hastily read it, which didn't take long as it was only one sheet of writing paper. Lucie described her mother's letter to Janet: 'dated Xmas – all well, but Mama worked to death and without a moment to write letters . . . or do anything but teach and superintend . . . She had not received my letter from Hastings.' A month later, at the end of February, another communication arrived from Malta which was even more disappointing: 'a letter from the [Austins'] maid to say how they were, and a hurried note from Mama to Miss Shepherd about money matters'.

But if the Austins were dilatory and uncommunicative, the Grotes were not. Lucie's letter to Harriet Grote telling of her entrance into the Established Church was perhaps the only laboured and tedious document she ever wrote. Miss Shepherd must have congratulated herself when she read it in the course of inspecting all the outgoing mail. Explaining her actions, Lucie spoke of doing her 'duty', of being 'blessed with grace to make Religion my guide; . . . if I place but perfect trust in Him and cultivate humility, His strength will guide me'. Harriet Grote – even more of a staunch, no-nonsense Benthamite than her husband – was not impressed or moved or even convinced by Lucie's avowals. She shot back 'a sarcastic and cutting letter' that deeply wounded Lucie and for the time being severed further communication. More than ever, Lucie feared her parents' reaction.

But the simultaneously much-anticipated and much-dreaded letter from Malta never came. Far away on that troubled island, Sarah Austin had greater worries than her daughter's religious persuasion. After fourteen months of sustained work, John Austin's health had broken down: depression, anxiety attacks, dyspepsia and insomnia all returned in full force and, in the intervals of nursing him, Sarah wondered how they would survive this latest (and as it would turn out, last) professional débâcle.

Then fate intervened. Just as it was becoming clear that Austin could no longer carry out his duties, word came from London that the Colonial Secretary, Lord Glenelg, had resigned, and that his successor, as an economy measure, was terminating Austin's commission and recalling him and his fellow commissioner, George Cornewall Lewis, to England. Hence the only letter Lucie received from Sarah in the spring of 1838 was a scribbled note saying that Austin was ill, the commission's work ended, and that they would sail as soon as Austin was well enough to travel.

★

They arrived back in London in July 1838. Austin was still far from well and Sarah was both harassed and quite desperate for money. They had managed very comfortably in Malta on a generous living allowance, but the Colonial Office had yet to pay Austin and Lewis their salaries. Thus John and Sarah returned to England nearly as penurious as they had left it almost two years earlier.

As soon as the Austins found furnished rooms in Queen Street, Mayfair, Lucie left Miss Shepherd's – a departure that was almost as reluctant as her arrival had been. Just when she had finally become contented at school and close to the other pupils and Miss Shepherd, she was being uprooted once more. And a host of unknowns now loomed ahead. She would be thrown once again among her parents' 'infidel' friends. Even worse, she would have to 'come out'. Lucie was now seventeen, and though the Austins were financially hard-pressed, they still moved in social circles where young ladies were obliged to be presented to the Queen. That summer, Lucie nervously curtsied to the young Victoria, who had been on the throne only twelve months and was just two years older than Lucie.

Then Lucie was cast into the turbulent social waters of the London 'season'. Austin remained ill and Sarah was labouring ten hours a day on a translation of Leopold von Ranke's 3,000-page *Ecclesiastical and Political History of the Popes*. But busy as she was, Sarah still made time to accompany Lucie to 'at homes', teas, dinners and balls. The important thing was that Lucie be successfully launched in society, find an intelligent, handsome and solvent husband, and avoid the anxious, careworn, beleaguered fate Sarah herself had endured for so many years.

Henry Reeve proved an unexpected ally in Sarah's campaign to secure a better life for her daughter. Through a combination of hard work, social acumen, and the ability to ingratiate himself in high places, 'Lord Reeve' had done very well for himself. The previous year he had been appointed Clerk of Appeals to the Privy Council through the good offices of the great Whig peer, Lord Lansdowne.★ Lansdowne was so impressed by Reeve that Henry became a frequent visitor to Lansdowne House in Berkeley Square, London and also a guest at house parties at Bowood, Lansdowne's country seat in Wiltshire. Writing to his mother from Bowood on one such occasion, Henry enthused, 'I am here in clover as you may suppose. To pass over the cookery in silence, I cannot conceive anything more exquisitely delightful than a dwelling in which the splendour of opulence is only the foil to the splendour of art, and in which one breakfasts with Titian, Rembrandt, and Michelangelo. I roll in soft cushions and see real visions.'

Lord Lansdowne was on close terms with a number of the Austins' friends, but it seems to have been Henry Reeve who secured an invitation for Sarah and Lucie in early 1839 to one of the grand balls held in Lansdowne House. Lucie had just turned eighteen, and with her incandescent, dark beauty was much in demand. Among her dancing partners was a tall young man with the classical features of a Greek god. Later, Lucie saw him dancing with the beautiful, large-eyed Caroline Norton, the granddaughter of Sheridan and a well-known poet — she was called 'the female Byron' — in her own right.

But Mrs Norton's name was badly tarnished when Lucie first saw her across the crowded ballroom at Lansdowne House. Three years earlier, when Lucie was still at Miss Shepherd's, Caroline's husband, George Norton, had brought a suit against the Prime Minister, Lord Melbourne, accusing him, in the

---

★ Henry Petty-Fitzmaurice, third Marquis of Lansdowne, was a consistent and powerful supporter of liberal reform. In 1838, when Lucie first met him, he was President of the Council in Melbourne's second administration. At Lansdowne House and Bowood, Lord Lansdowne entertained writers, artists, scientists, scholars, politicians and aristocrats.

phrase of the day, of 'alienating his wife's affections'. The Norton marriage had been disastrous from the very beginning, but Norton's case was actually politically engineered by Melbourne's Tory enemies. So untenable did the jury find it that they acquitted Melbourne and Caroline without even leaving the jury box to deliberate. Melbourne's name was cleared, but though Caroline was legally declared innocent of having committed adultery, her reputation was irrevocably damaged. Even in 1839 she was still not received in many quarters; Lord Lansdowne was exhibiting great generosity of spirit and indifference to scandalmongering by inviting her to Lansdowne House.

Lucie was intrigued and moved by Caroline's story, which also involved her courageous – and at that time still unsuccessful – efforts to gain custody of her three children from Norton, who, it was rumoured, also confiscated her considerable literary earnings. The degree to which Lucie had already shed the conventional social and religious pieties which she had acquired, chameleon-like, at Miss Shepherd's is evident in her fascination with and admiration for Caroline Norton, though when she first met her at Lansdowne House, she could not have guessed that Caroline was to become one of her closest friends.

At the ball, Lucie may have been even more struck by the tall young man who had danced with both her and Mrs Norton. She learned, perhaps from Henry Reeve, that he was a twenty-eight-year-old baronet named Alexander Duff Gordon who held a junior clerkship in the Treasury. A rather humble post, but he nevertheless appeared to be one of God's chosen ones: handsome, charming, witty and intelligent, though as Sarah later put it in her habitually negative way, Alexander possessed 'nothing but a small salary, his handsome person, excellent and sweet character and his title (a great misfortune!)'.★

★

★ Sarah wasn't exaggerating Alexander Duff Gordon's financial insignificance. His father, Sir William Duff Gordon, inherited the baronetcy and sherry cellars of his maternal uncle, Sir James Duff, who was the British Consul in Cádiz during the Peninsular War. When Sir James died in 1815, he left large debts

At first, Lucie and Alexander were drawn to each other by their complementary beauty and temperaments: she dark, mercurial, loquacious; he fair, gentle (his mother lamented that he could never scold), and soft- though well-spoken. But soon they perceived in each other a deeper, rarer affinity. Alexander had never met a woman who was so original, who wore a quite masculine erudition so lightly and gracefully, who was so curious and ardent and laughed so spontaneously, who was so splendidly and unselfconsciously beautiful. Other than her cousin, Henry Reeve, Lucie had almost no experience of eligible young men, but certainly she found Alexander more interesting and attractive than the subdued suitors she had encountered in Jane Austen's novels, and more believable and sympathetic than Byron's extravagant heroes.

Alexander was also everything that her parents were not: he was constitutionally cheerful, strong and healthy in mind and body, socially adept but also artlessly genuine, and he was generous, considerate and unfailingly humane. It mattered greatly to Lucie, too, that he was a passionate admirer of German literature and had already produced several translations, and that he held liberal, Whig political views. Alexander possessed a host of other endearing qualities as well: he excelled at charades, could draw cleverly, rode brilliantly and patiently tolerated bores – including, in time, the often trying John and Sarah Austin.

In time, too, Lucie had to cope with the Duff Gordon family, which in 1839 consisted of the dowager Lady Duff Gordon and her grown children, all of whom lived with her at 34 Hertford Street, Mayfair: Alexander, Cosmo, Georgina and Alice. Georgy (as she was called in the family) and Alice were still in their

---

which were inherited by Sir William and then, after he died in 1823, by his wife. Lady Duff Gordon sailed to Spain with her four children in 1824 to sell the sherry concern and clear the family debts. She was left with just enough to support herself and her two daughters, but her sons, Alexander and Cosmo, had to earn their own living.

twenties when Lucie first met them, but they already seemed consigned to 'perpetual spinsterhood' and a symbiotic kind of intimacy: they even shared a single egg for breakfast, Georgy taking the yolk and Alice the white. They were intelligent and attractive, like their brothers, but had no real outlet for their talents. Like so many other frustrated women of their day, they spent an alarming amount of time being vaguely ill.

Their mother, however, was hardy and strong, as well as highly intelligent, and she exerted a powerful influence over the course of her sons' lives, especially her favourite, Alexander. Lady Duff Gordon was exactly fifty when Lucie first met her in 1839, and she had raised her children and managed her own affairs with complete independence in the sixteen years since her husband's death. We know a great deal about Lady Duff Gordon because from the time of her marriage she kept a regular, detailed diary that never varied in its daily format: the day's weather, the health of Georgy and Alice, the activities of Alexander and Cosmo, callers, outings, reflections on political events and whatever book Lady Duff Gordon happened to be reading. Religious sentiments are also liberally sprinkled throughout the diaries, and at the end of each year, Lady Duff Gordon wrote a retrospective account of the personal and public events of the past twelve months, and described and analysed the feelings they gave rise to.

Lady Duff Gordon's diaries, in fact, reveal an admirable if rather formidable woman, a product of both the eighteenth and nineteenth centuries (she was born in 1789 and was to live until 1875): strong, intelligent, and resourceful, but not the least bit unconventional. She held fast to all the traditional values, social forms and religious beliefs of her class and time. She never missed Sunday worship, and even when she dined alone, she did so in evening dress and long black suede gloves. She was a woman too who had very little interest in or knowledge of anyone outside her own aristocratic milieu. In time she was destined to be a kind of covert antagonist to Lucie: covert because though their relations were not warm, they never engaged in open hostilities, and indeed Lady Duff Gordon didn't articulate her real grievances against her daughter-in-law until both Lucie and Alexander were dead. In the spring of 1839, however, Lucie and Lady Duff Gordon were just becoming acquainted, and the only thing that her future mother-in-law could hold against Lucie was the Austins' social obscurity.

Lucie and Alexander contrived to see a great deal of each other throughout the spring and summer – at Bowood and Lansdowne House, in various London drawing-rooms, at the theatre and the opera, and most of all, when the weather was fine, in Hyde Park or Green Park where they spent hours walking and talking together, and falling more and more deeply in love. Geography conspired with them, for the Austins' rented lodgings in Queen Street were only a few minutes' walk from Lady Duff Gordon's home in Hertford Street and both were very close to Hyde Park and Green Park.

Despite his small salary at the Treasury, Sarah was much impressed by Alexander and soon he became a regular caller at Queen Street. John Austin was usually indisposed – he long remained a shadowy figure to his daughter's suitor – but Sarah and Lucie were always delighted to see Alexander. He showed great interest in the interminable Ranke history of the popes that Sarah was still translating, and warmly praised the pages she showed to him. They all enjoyed chatting in German and talking about German writers, and Lucie entertained Alexander with tales about Heinrich Heine in Boulogne.

Alexander brought sunlight and fresh air, hope, purpose and laughter into the rented rooms at Queen Street. Lucie basked in this new atmosphere and perhaps even allowed herself to imagine what living in it all the time might be like. Sarah wondered to herself, and then inquired of Alexander, whether he might be of some practical assistance to them. Months had passed and John Austin had still not been paid the £1,500 annual salary he had been promised when he went to Malta; for his two years of service, the Colonial Office in fact owed him £3,000. Alexander had been working in the Treasury since he left Eton and had longstanding connections in the government. Could he perhaps make inquiries on their behalf and discover when or how Austin's pay might be forthcoming? Of course Alexander immediately promised Sarah that he would do everything in his power to bring the matter to a successful conclusion.

But before he had any definite news about Austin's salary, he rushed headlong into proposing to Lucie. He had been contemplating this step for some time, but he broached it with what seemed complete and unpremeditated spontaneity. They were walking in the park one day, as they had so often before, when Alexander said to Lucie, 'Do you know people say we are going to be married?' and then, before Lucie could respond, he hit home with, 'Shall we make it true?' Lucie scarcely paused before answering in her usual forthright manner, 'Yes.' She was only eighteen, had been 'out' less than a year, had never before had a suitor, knew virtually nothing of the realities of married life, but she knew what she wanted and had no doubts. In the middle of Hyde Park, on a glorious summer's day in 1839, the world for Lucie and Alexander seemed to lie all before them, green and new, and they feared absolutely nothing.

★

It was a good thing they were so fearless because they encountered much hostility and opposition when they informed their parents of their wish to marry. Lady Duff Gordon strenuously objected to the idea of her favourite son allying himself with the daughter of an obscure jurist of small means and his scribbling, bluestocking wife. John Austin was even more aghast; apparently the idea of Lucie marrying had never crossed his mind. He was completely thrown by the prospect. He argued that Lucie's youth, Alexander's small salary at the Treasury and Lady Duff Gordon's opposition were all insuperable barriers.

Austin's reaction during a painful interview with Alexander

at Queen Street was so alarming, in fact, that both Alexander and Lucie immediately wrote him careful, reassuring letters that they would abide by his wishes and patiently await more propitious circumstances before raising the matter again.

MY DEAR SIR,

I have to express to you my sincere regret for the anxiety which I have caused to you and the grief to your Daughter, by my precipitancy in proposing marriage to her before I had sufficient means to justify the course I pursued – and as my Mother is unable to increase my income, and you objected to your Daughter's extreme youth, you will, I trust, consent that the matter should remain in abeyance for the present. And as you were good enough to approve of my connexions, and are free from all personal objections to me individually, I hope you will permit me at some future period, in a year or two hence, should I retain still a place in your Daughter's affections, to renew my proposal with improved circumstances and place the decision before your Daughter's more matured judgement – far is it from my wish to fetter so young a person, or involve her in any engagement. Meanwhile, I will not seek in any way to unsettle her mind, or urge her to any decision, and will avoid giving unnecessary pain by the chance of meeting Lucy, by absenting myself from any place I might happen to meet her; this is my duty to your Daughter and to you.

My views of happiness differ from my Mother's, as my conduct will show, and I will study to deserve your Daughter at some future period, should she still have for me the same feelings and it should not meet opposition from you. With sincere sorrow for this annoyance I fear I have caused. Believe me, dear Sir,

YOURS MOST TRULY,

ALEXANDER DUFF GORDON

Lucie's letter was even more heartfelt and reassuring:

MY DEAR FATHER,

I am much grieved I shld. have been the cause of so much uneasiness to you. I wd. wish to relieve you from as much as lies in my power. Will you consent to dismiss the subject of Sir A. G.'s proposal from yr. mind till yr. present business is over and yr. affairs in such a state as to enable you to give some more positive answer? I will promise in the meantime to behave in such a manner as shall meet yr. approbation as far as I can, & to have no communication with Alexander but such as you shall approve – the suspense I confess will be painful, but it will be comparative happiness to the grief of parting with him altogether, a step I trust I shall not be compelled to take. I will promise to occupy my mind with other things and not give way to any repining or cause you annoyance by discontent. I would fain be allowed to hope that some years hence when Alexander's salary is increased & the objection of my extreme youth removed, we may be allowed to marry, with this hope I feel confident I can make my mind easy & calm & submit cheerfully to see him but seldom, or if you desire it, not at all – this I say believing, as I do, his feelings towards me to be the same as mine towards him, & not feeling any fear they will undergo change.

If you will consent to this arrangement I shall feel very grateful to you & it is what I doubt not Alexander will concur in.

YR. MOST LOVING CHILD,

L. AUSTIN

Mollified by these letters, Austin retired from the field to bed. But Alexander was unwilling to let the matter rest and redoubled his efforts to secure Austin's unpaid Malta salary from the Colonial Office. One morning while Sarah was writing letters and Lucie reading in the Queen Street sitting room, he burst in with the news that Austin was about to be paid the £3,000 owed to him. And when the money shortly came through, it had the desired effect. Austin backed down and withdrew his objections to Lucie and Alexander marrying. Sarah wrote to a friend, 'Alexander Gordon has fallen in love with my dear child and . . . this £3,000 will enable us to help them when they marry.' Lady Duff Gordon was somehow placated as well or perhaps Alexander stood up to her for the first time in his life, and she consented to accept Lucie as a daughter-in-law lest she lose her beloved son. By the early autumn of 1839, Lucie and Alexander were formally engaged.

Now they were almost constantly together, in London and elsewhere. In October, Lucie took Alick (as she now called him) up to Lancashire to visit the Norths at the Shuttleworth seat, Gawthorpe Hall. The younger North children adored Alexander because he was handsome and amusing and drew wonderful devils and other fantastical creatures in their scrapbooks. Mrs North, however, was alarmed when Lucie and Alexander rambled about the surrounding hills wrapped up in one plaid, both of them smoking cigarettes. They liked to smoke, too, up on the roof of Gawthorpe and Mrs North feared the neighbours would mistake Lucie for Janet, who, of course, would rather have died than been caught out smoking a cigarette.

In late October, shortly after Lucie and Alexander returned from Lancashire, the Austins (but not Alexander, who was tied up at the Treasury) went to Richmond for several days, where they were visited by Henry Reeve. He found them in a rather exhausted state, owing to a fire that had broken out the night before. As Henry recorded the incident in his diary, all three Austins behaved in a characteristic manner: 'Lucy's bed was wholly consumed, and it seems incredible the house escaped; but ... mother and daughter exhibited their wonted energy and presence of mind, to the astonishment of admiring ostlers from the Star and Garter. My aunt pushed a man with a pail in his hand into the thickest smoke, and then followed him with another. Lucy signalised herself at the pump, and raised a flood of water from the bowels of the earth. In short, they got the fire under.' And where was John Austin all this time? According to Henry Reeve, very much in the background, 'teeth chattering, knees shaking, paralysed', though the next day 'he had the face to use big adjectives and talk of energy'.

Soon after they returned from Richmond, the Austins left Queen Street for more spacious lodgings in Hornton Street, Kensington, a move made possible by the payment of Austin's salary. But no sooner had they unpacked than Lucie was swept off to Herefordshire by the Duff Gordons to visit the family of Alexander's uncle, George Cornewall Lewis, at their home, Harpton Court. Lucie had already heard a good deal about Cornewall Lewis, who had been her father's fellow-commissioner in Malta. Now she met him for the first time, and became better acquainted with her future in-laws, the Duff Gordons – a family so different in every way from her own. It is highly unlikely that she smoked in front of Lady Duff Gordon or wandered about outdoors wrapped in a blanket, unchaperoned, with Alexander. Her training at Miss Shepherd's undoubtedly proved useful in Herefordshire but, unfortunately, she could neither sing nor play the piano. Music was a passion of Lady Duff Gordon and her daughters, though Alexander was tone deaf and considered musical performances unpleasant interruptions of conversation.

During her stay in Herefordshire, Lucie told Lady Duff Gordon of her baptism and entrance into the Established Church under the aegis of Miss Shepherd, a confession which at least partly won over her future mother-in-law. In addition, they discovered a shared love of literature and discussed the latest novels and their favourite poets. In every way, Lucie was a model of discretion while she was with the Duff Gordons: polite, considerate, cheerful, and careful to steer clear of controversial subjects – especially when they touched on political or religious matters. In Herefordshire, Lucie practised her gift for assuming the protective coloration of a particular environment without in the least betraying or surrendering her own unique sense of self. Thus she could be infinitely variable but never false or hypocritical. Soon she had gained Lady Duff Gordon's respect and even grudging affection.

While she was still in Herefordshire, Lucie and Alexander set the wedding date for 16 May 1840, a little more than a month before Lucie's nineteenth birthday. After returning to London in late January, she was soon immersed in complicated plans and preparations: fittings with dressmakers, a guest list to be drawn up and invitations engraved, arrangements for the wedding breakfast settled. And then there was the legal side of things. Lucie had no dowry *per se*, but a marriage settlement was drawn up stipulating that Lucie's property, including certain annuities she would inherit from her mother after Sarah's death, be made over to Alexander.* In addition, Lady Duff Gordon settled £600 of three-per-cent annuities on her son at his marriage.

Sarah Austin saw to all the preparations for Lucie's marriage with the efficient competence she had acquired over the years managing her husband's affairs. But did she turn her attention to more intimate things as well and sit down with Lucie one evening and frankly discuss the facts of life with her? Given Sarah's thoroughness and highly developed sense of duty, the answer is probably yes. But it is unlikely that whatever she said was much of a revelation. Lucie's wide and unfettered reading in the classics, Shakespeare, Restoration and eighteenth-century drama and countless French, German and English novels left little scope for new information about sexual passion — outside as well as within marriage.

★

Shortly before nine in the morning on 16 May 1840, assorted Austins, Taylors, Duff Gordons and numerous relations and friends (the Carlyles, Grotes, Mills, Sydney Smiths and many more) converged on Kensington Old Church. A carriage drew up and Lucie alighted with her mother and Henry Reeve. John Austin was too ill to attend the marriage of his daughter.† After

---

* This was standard procedure before the Married Woman's Property Act of 1870. Lucie's marriage settlement, now in the possession of Sir Andrew Duff Gordon, is one of those huge nineteenth-century parchment documents, bristling with red wax seals and written in the elegant but almost indecipherable script of Victorian legal clerks. It was signed, on 15 May 1840, by John Austin, Sarah Austin, Lucy Austin, Alexander Duff Gordon, George Cornewall Lewis and Alfred Austin.

† His name is thus conspicuously absent from the marriage certificate, which was signed by Sarah Austin, Charlotte Austin, Cosmo Duff Gordon, Alice Duff Gordon and Honora Taylor.

the Revd Gilbert Lewis had performed the ceremony, Lucie in white ivory lace and Alexander in a dark frock-coat emerged from the cool, vaulted church into the sunlight of a brilliant spring morning. Their 'majestic beauty' – their splendid youth and radiant joy – took away the breath of all those present.

All her life Lucie collected, appropriated and had bestowed upon her names, jestingly or otherwise. So far she had been her parents' and Jeremy Bentham's and John Stuart Mill's 'Toodie', Carlyle's 'Lucykin', Alice Spring-Rice's 'Roger Austin', Miss Shepherd's 'Miss Austin', the Welsh Taylors' 'Thonys', and perhaps other lost sobriquets as well. But now on the steps of Kensington Old Church, her arm entwined in Alexander's, she joyfully assumed what she and all those gathered round her believed to be her ultimate, definitive identity as Lady Duff Gordon.

Part II

LADY DUFF GORDON

Chapter Five

For their honeymoon Lucie and Alexander went to Germany. First they travelled to Bonn, where Lucie celebrated her nineteenth birthday in June, visited her favourite childhood haunts and introduced Alexander to the erudite August von Schlegel, with whom they had tea. Then they went on to Augsburg and called at the atelier of the famous artist Wilhelm Kaulbach, 'a wonderful genius', Lucie wrote home to Sarah, 'and a beautiful portrait painter'. In Munich they admired the Gothic architecture and browsed for hours in bookshops, where Alexander shocked the booksellers by asking for a copy of Friedrich Strauss's *Leben Jesu*.★ At the Munich Library they pored over illuminated manuscripts and other treasures, including Albrecht Dürer's self-portrait, which seemed to Lucie the most lifelike and moving portrait she had ever seen: 'his face so sweet and so sad . . . and so beautiful, no print could ever catch the life in the face and in the very hair and beard . . . it was like seeing himself'.

It all sounds a terribly intellectual, high-minded honeymoon – the calls on learned philosophers, the mornings in libraries and afternoons in galleries, the esoteric old books they discovered in rare booksellers'. But, of course, these cerebral days gave way to nights when Lucie and Alexander's marriage was not merely one of true minds. Before her marriage Lucie had been a physically as well as mentally adventurous young woman. She was the daughter, too, of a sexually uninhibited (at least on paper) mother. Now Lucie was married to an exceedingly

★ In *Das Leben Jesu: kritisch bearbeitet* ('The Life of Christ, critically examined'), published in 1836, Strauss subjected the Gospel accounts of the life of Jesus to close historical scrutiny and concluded that they were based on myth rather than historical fact. George Eliot translated the book into English in 1846.

50126

handsome husband, ten years her senior and probably sexually experienced. And they were passionately in love. She must have found the sexual expression of that love an exciting revelation.

They returned to London in late September and moved into a house in Westminster, 8 Queen Square, adjacent to the statue of Queen Anne and just across the square from the house where Lucie was born and grew up. Number Eight was rather large for just Lucie and Alexander, but it was close to the Treasury, where Alexander continued to hold his not very remunerative clerkship. To augment his income, they talked of taking in lodgers and, of course, children would arrive to fill up the large, airy rooms.

How does one fathom the secret of a happy marriage? For that is what we are confronted with now – on the threshold of which Victorian stories are supposed to end, not get properly underway. Tolstoy later expressed the prevailing view when he said that all happy families are alike, and unhappy ones unique, as if happiness were inevitably banal and predictable. But Lucie and Alexander's great happiness in the early years of their marriage was neither; their love was, in fact, exceptional in its foundation of complete intimacy, and – rarer still – equality. Lucie's idiosyncratic upbringing, her emotional independence and intellectual self-confidence meant that she met Alexander as an equal. And he, the son of a strong, dominant mother, admired (rather than felt threatened by) Lucie's intelligence and self-sufficiency. In this, they defied most of the rules of the marriage game as it was then played, with its high stakes of family, position and money. None of these figured in Lucie and Alexander's union. Family and rank are perhaps negligible considerations, but money is another matter, and Lucie and Alexander's indifference to it in time would create trouble and even heartache – but that was years off as yet.

Soon Lucie and Alexander became one of the most admired and talked-about couples in London: a golden pair with their good looks, wit, and radical political views. Lucie gained a reputation for being a delightful, albeit rather Bohemian hostess. Guests were amazed, for example, when she stayed in the dining-room to smoke a cigar with the men after dinner. Her clothes could be odd, too; sometimes she appeared in the most elegant of evening dresses, her heavy dark hair coiled up on her head and studded with jewels. But on other occasions she would wear garish, incongruous get-ups that made her look more like a gypsy or opera singer than a society hostess.

Such flamboyance, however, didn't deter callers. Soon, like her mother before her, Lucie presided over a salon at 8 Queen Square, though far more eclectic and high-spirited gatherings congregated until the small hours at the Duff Gordons' than had ever convened in Sarah Austin's chilly parlour. Ageing Utilitarians, novice journalists, artists, Duff Gordon connections, Spring-Rices and Norths, Italian refugees and German philosophers all jostled one another in Lucie's drawing-room, and in the midst of her guests, Lucie held forth. Even her mother-in-law, the dowager Lady Duff Gordon, had to concede Lucie's 'powers of conversation and clearness of intellect'.

When Lucie was in full flow, Alexander sometimes receded into the background, only inserting a word now and then, when the opportunity arose. Old Sydney Smith, a frequent visitor to the Duff Gordons, remarked to Sarah Austin that 'Sir Alexander is making some progress in the arts of conversation. I have watched him through whole sentences.'

Sydney Smith was only one of the Austins' old friends to turn up at the Duff Gordons. Others included the Carlyles, the Grotes, Henry Reeve and his mother, Lord Lansdowne, and John Stuart Mill and Harriet Taylor. (Mill and Harriet Taylor were still together after ten years, though it would be another decade before John Taylor's death would enable them to marry in 1851.) Gradually, however, the old regime was joined and then outnumbered by interesting figures of Lucie and Alexander's own generation: the poet and writer on social and political issues Richard Monckton Milnes, the biographer and journalist John Forster, the two reigning novelists of the day, Charles Dickens and William Makepeace Thackeray, the artist Richard or 'Dicky' Doyle, and the dramatist and future editor of *Punch*, Tom Taylor. Tennyson arrived one day with Carlyle (their unlikely friendship was based on a shared passion for smoking) and startled Lucie when they were introduced by stretching all six feet of himself out on the carpet at her feet and asking, 'Will you please to put your feet on me for a stool?' Tennyson was no Lothario and he was at this very time trying to extricate himself from a longstanding engagement to a woman he wearily wed some ten years later. Nevertheless, one evening at the Duff Gordons' he burst out to Alexander, 'I never loved a dear gazelle, but some damned brute, that's you, Gordon, had married her first.'

Almost all of Lucie's many admirers were men, as indeed were most of the visitors to Queen Square. Somehow the wives, if the men were married, invariably remained at home. It is unlikely that Lucie ever met the perpetually pregnant Catherine Dickens or the mentally unstable (and eventually institutionalized) Isabella Thackeray. But she did make one important, lasting friendship with a woman at this time and that was with the controversial Caroline Norton, who even now, more than four years after being cleared of her estranged husband's charges of adultery with Lord Melbourne, was not received in many fashionable circles. On principle Lucie and Alexander made a point of refusing all invitations to homes where Caroline Norton was not welcomed. Lucie admired, indeed almost worshipped, Caroline, who was thirteen years her senior and a highly successful poet and novelist. Despite all her sorrows – her disastrous marriage, her failure to gain custody of her three young boys, the continuing heartache of her relationship with Melbourne – Caroline could be the most clever, amusing and sympathetic of friends: a beautiful, warm-hearted, intelligent and brave woman. Lucie was awed by her unflagging spirits as Caroline battled against the child-custody laws, wrote volumes of verse and edited literary annuals to support herself, and shone in the enlightened pockets of London society still open to her.

One of these was at the famous breakfast table of the poet Samuel Rogers, who doted on Mrs Norton and was willing to overlook her intellectual gifts (which he disliked in women) because of her great beauty. He made the same concession for Lucie when Caroline introduced the Duff Gordons to Rogers and soon they, too, became regular Sunday-morning guests at Rogers's home in St James's Place. A Rogers breakfast was always a small, select gathering which certainly didn't assemble there for the food: tea or coffee, brown bread and butter, stewed fruit in the winter and strawberries in the summer.

Nor was the nearly eighty-year-old host prepossessing. Rogers was said to be 'the ugliest man in Europe, perhaps in the world'. There was something repellently corpse-like in his appearance – 'a silvery phosphorescence of decay' – that called forth all sorts of macabre jokes, some of them repeated to his face. In the summer people would say, 'How can you go and dine with Rogers in this hot weather? He's been dead these thirty-two years and cannot be expected to keep.' Rogers, though a wealthy banker and art collector as well as a poet, always walked about London in all weathers, so that Lord Alvanley asked him one day when Rogers described how he had walked home from a late party in the pouring rain, 'Why, as you can afford it, don't you set up your hearse?' On another occasion, when Rogers told Sydney Smith that a wren had been eyeing him in a curious way, Smith retorted, 'Why, I wonder? If it had been a carrion crow, one could have understood.'

Rogers's poetry – of which he had a rather inflated opinion – was so laboured that Sydney Smith said of it, 'when [Rogers] is delivered of a couplet with infinite labour and pain, he takes to his bed, has straw laid down, the knocker tied up, expects his friends to call and make enquiries, and the answer at the door invariably is: "Mr Rogers and his little couplet are as well as can be expected."'

Rogers collected art – Raphaels, Titians, Giottos, Rubens, Rembrandts and others, many of which hung in his dining-room and gazed down on his guests as they ate their meagre breakfast – but even more he collected people. In the past Pitt and Sheridan had graced his table. Now, in old age, he was an eager talent-scout and prided himself on picking out young genius. Thus it says much for the Duff Gordons that he pressed his invitations on them, though he was more taken with Lucie than with Alexander, who usually remained silent at breakfast. Alexander had good reason to be silent, and even the voluble Lucie must have weighed her words carefully before speaking in Rogers's presence. For the old poet was renowned for his caustic and severe repartee; as another of his rare female friends, the actress Fanny Kemble, put it, 'he has the kindest heart and the unkindest tongue in London'. Carlyle was even blunter: Rogers, he said, was 'an elegant, politely malignant old lady'.

★

Lucie's great happiness in her marriage and her success in London society were perhaps not unrelated to the fact that the Austins were no longer on the scene. In 1841 they retreated once again to the continent to economize – to Germany, in fact, where they went first to Carlsbad so that John Austin could take the waters for his continued ill health, and then to Dresden and Berlin. By this time Pückler-Muskau was back from his extensive travels and, the following year, he and Sarah finally met in Berlin. This long-anticipated, long-deferred event was, perhaps inevitably, a great disappointment – a case of 'all passion spent'. The two once-passionate lovers, now both stolidly middle-aged (Sarah was forty-nine and Pückler fifty-seven), couldn't possibly live up to the fantasy scenario they had spent years elaborating in their letters. Pückler had found romantic and sexual interest elsewhere; Sarah's passion had been extinguished by poverty, worry, depression and illness. They had little to say to each other, exchanged books, made their farewells, and never communicated again. That mournful chapter closed, Sarah turned her full-hearted attentions once again to her ailing and dispirited husband and to translating work – the more abstruse and arduous the better.

Meanwhile, she heard nothing but good news from and of Lucie in London, which cheered her. In October 1841, Sydney Smith wrote to Sarah in Dresden, 'I am just come from Bowood. Lord Lansdowne's admiration of your daughter is if possible equal to that he entertains for you. He was loud in his admiration of her sense and her beauty.' Lucie, in fact, was eclipsing her mother's reputation in London society. And there was a freedom for her in having her mother's unrelieved seriousness and her father's gloom at a distance.

Nevertheless, when Lucie discovered that she was pregnant in June 1841, she turned immediately to Sarah with the glad, but also perhaps somewhat bewildering, news. To be a mother at twenty was, of course, perfectly normal and predictable. A handsome, gifted couple such as the Duff Gordons would be expected to produce a whole brood of handsome, gifted children, and to do so with their usual élan. And yet Lucie, like Sarah twenty years earlier, may have wondered if she was ready for motherhood and how it might affect her intimacy with Alexander.

But any doubts she may have entertained had no visible effect on her pregnancy. Lucie bloomed during the summer and autumn of 1841. She grew ripe and plump – almost Rubenesque – and remained so after the baby was born. Like many expectant mothers, she hoped for a boy. And being still her mother's daughter, she carefully prepared for its arrival: not merely by having all the little clothes and gowns it would need knitted and sewn, but also by studying what was available at the time on the subject of childcare and the education of children. She was, in fact, reading Rousseau's *Émile* when she went into labour and kept at it until the pains became too distracting to concentrate.

Janet Anne Duff Gordon – a large, hearty baby – was born

on 24 February 1842. It was an easy birth and after the first, subdued disappointment Lucie felt over having a daughter, she was as delighted as Alexander was with the baby. Sydney Smith was one of the first to congratulate the young parents and also the nervous grandparents in Dresden on the 'new creation'. But he also confided to Sarah Austin, 'a first act of this kind Malthus himself was always willing to overlook, but I hope they will not go on creating . . . I suspect [the baby] . . . will turn out a very sensible, agreeable person but I am not sure of it.'

Sydney Smith himself felt keenly now the close of life bearing down on him, and so may be forgiven his scepticism over those, like little Janet Duff Gordon, who were just embarking on it. He wrote in this same letter to Sarah, 'what most annoys me is the proximity of Death – for I am nearly seventy-two – and I am afraid of the very disagreeable methods in which we leave the world – the long death of palsy, the degraded spectacle of aged idiotism. As for the pleasures of the world, it is I think a very middling, ordinary sort of place and if one could be sure of dying in a fit of laughter or in some ecstasy, I should not care much for what I lost.'

When Janet was only three months old, Lucie and Alexander took her to Bonn to visit the Austins, who were entranced with their tiny granddaughter. And the following summer, when she was one and a half, Lucie and Janet, with Janet's nurse, 'Narty', went to Boulogne for a longer holiday with the Austins. By this time Janet was walking and up to perpetual mischief. Lucie wrote to a friend, 'children are delicious, the naiveté with which they display every human vice is indescribably charming'. And Sarah confessed she was 'the most foolish of grandmothers . . . and never so happy as when all my schemes are disconcerted and all my things thrown into confusion by this little creature'. Janet was fascinated by Sarah's labours at her desk and was constantly grabbing at the pages of manuscript and – most desirable of all – the dangerous inkwell. Like Lucie as a very small child, one of the first images to be planted in Janet's memory was that of a woman writing industriously at a desk strewn with open books and papers.

★

Shortly after they returned to London and Queen Square, Lucie, too, was preoccupied with writing for hours at a stretch in the back parlour. The arrival of Janet coincided with her decision to turn her own hand to translations. She and Alexander were now beginning to worry about money and how to manage on his meagre salary at the Treasury. Lucie wanted to make a financial contribution. But she may have been motivated, too, by a sense of restlessness – a feeling that she wasn't completely fulfilled by her life as a young wife, mother and hostess. She loved little Janet, but she didn't dote on her as Alexander did, and of course it was the nurse Narty who actually cared for her. The Duff Gordons' literary friends – Macaulay, Rogers, the Carlyles and the adoring Tennyson – all encouraged Lucie to write. And Caroline Norton as well as Sarah Austin must have been a potent example.

But like her mother, Lucie shrank from original work. Translation is in many respects the most ladylike and self-effacing of literary endeavours. And also the least frightening, for one is never confronted with a blank page. Yet it requires great intelligence and verve and a resonant, tactful style. Lucie's first rather modest effort was a children's book (the other great domain of women writers) entitled *Stories of the Gods and Heroes of Greece* by Berthold Niebuhr, the eminent German historian whom the Austins had known when Lucie was a child in Bonn. The slender book, in fact, consisted of retellings of several Greek myths for Niebuhr's young son, who had been Lucie's playmate. Lucie's rendition of Niebuhr's simplified versions of the stories of the voyage of the Argonauts and Hercules and Orestes are told with the lilt and cadence of fairy-tale. Her translation of the tale of the golden fleece must have charmed little Janet: 'Now the fleece was nailed to an oak, and at the foot of the oak lay a dragon who never slept and who ate up anyone that tried to touch the fleece except King Acestis; and the dragon was immortal so that Medea could not help Jason to kill him. But he was very fond of sweet cakes in which she had mixed a sleeping potion; and Jason took them and threw them to him, and the foolish dragon ate them all up and fell asleep directly. Then Jason drew out the nails which fastened the fleece to the tree, hid it under his cloak and carried it on board the ship. And Medea went with him and he married her and took her to Greece.' And, of course, they lived happily ever after.

Lucie diffidently published Niebuhr's little book under her mother's name and Sarah Austin contributed a pedantic preface discussing Niebuhr, the superiority of Greek over debased and corrupted Roman myth, the phonetic spelling of Greek names and the contribution of German scholarship to classical studies. This heavy-handed introduction made a strange contrast to Lucie's simple and charmingly told tales, but she wanted her mother's imprimatur for this initial step of her writing career.

She also relied on Sarah's learning and editorial advice in her next, far more ambitious project: a translation of a strange volume that had caused something of a sensation in both Germany and England: Wilhelm Meinhold's *Maria Schweidler Die Bernsteinhexe*, or as it became known in English, following Lucie's translation, *The Amber Witch*. A long, intriguing review of the book in the original 1843 German edition appeared in the *Quarterly Review* in June 1844 and it may have been this unsigned article which first drew Lucie's attention to the book. If so, she knew very well what she was getting into, and nothing could have been further from the child's play of Niebuhr's Greek myths. The *Quarterly Review* said that 'the unrivalled charm throughout this ... book' was 'incommunicable, we fear, in any translation ... Who could translate it? Scarcely even Mrs Austin. The somewhat antiquated and provincial language, with its odd pedantic scraps of Latin ... could hardly be preserved by a translator.' But Lucie was intrigued and not the least bit discouraged by these caveats and the suggestion that even her mother might be daunted by *Maria*

Schweidler. In addition, the whole subject of witchcraft fascinated her. She ordered a copy of the book from Germany, stayed up all night reading it and realized that she had a classic on her hands which she could introduce to the English reading public.

What Lucie didn't know, however, was that *The Amber Witch* was a clever literary hoax: a fiction perpetrated by Meinhold that pretended to be a genuine seventeenth-century chronicle of a case of witchcraft during the Thirty Years War. It tells the story of a beautiful, clever young girl named Maria Schweidler who saves her clergyman father and a number of their neighbours in the island of Usedom from starvation and want when she accidentally discovers a large vein of amber one day when she is out picking berries. She and her father secretly sell the amber to Dutch merchants. But their sudden wealth and then the mysterious deaths of cows and pigs in their village arouse the suspicions of the villagers and after many trials and tribulations – and a good many sub-plots – Maria is tried for witchcraft and tortured. To end the great distress of her poor old father, she confesses. But at the eleventh hour she is saved by a handsome village boy who has evidence of her innocence, and the story ends with their marriage.

The book is an ingenious amalgam of documentary realism and fairy-tale related in archaic seventeenth-century German. Meinhold hoped to hoodwink the controversial biblical scholar Strauss and expose his pseudo-scientific school of historical criticism, and for a time, in some quarters at least, he succeeded. But Lucie was far more interested in the historical background of *The Amber Witch* than with the provenance and authenticity of the text. She read everything she could lay her hands on about the Thirty Years War and witchcraft. And she also read a great deal of seventeenth-century English literature to enable her to render Meinhold in a suitably antiquated English style. She succeeded in this so brilliantly that some reviewers claimed she had produced a translation actually superior to the original. Meinhold himself, who belatedly

acknowledged that the story was a fiction after Lucie's translation appeared, was so impressed with it that he dedicated his
next book, *Sidonia the Sorceress*, to her.

Lucie's publisher, John Murray, was also delighted with *The
Amber Witch*, which was published in early 1844 and went
through three editions by the end of the year. Though she was
paid a flat translation fee of £50 and did not receive royalties,
the book's sales were very gratifying to Lucie and with its
success she was launched on a career as a woman of letters. And
– no small matter to her – with the £50 she had the leaking
roof of the Queen Square house repaired.

This same year – 1844 – a book came out with the strange
title *Eothen*, which Lucie seriously considered translating into
German: an eccentric, droll travelogue by a complete unknown
named Alexander Kinglake. Kinglake had been at Eton in the late
1820s with Alexander, but he was two years ahead of him, so they
scarcely knew each other. Then he had gone on to Cambridge,
where he was acquainted with Thackeray and Tennyson, but it
was only after *Eothen* was published to universal acclaim that he
became known to the Duff Gordons. Though she soon dropped
the idea of translation because she didn't think Kinglake's 'lively,
brilliant and rather insolent style' could be rendered into
German, Lucie was eager to meet him after she had read the
book and also a long article that he published in December 1844
on 'The Rights of Women' in the *Quarterly Review*.

'*Eothen*' is the Greek word for 'from the East' and Kinglake's
book recounted his travels across Eastern Europe to
Constantinople, Greece, the Lebanon, Palestine, and finally
Egypt. But it didn't really partake of the Orientalism that had
infected the English literary sensibility ever since Byron. *Eothen*
is an inward-looking book and inveterately English. It is as
much about Kinglake's wry perceptions, reactions and intermittent homesickness as it is about exotic foreign lands. Kinglake
had an eye for the absurd rather than the sublime, and also for
the morbid and the dangerous. The plague which raged in

Egypt and many of the other places he visited is introduced on the first page, and it remains a dark motif throughout: the black mourning thread woven into Kinglake's golden tapestry of the East.

'The Rights of Women' article – somewhat inaccurately titled – carried on Kinglake's interest in the East, for it was a long review essay on Monckton Milnes's recently published collection of verse, *Palm Leaves* (very much in the Byronic oriental mode), and Sophia Lane Poole's *The Englishwoman in Egypt: Letters from Cairo*. In an urbane and ironic style, Kinglake discussed the relative position of oriental and English women as portrayed in Milnes's sentimental verse, in Mrs Poole's realistic, searching account, in the prolific Mrs Sarah Stickney Ellis's *The Women of England* and *The Wives of England*, and finally in Anna Jameson's historical study of the role of women in English poetry from the Troubadours to the Romantics.

'The Rights of Women' was precisely the sort of knowing, deftly written article which delighted Lucie, and she asked Alexander to arrange a meeting with Kinglake through Thackeray or Tennyson. This came off and was a great success, and soon Kinglake, a small, rather odd-looking, confirmed bachelor, became a *habitué* at 8 Queen Square. From the beginning, he was smitten and also awed by Lucie. Years later he vividly described her at this time: 'the classical form of her features, the noble poise of her head and neck, her stately height, her . . . pure complexion, caused some . . . at first to call her beauty statuesque, and others to call it majestic, some pronouncing it to be even imperious. But she was so intellectual, so keen, so autocratic, sometimes even so impassioned in speech, that nobody, feeling her powers, could well go on feebly comparing her to a statue or a mere queen or empress.'

Though Kinglake was no orientalist himself – indeed, he had often been bored and miserable on his travels – he was fascinated by Islamic cultures, and Lucie was soon infected with this fascination. She read Sophia Lane Poole's book and then that of her more famous brother, Edward Lane: *Manners and Customs of the Modern Egyptians*. Lane's meticulous exploration of Egyptian life brought back all the magic of the *Arabian Nights* which Lucie had loved as a child. Now she read it again in Lane's recently published translation.

Egypt and the East were, in fact, very much in the air in the mid-forties. When in difficulties – financial, moral or psychological – it was the place to repair to. In the summer of 1844 Thackeray was travelling in Greece, Turkey and Egypt in the wake of his wife's final nervous breakdown. Another Duff Gordon friend, Eliot Warburton, had just returned and was writing his own book on the East, published the following year as *The Crescent and the Cross*, which Lucie greatly admired. Lane himself was established in Cairo, labouring on what became his great life-work: an eight-volume Arabic–English lexicon.

All these books and authors were like seeds planted in Lucie's mind at this time, and her next translation reflected her new interest in the East. Lucie was a wide-ranging, unsystematic reader, drawn more to non-fiction – history, letters, memoirs, biography – than fiction. (When she did read novels, she preferred Thackeray to Dickens, and the Brontës to Jane Austen.) In the autumn of 1844 she came upon two obscure accounts of Abd el-Kader, the romantic Algerian leader who for more than a decade had been waging a guerrilla war against the French in Algeria. She decided to translate both in one volume for John Murray's popular 'Colonial and Home Library' series.

The first book, *The Prisoners of Abd el-Kader*, by a French naval lieutenant, M. de France, was a rather xenophobic production, a long, harrowing account of de France's captivity and life with Abd el-Kader's army. Lucie abridged as well as translated it, cutting the more self-serving and racist passages while emphasizing those which shed light on Abd el-Kader's character.

The Soldier of the Foreign Legion by a German named Clemens Lamping was much more interesting. Lamping came to Algeria as a mercenary to fight against Abd el-Kader, but he ended up being more conquered than conquering. Like Lane in Egypt, he became fascinated with Arab life – the language, customs, oriental women, Islam. His slender volume is almost a prose-poem evocation of the strange, seductive world he found in Algeria, a world which the romantic and apparently invincible figure of Abd el-Kader seemed to personify. Indeed, one can find passages in Lamping that not only seem to echo Lane, but also foreshadow Lucie's own *Letters from Egypt*. Kinglake may have provided her with a ticket to the East, but it was Lamping who gave her the map to pursue her way there. He introduced her to the 'paradise' of coffee-houses, the spectacle of Eastern weddings, the cacophony of dark-alleyed Algiers, the dignity and simplicity of nomadic Berber life, and the magic of long, silent desert nights under the stars. Lamping created an Arabian Nights aura that haunted Lucie until she, too, travelled East and dwelt in the midst of similar, dreamy landscapes.

★

But for the present she was strictly an armchair traveller and had no idea that she was ever to be more than a vicarious one. Before she finished translating de France and Lamping (the two books were eventually published together as *The French in Algiers* in 1845), Lucie discovered that she was pregnant again. No doubt this was welcome news to both her and Alexander, but at the same time they were worried about money. Lucie tried to negotiate with Murray for a larger payment for *The French in Algiers* than she had received for *The Amber Witch*, but in the end agreed to the same flat translation fee of £50. As soon as she had submitted the manuscript, however, she asked if her 'wages', as she called them, could be paid in full at once rather than upon publication of the book. 'I have a heavy bill from my carpenter,' she told Murray, 'which is to be defrayed by *Algeria*.'

The baby was due early in the year, but before then, in late December 1844, there was another, wholly unexpected arrival at 8 Queen Square – one that seemed to walk out of the Eastern books Lucie was reading and translating. Late one bitterly cold night, Lucie and Alexander returned home from a theatrical party at Dickens's to find a small, black figure crouched on their doorstep. Lucie recognized the child at once – he was the young African servant of an Italian who lodged in the same house as Lucie's friend, Signor Prandi, the Italian teacher at Miss Shepherd's. Lucie and Alexander immediately brought the child indoors and placed him before the fire and plied him with hot rum, and he explained that his eyes ailed him and that his Italian master had turned him out because he didn't want to be saddled with a useless, blind servant-boy. He had fled to the Duff Gordons, he said, so that he could 'die on the doorstep of the beautiful pale lady' who had been kind to him.

Of course, Lucie and Alexander immediately took him in. The boy was about twelve, a Nubian from the Sudan named Hassan el-Bakkeet. Janet couldn't pronounce his name and called him Hatty, and Hatty he became henceforth. He spoke impeccable English because he had come under the protection of English missionaries while very young. Just how he had been acquired by the Italian was unclear, but from the moment he crossed the threshold at Queen Square he was utterly devoted to Lucie and soon became the inseparable playmate of Janet. Lucie had his eyes cured and gave him lessons. Before a month was out, he was an integral member of the family.

Caroline Norton was charmed by Hatty and drew him while he read to Janet, who was nestled in his lap. But not all the Duff Gordons' friends were as taken by the new addition to the family. A visiting American writer was shocked to see Janet in Hatty's arms and asked Lucie how she could allow a negro to touch her child. A maid was also difficult when Hatty fell ill and the doctor prescribed leeches. Lucie showed the maid how to apply the leeches to Hatty's chest, but she recoiled and burst out, 'Lawks, my lady, I wouldn't touch either of them.' Where-upon Lucie did it herself.

Lucie treated Hatty as one of her own, and cut friends who disapproved, just as she cut people who denounced Caroline Norton. But there was something of an irony in her champion-ship of Hatty. Because he had been raised by pious British missionaries, he was a bit of a snob himself. He was much impressed by Lord Melbourne and Lord Lansdowne and other titled guests at the Duff Gordons'. And when Prince Louis Napoleon came unexpectedly to dinner, Hatty whispered to Lucie, 'Please, my lady, I've run out and bought two-pennyworth of sprats for the honour of the house.'

The 'honour of the house' also made him smart under any real or imagined humiliation it might suffer. Soon after Hatty joined the family Lucie gave refuge to a young female servant who had recently had a child, but omitted, as Janet later put it, 'the precaution of marriage'. Lucie assembled all the other servants and sternly threatened to dismiss anyone who troubled or spoke against the new maid, Mary. According to Janet, 'small, jet-black Hassan, possessed with an idea of the dignity of his sex, conceived it his duty to become the spokesman of the rest, and . . . advancing a little in front of the neat-aproned, tall maid-servants, he promised in his and their name a full and careful obedience to the mistress's orders; then wringing his hands and raising them over his head, he added: "What a lesson to us all, my lady."'

★

In early February 1845, just before Janet's third birthday, Lucie gave birth to a son, and Hatty announced triumphantly to all callers, 'We have got a boy!' The baby's birth rather eclipsed Janet's birthday celebrations, and as she later confessed, seeing her parents' joy and absorption in her new brother made her wish keenly that she were a boy.

The baby was large and strong and handsome and they named him Maurice after Lord Lansdowne (Henry Petty-

Fitzmaurice) whom they asked to be godfather. The christening was put off, however, until the summer, and throughout the early spring Lucie was absorbed with her beautiful child, who was rarely out of her sight. She had contracted with Murray again to translate a lengthy German book of famous criminal trials – just the sort of esoteric and bizarre thing that appealed to her – but she let it slide now. She was immersed in domestic life, and with the new baby her happiness seemed complete. She had a handsome, loving husband, two beautiful children, a wide circle of affectionate and amusing friends. Even the death of Sydney Smith that spring couldn't seriously detract from Lucie's contentment and sense of well-being. His had been a long, useful life and she hoped that he had died as he wished, 'in a fit of laughter or some ecstasy'.

As the days and weeks passed, a warm, balmy spring with soft breezes took possession of the city. The trees and bushes in Queen Square came into full leaf, followed by daffodils, primroses and lilacs. On 24 June, Lucie celebrated her birthday and the sun poured down from a cloudless blue sky just as it had on the little square twenty-four years earlier. A month later, on 30 July, Maurice was christened at St George's, Hanover Square. The godparents, Lord Lansdowne and Caroline Norton, were both present, and after the church ceremony there was a celebratory breakfast at Queen Square.

But the next day Maurice woke up flushed with a fever, and Lucie wondered if he'd caught a cold at the christening. She sent for the doctor, who assured her there was nothing to worry about. But the baby wasn't better the following day nor the next. Nothing the doctor prescribed could bring down the fever, and the baby became too weak and listless to feed. Lucie sat up with him night after night, bathing his small, hot brow with wet compresses, rocking him when he feebly cried. In the early hours of 4 August, he suddenly emerged from his languid state, went red and stiff and had convulsions. A short time later he died in Lucie's arms.

Alexander was so overcome with grief that Lucie had to see to everything herself, all the while feeling a terrible sense of unreality and disbelief. On the evening of the 5th she sat down and wrote to Lord Lansdowne: 'The poor child whom you saw christened last week died at 2 o'clock yesterday morning after suffering fearfully since the afternoon of Sunday. Of course, none but ourselves can see in the death of so young a creature any very great grief, but to me it seems a terrible loss. The child was so strong and so handsome that I had indulged hopes of so much happiness from what he would one day be to me, and now I find it hard to bear the destruction of them . . . My poor husband is so cut up that I am forced to do all that has to be done . . . I feel that I have no right to lament, for all has gone so well with us that some misfortune was due . . . [But] you will be sorry for my grief . . . and able to imagine that blank left in my life by the loss of a creature who had never been absent from me one night or day since its birth.'

Lucie grieved not merely for the baby that was; as she told Lord Lansdowne and others, she mourned even more the child that would have been. Lucie could not say – as she had of Jeremy Bentham or Sydney Smith – that the child had had a long, full life. He had lived barely six months, and now Lucie was haunted by the long perspective of his lost years.

After writing to Lord Lansdowne, Lucie sent word to her parents, now living in Paris, and then she saw to all the funeral arrangements. Despite her vague religious beliefs, it was a comfort to her that the child had been baptized. She ordered a small coffin to be made and went to see the vicar. Scarcely a week after the christening, the funeral was held with only Lucie, Alexander and Caroline Norton present. Caroline, especially, could feel Lucie's great sorrow, for Caroline's youngest son, a boy of eight, had died three years earlier while in the custody of her estranged husband.

That evening, after the funeral, Lucie packed away the christening gown and all the little clothes and blankets and had the cradle carried back up to the loft. A mother is bound to her infant physically – bone of its bone, flesh of its flesh – as well as emotionally. It was many days before Lucie's breasts were no longer swollen with milk, and many nights before she stopped waking instinctively in the dark, listening for the baby's cry.

And even then, she wrote to a friend, 'I find it still impossible to shake off the depression caused by my boy's death. The more I think of it, the worse it seems to me and the harder to bear. People torment me with the stupid and senseless consolation of "You can easily have another." I have too little faith in the mercy of Providence to incur the risk of having my heart broken over again . . . The misfortune, the sorrow is *there, c'est un fait accompli*, it may be borne, like everything else, but it can't be repaired.'

After she had done all that she had to do, and the poor baby was buried and all his little things put away, Lucie's acute grief moderated into a dull despair. She wrote to Kinglake that she felt 'indifferent to everything and almost everyone, for I cannot disguise from myself that I care less even for my [remaining] child'. This numbness, the sluggish passivity of grief, was the first step – not towards repair, but towards another kind of wholeness, a different sort of life ahead. But the nearness of death, and the swiftness of its descent, would remain with Lucie through all her coming years.

Chapter Six

One morning in late August 1845, Jane Octavia Brookfield rose from her sofa – all five feet nine inches of her – in the sitting-room of Halberton Vicarage, where she was on an extended visit. The maid had come in and handed her a letter from her husband, the Revd William Henry Brookfield, who was back in London in their rented rooms in Great Pulteney Street. Though they had been married for only four years, the Brookfields were often apart. Theirs had been a protracted, epistolary courtship, somewhat like that of John Austin and Sarah Taylor, and they discovered shortly after their marriage that they got on together best when they were separated.

Like the Duff Gordons, who were almost their exact contemporaries, the Brookfields were short of money, which created a good deal of tension and misunderstandings. Brookfield's most obvious assets – a dry wit and urbane charm – were not highly prized by the Church, and his clerical career had not flourished. He was now the meagrely paid curate of St James's, Piccadilly and St Luke's in Berwick Street, but he preferred to hark back to his halcyon days at Trinity College, Cambridge, where he had first met his good friends, Thackeray and Tennyson. Friends, to Brookfield's chagrin, who, despite all sorts of handicaps and setbacks, had done so much better than himself.

Jane Brookfield was chagrined too, but instead of rousing herself to do something about her husband's obscure professional status, she subsided into semi-invalidism. This didn't, however, prevent her from travelling a good deal. She was often away from London, experimenting with hot air treatments or sulphur baths, or simply languishing on the sofas of understanding relatives and friends. Hence her prone position in the sitting-room of Halberton Vicarage, where she opened her husband's letter and read:

MY DEAR WENCH,

Yesterday . . . at six o'clock who should step in but Eothen [Kinglake]. He is going to Algiers tomorrow . . . He came . . . to invite us to eat whitebait at Greenwich, it being his party – to meet Mrs [Caroline] Norton, Lady Duff Gordon, Sir Duff ditto, Sidney Herbert . . . and perhaps Milnes . . . Kinglake vows that there [is] nothing to hinder you going (for I expressed my doubt [because of Caroline Norton's presence]) . . . she visits everywhere – and he himself believes nothing against her . . . [He says she] is decidedly pretty, a nice person, very unaffected, and a shade free and easy, but it seems only the overflowing of an open disposition. Kinglake was very agreeable – took occasion to remark that I had been happy in my marriage (I sighed like Billy Pearson and said 'Ah, you don't know, old fellow') that you appeared to have a perfect temper, and to 'fall into my batchelor [sic] ways'. Thackeray observed on Saturday night that you had the sweetest voice he ever heard. And now, you wretch, have I told you enough? I don't know what mischief I haven't done by repeating men's praise of you – a thing I generally avoid . . . God bless thee.

EVER MOST AFFECTIONATELY,

W.H. BROOKFIELD

Thackeray was already quite desperately (though platonically) in love with Jane Brookfield, who was beautiful, as witty as her husband, and perhaps even cleverer. And according to her husband, Thackeray wasn't Jane's only devotee; he complained in another letter of her 'seven hundred and ninety-nine lovers', all clamouring for her return to London.

Despite her husband's reassurances, Jane was reluctant to encounter the notorious Mrs Norton, so she didn't return for Kinglake's farewell party in Greenwich, which meant that she also didn't, as yet, meet the Duff Gordons. For Lucie, despite her grief over Maurice and the wretchedness and despondency that had engulfed her since his death, felt she must say goodbye to dear Kinglake, who was off to Algeria, where he hoped to meet the famous Abd el-Kader – influenced in his expedition, in part, by Lucie's translation of *The French in Algiers*.

Lucie and Alexander went to Greenwich by boat on a glorious late summer's afternoon at the end of August. It was the first time she'd been out since the baby's funeral and when they arrived at the Trafalgar Tavern, which had its own dock on the Thames at Greenwich, the gloom that had enveloped her for the past month suddenly lifted. She was among friends – Caroline Norton, Monckton Milnes and Sidney Herbert as well as Kinglake himself – there was music and everyone was talking and jesting at once. To her surprise, Lucie soon found herself talking and laughing too. The Trafalgar was famous for its whitebait dinners. The whitebait was caught on the spot and cooked immediately in copper cauldrons over a charcoal fire. The resulting meal was delicious, especially when washed down with champagne and claret.

★

Lucie was so buoyed by the evening – and so grateful for its respite from bereavement – that she came home with a sense of being in and belonging to the world again. She opened up her desk in the back parlour and took out the hefty volume of German criminal trials which she had contracted with John Murray to translate, her notes and rough drafts, plus back issues of the *Law Magazine*, all of which she had scarcely looked at since the baby was born the previous February. Almost at once she was utterly absorbed and, in the coming weeks, as autumn and then early winter closed in, she gave herself up to the quite Herculean task of rendering Anselm Ritter von Feuerbach's 1,300-page *Aktenmassige Darstellung Merkwürdiger Verbrechen* ('Narratives of Remarkable Crimes, Compiled From the Official Records') into an abridged and faithful English translation.

The book had been suggested to Lucie by her father's old friend, Nassau Senior, and Lucie corresponded with Senior and

John Austin himself in Paris over various points as her work progressed. She also did a great deal of research on German and English law – reading the standard texts recommended to her by John Austin and diligently going through the back numbers of various legal quarterlies. This research formed the basis of her lengthy preface, in which she also assessed Feuerbach's career as 'a man celebrated as a judge, a legislator, and a writer', who had been 'the President of the highest criminal court in Bavaria' and the chief architect of the Bavarian penal code.

But what Lucie found fascinating in Feuerbach was not so much the intricacies of the Bavarian legal system and the light it shed on English law as Feuerbach's 'extraordinary power of penetrating the recesses of the human heart, and of divining the secret motives of human action'. Feuerbach's crime narratives pitched Lucie into a squalid underworld of theft, fraud, fornication, violence and murder: a brutal husband and father murdered by his family when they could take no more of his sadistic violence; a German Jack the Ripper – a serial killer who slit the throats of his female victims; a vintner who stabbed to death his mistress and her lover when he found them in bed together; a grotesque old housekeeper who poisoned her employers and their children, one after another, with arsenic; the motiveless bludgeoning to death of a beautiful young woman travelling to meet her fiancé.

For the most part, Feuerbach's criminals were an unsavoury lot, usually from the lower classes. A striking exception, however, was the case of the Catholic priest Francis Riembauer, a secret Don Juan, who murdered one of his mistresses, the mother of his illegitimate child, and then killed another woman and her daughter after they discovered the corpse of the mistress. All these murders were graphically described by Feuerbach, as were the scenes when the criminals were, in Lucie's words, 'led to the spot where the crime was committed and the bleeding corpse, or, it may be, the mouldering remains are suddenly shown to him'.

Far from distressing Lucie in her bereaved state, Feuerbach's lurid case-histories utterly engrossed her, and she felt sure they would create a sensation among English readers. For Lucie was writing in a day before thrillers and crime novels had become widely current. Hence she drove a hard bargain with Murray, who initially offered her the same £50 flat translation fee she had earned for *The Amber Witch* and *The French in Algiers*. This she politely refused, pointing out that she had not only translated Feuerbach but also distilled his unwieldy 1,300-page book into just under four hundred pages covering fourteen representative cases.

At this stage Alexander entered into the negotiations, as in fact he had done in the end with Lucie's earlier books. A married woman, of course, could not transact a legal contract at this time, and all her earnings automatically became the possession of her husband since she was also barred from owning property. But Alexander's previous involvement in Lucie's publishing agreements had amounted to no more than signing her contracts and writing receipts for cheques she received in his name from Murray. With the Feuerbach book Alexander was more aggressive, backing her demand for more money so that, by October 1845, Alexander and Lucie had got Murray to agree to a £200 translation and abridgement fee – four times what Lucie had previously earned – £150 to be paid on the publication of the first edition of 1,000 copies and an additional £50 when the second edition appeared.

The book, published under the English title *Narratives of Remarkable Criminal Trials*, was, as Lucie had foreseen, an enormous success and she now became known as a woman of letters well beyond the literary circles she already moved in. It was also favourably reviewed both in the popular press, which dwelt upon the sensational nature of the crimes, and in scholarly and legal journals.

In October, shortly after Lucie delivered the Feuerbach manuscript to Murray, Lord Lansdowne pressed her to come to

Bowood and she and Janet took a fortnight's holiday there at the end of the month. When she returned to Queen Square she found an invitation from Dickens to come to his production of Ben Jonson's *Every Man in His Humour* playing at the St James's Theatre. The production was the talk of the season, and Dickens playing Bobadil and John Forster playing Kitely had received rave notices in *The Times* and other papers.

Lucie persuaded Caroline Norton and Lord Melbourne to go with her to see Dickens's production on the evening of 15 November, and when they got to the theatre they met Tennyson and Henry Reeve, both of whom Lucie hadn't seen in months. It was now nearly ten years since Caroline Norton's husband had sued Melbourne, for 'alienating his wife's affections', but it was still quite daring of Caroline to appear in public with Melbourne. It was also something of a risk for Lucie to invite them to this particular entertainment, for she well knew that Melbourne was easily bored. Once settled in their box, before the curtain rose, he predicted that it was bound to be a tedious evening. Throughout the first act, he groaned and complained in an undertone. But at the interval, he lost all restraint and 'exclaimed in a stentorian voice, heard across the pit: "I knew this play would be dull, but that it would be so damnably dull as this I did not suppose."' To Lucie it felt as if the entire audience craned their necks towards the box after this pronouncement, but she and Caroline Norton affected sublime indifference to the spectacle Melbourne had made.

★

Early in the new year of 1846, Lucie and Alexander decided to take in a lodger, largely because they needed the extra income. At Thackeray's one evening, they met a small, rather self-effacing young man with the incongruous soubriquet of 'the Thunderer of *The Times*'. This was the journalist C. J. Bayley, who wrote controversial articles on the Corn Laws and other important issues for *The Times*. He was a bachelor, looking for a congenial roof to put over his head. Lucie found Bayley charming and, across Thackeray's dining-table, she and Alexander impulsively invited Bayley to come and live at 8 Queen Square as soon as he could arrange his affairs.

Within a week he moved in, taking over the small parlour behind the dining-room where Lucie used to write. This became 'Bayley's Sanctum' and Bayley himself 'Our Lodger' and 'dear little Bayley'. Soon he was Janet's 'playfellow and slave', Alexander's after-dinner companion and Lucie's confidante.

Like everyone else at the time, Lucie and Alexander were closely following the agitation of the Anti-Corn Law League, with which they and Bayley in his editorials sympathized. The wet summer of 1845 and the failure of the Irish potato crop had brought famine to Ireland. Throughout the winter and the spring of 1846 everyone talked of nothing but the famine and whether or not the Conservative Prime Minister, Sir Robert Peel, would go back on his word and repeal the Protectionist Corn Laws in order to alleviate the massive distress in Ireland and England. At last, in June, Peel did repeal the offensive laws, despite the opposition within his own party of Lord Bentinck and Disraeli. This split amongst the Conservatives was fatal, and three weeks after the repeal, Peel's government fell – much to the delight of everyone at 8 Queen Square, including Janet, who regarded Peel and the endlessly debated Corn Laws as her 'personal enemies' because they took up so much of Bayley's and her parents' time.

This same June of political turmoil was also a month of atmospheric turbulence and unprecedented heat: 'murderous weather' in Queen Square, London, and the whole of England. Daily temperatures averaged 84 degrees in the shade and 105 in the sun. 'Wherrymen, out in boats on the Thames all day, died of sunstroke; farm-labourers died of heat-stroke after a day's mowing; many people all over the country were drowned while bathing.' Typhus broke out in London and so did fires after weeks of drought. And then suddenly violent storms swept through the country, flooding dried brown fields, and killing people with random bolts of lightning. The raindrops were so large that they reflected light like prisms and cast weird, wavering rainbows on window-ledges and bare floors. Janet was enchanted though the thunder terrified her. Lucie was strangely excited by the uncanny weather, but in Great Pulteney and Wimpole Streets, Jane Brookfield (who still hadn't met the Duff Gordons) and Elizabeth Barrett (who probably never did) both stayed rooted to their sofas through enervating heat and cataclysmic storms.

Into this alternately parched and tempestuous climate wandered two arresting figures from Germany whom Lucie and Alexander first encountered at the home of either Monckton Milnes or the Carlyles. They were Gräfin Ida Hahn-Hahn, a divorced, one-eyed novelist with false teeth and 'a face like a squashed muffin', and her inamorato and travelling companion Oberst Baron Adolph von Bystram. Lucie had read Gräfin Hahn-Hahn's enormously popular *roman-à-clef, Die Gräfin Faustina*, when it first appeared and caused a sensation in 1841. Five years later when the authoress, her lover in tow, swept into London with the turbulent weather, Jane Carlyle observed of her, 'She is a sort of George Sand without the genius . . . [but] a good deal more . . . gumption — a clever woman, really — separated from her husband, of course, and on the whole very good to read when one is in a state of moral and physical collapse.'

Lucie had probably read Gräfin Hahn-Hahn's novels and also perhaps her travel books, one of which recounted her adventures in Egypt and Nubia. Now there was plenty of opportunity to observe her in person as she was being lionized by literary London all summer. Everyone was giving parties for her, though there was a considerable amount of social discomfiture over her appendage, Baron von Bystram, of whom Monckton Milnes said to a friend, 'at first he was called her cousin, then her secret husband, then her guardian, then I don't know what, but as "travelling companion" it was not considered decorous that he should be known. If she had been handsomer, we might have permitted it; but as it was, the public mind was offended.' But Lucie, with her liberal views, wouldn't have been shocked by the Gräfin's irregular liaison. She and Alexander probably went to the Carlyles' party for her on 24 June. And they may have been present, too, when Samuel Rogers had her and Bystram to breakfast and observed after they departed, 'Those are the two ugliest adulterers I have ever had in this house.'

★

In early August, Lucie and Alexander were invited to a party at Dickens's. Janet watched Lucie as she did her long dark hair and put on her evening dress and thought she looked 'like a beautiful fairy queen'. Dickens's parties were apt to be theatrical affairs and on this occasion Lucie became involved in a complicated charade that she not only performed in but also stage-managed and directed. Alexander, meanwhile, suddenly felt ill and rather than disturb the spirited charade, he slipped out unnoticed and made his way home in a cab. At midnight Janet was woken up by a violent ringing and knocking at the front door. A policeman had found Alexander clinging to the railing, and at first thought him drunk, but then quickly realized that he was simply too weak to climb the steps. The doctor was sent for and diagnosed cholera. Shortly afterwards, Lucie arrived home, quite panic-stricken over Alexander's disappearance, and then even more distressed by his illness. The next morning, Janet realized her mother had been up all night with her father; Lucie looked so 'strange . . . in her red dressing-gown, even paler than usual, her magnificent hair coiled round and round her head with a jewel stuck in here and there'.

For the next four or five days Alexander remained violently ill – with a high fever, acute stomach pain, vomiting and diarrhoea. The doctor came twice daily and told Lucie frankly that Alexander's life was in danger. Lucie, scarcely sleeping or eating, nursed him round the clock, locked in what seemed a hopeless battle against death. Losing her baby had been heartbreaking, but losing Alexander would be unendurable.

Gradually, Alexander improved, the fever subsided, he was no longer delirious and recognized her again. At last the doctor pronounced him out of immediate danger, but prescribed a long and gradual convalescence. Lord Lansdowne put his villa in Richmond at their disposal and as soon as it was safe for Alexander to be moved, Lucie took him there. Janet remained at Queen Square with her nurse, but Kinglake, who was about to set off on another expedition to Algeria, came to Richmond to cheer Alexander and help Lucie, as she said, 'with the gentleness and kindness of a woman'.

They remained in Richmond until the end of the year and, as Alexander grew stronger, more and more visitors arrived so that imperceptibly the hospital atmosphere was replaced by that of an informal house-party. 'This house is Bowood on a diminished scale,' Lucie wrote to her mother. Hatty 'is an inch taller for our grandeur . . . he thinks me a great lady and himself a great butler'. Lansdowne himself came to stay for several days, followed by Caroline Norton, who called Alexander her 'semi-hub'. Lucie's aunt, Charlotte Austin, who spent a great deal of her life in people's sickrooms, came to help. Bayley arrived from Queen Square each weekend. Milnes and Thackeray called and also friends of Alexander's that Lucie knew less well: the artists Charles Eastlake, Edwin Landseer and Henry Phillips, all of whom had been pupils of the painter Benjamin Robert Haydon, who had committed suicide in the midst of the heat wave in June. Thus, indirectly, did death continue to intrude and haunt Lucie. She wrote to Sarah Austin from Richmond, 'It sounds absurd to say, but I have not yet recovered the fright of Alexander's cholera, it has made me nervous about him in every way. He has [however] been stronger and better lately . . . I think, and is growing fat.'

★

By Christmas, Lucie and Alexander were back home again at Queen Square and two months later, on 24 February 1847, they held a gala party to celebrate Janet's fifth birthday. Like Lucie as a child, Janet had virtually no friends her own age, so when she drew up a guest list it included only adults: Caroline Norton, whom she called Aunt Carrie, her 'slave' Bayley, Lord Lansdowne, Tom Taylor because he told such good jokes, 'Dicky' Doyle who drew pictures for her, and Thackeray who first introduced her to oysters and made fanciful sketches while she sat on his knee.

Macaulay (Sydney Smith once described the historian as a book in breeches) was not invited because Janet felt he talked too much, a fault she also criticized in her grandfather, John Austin. She was quite harsh, too, on Carlyle and Tennyson. Lucie was one of the few people in London who could out-talk Carlyle, especially on the subject of German literature. Janet would watch their lively disputes as if she were following a tennis match – back and forth, back and forth; Lucie saying one thing, Carlyle slamming a retort back to her, Lucie trouncing him with another riposte. One afternoon Carlyle burst out in his Scotch accent, 'You're just a windbag, Lucie; you're just a windbag.' Janet was enraged at this insult and piped up, 'My papa says men should be civil to women.' This took Carlyle aback considerably, but he relented and said, 'Lucykin, that child of yours has an eye for inference.'

Janet had not been raised to know 'her proper place'. She offended Mrs Grote when shown a portrait of Harriet Grote as a beautiful young woman by refusing to believe Mrs Grote had ever looked so lovely. And one day when she was out walking in St James's Park with Carlyle, trotting alongside him to keep up with his long strides, his wideawake hat blew off. A 'civil working man' ran after it and retrieved it for Carlyle but, when he presented it to him, instead of offering the man five pence, Carlyle merely said, 'Thank ye, my man; ye can say ye've picked up the hat of Thomas Carlyle.' Young as she was, Janet was mortified.

She disliked Tennyson because of the way he would come round of an evening and keep everyone prisoner for hours while he droned on and on in a monotone, reciting his poetry. And in Janet's opinion he didn't improve with time. Some years later, after he had become Poet Laureate, Janet went to stay with the Tennysons at Freshwater, on the Isle of Wight. One day, while out walking with Tennyson, 'the great poet's shoe-string came untied, and imperiously pointing to his foot, he said: "Janet, tie my shoe."' Janet 'resented so imperative a command, besides which the strings were extremely dirty', so she answered, '"No, tie your own shoe. Papa says men should wait on women, not women on men."' Tennyson afterwards told Alexander that Janet was 'a clever girl, but extremely badly brought up'.

In some respects, she probably was, and it was certainly true that she considered her father almost a god, and hence quoted him as a kind of oracle to Carlyle and Tennyson. Janet adored Alexander, whom she called 'Dear Old Boy' rather than Papa or Father, and they were known as 'the inseparables'. Lucie once complained that Alexander's theory of raising children was 'to utterly spoil them'. Janet was indulged in some ways, but in others she may have been neglected. Certainly she was left to her own devices a good deal of the time. At the age of six she still didn't know how to read, a fact which shocked Dickens, who gave her an enticing book called *The Seven Champions of Christendom* to spur her to learn. Later a series of governesses were hired to instruct her, but Janet remained haphazardly educated and largely self-taught.

Lucie may have lavished less care or attention on Janet than she would have had Janet been a boy. Janet, at least, felt this to be so, with the result that she became an inveterate tomboy. She loved to ride, especially with her father, and later to hunt. She spent as much time as possible outdoors and had no use for dolls. When she got scarlet fever, her hair was cropped, and after she recovered, she kept it short, like a boy's. And like her mother, she preferred the company of men.

★

Lucie Duff Gordon in 1852 by Henry Phillips. Though the portrait was painted ten years before she went to Egypt, Lucie is wearing an oriental wrap and linen tunic shirt.

Sarah Austin in 1834, at the height of her 'postal affair' with Prince Pückler-Muskau. By John Linnell.

Lucie as a schoolgirl, drawn by friends at Miss Shepherd's school.

Lucie Austin at the time of her engagement to Alexander Duff Gordon.
By Robert Cruikshank.

Left: Alexander Duff Gordon, of whom Sarah Austin said shortly before he married Lucie, 'Alexander has nothing but a small salary, his handsome person, excellent and sweet character and his title (a great misfortune!).' By George Frederic Watts; *Right*: Lucie's mother-in-law, the dowager Lady Duff Gordon, in middle age. By George Frederic Watts.

8 Queen Square, Westminster, with the statue of Queen Anne. Lucie and Alexander lived here for the first ten years of their marriage, just a stone's throw from 1 Queen Square where Lucie was born and spent much of her childhood.

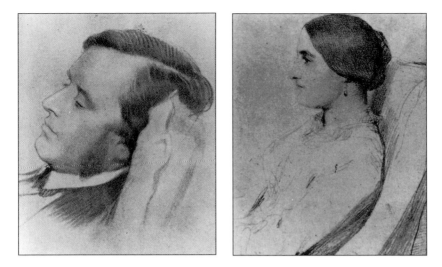

Above: Drawings of Lucie and Alexander several years after their marriage. By George Frederic Watts; *Below*: Janet Duff Gordon with her devoted playmate, the Sudanese boy Hassan el-Bakkeet, or 'Hatty' as everyone called him. Drawing by Caroline Norton.

The Duff Gordon 'coat of arms' devised by Dicky Doyle after Lucie and Alexander moved to Esher. Lucie and Alexander on horseback flank the crest, which shows Lucie's quill pen and one of the books she has translated; above the crest are a bunch of Lucie's cigars, a keg of Duff Gordon ale and Alexander's pipe.

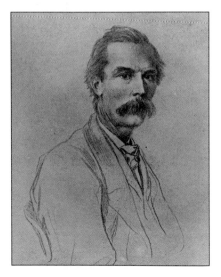

A drawing of Henry Ross, who was more than twice Janet's age and a year older than Lucie. By George Frederic Watts.

Janet Duff Gordon at the time of her marriage to Henry Ross in 1860.

Above: Maurice Duff Gordon in his early twenties; *Below*:
Lucie's beloved youngest daughter, Urania.

Throughout 1847, Lucie felt vaguely restless. She wasn't working on a translation: though she suggested several to John Murray, he wasn't taken with her proposed books. She turned her attention then to setting up a library for working men in East London, in Bow. This also involved informal teaching of a sort; she went to Bow once a week and discussed Shakespeare and other authors with the factory workers and labourers who came to her reading room. Though Lucie was the tutor, the insights and ideas of her pupils intrigued her; they gave her a very different perspective from the sophisticated literary circle of her friends.

In June, Alexander became embroiled in a quarrel between Thackeray and John Forster that reflected the tension that existed throughout the forties and fifties between the two reigning novelists: Dickens and Thackeray. Dickens's *Dombey and Son* and Thackeray's *Vanity Fair* were both being published in monthly parts and the authors and their respective bands of readers were closely following the sales of the two novels. The quarrel came about because Dickens's volatile friend, Forster, became incensed when Thackeray published an unflattering sketch of him which exaggerated his corpulent build, and Forster told their mutual friend, Tom Taylor, that Thackeray was 'false as hell'. Taylor unwisely passed on this insult to Thackeray himself, who was infuriated and cut Forster dead the next time they met. Thackeray then summoned Alexander, told him he intended to challenge Forster to a duel, and asked Alexander to be his second. Alexander did all he could to dissuade Thackeray from this extreme course, but to no avail. Reluctantly, he delivered Thackeray's challenge to Forster, who in turn asked Dickens to be his second.

It was an absurd situation. Dickens relished the dramatic prospect of a duel, but Alexander continued to do everything he could to avert it, and in the end, he succeeded. Alexander extracted a conciliatory letter from Forster, persuaded Thackeray that he was being hypersensitive and soothed his bruised feelings.

A reconciliation party was held at the Trafalgar Tavern in Greenwich for the principals and their seconds. Dickens remained disappointed that the duel hadn't come off, but he had only praise for Alexander's tactful handling of the situation: 'nothing could possibly be more frank, sensible, or gentlemanly in the best sense,' Dickens said, 'than Gordon's behaviour through the whole affair.'

Soon after Alexander had resolved the argument between Forster and Thackeray, the Duff Gordons were drawn into the affairs of the Brookfields, whom they had met by this time in some London drawing-room or another (presumably one where Caroline Norton was not present). Lucie was fond of taking up people and causes, and something about the Brookfields – their wit and intelligence and their precarious financial state, no doubt – made her want to help them. The Brookfields were in quite desperate straits by mid-1847 because they had suffered during the 'railway crisis' that year when Brookfield's scanty savings, invested in railway stock, had depreciated dramatically. There was no prospect of Church preferment for him, so several of his friends suggested that he become a school inspector. When Lucie got wind of this idea, she immediately planned a dinner party for the Brookfields and Lord Lansdowne, who she knew could help secure an inspectorship for Brookfield.

The dinner was a great success in that Lansdowne did, in fact, oil the wheels for Brookfield's being awarded an inspectorship the following year. But in a letter to his mother, written soon after the party, Brookfield dwelt a good deal more on his hosts and the menu than the opportune introduction to Lansdowne:

> We dined with [the Duff Gordons] . . . the other evening at a very little party. Lord Lansdowne, Lady Charlotte Lyndsay, a Mr Bruce, a foreign author, and our two selves. The dinner was peculiar in its way. The Gordons are peculiarly far from 'fine'. He is most gentlemanly . . . and would seem perfectly unconscious that such and such things were considered vulgar; she, on the other

hand, would seem rather as if she gloried in their very commonness:
but not so much – I don't mean to malign her. The dinner was
soup and cod's head and shoulders, followed by the bouilli, of
which the soup had been made; two fowls and a chap, followed by
a pheasant, a tart, a jelly and black puddings; the black puddings
followed by an orange pie – made just like an apple pie but not
nearly so good; cheese and salad; sherry, bottled ale and bottled
porter, with a bottle of claret after dinner . . . Lady Gordon had
dressed the salad herself in the kitchen. But the difference with
which he would mention such a thing as a simple matter of fact –
and she with just the least little tinge of bravado would strike an
acute observer. Now if you heard Sir Alex ask whether you would
eat Beccaficoes à la Reine or Black puddings . . . you could not
possibly distinguish which came from the belly of a sow and which
from the Groves of Sardinia.

Despite Brookfield's reservations about the Duff Gordons'
hospitality, he at least clearly enjoyed it, but several months
later, when they were looking for cheaper lodgings, the
Brookfields felt themselves in a quandary when the Duff
Gordons invited them to move into 8 Queen Square. Jane
Brookfield was, as usual, staying with friends in the country,
when her husband wrote to her of how the Duff Gordons had
'rushed [in] . . . with their usual unembarrassed good nature'
one day to suggest that the Brookfields take over the ground
floor of the Queen Square house and pay half the rent in return.
(It is unclear what they meant to do with 'dear little Bayley';
perhaps he was to move up to the first floor along with them.)
Brookfield, who confessed that Lucie and Alexander 'are people
I [have] . . . rather a weakness for', was quite taken by the
proposal and told his wife that 'Lady Buff', as Lucie was
known to her friends, said 'she should be able to coddle you'.

But Jane thought less of being coddled than the myriad social
consequences of living with the Duff Gordons. She wrote to her
husband of their offer: 'I think it exceedingly kind of course –
but . . . it would be exceedingly imprudent on many accounts

to accept [it] . . . I could cordially like Lady Duff Gordon for a mere acquaintance and feel admiration for all her good qualities, but it would go against me to be so much mixed up with her as to be living together.'

Jane was specifically worried about the Duff Gordons' Bohemian ways and, above all, the company they kept. 'Consider how very little we know of the Gordons in private life, what their ways are as to religious observances, for instance – and if "birds of a feather flock together" should not we be careful to know . . . what their ways are . . . Cannot you call up visions of cosy little Sunday dinners with Mrs Norton . . . and I would not vouch for your or my virtuous sense of congruities restraining our joining in such *délassments*.' And to cap her argument, Jane invoked Lucie's 'notoriously equivocal manners, however free from a shadow of actual blame her conduct is'. Jane told her husband, 'I could never be intimate with Lady Buff because she appears to have neither a woman's delicacy nor reverence.'

Brookfield reluctantly bowed to his wife's scruples and told Lucie and Alexander that, regretfully, they wouldn't be able to accept their kind offer. But in his reply to Jane's letter, he couldn't resist relating how he'd been at the Duff Gordons the night before, that Lucie 'looked very handsome [and] said nothing in the least queer'. Brookfield even went so far as to ask Jane to 'write a few plain good-natured unhumbugging (and all the better if slightly droll) words to Buff (8 Queen Square) thanking [her] for the notion being entertained. It really was very good-naturedly done even considering also that they intended to benefit themselves slightly at the same time.'

So the Brookfields didn't move in with Lucie and Alexander and Bayley continued to occupy the back parlour at Queen Square. For much of the summer of 1847 he was, in fact, in sole possession of the house, for in early August Lucie, Alexander and Janet went to the continent, where they joined the Austins in the Ardennes. Shortly after they arrived, they discovered that Prince Pierre Buonaparte was staying in the same hotel, and when he was introduced to Lucie, he exclaimed, '*Mais, Madame, vous êtes des notres. Vous êtes une Buonaparte,*' and leading her to a large mirror in the hotel foyer, he said that though people told him that he resembled Napoleon, Lucie, in fact, was '*son image*'. There was, in fact, an uncanny resemblance that was confirmed by others.

From the Ardennes, the Duff Gordons went to Dinant-sur-Meuse and then on to the grottoes of Han, which thrilled Janet: they walked for what seemed like miles underground, Lucie and Alexander half bent over, down narrow passages which opened up into vast caves with huge stalactites hanging from the roof. In September they went on to Belgium and Czechoslovakia, finally returning to London and Queen Square in late October.

★

Almost immediately their hectic London social life started up again: evenings at the theatre with Caroline Norton, whitebait suppers in Greenwich, theatricals at Dickens's, Sunday breakfasts at Samuel Rogers's. In December, Tennyson held a small dinner-party at his bachelor lodgings at 42 Ebury Street in Chelsea. He'd just moved in and was nervous about entertaining the friends he'd invited: the Duff Gordons, the Brookfields and Harry Hallam. Brookfield dropped by on the afternoon of the day the party was to be held and found Tennyson surrounded by workmen who were dismantling his bed and moving out other furniture from his bedroom. Tennyson explained that he had only one sitting-room and was clearing out his bedroom so that the ladies would have somewhere to sit while the men smoked after dinner. Brookfield persuaded him that all the trouble he was going to was unnecessary: Lucie Duff Gordon herself smoked, and Jane Brookfield would be able to tolerate the tobacco fumes for an hour or two.

★

In January, Lucie and Alexander went to a house party at Bowood to which Lord Lansdowne had invited, among others,

149

Emily Eden, the unmarried sister of Lord Auckland, the former Governor-General of India. Emily Eden had gone out to India with her brother and acted as his hostess, and though she loathed the country, she published a book of her Indian sketches, *Portraits of the People and Princes of India*, which Lucie had probably seen. Now, at Bowood, everyone was talking about *Jane Eyre*, which had come out the previous October, and speculation was rife over the identity of its author, Currer Bell. Thackeray, who was also a guest, admired it enormously, as did Lucie. Emily Eden, predictably, did not.*

Perhaps no two women could have been less alike than Emily Eden and Lucie, and it is not surprising that they didn't take to each other at Bowood. In a letter to a friend Emily said of Lucie, 'I think her anything but agreeable, but I strongly suspect that instead of our cutting her, she was quietly cutting all of us, merely because she thinks women tiresome . . . I [tried] to be civil to her, but was repulsed . . . She came down to luncheon every day in a pink striped shirt, with the collar turned down over a Belcher handkerchief, a man's coat made of green plaid, and a black petticoat. Lord Grey . . . called her the Corsair; but she was my idea of something half-way between a German student and an English waterman.'

When Lucie and Alexander returned to Queen Square from Bowood in early February 1848, they found a letter from John Austin in Paris, describing the escalating political turmoil there. The letter was, in fact, a harbinger of widespread political unrest that would persist for the next year and more: revolution in France and elsewhere in Europe, and Chartist demonstrations and the possibility of upheaval in England as well. In March, the French king Louis Philippe abdicated and fled to England, and so, too, did his Prime Minister, François Guizot. Guizot,

---

* Unbeknownst to Lucie and the other guests at Bowood, Emily Eden was herself a novelist with two novels, *The Semi-detached House* and *The Semi-attached Couple*, secreted away in her drawer at home. She eventually published them anonymously some ten years later.

who was a celebrated historian as well as a politician, was a friend of the Austins who had told him to go directly to the Duff Gordons upon reaching England. Lucie and Alexander, of course, warmly welcomed him. But Janet was bitterly disappointed: she had expected a dashing hero covered with gold embroidery and splashed with blood. Instead, Guizot was a small, reserved, unprepossessing man, and Janet announced that it had not been worth her while to put on her best frock to meet him.

In April, everything came to a head in England. The fiery Irish barrister and former MP for Cork, Feargus O'Connor, called for a mass Chartist meeting on Kennington Common on the 10th, and from all over the country Chartist demonstrators streamed into London, the defence of which was entrusted to the Duke of Wellington. A violent repetition of what had happened in France seemed imminent.

Though Lucie and Alexander were sympathetic to the Chartist demands – universal male suffrage, annual parliaments, vote by ballot, equal electoral districts, payment of MPs and abolition of property qualifications for them – they deplored violent means to gain these ends. Their house in Westminster was in a particularly vulnerable location, so Alexander enrolled as a volunteer constable and Lucie's workmen friends from her Bow library came to Queen Square to protect her. By this time the Austins had also escaped from France and were settled in Weybridge in Surrey, and to her mother there Lucie wrote of the events at Queen Square on the night of 9 April: 'I never wish to see forty better gentlemen than we had here last night. As all was quiet, we had supper, cold beef, bread, and beer with songs, sentiments, and toasts, such as "Success to the roof we are under", "Liberty, Brotherhood, and order". Then they bivouacked in ... different houses till 5 this morning, when they started home ... Tom Taylor was capital, made short speeches, told stories, and kept all in high good-humour; and Alexander came home [from patrolling the streets as a constable] and was received with glee and affection, and all agreed the fright, to us at least, was well made up by the kindly and pleasant evening. As no one would take a penny, we shall send books to the library . . . and I shall send cravats as a badge to the "Gordon Volunteers".' The next day the 'Gordon Volunteers' drifted back to East London, by which time it was clear that the dreaded English upheaval was not to be. Feargus O'Connor was told that a march on London would not be tolerated and he acquiesced. He disbanded his force of 20,000 Chartists on Kennington Common and all their demands were put into abeyance for the time being.

★

After all the Chartist excitement had died down, Lucie began work, in collaboration with Alexander, on a translation of the German historian Leopold von Ranke's *Memoirs of the House of Brandenburg*. It was a mammoth undertaking, even for the two of them, and when the book was published the following year by John Murray it appeared in three stout volumes – some 1,400 pages in all. Ranke was an old friend of Sarah Austin, who had translated his *History of the Reformation in Germany* and *The Ecclesiastical and Political History of the Popes*, and Lucie and Alexander consulted Sarah frequently as their work progressed. During a visit to London, Ranke himself also turned up at Queen Square one day for luncheon. He strode up and down the drawing-room, like a wind-up toy, quite stunning Janet, who could not follow his running monologue, as he shifted abruptly from German to French to English, Italian and Spanish, with a Latin phrase thrown in now and then.

Memoirs of the House of Brandenburg was the first of Lucie's historical translations; in the fifties she published two more: Ranke's *Ferdinand I and Maximilian II of Austria* and Moltke's *The Russians in Bulgaria and Rumelia in 1828 and 1829*. These were all highly competent, readable, and thorough – very much in the vein of Sarah Austin, who may, in fact, have brought them to Lucie's attention. But they were not among Lucie's favourite books, nor did she become deeply absorbed in them. She often found them, in fact, a chore. While working on the Brandenburg book she wrote to her old friend Alice Taylor (*née* Spring-Rice): 'I am hard worked at a tedious daily-bread sort of translation which is gradually destroying what little intelligence my other tasks have left me.' Ranke and the other historians whose work Lucie translated simply didn't move and engross her the way the Abd el-Kader narratives in *The French in Algiers* or Feuerbach or, several years later, a French novel based on Swift's life, *Stella and Vanessa*, all did. These translations were windows of one sort or another – into other cultures and countries, into the violent world of crime, into romance.

When she and Alexander had nearly finished *Memoirs of the House of Brandenburg*, Lucie discovered that she was again pregnant. It was three years since her baby had died and she had, at last, buried her grief. But both she and Alexander still longed for a son. The joy they felt when a healthy baby boy was born on 15 March 1849 was all the greater for the loss they had suffered three years earlier. And the vital connection between that loss and their present joy was reflected in their decision to again ask Lord Lansdowne and Caroline Norton to be the baby's godparents. Even more significantly, they named their new son Maurice as before.

Once again Lucie was totally absorbed by her beautiful child and again, too, Janet must have nursed her own secret grievance over her mother's delight in her little brother. In July, when the baby was four months old, the three of them, accompanied by Hatty, went to spend the summer with the Austins at their home, Nutfield Cottage – a large, rambling house – in Weybridge. Maurice was a warm, sunny, open child with smiles for everyone, but he became strangely enamoured, above all, with dour John Austin, who never showed the least interest in young children. Sarah wrote to a friend how 'the [little] creature has attached himself with a sort of passion to his grandfather'.

Both John and Sarah Austin, who were now nearly sixty, had mellowed considerably since their return to England the year before. The recent death of Austin's father had finally granted them a measure of financial security and they settled down to a life of quiet retirement in Surrey. Sarah no longer agonized over Austin's professional failures; she continued her own translating work but now, relieved of financial anxieties, she could pick and choose those books she was interested in. On a reduced scale, she still had a salon of sorts in Weybridge, for many of her illustrious friends made their way down to Surrey to see her. But her greatest happiness came from seeing her husband, at long last, relatively contented and in improved if not positively good health. Sarah drew enormous satisfaction, too, from Lucie's happiness and her two beautiful, lively grandchildren.

The autumn of 1849 was so mild that Lucie decided to stay on in Weybridge with the children and Hatty. Alexander came down at weekends, sometimes bringing Bayley along with him. But Bayley's happy days with the Duff Gordons were numbered; he had accepted an appointment as secretary to the Governor of Mauritius and was to leave them early in the new year.

In early October, when Lucie and the children were still with the Austins, Hatty caught a bad cold, which developed into bronchitis. As the days became shorter and darker, he could not shake off his hollow cough, and he became weak and short of breath and intermittently feverish as well. Nutfield Cottage was chilly and damp, and Janet and Maurice came down with colds too. By the time they all went back to Queen Square in November it was clear that Hatty, who had never been in robust health, now had consumption, and Lucie blamed herself for his illness, which she felt sure was the result of their remaining too long at Weybridge.

Christmas was a nightmare. Hatty was rapidly wasting away, Janet was 'bilious and ailing', and the baby was acutely ill for several days with a high fever which terrified Lucie. Lucie herself developed a persistent cough which, along with her great anxiety over the children and Hatty, made for broken, sleepless nights. Only Alexander remained well and he was hard-pressed summoning the doctor and caring for the others. He sat up night after night with poor Hatty until the boy finally died in his arms on Christmas Day. Lucie's grief was enormous and Janet was heart-broken.

★

On New Year's Eve 1849, Lucie was still suffering from catarrh, but she sat up late alone writing to her old friend Janet Shuttleworth, mulling over the events of the past year. She may have brooded, too, over the decade that was ending – ten years during which she had married, travelled, published five books, given birth to three children and buried one. She was twenty-eight, beautiful, intellectually accomplished, socially well-connected. She had much to be thankful for – her happy marriage, above all – but she was scarred, too, by the death of her first son and the passing of Hatty.

In such a mood, at such a time, she may have tried to imagine what the future would hold. Lucie's expectations might reasonably include more children, more friends, more books, more settled, domestic happiness. And yet on this last cold, dark night of the 1840s, as she wrote to Janet Shuttleworth before the fire, her cough already foreshadowed another kind of life ahead.

Chapter Seven

January, February, early March 1850: midwinter of mid-century. Low, leaden skies, fog and bare trees. Days which seemed a perpetual dusk; the sun had apparently decamped to warm some other planet. Here the lamplighters appeared at four or half past, ushering in the long winter night. At the end of one such night in January, in a grey, frosty dawn, 'dear little Bayley' departed for Mauritius and tropical heat and light. He kissed Janet, shook hands with Alexander, and then, turning to Lucie, pressed his gold pen into her hand and begged her to write often.

A month or so later, on Janet's eighth birthday, Lucie sent the first of her many long letters to Bayley, her 'much lamented lodger'. There had been no birthday party; the weather remained dispiriting and everyone except Alexander was out of sorts. Janet was in bed with another attack of bilious fever; Maurice was teething in earnest and fretful; Lucie herself still had 'a horrible cold'. But she was cheered by the latest scandal which she passed on to Bayley with relish. 'Pretty Mrs Alfred Montgomery has left her husband, they have quarrelled; and Lady Holland won't return to hers, and Lady Lincoln who left her husband two years ago is driving about Rome with a baby of 10 months whom she has christened Horace Walpole.'

All this paled, however, beside Lucie's news that after eight years of marriage, and nearly as many of serious invalidism, Jane Brookfield had produced a child, 'a fine wench', as her husband informed the Duff Gordons. Thackeray – who had considered himself the apex of the triangle he formed with the unhappy Brookfields, who had listened by the hour at the side of Jane's sofa to her tales of marital misery and estrangement – was crushed. He turned up on the Duff Gordons' doorstep in search of consolation. Thackeray: a great, bluff, clubbable man with a mad wife and two little daughters to raise, now reduced to despair by Jane Brookfield's unaccountable maternity. The whole world knew that her husband refused to stay in houses where he couldn't have a separate dressing-room. It was all precisely the sort of tragedy in a teacup to quicken Lucie's cold-muffled imagination and sympathy.

Almost as amazing as the news that Jane Brookfield was a mother was the fact that Tennyson became a husband a few months later at the age of forty-one. His bride, Emily Sellwood, to whom he had been engaged off and on for fourteen years, was thirty-seven and well past her first bloom. She was also, like Jane Brookfield, in delicate health. Hence Lucie's bulletin to Bayley: 'Tennyson is married to a woman who is so ill that she cannot walk, and he wheels her about.'

1850 was a crucial year to Tennyson professionally as well as personally because it saw the publication of *In Memoriam*, his long elegy to his beloved friend Arthur Henry Hallam, who had died in 1833. Tennyson had been writing the verses which comprise the poem for the past sixteen or seventeen years, and this slow gestation and Tennyson's gradual emergence from abject grief to a transcending affirmation and embrace of life produced a work which, though grounded in personal experience, expressed a peculiarly Victorian combination of melancholy, hope and faith in the future. It was a poem, too, in which Lucie could trace the lineaments of her own bereavements and her survival of them, and thus it spoke to her more immediately than *The Princess,* which Tennyson had told Lucie she'd inspired.

With the publication of *In Memoriam* and the critical acclaim it received, Tennyson seemed the obvious candidate to succeed Wordsworth as Poet Laureate when the old Romantic poet died in late April. In May, however, Prince Albert offered the laureateship to the Duff Gordons' old friend, Samuel Rogers. Rogers had yearned for this honour for upwards of fifty years, but now he reluctantly declined it, describing himself at eighty-seven as 'a shadow . . . soon to depart'. With Rogers out of the running, the other contenders were, in addition to Tennyson: Leigh Hunt, the verse dramatist Sheridan Knowles, the poet and dramatist Henry Taylor (who had married Lucie's girlhood friend, Alice Spring-Rice) and – the first woman to be mooted for this august post – Elizabeth Barrett Browning. Some felt that the Queen should have a female laureate but, in the end, Victoria deferred to her husband's judgement: Tennyson was named Poet Laureate and commenced his metamorphosis from eccentric, morose genius to Victorian sage.

★

In the late spring, Lucie and the children went back to the Austins at Nutfield Cottage in Weybridge, where Alexander visited them at weekends as before. Colds and ailments of one sort or another had plagued them all winter and Lucie now felt that the country, at least in the spring and summer, was healthier than London. In Weybridge, Janet and Maurice could play outdoors in the country air and Lucie could ride. Occasionally she went up to London, as she did in July when she attended a concert at Lansdowne House in Berkeley Square, dressed, according to Thackeray, 'in a tawdry, rainbow gown, particularly odious'. Not one of her more successful sartorial experiments.

The day after the concert Lucie returned to Weybridge, where she could be as careless as she wished about clothes and devote her days to translating a novel about Swift's romantic embroilments, *Stella and Vanessa*, by a French writer named Leon de Wailly, already known to Lucie as the translator of Burns and Shakespeare, among others, into French. *Stella and Vanessa* was Lucie's first excursion into fiction, though the book was underpinned by historical fact. She had come across it serialized in a popular French magazine and immediately saw its commercial possibilities: a novel, as she said in her preface, which explored 'the singular and unexplained relations of Swift with the two distinguished and charming women whom it was his lot and his pleasure to make miserable'. Lucie didn't share de Wailly's 'partisanship' for 'his hero', Dean Swift, in 'this strangest chapter of English domestic history'. But she had nothing but praise for 'the depth and finesse of [de Wailly's] . . . knowledge of human nature, the minuteness and delicacy of his delineations of character and manners, and the ease and simplicity of his style'. Richard Bentley published the book in August and it was such an immediate success that Lucie used her earnings to pay for a three-week holiday for herself and the children in Sandgate.

When they returned in the early autumn, Lucie and the children went back again to Weybridge rather than Queen Square, and here Lucie learnt that one of Alexander's colleagues at the Treasury, a man named Pennington, who had held the post of auditor, had had a stroke in August. From Weybridge, Lucie wrote to Lord Lansdowne to ask if he might use his influence to secure the auditor's post – which was worth, she said, £1,000 or £1,200 a year – for Alexander. Lansdowne, who was now President of the Privy Council and a senior member of the Cabinet, did indeed approach Lord Russell on Alexander's behalf, but nothing came of his intervention. Lansdowne then tried to make a generous gift of money to the Duff Gordons, but this they could not bring themselves to accept. By way of a compromise, it was agreed that Lansdowne should assume all responsibility for Maurice's education and maintenance. But since Maurice was still a very small boy, at home with his nurse, Lansdowne's generosity brought no immediate financial relief to Lucie and Alexander.

Money worries, however, were a familiar nuisance and Lucie carried on with most of her old insouciance despite them. In the autumn of 1850 she set up a library and reading room for working men in Weybridge, run on the same lines as the one she had established in Bow and with equal success. It was a modest operation – Lucie had no programme, no scheme, no vision. She merely arranged for the hire of a room and collected subscriptions to pay for it and books. Her horizons were probably broadened as much as those of her working-class readers and students. Weybridge, Queen Square and all the homes and circles the Duff Gordons frequented comprised, after all, a small, homogeneous world. Esoteric foreign books were one route out of it, but so, too, were the shabby Weybridge reading-room and Lucie's sixty-odd members who congregated on Monday evenings to read and discuss Shakespeare.

★

During the winter of 1850, Lucie was also drawn into the world of an unusual boarding-house called The Limes near Nutfield Cottage in Weybridge. It was run by a cultured lady named Mrs Macirone, who had a vaguely deceased Italian husband and two musical daughters, Grinlia and Emelia. Mrs Macirone's lodgers were all aspiring young artists – writers and painters, for the most part, with a few journalists thrown in. A pale, spiritual band, low on money, but full of promise and visionary ideas.

The Duff Gordons' friend Tom Taylor★ lodged at The Limes and he introduced them to an appealing couple – newly-weds in fact – named George and Mary Ellen Meredith. Lucie already knew something of the bride's tragic story. Mary Ellen Meredith was born, like Lucie, in 1821, the daughter of the novelist Thomas Love Peacock, whose witty satires (*Headlong Hall*, *Nightmare Abbey* and *Crotchet Castle*) Lucie had read and much admired. Like Lucie, too, Mary Ellen had had a boy's education, but her childhood was far from happy. Mrs Peacock, like Mrs Thackeray after her, went mad, leaving her husband with four young children to raise. When Mary Ellen was in her early twenties, she was rescued from her unhappy family by a handsome young naval officer, Lt. Edward Nicolls, or 'Darling Eddy' as she called him in letters. They married in January 1844; by March, Mary Ellen was pregnant; a month later,

---

★ Tom Taylor was a civil servant, dramatist and journalist; he wrote regularly for *The Times* and later was editor of *Punch*.

Darling Eddy drowned in a storm at sea. Before she turned twenty-four, then, Mary Ellen had become a wife, a widow and a mother. In her grief she began to write – poems and essays for the most part, but also on culinary subjects, for Mary Ellen was a creative and accomplished cook.

In 1848, when her little daughter, Edith, was four, Mary Ellen met George Meredith, a solicitor's clerk seven years her junior who wrote poetry and had fervent literary ambitions. He worshipped Peacock, adored little Edith, and was captivated by the tragic young widow, Mary Ellen. Meredith was reticent, however, about his own connections. It is highly unlikely that Mary Ellen or Peacock knew that Meredith's father had been a tailor before emigrating to South Africa and marrying (after George's mother died) his cook.

Despite the fact that they had little money and George no settled profession, in 1849, when Mary Ellen was twenty-eight and Meredith twenty-one, they married and went – as the Duff Gordons had – to Germany for their honeymoon. For George was a great admirer of German literature, which he read with ease though he spoke the language indifferently. On their return, the Merediths established themselves at The Limes, and it was here, in Mrs Macirone's sitting-room, that Lucie first heard Mary Ellen's sad story in her own words, and discussed with Meredith the latest German novels. Janet Duff Gordon and little Edith Nicolls became fast friends and, at the end of each day that Janet spent playing with Edith at The Limes, Meredith would walk back to Nutfield Cottage with her perched on his shoulder, telling her strange tales as they crossed the fields. Or he would recite to her some of the stanzas from his work in progress, a kind of *Arabian Nights* entertainment called *The Shaving of Shagpat*. Janet called the ardent young Meredith 'My Poet'.

Idyllic days, these, and the young Merediths were delighted to be 'taken up' by the Duff Gordons. There were dinners at Nutfield Cottage, tea-parties at The Limes, and much informal coming and going between the two houses. Lucie and Alexander encouraged Meredith's literary ambitions and introduced him to their friends, including Caroline Norton, who became the inspiration, some years later, for Meredith's novel, *Diana of the Crossways*. Mary Ellen showed Lucie an article she was writing: a witty, original 'Essay on Gastronomy and Civilization' which was published the following year in *Fraser's Magazine*.

Reading this clever piece, Lucie may have glimpsed the trouble which lay ahead. 'The stomach, not the heart, as poets write, is the great centre of existence and feeling,' Mary Ellen wrote. George Meredith had chronic indigestion; he was a fellow-sufferer of John Austin and Carlyle: a man who couldn't bear to watch his wife eat eggs in the morning. A dyspeptic matched with a gourmet does not make for a serene marriage: their temperaments, their world views, their pleasures and passions will almost certainly be at odds. And the Merediths had other practical problems to plague them as well. A chronic shortage of money, above all, and then Mary Ellen kept getting pregnant and losing her babies, which miscarried or were born dead.

Lucie and Alexander watched the Merediths' ebbing fortunes with concern and tried, as always, to help: Lucie wrote letters on Meredith's behalf to friends with money and influence, but to little effect. Meredith was a queer specimen with little charm or humility. For three years Mary Ellen and George lived on at The Limes, getting more and more deeply in debt, losing babies, writing poems, novels and articles that few wanted to read and no one wanted to publish. Finally, in 1853 – the year their only surviving child, Arthur, was born – they left Esher and moved in with Peacock at Lower Halliford, and the Duff Gordons lost track of the once golden and romantic young couple.

★

But well before the beleaguered Merediths evaporated into thin air, Lucie had her own trials in the winter of 1851. First Janet and then Maurice fell ill with measles while Lucie was visiting her uncle, the successful barrister, Charles Austin, in Suffolk. (Alexander had remained in London, at Queen Square.) As soon as the children were well enough to travel, Lucie returned to Weybridge — a harrowing journey in frozen weather with two feverish, fretful children. She had been nursing them day and night for three weeks, snatching a few hours of sleep and a cold meal when she could. Almost immediately after arriving at Nutfield Cottage, when the children had been carried in and put to bed, Lucie herself collapsed. She'd had an harassing cough for weeks, but now it gave way first to bronchitis, and then to pneumonia. Her temperature soared, her pulse became almost imperceptible, she drifted in and out of consciousness, and only half-recognized Alexander when he arrived after Sarah had sent an urgent message to him in London.

It was almost exactly two years since Hatty had caught his fatal illness at Nutfield Cottage and the house was as damp and cold as ever. Alexander insisted that Lucie be moved to London, but the local surgeon declared she was too ill to travel even that short distance. Alexander was reduced to a kind of savage despair at their helplessness. Sarah felt trapped in a nightmare. In late January she wrote to a friend, 'for . . . a fortnight [Lucie] . . . has been labouring under a fearful attack of bronchitis — incessant cough, high fever, and all the most terrible symptoms. Last Thursday I began to feel as if in a black dream.'

Lucie herself would only have been aware of alternating waves of heat and cold which swept over her, of wet sheets and clammy leeches, of a terrible heaviness and oppression in her chest. She lay in a suspended state of sensations: thirst, a throbbing in her head, a humming in her ears. Paroxysms of coughing and gasping for breath. A murmur of voices and then silence.

There was a crisis at the darkest point of one bitterly cold night. Alexander was called, Janet awakened and John Austin summoned; Sarah was already at Lucie's bedside as she had been every night since Lucie returned from Suffolk. They gathered about Lucie's bed and formed a very Victorian, anguished tableau: pale, spiritualized womanhood about to depart this vale of tears, surrounded by handsome husband, sobbing child and broken-hearted old parents.

Such scenes and their funereal aftermaths really happened – all the time. But on this January night in 1851 Lucie was narrowly spared. With the approach of morning, her fever began to subside; her shallow breathing quietened; she slept. And when she awoke, she knew where she was and with whom and that she was gravely ill, but not dead. In the days that followed she gradually rallied. Soon after the crisis, Sarah wrote almost euphorically to a friend, 'God be praised! [The fever] is now dispersed. For three days past her recovery has been steadily advancing. She is permitted to speak and to take a little food, and nothing . . . remains but the necessity for extreme care.'

Throughout the spring and summer of 1851, Lucie continued to improve slowly. Tom Taylor, the painter Henry Phillips and Kinglake all came to visit. Lord Lansdowne sent baskets of fruit and hothouse flowers. Caroline Norton arrived with a parcel of books and all the latest gossip. By late March, Lucie was well enough to travel, and she went with the Austins to Ventnor, on the Isle of Wight, in the hope of speeding her recovery. But the excursion was not a success. Lucie wrote to Lord Lansdowne that the weather was 'horribly cold and I am not at all well and cannot walk'. She and the Austins hastened back to Weybridge, where Lucie had a relapse and was confined to bed again with a bad throat, chest inflammation and 'nervous headaches'.

As the weeks and months passed and Lucie's health remained precarious, some of her friends wondered if she was becoming an invalid and would end up conducting her life as did Jane Brookfield and Emily Tennyson: from a sofa. She was greatly changed and wrote to Bayley that 'I . . . had a very narrow escape for my life . . . I fear you [will] . . . think me very much altered . . . I have lost much of my hair, all my complexion, and all my flesh, and look thin and ill, and old, and my hair is growing grey. This I consider hard upon a woman just over her thirtieth birthday.' But what was 'worst of all', Lucie told Bayley, only half in jest, was 'that Alexander loses no opportunity of mentioning to me that I have lost my looks, and I therefore break the melancholy fact to you lest he should be beforehand with me, for it seems to be a subject of immense gratification to him'.

But the transformation in Lucie went beyond her greying hair (which, unlike Sarah Austin, she never dyed), weight loss and dulled complexion. Her 'narrow escape' had changed her internally as well. She wrote to Bayley in the spring that though she had largely recovered, she remained 'preternaturally weak, languid, and nervous. Today I ought to be dining in London with Lord Lansdowne at Senior's (where Alexander . . . is spending some days), but my eyes are weak and painful, and myself low and seedy and exactly what is called "not up" to anything.'

The languor, nervous headaches, low spirits and 'seediness' came and went; occasional good days – of sociability, energy, industry – followed bad ones, spent in bed with the curtains drawn. But a fundamental resilience had been lost. To Bayley Lucie confessed, 'I . . . feel as if the spring of me were broken and as if I should never go again; I haven't energy to look out of the window unless I am forced. Everything oppresses and tires me.'

What Lucie had endured was not merely a dangerous physical ordeal. Illness is the nightside of life; it takes us unwillingly from the land of health into another world, just as dreams spirit us out of the world of consciousness at night. Thus illness is a kind of travel – and exile. Especially for those, like Lucie, who have so narrowly escaped death. Returning to health and the land of the living, the most everyday, familiar things, places, and faces may seem strange and alien. Disorientation – a sense of dis-ease – lingers after all the physical symptoms have vanished. One is not oneself. And home is no longer what it used to be.

★

To complicate matters for Lucie and increase her disquiet, she and Alexander really had no proper home of their own now. For nearly two years, Lucie had spent most of her time with the Austins in Weybridge while Alexander remained in Queen Square. Lucie now felt the toll of her long stay with her parents. In her own uneasy state of mind, she found her father's gloom more oppressive than ever, and she chafed at what she called Sarah's 'maternal despotism' – her dictatorial way in the sickroom and her handling of the children. Despite Lucie's breakdown and close brush with death in Weybridge, Lucie and Alexander both felt that there were advantages to living in the country. The air was healthier, even in the winter, and they calculated that they could live more economically if the Queen Square house could be let. As soon as she was strong enough, she and Alexander began to look for their own home in Surrey.

In late spring they found what Lucie described to Bayley as 'a charming house' in Esher, 'on the top of a high, sandy hill, so dry and healthy and warm and pretty'. Belvedere House, as it was called, had originally been an inn with an adjacent cottage; at some stage these had been joined at right angles, making an L-shaped dining-room on the ground floor with an L-shaped drawing-room above it. It was a comfortable, ramshackle house, full of old furniture and china, with plenty of bedrooms for the Duff Gordons and their guests, and crooked staircases and pokey corridors for Janet and Maurice to play in. Outdoors the house was surrounded by an old-fashioned garden with big mulberry trees, roses and scarlet geraniums. The lawn sloped upwards from the back of the house to the palings of Claremont Park where Louis Philippe had died the year before and where the Duchess of Orléans and her two sons still lived. The magnificent beeches of the park overhung the end of the Duff Gordons' gooseberry garden. Not far away were the River

166

Mole and Wolsey's Tower and, in the distance, Windsor Castle.

When they moved to Esher in the early summer, Lucie found the house and surrounding countryside enchanting. She was also cheered for more practical reasons. The rent for Belvedere House was only £84 a year, including the greenhouse and stable. Alexander, thanks to Lansdowne's influence, had been promoted from an assistant to a senior clerkship at the Treasury and was now getting £100 more a year, and they had managed to let the Queen Square house. 'So I hope we shall be very tolerably well off,' Lucie confided to Bayley. Another matter for relief was that four miles now separated them from Weybridge and the Austins – they were close enough to arrange visits easily, but sufficiently distant to prevent there being daily meetings. Even better, Esher was on the railway, one station beyond Kingston, fifteen miles from Hyde Park Corner. This meant that Alexander could live with Lucie and the children in the country during the week as well as the weekends and travel daily up to London.

The weather was glorious all spring and summer and at the weekends Lucie and Alexander had a steady stream of visitors from London; so many, in fact, that Belvedere House was soon known as 'the Gordon Arms'. Their friend Dicky Doyle, the popular *Punch* illustrator, designed a clever Duff Gordon coat-of-arms which showed Lucie's cigars, Alexander's pipe, an open book and quill pen, and a cask of the famous Gordon Arms beer. Thackeray heralded his arrival one weekend in verse:

> A plain leg of mutton, my Lucie
> I pray thee have ready at three;
> Have it smoky and tender and juicy
> And what better meat can there be?

> And when it has feasted the master
> 'Twill amply suffice for the maid:
> Meanwhile I will smoke my canaster,
> And tipple my ale in the shade.

Kinglake gave Alexander a handsome chestnut mare named Celia and Janet a pony which she called Eothen. Lord Lansdowne presented Lucie with a horse appropriately named Lucy-fer and gave Janet a new piano. Tom Taylor arrived one weekend with a 'great fat spaniel', which, according to Lucie, 'committed every offence against decency and cleanliness that a dog could be guilty of' and was not suffered to stay on after Taylor departed. New acquaintances such as the artists John Everett Millais and George Frederic Watts also found their way to the Gordon Arms. On particularly fine days, there were picnics in the surrounding woods and boating parties on the Mole, in the course of which the wine and ginger-beer, which were hung overboard to cool, were sometimes lost, and Alexander and several of the more hardy male guests had to dive into the Mole's deep waters to search for the missing bottles.

By August, Lucie's health seemed almost fully restored, and she crossed the channel with Alexander for 'a three weeks' lark' in Paris, where they stayed in the rooms of the Austins' old friend, the philosopher Barthélemy St Hilaire. A heat-wave descended on the city along with the Duff Gordons; the 92 to 95 degree temperatures perfected Lucie's cure, and she felt better than she had in years. But when they returned to Esher in early September she injured her thigh while out riding; the wound swelled up and became infected and had to be opened by the local surgeon, a Dr Charles Izod, who became a great friend of the Duff Gordons. Izod also told Lucie to keep smoking cigars, to ease her cough which had returned with the onset of cooler weather in the autumn.*

Her cough and thigh wound kept Lucie in bed off and on throughout October and November. She was too ill and Alexander too busy to take Janet to the Great Exhibition in London housed in Paxton's Crystal Palace – an enormous

---

* Dangerous advice, of course, but at the time it was generally believed that smoking alleviated rather than exacerbated lung complaints.

conservatory of glass and iron in Hyde Park containing some 100,000 exhibits from all over the world. The painter Henry Phillips kindly volunteered to go to the Exhibition with Janet, and afterwards they went on to the British Museum to see the great bas-reliefs of the Assyrian kings from Nineveh which the Duff Gordons' friend Henry Layard had excavated in the mounds near Mosul.

★

Lucie remained 'seedy' and unwell, though not seriously ill, well into the new year, 1852. Alexander's mother, Lady Duff Gordon, found her daughter-in-law's protracted indisposition tiresome and hinted that the problem was as much a mental as a physical one – that, in fact, Lucie was malingering. Having made her views known, Lady Duff Gordon herself then swept off to Rome for the winter with her daughters Georgina and Alice. In early January, Alexander reported to her that Lucie 'is decidedly gaining strength. She sleeps and eats better and is getting fat. Horse exercise does wonders for her and from the beauty of the weather she gets out every day.'

But the new year did not continue auspiciously. A cold snap and violent east-winds revived Lucie's cough and, for the first time, she began to have symptoms too of rheumatism. Both Lucie and Alexander were greatly oppressed by the news that their close friend, the writer and inveterate traveller Eliot Warburton, had drowned at sea when the boat he was on, the *Amazon*, bound for the West Indies, caught fire. Lucie, especially, grieved for Warburton's young wife and two little boys.

In early February, calamity hit closer to home. Sarah Austin had a heart attack, and for some weeks it was doubtful that she would survive. She had become greatly overweight since the Austins' return from the continent and her obesity, of course, placed an extra burden on her heart. She complained of a constant sensation of lightheadedness and faintness which she attributed to lack of nourishment, though it was really caused by her weak heart; and eating large quantities of food did not banish her symptoms. In April, Alexander wrote to his mother in Rome that Sarah 'makes no progress and will never be strong again'.

But just as worrisome as Sarah's weak heart was John Austin's deep depression over his wife's illness. Lucie and Alexander were as anxious about him as about Sarah, for they couldn't imagine how he would manage should Sarah die. Alexander confided to his mother that 'Padre Austin's black morose face and miserable apprehension make our visits very dreary. Lucy is very unhappy about him . . . I can't think what will become of him if she dies. I could not in justice to my children or to Lucy have him to live with us. He is too depressing, it would be awful to have a black demon always sitting on one's back.' Fortunately things did not come to this pass. Gradually Sarah regained her strength, though it was some months before Alexander could write to his mother that Sarah was 'much better . . . much thinner . . . [and] with great care she may live to the usual six score of years and ten'.★ Alexander added, however, that 'care and prudence are not in the category of her virtues'.

Before Sarah's heart attack, Lucie had planned a gala birthday party and ball for Janet's tenth birthday at the end of February. As the date approached she was terribly anxious about both her parents, but she decided to go ahead with the celebration, and it was a great success. The guest list consisted, as Alexander put it, of 'grown-up children', though Meredith's little step-daughter, Edith Nicolls, must have been invited too. Nearly everyone who had attended Janet's fifth birthday party in Queen Square returned for her tenth in Esher. In addition, Lucie hired a conjurer and musicians. Forty sat down to supper and the ball went on until half past two in the morning. Alexander reported

★ Presumably, Alexander meant three or four score years and ten; it is unlikely that he was hoping that his mother-in-law would live to be 130 years old.

to his mother that 'it all went off very well and nothing was broke'.

Among those invited to Janet's birthday party was Henry Phillips, who, in January 1852, had fallen down the stairs at Waterloo Station and broken his kneecap. He was still too incapacitated in February to come to Janet's celebration, but when he was able to hobble about on crutches, Lucie suggested that he join them in Esher and recuperate fully at the Gordon Arms. Phillips was finding his solitary invalidism oppressive and was delighted to take up Lucie's invitation, and in return for the Duff Gordons' generosity, he proposed that he paint Lucie's portrait while he stayed with them.

He arrived in early March and because his leg was still too painful to stand on for any length of time, Phillips rigged up a contraption of pulleys and cords that enabled him to paint on a suspended canvas while he sat or even lay on a couch. On 17 March, Alexander reported to his mother that Phillips had begun Lucie's portrait 'which promises well'. But Lucie herself had caught a cold and had swollen eyes and an earache. Nevertheless she and Phillips persevered and by early April they conspired to produce a masterpiece.

In Phillips's portrait Lucie appears neither ill nor 'old and grey', as she described herself in letters at the time. Instead, she is luminous. She is wearing a plain, white tunic blouse, fastened at the neck with a jewelled stud, and round her shoulders and arms is draped a magnificently embroidered, Oriental-looking shawl. Her complexion is pale but glowing and her heavy dark hair is loosely pulled back from her high brow. Her eyes are dark and the expression on her face serene, but not remote. She appears at the same time both statuesque and warmly attentive to the vista at which she gazes. For it is a profile portrait, and we cannot follow her line of vision and glimpse what she so clearly sees. But Phillips could, and the reflected glory of Lucie's vision bathes and illuminates the painting.

The day after it was completed, George Frederic Watts – that gentle, reclusive artist who lived with the Prinseps in Little Holland House, Kensington – came to inspect and advise on it. He was a close friend of Phillips, but Lucie and Alexander probably knew him through Lady Duff Gordon, whom he had painted and who had long been a kind of patron to Watts. Watts concurred with Alexander that the painting was 'glorious' and urged that it be exhibited. And so it was wrapped up and crated and sent up to London shortly before Phillips left the Gordon Arms late in the spring.

Lucie and Alexander themselves went up to London soon after Phillips's departure to see Lucie's portrait displayed at the Royal Academy. It was the first time Lucie had been to London for nearly a year. They stayed at Lansdowne House in Berkeley Square, where Lord Lansdowne had had a room newly painted and papered especially for them. He was grateful for their visit, for Lady Lansdowne had recently died of breast cancer, after much pain and suffering, and he had been desolate and lonely ever since.

From Lansdowne House Lucie and Alexander went to the Tennysons' in Twickenham for the christening of their first son, Hallam Tennyson, on 5 October 1852. The previous year Emily Tennyson had had a child who was strangled by its cord at birth. Given her delicate health and her age (Emily was thirty-nine in 1852 and Tennyson forty-three), it seemed almost a miracle when Hallam – a strong, healthy child – was born so soon after the stillbirth. Though Tennyson said the baby looked 'like a brickfaced monkey', he was a doting father. Observing him, Elizabeth Barrett Browning (herself a middle-aged mother of a lively three-year-old) said, 'I do like men who are not ashamed to be happy beside a cradle.'

Mrs Browning – that most renowned of nineteenth-century female invalids – was herself too ill to attend the christening, but Lucie and Alexander met her husband there; indeed Browning held the baby throughout the christening service, 'happily bouncing it in the air', which prompted Tennyson to grumble later, 'how he did flourish about'. The other guests included a number of Duff Gordon friends: Henry Taylor (but not his wife, the former Alice Spring-Rice, who had herself just had a baby), Monckton Milnes, Jane Carlyle ('in wickedly funny form'), Thackeray, and the Brookfields.

★

After this London interlude, Lucie and Alexander went back to Esher in late October and Lucie didn't stir again until the following spring. It was at about this time that, as Janet later put it, 'my parents suddenly realized that I knew little else but how to saddle a horse and how to ride him'. Strangely, Lucie had no intention of giving Janet the sort of rigorous education she'd received from Sarah Austin, nor did she wish to teach Janet herself. She may have felt that Janet wasn't clever enough or perhaps she didn't want to impose on her the regimen she had endured as a child. But Lucie did want Janet to become competent in modern languages and music, and so in late 1852 she hired a German governess named Mathilde von Zeschau, the daughter of a retired major in the Saxon army, to teach Janet German and music. Lucie liked Mathilde immediately and described her to Bayley as 'pretty, agreeable and 22'. Even more, she admired Mathilde's 'pluck' and resourcefulness 'in going out as a governess without being absolutely forced to do so' since her father was affluent enough to support her. But despite all Mathilde's admirable qualities, Janet's German did not flourish, with the result that in the spring of 1853 Lucie decided to send both Janet and Mathilde off to Dresden for a year where Janet could live with Mathilde's family and go to a German school.

As soon as they had departed for Germany in April 1853, Lucie and Maurice went to Ventnor, on the Isle of Wight, for a holiday with the Austins. Though Lucie's health was much improved since her stay there two years earlier, it was not a peaceful or relaxing time. Sarah wrote to Lord Lansdowne of Lucie's 'anxieties and disappointments' which centred round

Alexander's unsatisfactory situation at the Treasury. Though he had been promoted to senior clerk, he was passed over for the post of auditor, and Sarah confessed to Lansdowne that 'the pertinacity of Alexander's failures puzzles me'. Lord Monteagle had indicated that there seemed to be 'an obstacle at the Treasury', but this did not really explain why, after more than twenty years of service, Alexander should still be earning such a meagre salary. In addition, he was, in Lucie's opinion, sorely overworked; Lucie herself confided to Lansdowne that she felt 'divorced' because Alexander 'never comes home till 7 and two or three times a week not till 10.'

Confiding her worries to Sarah did not bring Lucie much relief. Nor did Alexander's appointment to the purely ceremonial post of Gentleman Usher to the Queen, which carried a stipend of only £10. But Lucie at least was able to see the humour in Alexander's new position and its duties. She wrote to Lord Lansdowne how on 'the festival of the holy Epiphany Alexr had to go in court dress to the Chapel Royal and there as Gentleman Usher present 3 bags of gold, myrrh and frankincense to three deans or bishops. There is a double incongruity of a man so careless of all forms performing a ceremony at once courtly and religious which strikes me as wonderfully ludicrous.'

Perhaps to distract herself from Alexander's failure to get ahead at the Treasury and perhaps, also, to contribute to their increasingly inadequate income, Lucie decided to take on some translating work again. But when she approached John Murray, he was not impressed by her proposals: a French romantic fable, *The Village Doctor* by the Countess of D'Arbouville, and a relatively short work by Leopold von Ranke, *Ferdinand I and Maximilian II of Austria*, which traced the causes of the breakdown of the German Empire after the Reformation. Both books were scarcely more than a hundred pages and, in the end, they were published in two new 'travellers' series' of short, pocket-sized books, brought out by Chapman & Hall and

Longman. These were sold chiefly at railway stations for only a shilling and thus brought Lucie little prestige and even less money.

The following year her translation of Count H. C. B. von Moltke's much longer military history, *The Russians in Bulgaria and Rumelia in 1828 and 1829*, did better, but this was probably because of the book's relevance to the Crimean War, which had broken out by then. But Lucie's name was omitted both from the book's title page and the preface (which in all previous translations she had signed and dated). Either the publisher, John Murray, didn't want to advertise that this military history had been translated by a woman, or Lucie herself was reluctant to acknowledge the book for some reason, perhaps because she felt her currency and credibility as a translator had suffered after her slight 'travellers' library' efforts. In any event, these books failed to earn enough money to compensate for the time and energy she expended on them. The Moltke volume turned out to be her last translation, though some years later she edited Janet's first excursion into the field: a translation of H. C. L. von Sybel's *The History and Literature of the Crusades*.

★

1853, then, closed inauspiciously. The 'pertinacity of their failures' – not on any grand scale, but in a wearisome, demoralizing way – oppressed Lucie. Sarah wrote to Lord Lansdowne of Lucie and Alexander that 'my comfort is that they are not ambitious'. From one point of view, Lucie's and Alexander's do appear to be 'lesser lives': they hover on the fringes of the lives of more famous, powerful, wealthy people. They may not have been ambitious but, as the biographer of Mary Ellen Peacock Meredith has observed, 'we know a lesser life does not seem lesser to the person who leads one. His life is very real to him; he is not a minor figure in it.'

Lucie was very worried now about money, about Alexander's moribund position at the Treasury, about her own recent lack of success as a translator. She may also have silently rebelled against her 'lesser', tangential position in the lives of her many celebrated friends – as if, somehow, she glimpsed her fate to be buried in the small print of footnotes in stout volumes of letters, diaries and biography fifty and one hundred years hence. In the *Journal*, for example, of Emily Tennyson, where Lucie is identified as 'the brilliant literary hostess and friend of Heine', or in Thackeray's *Letters*, where she is described as 'the witty and unconventional wife of Sir Alexander Duff Gordon', or in scholarly introductions to Tennyson's *The Princess* and George Meredith's novel *Evan Harrington*, both of which have characters inspired by Lucie.

If Lucie glimpsed her posthumous footnote career, she wouldn't have been unduly troubled about posterity's estimation of her. It wasn't the obscurity of a 'lesser life' that troubled her, but its monotony, predictability and distance from the centre of things. She lacked the artist's voracious sense of self. But she still yearned for colour, drama, intensity, the unexpected and the extraordinary. Thus when a dark young Indian prince (as she thought) – an *Arabian Nights* figure if ever there was one – walked across the threshold of the Gordon Arms at the beginning of 1854, she was more than eager to take him in.

Chapter Eight

As the crow (or Airbus) flies, the distance between Cawnpore in Northern India and Esher in Surrey, reckoned in miles, is roughly 6,000. In 1854, no one travelled with such arrow-swift directness. Following the much longer, established sea-route from Calcutta to Southampton – sailing from the Bay of Bengal, crossing the Indian Ocean, rounding the Cape of Good Hope, heading north past the bulge of West Africa and entering the chilly stretches of the North Atlantic – would take several months. But those who made this protracted and sometimes dangerous journey (many ships were lost in that treacherous series of oceans) also crossed frontiers of culture, language, beliefs – mapless territory which could be as difficult to negotiate as the suspension of winds off the equator or sudden squalls in the Bay of Biscay.

Of course, ever since the East India Company was established in the seventeenth century this was a frequently made voyage and the majority of those who embarked on it travelled solely in terms of miles. Emily Eden, for example, who had found Lucie Duff Gordon's attire so objectionable at Bowood, managed to live in India for more than six years, securely cocooned in her imperturbable Englishness – as deaf and blind to India as a statue of Krishna in the middle of Piccadilly would be to English culture.

The much smaller band of travellers who journeyed in the opposite direction – Indians bound for England – seem to have been more aware of the cultural, historical and religious expanses they covered. Certainly this was the case with a handsome young Indian named Azimullah Khan who arrived at the Gordon Arms in Esher in January 1854, impeccably turned out in a British greatcoat and top hat, with a brass-buckled

Gladstone, three corded-up trunks, and a servant in native dress. It is unclear precisely how and why Azimullah made his way to the Duff Gordons' in Esher rather than to some other politically radical oasis, or indeed to a seedy boarding-house in Putney or Bloomsbury where he might have found some of his fellow countrymen. He had come to England to transact a delicate and intricate piece of business with the East India Company on behalf of a putative Indian maharajah named Nana Sahib. Lucie and Alexander had numerous friends and acquaintances in the employ of the Company, including John Stuart Mill, who could have drawn their attention to the Nana Sahib matter and made them eager to throw open their doors to his envoy. Whatever Azimullah's exact path to Esher may have been, his mission in coming to England was unambiguous, and it was precisely the sort of venture to attract and make a partisan of Lucie.

Nana Sahib was the adopted son of an Indian prince named Baji Rao II who had surrendered to the British in 1818 at the end of the Maratha Wars. In exchange for his kingdom, the East India Company conferred on Baji Rao a generous annual pension of roughly £80,000. This figure seems extravagant, but because Baji Rao was a sickly, dissolute man who appeared to have one foot in the grave, the Company didn't expect to have to pay the pension for very long. And it was clearly stipulated that the annuity would cease with Baji Rao's death and not pass on to his adopted son, Nana Sahib.

To the Company's annoyance, the old Prince lived on until 1851 but, when he finally died, the pension was immediately stopped. Nana Sahib had known all along that it would be, but he had heavy responsibilities, a large family and an even larger establishment near Cawnpore to maintain. He also felt a real grievance against the British, not merely for withholding the pension, but for dispossessing his stepfather of his kingdom. Soon after Baji Rao's death, Nana Sahib began petitioning the East India Company for the restoration of the pension. Months and then years passed and Nana Sahib's strenuous efforts to recover the pension all failed. He then decided to apply directly to the Company directors in London. But Nana Sahib didn't speak English and as a Hindu he would lose caste if he crossed the sea. So he began searching for someone to send as his representative: a Muslim who could travel abroad, someone conversant with English ways, who spoke the language fluently, someone deferential but firm, charming but also cunning.

Cawnpore was not a large city; it was, in fact, a colonial backwater, but it yielded the perfect candidate for Nana Sahib's mission: Azimullah Khan. Still in his twenties, Azimullah was the son of a maidservant, but English missionaries had noticed his remarkable intelligence as a small child and sent him to the Cawnpore Free School. Here Azimullah became fluent in English, and familiar with English manners, customs, ways of thinking, and values, all of which fascinated him. After finishing school, he was a teacher for a time and then a *munshi* to various British military officers in Cawnpore. But one of these accused Azimullah of bribery and corruption and he was summarily dismissed. Deprived of employment, he settled down to translating Shakespeare into Hindi and learning French. It was at this juncture that Nana Sahib came across Azimullah and made his offer to send him to England. Nothing in Azimullah's wildest dreams could have suited him more.

He arrived in the dead of winter, in January 1854. The roads were all blocked with snow and ice, but somehow he managed to make his way from Southampton to Esher, as if the heat and colour of the world from which he came blazed a trail through the frozen white landscape to the Gordon Arms. Here the first thing he came upon was 'little Maurice, quite knee deep, snowballing the dog and garden'.

Several days later Lucie wrote enthusiastically to Bayley in Mauritius, 'Your place as lodger is now filled by Azimullah Khan, a very grand-looking and very amiable, charming young Musselman Maharajah, who calls me his European mother, as the civillest thing he can say.' Lucie, of course, at thirty-three, was far too young to be Azimullah's mother. But an even more fanciful notion was that Azimullah was a maharajah, an idea that probably sprang from the fact that Azimullah's surname, 'Khan', meant 'king'.

Lucie did everything in her power to aid Azimullah's undertaking for Nana Sahib, and also to establish Azimullah himself in her own social circle. As usual, she turned first to Lord Lansdowne. Azimullah wanted no less than to be presented to the Queen, but Alexander had cautioned that it was unlikely that he would be received because of his claim against the East India Company. Lucie asked Lansdowne if he agreed: 'begging my husband's pardon, I can hardly believe that our court can take upon itself to prejudice a question of the kind or so openly to favour the E.I.C. against another subject of the crown. I should like to know what you say.' If Lansdowne, like Alexander, was pessimistic about Azimullah's chances of meeting the Queen, Lucie asked if he could obtain a ticket for the opening of Parliament for him, so that he could at least view the Queen from afar.

In the meantime, Lucie introduced Azimullah to all her friends, and soon he was suavely moving through fashionable Mayfair and Belgravia drawing-rooms on his own as well as in the company of the Duff Gordons. He was just the thing to enliven a dinner party: handsome, exotic, highly intelligent, but also enough of a chameleon to assume the coloration of his new English friends' values and beliefs. Deferential and plausible, Azimullah didn't challenge anyone's diehard racial assumptions. He knew 'his place', but he also carved out his own niche in the more daring and tolerant reaches of English society. The Queen and the Court may have remained inaccessible, but Lord Lansdowne invited Azimullah to Bowood; Phillips painted his portrait; Samuel Rogers had him to breakfast and Caroline Norton had him to dinner. Lucie even took Azimullah to dine with her mother-in-law, in Hertford Street, and after dinner rushed off with him to the opera, no doubt leaving Lady Duff Gordon with dramatically elevated eyebrows.

Inevitably, Azimullah's deft combination of the familiar and the foreign enabled him to make a number of conquests, especially female ones. It was rumoured that he was secretly engaged to one young lady; more probably he had affairs with several married women. Most likely Lucie was aware – in a vague sort of way – of these romantic adventures. Certainly her own relationship with Azimullah was very close, but with her he assumed the role of a protégé. She told Lord Lansdowne how they sat up late night after night talking: 'you would be amused at the incessant questioning that goes on . . . I have gone through such a course of political economy and all social sciences . . . and had to get so many books for my pupil to devour that I feel growing quite solemn and pedantic. Azimullah . . . will go home with very reforming notions to his own people.'

For more than a year, Azimullah remained at the Gordon Arms, desultorily pursuing Nana Sahib's suit for the restoration of the pension. Of course, he sent back regular bulletins to his sponsor, and though there was little news regarding his mission, Nana Sahib was delighted to hear of the generosity and hospitality shown by the Duff Gordons to his agent. As a token of his gratitude, in fact, he sent to Lucie a necklace of emeralds, rubies and pearls, and a bolt of exquisite kincob cloth, woven of deep rose silk and real gold threads.

★

In March 1854, just two months after Azimullah arrived in England, the Crimean War broke out. From the beginning it was clear that, as Tennyson was to put it, 'someone had blundered'. And not just at the Battle of Balaclava. The Duff Gordons' friends Kinglake and Henry Layard both travelled to the front (Kinglake was later to write the definitive history of the war), and so, too, did a host of foreign correspondents. This, in fact, was the first war covered by the press, and both their coverage and the war itself aroused tremendous controversy in England. Lucie followed the newspaper reports closely and like many others was 'haunted', as she told Lord Lansdowne, by 'the dangers and sufferings of all that best blood of England'. In this instance, hers was the patriot's view and she also shared the general opinion that the press had no right to criticize the conduct of the war. 'How disgusting is the tone of the newspapers,' she wrote to Lord Lansdowne. 'That we should live to see anonymous fellows daring to throw out insinuations against the courage of our Generals!' Whether, on the other hand, she was carried away by Tennyson's 'Charge of the Light Brigade' when it was published in the *Examiner* in December is questionable. She might even have seen the humour in Tennyson's altering the number of the Light Brigade who rode into the Valley of Death from seven to six hundred in order to keep to his metre.

In the summer of 1854, Janet and her governess returned from a year in Dresden, and Lucie reported to Bayley that Janet was not only speaking fluent German but also hunting 'vigorously with the foxhounds and thinks me cruel not to let her kill both the horses after the staghounds. She rides perfectly and with the utmost courage.' Lady Duff Gordon, however, was far less impressed with her granddaughter, whom she found in need of a 'less good opinion of herself', and wanting 'manners and breeding and all feminine graces (as her mother did before her), and respect for God and man'. Maurice, now five, Lucie told Bayley, had 'grown very tall and amiable', and Alexander 'extremely portly and dignified-looking'. Lucie, herself, however, though somewhat 'better in health', looked old, she said, with her 'hair quite grey'.

Yet she felt energetic and young enough to accompany her old friend Janet Shuttleworth, or Lady Kay-Shuttleworth* as

* When Janet Shuttleworth married James Kay in 1842, he assumed her name and arms by royal licence. A tireless worker for the poor, public education, and other liberal causes, he was made a baronet in 1849. Sir James and Lady Kay-

she was now, to Hamburg for six weeks in October and November. Janet Kay-Shuttleworth was, in fact, seriously ill and hoped that a spell on the continent would be restorative. Instead, she remained unwell and Lucie, too, fell ill. 'The air of Hamburg disagreed with me,' she wrote to Mrs Grote, 'and I came home very poorly.' This was the first time Lucie had been to Germany since her honeymoon and, in the cold, damp and 'disagreeable' air of Hamburg, all the old magic of Germany seems to have been spent for her.

After spending the winter together at Esher, Alexander and Janet visited Duff Gordon and Cornewall Lewis relatives in Wales and Herefordshire for much of the summer while Lucie packed off Maurice and his nurse to the sea and she herself went to Bowood. They all came together again briefly at the end of August, but Lucie, especially, continued to feel restless. She was helping her cousin, Henry Reeve, with a translation of de Tocqueville's *Ancien Régime*, but otherwise had little to occupy her.

★

In September Lucie impulsively decided to take a holiday in Paris and she persuaded Alexander to come with her. It would be, she said, a belated fifteenth-anniversary celebration for them – the first time they had had a holiday alone together since their honeymoon. Initially all went well: the early autumn weather was glorious and they found charming rooms in the Champs-Elysées. They toured the galleries, made an excursion to Versailles, ate delicious meals at odd hours in Montmartre, haunted the booksellers on the Left Bank.

But then they heard that Heinrich Heine – Lucie's old friend from Boulogne – was dying in extreme poverty, not far from their own lodgings, and of course Lucie immediately rushed off to see him. Heine was partially paralysed and nearly blind from

---

Shuttleworth are chiefly remembered today as the rather aggressive friends of Elizabeth Gaskell, Charlotte Brontë and other literary figures whom they liked to entertain at their home, Gawthorpe Hall, in Lancashire.

a venereal disease of the spinal cord, and subject to agonizing pain and haemorrhages. Lucie found him lying on a heap of dirty mattresses, his emaciated body no bigger than a child's under the sheet, his hollow eyes staring out from his pale, wasted face. When Lucie bent down to kiss him, his beard felt like swan's down and she could scarcely keep back her tears. Heine raised his eyelids with his long bony fingers, and when he saw Lucie with Alexander next to her exclaimed, 'Gott! die kleine Lucie ist gross geworden, und hat einen Mann!' (God! Little Lucie has grown up and has a husband!)

Despite his great physical suffering, mentally Heine seemed to dwell for the most part in the past, and Lucie's sudden appearance brought back to him the happy period in Boulogne twenty years earlier. His old sarcasm was softened if not entirely extinguished and, in addition to the past, he dwelt upon the fate of his works – which was the only sort of immortality he hoped for. He offered Lucie the copyright to all his books and gave her *carte blanche* to translate them into English as she saw fit.*

For the rest of their time in Paris, Lucie visited Heine twice or more a week, always conversing with him in his mother tongue. And thus the holiday turned into a deathbed vigil from which Alexander, inevitably, was largely excluded. When the time drew near for them to return to England, Lucie tried to break the news gently to Heine, but he begged her to keep the date a secret because, he said, he could not bear to say 'Lebewohl auf ewig' (an eternal farewell). But on her last day with her old friend – though she had not told him that it was the last – Heine said that Lucie had reappeared at the end of his not very long (he was only fifty-eight) nor greatly happy life as 'ein schöner gütiger Todesengel' (a beautiful angel of death), bringing him greetings from youth and Germany. Several months later, when Lucie and Alexander had returned to England, Lucie read in the

---

* Lucie, however, never translated any of Heine's works.

papers one morning that Heine had died and been buried at his request without religious ceremony in Montmartre Cemetery.

★

Lucie's frame of mind upon returning from Paris was understandably melancholy, and she continued to be haunted by memories of Heine, dying in pain and squalor in his Parisian garret. She roused herself, however, to go with Alexander to a house party over Christmas to which they had been summoned by the great society hostess and literary lionizer Lady Ashburton, wife of the second Lord Ashburton, scion of the wealthy Baring family. No less than twenty-five guests assembled at the Ashburton estate, The Grange, near Alresford in Essex, including such Duff Gordon friends as the Brookfields, Tom Taylor, Henry Taylor, Dicky Doyle, Tennyson and the Carlyles.

It was a gathering of the brilliant and the glittering, but not all the sparks that flew were cerebral. As everyone there knew, Carlyle, in his own peculiar, acerbic way, was besotted with Lady Ashburton. Though this was a platonic passion, it had caused Jane Carlyle much anguish and she had come to The Grange under duress. Her smouldering jealousy was not subdued by Lady Ashburton's careful condescension to her, nor by her hostess's gift of a silk dress which might have been an appropriate present, as Jane caustically observed, for a housekeeper. It certainly was not a tactful gift for a proud and deeply unhappy woman who was dismayed by the magnificent gowns and jewels of the other female guests. If Lucie brought along one of her 'tawdry rainbow' gowns or wore her man's tailored plaid jacket to luncheon, Jane may have felt consoled by the presence of at least one other woman indifferent to fashion.

Sublimely unaware of the tensions that swirled about him, Tennyson was persuaded to give a recitation. Unfortunately, he chose to read his controversial new poem, *Maud*, a work which traced an unstable young man's obsession with his dead love, Maud, to the brink of madness: an obscure psychological odyssey ending with his salvation fighting in the highly unpopular

Crimean War. When *Maud* was published earlier in the year, the critics had been baffled, astonished, even appalled. One reviewer said there were too many vowels in the title, and that it didn't really matter which was deleted. Tennyson, the most prickly and sensitive of men, responded to the barrage of criticism the poem received by reading it on every possible occasion in the hope that its meaning and merits would thereby become clear.

To those at The Grange who had already been present at one of these recitations of *Maud*, the prospect of being subjected once again to its more than 1,000 lines was unendurable. Carlyle went out for a long walk, accompanied by Brookfield and several others. Lucie and Alexander probably stayed behind with the remaining politely attentive guests assembled in the library. But Tennyson was perturbed at their very politeness and wondered why they failed to interrupt him with exclamations of 'how beautiful!' and other appreciative noises. Jane Carlyle, captive in the library with her adversary Lady Ashburton, who smiled benignly up at Tennyson as he droned on interminably, was furious. She later exploded to a friend that Tennyson had ruined the house party by going 'about asking everybody if they liked his *Maud* – and reading *Maud* aloud – and talking Maud, Maud, Maud, till I wished myself far away among people who only read and wrote prose or who neither read nor wrote at all'.

When Lucie and Alexander returned home from the Ashburtons' they learned that Alexander's uncle, Sir George Cornewall Lewis, had succeeded Gladstone as Chancellor of the Exchequer in Palmerston's new cabinet, and Lewis now offered to Alexander the post of his private secretary. This meant that Alexander could finally leave his unremunerative labours at the Treasury. And the following year, again through the influence of Lewis (now Secretary of State for War), Alexander was made a Commissioner of Inland Revenue.

The Inland Revenue post was both congenial and well paid.

In her diary, Lady Duff Gordon exulted over her son's good fortune: 'a permanent situation of £1200, quite in his own line of knowledge and interest!!! Exactly what will most suit him and with his other little emoluments will give him an income of 1500 p.a. for life. I rejoice in it in all ways.' Though Alexander would have a permanent office at Somerset House in the Strand, the post of Commissioner also involved extensive travel in Ireland and Scotland which Alexander greatly enjoyed. His duties included checking up on subordinate officers and putting down illicit stills. But Alexander was such a soft touch that many an owner of an illegal still or evader of the window tax got off with only a warning or a small fine.

★

Alexander was not the only one away from home now; increasingly it seemed that all the inmates of the Gordon Arms were shooting off in different directions. Maurice was on the verge of being packed off to Eton and there was talk of sending Janet back to Germany for further study. But before definite plans could be made, Janet fell ill of scarlet fever and was confined to bed, where she remained for six weeks, reading the complete works of Sir Walter Scott which Lucie borrowed for her from the London Library.

Janet was made all the more miserable while ill because Azimullah Khan – who had become her great friend – had been recalled to India in the spring of 1855 by Nana Sahib when it became clear that the East India Company would never budge over the matter of the pension. Azimullah, no doubt, would have preferred to linger in England and pursue his own more rewarding affairs, but when the order to return came, he had no choice but to obey and reluctantly said goodbye to the Duff Gordons and his numerous London friends and admirers. Azimullah then made his rather desultory way back to India, overland via the Crimea, where he paused long enough to get a very unfavourable view of the operations of the British army — impressions he carefully stored in his mind along with the other detailed knowledge of western ways of thinking and acting that he had gained during his lengthy stay with the Duff Gordons.

Although Azimullah returned to Cawnpore having failed at his original mission to regain the pension from the East India Company, he could still persuade Nana Sahib that in other, more subtle ways his sojourn in England had been a success. Put bluntly, he had supped with the enemy, and in future would have no qualms over biting the hand that had fed him. But for Lucie Azimullah's departure left a hole in the family: she had lost her protégé and confidant. Even more, she lost the window on an exotic world which Azimullah had brought home to her. For in his own way, Azimullah had been an ambassador as well as an envoy. And Lucie would sooner have suspected that Nana Sahib's quite genuine pearls were paste and his emeralds cut glass than she would have doubted Azimullah's integrity.

All too soon, however, events in India threw into doubt everything Lucie trusted and sympathized with in the affairs of Azimullah and Nana Sahib. At first she and Azimullah exchanged letters, Lucie ending hers with affection 'from your devoted English mother'. But early in 1857 their flow of letters ceased as, all across northern India, Indian soldiers (called sepoys) in the Bengal army began to rise up against their East India Company British commanders. The immediate cause of the 'Mutiny' was the new Enfield rifles with cartridges rumoured to be greased with beef and pork tallow and thus hateful to both Hindu and Muslim soldiers. But the introduction of the abhorrent greased cartridges, many Indians believed, was just the first step taken by the British to assail their religious beliefs; soon, it was feared, there would be mass forced conversions to Christianity.

Throughout the spring, the Mutiny spread – from Meerut to Delhi to Agra, and, in early June, to Cawnpore. Lucie and Alexander and the children, meanwhile, had gone to France for the summer. While they were in Dieppe ('pleasant but crowded and dear'), Lucie complained in a letter to Lord Lansdowne that they were cut off from all news 'of Indian affairs . . . and as ignorant . . . as if we had been in Central Africa'. When they arrived in Paris in late August, however, they quickly learned all about what Lucie called the new 'vista of disaster and hatred' in India.

It was unusually hot in Paris, but well below the 126 and more degrees that had reigned all summer in Cawnpore. Bit by bit, from newspaper stories, conversation at dinner parties, and talking to people on the street and in the parks, Lucie and Alexander pieced together what had happened at Cawnpore while they holidayed in France. In early June, the sepoys had risen and more than 800 Europeans took refuge in a crowded, poorly defended entrenchment which stood in the midst of a barren plain on the outskirts of the city. They were besieged here for twenty-one days under horrendous conditions; more than 250 died of wounds or disease. Then Nana Sahib offered the survivors safe passage to Allahabad if they laid down their arms. After a short debate over Nana Sahib's terms, those in 'the fort of despair', as it was now called, surrendered. But the next day, when they paraded down to the Ganges and started to board the boats provided to take them to Allahabad, a massacre was unleashed by Nana Sahib's forces concealed on both sides of the river. Hundreds perished.

Of those who somehow survived the river massacre, the men and boys were immediately rounded up and shot by sepoys on the river bank while the surviving women and children looked on helplessly. Then these women and children – more than 125 of them – were herded together and marched to a small house a mile or so distant called the Bibighar, which had originally been built by an English officer for his Indian mistress. Here they were incarcerated for three more weeks. Some went mad; others succumbed to wounds or died of cholera or dysentery. Babies were born and died too. On 15 July, news reached Cawnpore that a British relief party was approaching the city. Nana Sahib and his advisers, among whom none was more prominent than Azimullah Khan, decided there must be no surviving witnesses of the massacre on the river bank. Sepoys were ordered to shoot all the prisoners in the Bibighar. When they refused to carry out this order, butchers were summoned from the bazaar who slaughtered the women and children.

Two days later the British 'relief party' entered Cawnpore, but there was nothing and no one left to relieve. When the British troops saw the blood-soaked walls and floor of the Bibighar and the mangled bodies of the women and children that had been cast down a well, they embarked on their own course of atrocities. They tortured and killed every Indian they could lay hands on who might have been remotely involved in Nana Sahib's treachery, as well as many who clearly were not. Nana Sahib himself either drowned in the Ganges or cleverly faked his suicide and disappeared into Nepal. His deputy and agent, Azimullah, also disappeared into thin air. But when Nana Sahib's mansion was looted by the British soldiers they found bundles of letters – some of them clearly amorous – to Azimullah from various English ladies. Among these, there may have been several familiar (but not amorous) ones from Janet as well as a number of long, lively letters from Lucie, signed with affection in her unmistakable bold, round hand.

While the British soldiers were looting, ransacking and hanging scores of Indians from the gracefully arched trees that bordered the Ganges at Cawnpore, Lucie was trying to fathom the horror that had transpired there, and trying, as well, to comprehend and come to terms with Nana Sahib's and Azimullah's certain involvement in and responsibility for the atrocities at Cawnpore. Alexander took a staunch British view of things, and so Lucie poured out her feelings of outrage on behalf of the nameless, voiceless mass of Indians in letters to Lord Lansdowne and Layard, whose brother was then serving in India. She commiserated with Layard's anxiety for his brother, but then confessed, 'I am singular . . . in giving . . . my sympathy to the natives who are between two millstones – first tyrannised by the sepoys . . . and then harried by the English . . . The English victims at least will have vengeance and subscriptions, but who will pity the poor helpless mass of the people guilty of the offence of a dark skin and a religion of their own?' The racism that the Mutiny had provoked utterly repelled her, and she told Layard, 'I *execrate* the tone of everybody in England on the whole affair.'*

But above all, Lucie was haunted by the role and fate of Azimullah. Azimullah who had moved so adroitly, so smoothly, and, Lucie thought, so intelligently and respectfully through her world in England. It was Azimullah, she learned, who had negotiated the terms of surrender with General Wheeler, the Governor of Cawnpore and commander of the besieged fort. On behalf of Nana Sahib, Azimullah had promised all the Europeans in the fort safe passage to Allahabad, comfortable boats to transport them, medicine for the sick and wounded and ample provisions (meat, beans and rice), all the while setting a death-trap for more than 300 innocent people. This was the man Lucie had harboured for more than a year at the Gordon Arms, the friend she had stayed up late night after night talking to, the companion she had taken to the theatre and opera, her pupil and protégé – and also her Eastern mentor. What on earth, she wondered, had become of him?

No one in Paris knew, of course, and so Lucie wrote to Lord Lansdowne, who had entertained Azimullah on more than one occasion at Lansdowne House and Bowood. She confessed herself 'very anxious' about Azimullah's fate: 'I am quite unable to believe that he cd [sic] approve or endure the atrocious conduct of Nana Sahib & yet he must be too much in his power not to be hanged either by him or the English.' But Lansdowne had no information about either Nana Sahib or Azimullah, and

---

* Lucie certainly would have been dismayed, too, by her mother-in-law's diary reflections on the Mutiny. Reading 'a most painful account of all the horrors of the Indian Mutiny', Lady Duff Gordon pronounced: 'no greater fiend was ever allowed to walk the earth than Nana Sahib!!!'

Lucie resigned herself to the fact that she would probably never know their fates. Even more, she came to feel that the horrible events at Cawnpore and indeed the whole Mutiny would never be fully understood. 'The real truth of the whole outbreak,' she wrote to Lansdowne, 'I believe we shall never know – I mean the native side of the question.'

*

By the time Lucie wrote this last gloomy letter to her old friend, it was September and she had been in Paris for nearly two months. Alexander and Maurice had gone back to England, Alexander to temporary bachelor lodgings in London and Maurice to Eton. Janet and her governess Mathilde were about to depart again for Dresden, where they would spend the winter. Lucie herself lingered in Paris until early October, dining out with her mother's old friends, Victor Cousin and Barthélemy St Hilaire, and also with Caroline Norton, who was spending the autumn in Paris with her eldest son, Fletcher. The Austins, too, threatened to descend on Lucie, but at the last minute John Austin refused to come to Paris 'for fear of being ill from pure vexation' – whether because he recoiled from the prospect of French cuisine or French politics is not clear.

In the end Lucie went to Fontainebleau alone, where she continued to mull over the events in India and also politics in general – brooding which she gave voice to in long, rather theoretical letters to Lansdowne, one of which ended, 'what with Indian news and the spectacle of political hatreds of all sorts presented to one here I feel quite out of spirits and begin to entertain doubts as to the notions of human progress inculcated in me in my youth ... Am I very aristocratic or very democratic? I am sure I cannot say.' The events of 1848, the Crimean War and now the Indian Mutiny all undermined the liberal humanism Lucie had been raised on since she trotted around Jeremy Bentham's garden in Queen Square with the old Utilitarian himself. After 1848, John and Sarah Austin had veered sharply to the right and repudiated the radical convictions of their youth. Now, in the wake of the Mutiny, Lucie, too, seemed poised on the brink of taking a new political direction.

For a time, she looked to what she called to Lansdowne 'our great aristocracy' as 'the defenders of liberty'. But the Mutiny gave the lie to this view of a benign, aristocratic élite ruling 'inferior' peoples of colour for their own good. For various reasons, including rank disenchantment, Lucie began now to identify with those she called 'the natives', rather than their British rulers. This was not really a product of carefully thought-out political convictions, but rather a growing emotional allegiance – a cast of mind and heart rather than an ideology. Today it may seem naïve; in the autumn of 1857 it was radical in the extreme.

★

By late October, Lucie was back in England, but she dallied for three weeks in Southampton where she stayed with old family friends before finally returning to Esher. With Maurice at Eton and Janet and her governess Mathilde in Dresden, the Gordon Arms seemed silent and empty, and Lucie and Alexander spent a quiet Christmas together there, punctuated only by a rather gloomy visit to the Austins at Weybridge early in the new year.

But Lucie was not too cut off to miss the latest gossip. In the spring of 1858 this included the news that Mary Ellen Meredith had run off with the artist Henry Wallis, a man nine years her junior who three years earlier had produced a famous painting of the boy-poet, Chatterton, on his deathbed after swallowing a suicidal draught. The delicately handsome model for Wallis's painting had been none other than George Meredith. In April 1858 Mary Ellen bore Wallis's child, a boy whose name on his birth certificate was registered as Harold Meredith since Mary Ellen was still legally Meredith's wife. The baby's parents, however, called him Felix (Latin for happy) and, as soon as Mary Ellen had recovered from childbirth, they eloped to Capri.

Lucie had not seen either of the Merediths in nearly six years, but she was probably not greatly surprised by – nor disapproving

193

of – this revolution in their affairs. What did amaze her, however, in April 1858, was the realization that she herself was pregnant. It had been nine years since Maurice was born; Lucie was now thirty-seven, and no longer in robust health. Moreover, Alexander was often away from home on Inland Revenue business and also spending more and more time in London, dining and sleeping at his mother's house in Hertford Street. Thus it seemed something of a miracle that they were to have another child.

But after the shock, Lucie must have welcomed this surprise. Ever since her close brush with death in 1851, she had felt prematurely aged and 'grey', and physically vulnerable if not positively frail. It was not pleasant – this sense of deterioration – especially for a woman who, before she fell ill, had been so handsome and strong. Pregnancy was a reassertion of vitality and passion: her body had unexpectedly turned creative and fertile again. And then, too, the baby would assuage her restlessness, the sense of purposelessness which had plagued her ever since she had retired from London life to Esher and then given up her translating work. She may have even felt that, like Mary Ellen Meredith, she was embarking on an unexpected adventure, despite the fact that Lucie's baby was fathered by her lawful husband and Lucie – as yet – was not bound for warmer climes.

If Lucie felt a vague kinship with Mary Ellen, it was then odd, indeed, that at this very time George Meredith should re-enter the Duff Gordons' lives. Shortly after Janet returned from Dresden in the late spring of 1858, she was riding to Esher station one evening to meet her father, when a small boy fell in the street in front of her horse. Janet immediately dismounted and took the child to his house nearby on the Esher High Street, where the door was opened by a tall, pale man who peered at Janet and then tentatively asked, 'Are you not Lady Duff Gordon's daughter?' Before she could answer, he boldly rushed on, 'Don't you know me? I'm your poet!' The child Janet had rescued was none other than George and Mary Ellen Meredith's only son, Arthur Meredith, who, ever since his mother had run off, had lived with his somewhat bewildered and financially hard-pressed father.

George Meredith had only recently moved to Esher with Arthur and they were leading a rather disorganized existence in rented rooms in the High Street house. Lucie, of course, promptly took up the deserted father and son. She and Janet found them a cottage to let on Copsham Common, near the fir woods of Claremont House and close to the Gordon Arms. Meredith was still a struggling writer, and two days a week he went up to London where he was a reader with the publisher Chapman & Hall. On these days – and others when he needed peace and quiet to write – he brought Arthur to stay with the Duff Gordons, and Janet taught the boy German and took him on long walks in the woods.

Before very long, Meredith was entranced by seventeen-year-old Janet, who, since he'd last seen her, had metamorphosed from a rugged tomboy into a handsome and self-assured, though still boyish, young woman. Meredith began writing Janet poems and discussing his novels with her. The following year he went even further and embarked on a novel – '*my* novel', as Janet called it – whose central characters were based on Janet, Lucie and Alexander. This was *Evan Harrington*, a complicated love-story about the trials and tribulations of an aspiring tailor's son, the novel's hero, Evan (based on Meredith), who falls in love with a young, socially superior woman named Rose Jocelyn (based on Janet), the daughter of the civilized and engaging Sir Frank and Lady Jocelyn (based on Alexander and Lucie).★

While he was writing the novel, Meredith would come over

★ This, of course, was not the first time Lucie had appeared in a literary work. In addition to Tennyson's *The Princess*, she had figured in a novel published in 1854, *The Progress of Prejudice*, by the popular writer Mrs Catherine Gore. Lady Duff Gordon read the book soon after it came out and wrote in her diary, 'It is clever and amusing – some pretty, genteel characters in it. It is imagined that one of the heroines is intended for Lucie. It immensely flatters her beauty, and I see no resemblance in the character.'

to the Gordon Arms in the evening and read aloud to Lucie and Janet from the manuscript. Lucie was amused by Meredith's sympathetic portrait of her. Janet was thrilled at her central role, but her response to the novel was much more literal-minded. Instead of seeing herself as the inspiration of Rose, she felt Rose should be her exact replica, and so she continually interrupted Meredith with statements such as 'I should not have done so,' or 'No, I should never have said that.' She also persuaded Meredith to incorporate her dog, an Irish retriever named Peter, into the book.

Lucie was delighted to have Meredith as a neighbour once again but, as the weeks and months passed, she began to be alarmed at the intensity of Janet's relationship with him. Meredith, after all, was still married, and, even had he been free, Lucie would not have chosen him as a son-in-law. Janet furthermore had not even 'come out' yet, and Lucie thought her too immature to embark on a serious romance with any man. It was probably the desire to put some distance between her daughter and Meredith rather than Lucie's approaching confinement which led her to wangle an invitation for Janet to visit the Tennysons at Freshwater on the Isle of Wight in October. Here the hardy and bold Janet became unexpectedly attached to the retiring and ailing Emily Tennyson, whom, on fine days, Janet would pull about the grounds of the Tennysons' house in a long, low kind of carriage while the Poet Laureate pushed from behind.

At the beginning of November, when the baby was almost due, Lucie and Alexander moved into Lady Duff Gordon's London house at 34 Hertford Street, Mayfair. Because of Lucie's various illnesses in the nine years since Maurice was born, they anticipated a difficult birth, and thus arranged for Lucie to be attended by one of Lady Duff Gordon's many medical specialists, Dr Rigby. Lady Duff Gordon herself and her two daughters, Georgina and Alice, were not, however, on the scene, having fled the thick, yellow fogs of London for Bognor on the Sussex coast.

As feared, Lucie had a long and difficult labour, though the worst of her pain was relieved by chloroform. At last, on 5 November – one of those twilit winter days that seem a mere pause between two long nights – Urania Duff Gordon was born: a small but perfectly developed infant with pale, translucent skin, dark eyes, and tiny, delicate ears that looked like whorled shells of mother of pearl. In the first moments of her life, Lucie fell utterly in love with her as she had with no one else in her thirty-seven years.

So, too, did Sarah Austin, who rushed up to London as soon as she heard from Alexander that Urania had been born, and that mother and daughter were both safe and well.★ Sarah wrote ecstatically to a friend 'that Heaven has sent me a new grandchild – a granddaughter, a prodigy of beauty and vigour. This little creature comes late to us all – the "last rose of summer" to her parents – "the last flower of autumn" to us. I am full of thankfulness for [her].'

Urania, like Lucie years before, was a '*wunderkind*': beautiful, happy, lively and healthy. She was her mother's delight – all the more so because bearing and nursing the baby had taken a toll on Lucie's fragile health. By the spring, however, Lucie felt well enough to prepare for Janet's 'coming out'. Janet's presentation at court was not, however, a great success. She was awkward and uncomfortable wearing stays for the first time and found her train too cumbersome to curtsy gracefully. She also managed to drop her glove in front of the Queen and then was too terrified to pick it up.

When the ordeal of 'coming out' was over, Janet put on her riding habit again with a sigh of relief and she and Alexander set off for Eton to visit one of Alexander's old tutors, stopping on the way at an inn in Great Marlow. The landlady found father

---

★ Lady Duff Gordon, in contrast, didn't see Urania until she was six months old, the following May. The baby she found 'charming', but Lucie, she felt, had become unattractively overweight nursing Urania.

and daughter a dubious pair, and raised her eyebrows when they tried to explain that Janet was Miss Duff Gordon, the daughter of Sir Alexander. To this information the landlady retorted 'that she had lived in titled families and [had] never heard any young lady address her parent as "dear old boy"'.

★

Lucie remained in Esher all summer with the baby but, in the early autumn, when the cold and damp brought back her cough, she and Urania went to Brighton and took rooms in a charming house facing the sea front. Here, despite 'hailstones and cold', as she wrote to Lord Lansdowne, she was 'well-doctored', and regained some of her old strength. But just as she was beginning to feel 'better than I ever expected again', she received word from Sarah Austin that John Austin had had an acute attack of bronchitis and was gravely ill.

Lucie immediately rushed back to Surrey, but for some days she was too ill herself to go to the Austins' cottage in Weybridge. Alexander meanwhile was inaccessible in Ireland on Inland Revenue business, and so Lucie sent Janet over to Weybridge daily to see how John Austin was faring. For a while Janet concealed the severity of his condition because she knew Lucie was not strong enough to nurse him. But after a fortnight of falsely optimistic bulletins, Janet could no longer hide the fact that Austin's case seemed hopeless, and Lucie set off for Weybridge immediately, despite her doctor's entreaties not to go.

What now ensued the unsentimental Janet later described as 'heart-breaking': through the long nights Lucie sat by her father's bedside in the cold, damp house, 'white as marble, her face set and stern . . . her large eyes fixed on his face'. This man who had never relished life, who had indeed more than once contemplated taking his own, did not linger long. And after he died on 17 December, Lucie had a violent attack of haemorrhage from the lungs – her first. In the midst of her great grief, she guessed that this meant she had tuberculosis.

Lucie was immediately taken back to Esher and put to bed,

while Janet remained at Weybridge to care for her grandmother. Sarah was 'beside herself with grief', and kept her seventeen-year-old granddaughter up with her night after night as she wept and called out to her lost husband and mourned him as if their marriage had been the Eden she had imagined it would be as a young bride forty years before. Finally, shortly before Christmas, when Alexander was back from Ireland, Janet took Sarah home with her to Esher.

The following months of early 1860 were nightmarish – Sarah was prostrate with grief and Lucie was confined to bed with a hollow, harassing cough and intermittent 'blood-spitting'. Only the beautiful baby, Urania, now more than a year old and walking, could make her mother smile. Sarah spent a number of weeks at the Gordon Arms until she could face returning to the silent, empty cottage in Weybridge. When she finally did go back, she was once again overcome with grief, and wrote to a friend, 'I listen, I get up every instant, and I seek what I shall never find again. It is impossible to tell you how desolate I am.'

She spent her days and nights reading and rereading Austin's diaries and the letters he had written to her during their courtship – attempting to make sense of his profoundly inconclusive life, as well as trying to bring back what was now irretrievably lost. But gradually Sarah's absorption in his papers became less morbid; she turned from the letters to his legal writings – lectures, unfinished articles, pages of notes – a great mass of disorganized material – as well as *The Province of Jurisprudence Determined*, which had long been out of print. This all became Sarah's 'sad and sacred work': she contacted John Murray and signed an agreement to prepare Austin's legal writings for publication.

For twelve or more hours a day Sarah now immured herself in Austin's study, 'surrounded by every object that speaks of him', annotating, editing, elucidating, drafting and redrafting a biographical preface. She scarcely paused to eat meals, and laboured on relentlessly 'between bursts of grief, interrupted by tears and sobs', all the while overcome by what she described as Austin's 'life of unbroken disappointment and failure'. But now, she realized, she could – however belatedly – make some sort of restitution. Immersion in her husband's papers had left Sarah more convinced than ever of his genius. Heart-broken and ill, she now laboured to make this genius plain to others by producing a definitive edition of Austin's works.

While Sarah toiled on, Lucie's health remained precarious. With the warmth of spring, however, she seemed to improve for a time. Indeed, in August she was well enough to present a bugle to the 6th Surrey Rifles. Despite her radical politics, Lucie was moved by the new volunteer movement which had arisen in response to the threatened invasion of England by Napoleon III. To stir up John Bull spirit, Tennyson had written one of his less memorable poems, 'Riflemen Form!' And in June, the Queen had reviewed 20,000 volunteers in Hyde Park. Now two months later, on a much smaller scale, Lucie addressed the Surrey Volunteers from a dais on the village green. But her speech was scarcely jingoistic and after she had presented the silver bugle, she said, 'We earnestly hope that it may never sound but for your training in those martial exercises by which you are qualifying yourselves to act as our defenders. Defence not defiance is your watchword.'

★

Just a month or so after Lucie's 'capital speech' to the Surrey Volunteers, she had a relapse with haemorrhaging, and her friend, the Esher doctor Charles Izod, urged her to go to Ventnor on the Isle of Wight for the winter. Reluctantly, she set off almost immediately with Urania, Urania's nurse, and Sarah Austin – who took bundles of her husband's manuscripts with her – and they all settled at the Royal Hotel. When Alexander and Maurice arrived for Christmas, Sarah went back to Weybridge for a time, and from here she wrote of Lucie's condition to her old friend, Guizot: 'I cannot say my dear daughter is worse ... But she is not better. She has had no return of haemorrhage, but then the bitter cold has brought on cough and expectoration. In short, though ... danger is not *present*, it is always *near*, and that is enough to keep me on the rack ... One of the cruel things is that her doctor wishes her to be alone as much as possible, that she may not be tempted to talk. While I was there, I was seldom with her above an hour in the whole day. It was the only way of keeping her silent. The baby is an enchanting little creature, overflowing with health, spirits, and vivacity. She is her poor mother's delight and amusement.'

Lucie's life throughout the following winter and spring of 1860 was that of an invalid in a strange hotel room, separated from her family for all but an hour of the day. She could hear little Urania laughing and calling in the next room or out in the corridor, but everyone else crept about, whispering to each other if they needed to communicate. It must have felt like dying by slow degrees: lying in the narrow bed in that silent room, the curtains drawn against the life that went on beyond the window-panes. This illness was altogether different from the feverish, dangerous brush with death Lucie had had in the winter of 1851. Nine years before she had nearly been spirited out of life unawares, in a dreamy delirium. Now she was fully conscious, fully aware of her weakened state and closeness to death. She must have doubted during those long hours that she would ever leave this cell of a hotel room, ever return to Esher and the Gordon Arms, ever see Alexander and Maurice and Janet again, or watch her beautiful baby grow into the fair young girl and woman she promised to be.

★

All this while, back in Esher, Janet was confronting an entirely different destiny. The previous summer she and Alexander had gone to a house party at Aldermaston near Reading given by one of Henry Layard's friends, Mrs Higford Burr. Here they met Layard's great friend, Henry Ross, a director of Briggs Bank in Alexandria, Egypt, who had excavated with Layard at

Nineveh. In 1860 Ross was forty, twenty-two years older than Janet and a year older than Lucie. He was tall, dark and exotically weathered by his years abroad. When Janet sat next to him at dinner, she was fascinated by his stories of hunting wild boars and pig-sticking in the East. Ross was, as she put it, 'a wonderfully vivid raconteur' . . . and 'longing to hear more', Janet invited him to Esher.

When he arrived at the Gordon Arms in November, Lucie was still at Ventnor and Alexander away on Inland Revenue business, so Charlotte Austin, John Austin's spinster sister, was summoned to Esher to chaperone Janet and Ross. This was no easy task as they spent most of their time outdoors riding. Ross's proposal, in fact, seems to have been made from the saddle. As Janet later recalled, 'I took Mr Ross out with the Duc d'Aumale's harriers, and was much impressed by his admirable riding, his pleasant conversation, and his kindly ways. The result was that I promised to marry him.'

To her ardent admirer, George Meredith, however, Janet frankly explained why Ross rather than Meredith himself had won her hand, and what it all came down to was not a matter of equestrian skill: 'Henry makes £5,000 a year and will make more – we shall live on £1,000 a year, put by £4,000 – and at the end of five or six years, Click!' Meredith was crushed by Janet's betrothal but, though he spoke to others of Janet's 'amiable selfishness', to her he heroically wrote, 'God bless you, my dear girl. If you don't make a good wife, I've never read a page of woman.'

Meredith wasn't the only one who was astonished at Janet's engagement. To Sarah Austin, down in Ventnor with Lucie, it was 'like a clap of thunder', leaving her 'stunned' – especially when she and Lucie realized that Janet meant to marry Ross as soon as possible. Nevertheless, Sarah wrote to a friend that Ross was 'clever and agreeable' while conceding 'there is a little too much difference in their ages, but Janet never liked young men.' Lady Duff Gordon, far away in Genoa where she was wintering with her daughters, was 'agitated', as she put it, at the prospect of Janet's marriage. For, shrewd woman that she was, Lady Duff Gordon surmised that Janet did not love Ross. Hence she wrote both to Alexander in Esher and Lucie in Ventnor, 'I trust that there will be no marriage unless Janet *from her heart* wishes it!'

Lucie's and Alexander's reactions were more complicated. To Alexander, the prospect of Janet's marriage was a terrible blow. As Sarah said, he 'suffered much' at the thought of losing Janet, all the more so since it was settled that Janet would go out to Egypt with Ross directly after the wedding. For years, Alexander and Janet had been 'the inseparables', and Lucie's poor health had strengthened their bond. As Sarah put it, Janet had been 'the sunbeam in Alexander's life made so dreary by Lucie's illness'.

Lucie, too, reacted to Janet's approaching union with Ross in terms of her poor health. She was relieved and 'heartily glad to get her away from the depressing influence of illness and anxiety, and to know her enjoying her youth'. As for Ross himself, Lucie wrote to Janet Shuttleworth that he was 'a catch' and 'everything I could wish . . . he is so excellent and agreeable; and there is quite enough money and a new country to see, and an interesting life' ahead. But then Lucie added some rather odd praise of Janet that reflected their lack of real intimacy and also how very different, at heart, mother and daughter were: 'I am selfishly sorry to lose her, of course, for she was a most efficient and pleasant daughter.'

In some ways, Janet's flight into marriage seemed a repetition of Lucie's twenty years before. Janet, like Lucie, was marrying at a very young age (on both their marriage certificates, they were entered as 'minors'). Like Lucie, too, marriage for Janet provided an escape from a home life shadowed by illness and depression.

As had always been the case in her short life, Janet had her way: she and Ross were married on 5 December 1860. Because

Lucie was not well enough to return home, the wedding took place at St Catherine's Church, Ventnor, on the Isle of Wight. But in the end, the venue made scant difference; when the wedding day arrived Lucie – like John Austin before her – was too ill to leave her bed to see her daughter marry. As Sarah wrote to Lord Lansdowne afterwards, the wedding was performed 'in strange and uncongenial circumstances': Lucie was absent, Alexander was disconsolate. And so, too, was George Meredith, who had travelled down to the Isle of Wight, like a martyr, to see Janet marry. He insisted, too, upon signing the marriage certificate along with Alexander and Tom Taylor.

In Genoa, Lady Duff Gordon wrote up the wedding in her diary from a report she received from her friend Lady Antrobus, who had attended: 'Janet looked quite handsome in her wedding clothes and behaved very well. The wedding service was very ill performed by a Mr White which I was sorry to hear.' Even from Janet's point of view, the wedding was scarcely festive. Years later she laconically described it: 'my marriage took place very quietly ... my mother ... was very unwell, unable to leave her bed, and it was a bitter parting from her and from my dear father, who I knew would be very lonely without me.'

Almost immediately after the ceremony, Janet and Ross set off for Paris, *en route* to Alexandria. Alexander and Maurice also departed from Ventnor after Christmas, leaving Lucie alone again in her hotel room, with an hour's inconsequential conversation with Sarah at the end of day, if the doctor thought Lucie was up to it.

★

Usually she was, and her health improved sufficiently in the early months of 1861 to enable her to return to Esher at the end of March. But it wasn't really a homecoming, because both Lucie's Ventnor and Esher doctors now told her that she wouldn't survive another winter in England. Exile loomed; and for her own sake they urged her to leave by early summer. At first she tried to stall, insisting that she felt much improved, pointing out that she hadn't coughed up blood in months. She also had sufficient energy to edit Janet's translation of von Sybel's *The History and Literature of the Crusades*, a project Meredith had suggested, which was published under Lucie's name by Meredith's employers, Chapman & Hall. Lucie also, at Meredith's instigation, translated some old German ballads by Tannhäuser. But there was no talk of more substantial projects.

Instead, the directive to go abroad became even more insistent in May after Lucie collapsed with another attack of haemorrhaging. George Meredith wrote to Janet, now in Alexandria, that 'your mother has had another attack, a very severe one. It wears my heart to think of her . . . She must not spend another winter in England.'

To Janet Shuttleworth, Lucie herself confided that 'my attacks are sudden, and utterly annihilating while they last'. And she felt acutely that she was a burden to Alexander and Sarah. 'Mere insecurity of life is an evil one soon gets reconciled to,' she told Janet. 'The real evil, is the feeling of being a trouble and expense to my husband, and unable to contribute to his comfort.' Yet despite her guilty feelings, Lucie still fought the sentence of exile.

At the end of June, however, Sarah and Alexander prevailed upon her to consult several medical specialists in London, including Lady Duff Gordon's physician, Dr Quail. Their verdict was unanimous: she must go abroad. Alexandria, where Lucie could live with Janet and Ross, was mooted, but the doctors said it was too damp and that only the dry heat of Upper Egypt would benefit Lucie's lungs. Lucie feared it would be too expensive to hire a boat to go up the Nile, and so after further medical consultations it was decided that she should sail to the Cape of Good Hope instead, at the very opposite end of the African continent. Hence Sarah wrote to St Hilaire in early July: 'my poor Lucie . . . will probably start immediately for the Cape. I need not tell you what this means – a solitary home for Alexander and the children; for me *le vide*. But the doctors unanimously say that another winter in England would be fatal.'

For Lucie there was scarcely time to think after her passage was booked on the *St Lawrence*, due to sail from Portsmouth on 19 July. She had to make all the necessary preparations quickly lest one of her 'annihilating attacks' left her too ill to voyage out on this perilous quest for health – and life. The Gordon Arms was let and Lucie moved in with the family of her Esher doctor, Charles Izod. Little Urania, after much agonizing on Lucie's part and a heart-breaking farewell, was sent to live with Lucie's maiden aunt, Charlotte Austin. Maurice, of course, was still at Eton. Alexander moved in with Lady Duff Gordon and his sisters at 34 Hertford Street, Mayfair.

On the morning of the 19th, he breakfasted early with his mother and then took the express train to Esher to pick up Lucie. Accompanied by Dr Izod, they travelled by rail to Portsmouth where Alexander and Izod took Lucie on board the *St Lawrence* and saw her comfortably settled, with her maid Sally Naldrett, in her cabin. 'A most sad, anxious business!' as Lady Duff Gordon remarked in her diary. Then there was nothing more to do but say farewell, with Izod hovering at the door and Sally noisily unpacking the valises. An embrace; then Alexander and Izod were gone and Lucie was left to her own thoughts until the ship weighed anchor and, pointing south, cumbersomely got underway.

★

No one could have imagined this exile for Lucie Austin in 1821, for Lucie Duff Gordon in 1840. But human beings, like all living things, shed chrysalises, moult, slough off old skins, metamorphose, discard and assume names, rise from heaps of cold ashes. There was no way, however, that Lucie could foresee in the summer of 1861 that her banishment would not just be healing, but transforming. South Africa would be the bridge to a different kind of wholeness, the route to another identity. When Lucie left Esher in late July, George Meredith said that 'a light had gone out'. But at her final destination she would acquire a new name, Noor ala Noor, which means 'light from the source of all light'.

Interlude

LETTERS FROM THE CAPE

Chapter Nine

Five days out to sea, in 'squally' weather off the Scilly Islands, Lucie wrote the first of her more than fifty letters home – long, diary-like letters that revealed in detail the fluctuating state of her health and, even more, her fascination with the new world she was encountering. Letters addressed to Sarah Austin, Lady Duff Gordon, Charlotte Austin and Tom Taylor as well as Alexander. What follows is a distillation of Lucie's letters to her husband, written at frequent intervals throughout the circuit of her exile and return: traveller's tales tinged with illness and homesickness as well as amusement and wonder.

To Alexander Duff Gordon. On board the St Lawrence, *off the Scilly Islands, 24 July 1861, 6pm.*

Dearest Alick,

All night was squally and rough. Lovely, but the ship is pitching as you never saw a ship pitch: bowsprit under water. Most of the passengers sick. I very hungry. Sally* sick, but full of pluck. By 2 o'clock a gale came on; all ordered below. Captain left dinner, and about 6, the sea struck us on the weather side, and washed a good many unconsidered trifles overboard, stove in 3 windows on the poop; nurse and four children in fits. Mrs Taylor and babies afloat, but good-humoured. Army surgeon and I picked up children and bullied nurse, and helped to bale. Went to bed at 9, couldn't undress, it pitched so. Slept sound, but seedy next day. Lay in bed all Tuesday and took Gallick acid to stop blood-spitting. Well

---

* Lucie's maid, Sally Naldrett, a clever, hearty, fearless woman in her late twenties: the Sancho Panza to Lucie's Quixote in South Africa and Egypt.

again today, but the gale continues. Evidently I can never be sea sick; but holding on is hard work, and writing harder. But it is great fun. I hope I mayn't be really ill, for the ship's doctor has next to no drugs, and is about 17, the army one is very rough, but a good fellow. Dr Jones and family appear to have come out of St Giles workhouse. A Mrs Harrison and her daughter going to Calcutta are jolly and good-humoured. The Polsons seem pretentious, and Mr Adams is making great love to Miss P. though he informed me he was otherwise engaged.

Today the air is quite saturated and wet. I put on my clothes damp when I dressed and have felt so ever since. This is stupid and ill-written, for it is not easy to see or to hold a pen while I hold on to the table with both legs and one arm, and am first on my back and then on my nose.

Adieu. LDG

To Alexander Duff Gordon. Bay of Biscay, 29 July 1861, 4 bells, i.e., 2 pm.

Dearest Alick,

Today is so cold that I dare not go on deck and am writing in my black hole of a cabin, in a green light, with the sun blinking through the waves as they rush over my port and scuttle. The captain is awfully vexed at the loss of time, and a good deal of temper is developing among the passengers. I persist in thinking it a very pleasant but utterly lazy life. I sleep a good deal but don't eat much, and my cough has been bad: I spit blood a little too, but considering the real hardship of the life – damp, cold, queer food and bad drink – I think I am all the better.

The humours of our company would make you very angry. Miss Polson is a very sweet, engaging girl, but her parents are odious. They beat the girl who is twenty-three and very delicate and gentle. The Polsons have fought the Captain on every point. They want meals in their cabin at separate hours, fresh water *ad libitum*, candles, and cooking lamps, and she is now prostrate after fits of hysterics such as I could not have believed in. She found some relief in slapping her black boy and her German maid, but still suffers severely. He modestly asked me to use my 'extraordinary influence' with the Captain to have the uprights which help to support the main deck (where I sleep) sawn in two because they creak tremendously.

It is now blowing hard again, and we have just been taken right aback; luckily I had lashed my desk to my washing stand or that would have flown off, as well as I off my chair. I don't think I shall know what to make of solid ground under my feet.

The little goat* is very well, and gives plenty of milk, which is a great resource, as the tea and coffee are beastly.

The days seem to slip away, one can't tell how. I sit on deck from breakfast at 9 till dinner at 4, and then again till it gets cold, and then to bed.

Your affte. LDG.

To Alexander Duff Gordon. Friday 9 August, becalmed under a vertical sun. Lat 17 degrees or thereabouts.

Dearest Alick,

Today the sun is vertical and invisible, the sea glassy and heaving. I have been ill again, spitting blood, and obliged to lie still. It is madness for an invalid to come in a lower deck cabin: one is deluged through the scuttle. I have been flooded twice, cot and all, and when shut up the stifling is dreadful. I've caught a cold by 'sleeping with a damp man', as some said. The cabin opposite mine was utterly swamped during the last gale, and I found an Irish soldier in despair. He had got ague, and eight inches of water in his bed, and two feet in the cabin. I looked in and said, he can't stay there – carry him into my cabin and lay him in the bunk. So we got the boy into Sally's bed and cured

---

* Lucie took a goat with her to South Africa, having been told by one of her doctors that goat's milk was beneficial for consumptives.

his fever and ague. Sally had to sleep in a chair and to undress in the boy's wet cabin.

I constantly long for you to be here, though I am not sure you would like the life as I do. All your ideas of it are wrong; the confinement to the poop and the stringent regulations would bore you.

Yr. aff. Toodie

To Alexander Duff Gordon. 17 August, Saturday evening.

Dearest Alick,

Since I last wrote we got into the Southwest monsoon for one day, and I sat up by the steersman in intense enjoyment. A bright sun and glittering blue sea; and we tore along, pitching and tossing the water up like mad. It was glorious. At night I was calmly reposing in my cot, in the middle of the steerage, just behind the main hatchway, when I heard a crashing of rigging and no end of a row on deck. The Captain screamed orders which informed me that we were in the thick of a collision. I lay still and waited till the row or the ship went down; but alas! the other women rushed out like maniacs, and a diabolical scene ensued. Mrs Polson rushed at me, and implored me to get up and support her. I declined, and she clung to the officers and everyone within reach, shrieking and hystericking. Upstairs it was just as bad, and I found myself next day looked on as an infidel by all the women, because I had been cool, and declined to get up and yell. Presently the officers came and told me that a big ship had borne down on us, carried off our flying jib-boom and whisker (the sort of yard to the bowsprit). The Captain says he was never in such imminent danger in his life, as she threatened to swing round and crash into our waist, which would have been a case of going to Davy Jones. Sally was as cool as an icicle, offered me my pea jacket which I declined as I preferred going down comfortably in my cot. Finding she was no use to me, she took a yelling maid in custody. I had no conception that women could behave so ill – such bare, abject cowardice!

I am tolerably well in some respects, but I cough more and more. The doctor on board is worse than useless, and he refused to do anything I asked and wanted to give me all manner of violent drugs; he is only 20, and such a conceited ass.

We have had five court martials and two floggings in eight weeks among seventy men.

30 August. I saw a lovely dolphin three days ago; his body, five feet long, was of a fiery blue-green, and huge tail golden bronze. I was glad he scorned the bait and escaped the hook; he was so beautiful. This is the sea from which Venus rose in her youthful glory. All is young, fresh, serene, and cheerful. We have not seen a sail for weeks and most of the passengers have quarrelled; so I live quite alone, barring the Captain who is very kind to me. The Polsons are a perfect pest.

Your affte Toodie.

To Alexander Duff Gordon. Cape Town, 18 September 1861.

Dearest Alick,

We anchored yesterday morning, and Captain Jamieson, the Port Captain, came with a most kind letter from Sir B. Walker, his gig, and a boat and crew for Sally and the luggage. So I was whipped over the dear old St Lawrence's side in a chair, and have come to a boarding-house where the Jamiesons live. I was tired and dizzy and landsick, and lay down and went to sleep. My room is at least 18 feet high, and contains exactly a bedstead, one straw mattress, one rickety table, one wash-table, two chairs, and a broken looking-glass; no carpet, and a hiatus of three inches between the floor and the door, but all very clean and excellent food. I have not made a bargain yet, but I daresay I shall stay here. My landlady is Dutch, with very suspiciously black hair and eyes. The waiter is an Africander, half Dutch, half Malay, very handsome, and exactly like a French gentleman and as civil.

Mr Adams is going to run away with Miss Polson tonight and marry her tomorrow morning. Her parents have nearly killed her with cruelty, beating, &c.

I can't say how I longed for you all three in one way or another, at sea. Mossey [Maurice] to talk with, you to fancy you liked it; and Baby [Urania] for my own sake. But for her I am glad indeed I left her at home; a passenger ship is no place for children.

Kiss my Rainy [Urania] and my sweet Mossey for me. Thank your mother for her letter. I'll write a line to Mutter now to appease her mind if possible.

Your own Toodie.

To Alexander Duff Gordon. Cape Town, 2 October 1861.

Dearest Alick,

I have had as bad an attack of bronchitis as ever I remember, and been in bed till yesterday. I have a very good doctor, half Italian, half Dane, born at the Cape, and educated at Edinburgh, by name Chiappini.

Cape Town is rather pretty, but beyond words untidy and out of repair. As it is neither paved nor drained, it won't do in hot weather; and I shall migrate 'up country' to a Dutch village. A few days ago I drove to Mr Van de Byl's farm with Mrs Jamieson. Imagine St George's Hill (the most beautiful bits of it), sloping gently up to Table Mountain, with its grey precipices, and intersected with Scotch burns, which water it all the year round, sprinkled with oranges, pomegranates, &c and camellias in abundance. At the streamlets there are the inevitable groups of Malay women washing clothes, and brown babies sprawling about. Yesterday I should have bought a black woman for her beauty, had it been possible. She was carrying a few hundred weight on her head, and was far gone with child; but such stupendous physical perfection I never even imagined. Her face was like the Sphinx, with the same mysterious smile, jet-black; her shape and walk were goddess-like, and the lustre of her skin, teeth, and eyes showed the acme of health. I walked after her as far as her swift pace would let me, in envy and adoration of such stately humanity.

Malay means here Mohammedan. They were Malays, but now embrace every shade from the blackest to the most blooming Englishwoman. Yes, indeed, the emigrant girls turn Malay pretty often, and get thereby husbands who know not billiards and brandy – the two diseases of Cape Town. They risk plurality of wives, and profess Islam; but they get fine clothes and industrious husbands. I am going to see one of the Mullahs with Dr Chiappini soon, and to look at their schools and mosques.

Will you think me mad to have been mixed up in a runaway match? Poor Miss Polson came to me in distraction, her parents having treated her horribly, and then turned her out of doors, and told her to go to Mr Adams. I could not refuse to take her in under the circumstances, and she stayed a week, and we tried all we could to get her parents to let her go to the Dean who kindly offered to take her; but as they would do nothing but curse and threaten to lock her up if they caught her, Mr Adams married her three days ago.

Kiss my chicks for me, dearest Alick. It is very dreary to be away so long. Your ever loving Toodie.

To Alexander Duff Gordon. Cape Town, 28 October 1861.

Dearest Alick,

I have a friendship with one Abdul Jemaalee and his wife Betsy, a couple of old folks who were slaves to Dutch owners, and now keep a fruit shop of a rough sort, with 'Betsy Fruitier' painted on the back of an old tin tray, and hung up by the door of the house. Abdul first bought himself and then his wife, whose missis generously lumped in Betsy's bed-ridden mother. He is a fine handsome old man, and has confided to me that

£5000 would not buy what he is worth now. I have also read the letters written by their son, young Abdul Rachman, now a student at Cairo, and who has been away five years, four at Mecca.

6 November. Yesterday I had a dreadful heartache after Rainy on her little birthday, and even these lovely ranges of distant mountains, coloured like opals in the sunset, did not delight me.

Now I will tell you my impression of the state of society here, as far as I have been able to make out by playing the inquisitive traveller. The Dutch round Cape Town are sulky and dispirited; they regret the slave days and can't bear to pay wages. They hate the Malays who were their slaves, and whose 'insolent prosperity' annoys them, and they don't like the vulgar, bustling English. The English complain that 'the Dutch won't die' and that they are 'the curse of the colony'. But they, too, curse the emancipation, long to flog niggers, and hate the Malays, who work harder and don't drink and who are the only masons, tailors, &c. The Malays also have almost a monopoly on cart-hiring and horse-keeping. As Sally says, 'The English here think the coloured people ought to do the work, and they to get the wages; nothing less would satisfy them.' Few of the English will do anything but lounge, while they abuse the Dutch as lazy and the Malays as thieves, and feel their fingers itch to be at the blacks. The Africanders (Dutch and negro mixed in various proportions) are more or less lazy, dirty and dressy, and the beautiful girls wear pork-pie hats and look very winning and rather fierce. But to them Miss Coutts* and the Bishop have provided formidable rivals. They emptied a

---

* Angela Burdett-Coutts (1814–1906) was a leading Victorian philanthropist, with a particular interest (one shared by Dickens) in reforming 'fallen women', some of whom she had shipped out to Cape Town in 1861. She was also a prominent figure in London society and was made a peeress in 1871. The identity of the Bishop remains obscure; he was undoubtedly one of her many philanthropic collaborators.

shipload of young ladies from a 'Reformatory' [in England] into the streets of Cape Town, and what in London is called a 'pretty housebreaker' is here know as 'one of Miss Coutts's young ladies'. Miss Coutts is the Venus (not Urania) of Cape Town. See how a change of hemisphere will reverse reputations.

Simon's Bay, 18 November. I came on here in a cart as I felt ill from the return of the cold weather. What a divine spot! A sort of glorified Scotland, with sunshine, flowers and orange groves.

It is such a luxury to sleep on a real mattress, not stuffed with dirty straw; and to eat clean food, and live in a nice room. But my cough is very bad, and the cruel wind blows on and on. I saw the doctor of the naval hospital today, who advises me to go up to Caledon, seventy miles inland, away from the dreadful south-easter. I have no blood-spitting, but a very bad cough & immense expectoration, and I feel poorly and always cold.

I have spent £60 in two months. 15s a day is the least we can live for in Cape Town, or elsewhere, and washing, travelling, chemist's bills – all enormous. Thirty shillings for a cart here – twelve miles.

I do so long for Baby. A Madagascar woman offered to give me her orphan grandchild, a sweet brown fairy, six years old, with long, silky black hair, and such gorgeous eyes. The child hung about me incessantly.

Your aff. Toodie.

To Alexander Duff Gordon. Caledon, 9 December 1861.

Dearest Alick,

After I wrote last, I had another attack of bronchitis, owing to the renewed cold weather. Simon's Bay is decidedly colder than Cape Town. The naval surgeon of the Simon's Bay hospital came to see me, Dr Shea. He said I should never get right if I remained on the coast where the south-easter is worst, and ordered me off to Caledon at once. He made a bargain for me for a light Malay cart (a capital vehicle with two wheels) and four horses, for 30s a day; three days to Caledon from Simon's Bay; about 100 miles or so.

Luckily on Saturday the wind dropped, and we started at nine o'clock. Sally and I sat behind, and our brown Malay coachman, Choslullah, with his mushroom hat, in front, with my bath and box, and a miniature of himself about seven years old – a nephew – so small and handy, and with preternaturally quiet ways and a pretty baby face. At Erste River we slept in a pretty old Dutch house, kept by an Englishwoman and called the Fox and Hounds, 'to sound like home, my Lady'. The beauty of the country beats all description. Ranges of mountains beyond belief fantastic in shape, and between them a rolling country, desolate and wild, and covered with gorgeous flowers.

We got to Caledon at eleven and drove to an inn which I find is kept by an English ex-officer, Captain Davies, and a very nice ladylike wife, all very clean and neat.

I have had no return of bloodspitting since I came here, and am much stronger. I shall try this place and if it does not answer I will make another sea voyage home by Australia or S America. I can't tell you how I longed for you on my journey here. You would have been so delighted with the country and the queer turn-out – the wild little horses, and the polite and delicately clean Muslim driver. Nearly all the people in the village here are Dutch. The coloured population is a sad spectacle, so drunken and sullen-looking. Harvest is now going on, and the so-called Hottentots are earning 2s 6d a day, with rations and wine; but all the money goes at the canteen in drink and the poor wretches – men and women – are drunk all day, and look wasted and degraded.

Goodbye, dearest Alick. I begin to think the time very long before I get home. I weary after Rainy sadly. Love to Charly [Charlotte Austin]. I am very grateful for her letters about the brats – tell her so.

Yours ever affly LDG

To Alexander Duff Gordon. 29 December 1861.

Dearest Alick,

Last mail brought no letter from you and had it not been for your mother's, I should have been in a fever of anxiety. I harassed the poor old Dutch postmaster till his life was a burden to him, and got Captain Jamieson to enquire and ascertain that none came.

I am beginning now really to feel better. I think my cough is less, and the expectoration not so great, and I eat a great deal more. The glorious African sun blazes and roasts one, and the cool fresh breezes prevent one from feeling languid. I walk from six till eight or nine, breakfast at ten, dine at three; and in the afternoon it is generally practicable to saunter again, now the weather is warmer. I sleep from twelve till two. On Christmas eve it was so warm that I lay in bed with the window wide open, and the stars blazing in. Such stars! They are much brighter than our moon.

I wish so you were here to see the curious ways and new aspect of everything. This village which is very like Rochefort, but hardly so large, is the *chef lieu* of a district the size of one-third of England. A civil commander resides here, a sort of *préfet*, and there is an embryo market-place, with a bell hanging in a brick arch.

7 Jan. For the last four days it has again been blowing a wintery hurricane, and I am not so well, and have even had a very slight tinge of blood in the expectoration.

I hope my long yarns won't bore you. I put down what seems new and amusing to me at the time, but by the time it reaches you, it will seem very dull and commonplace.

15 Jan. No mail in yet. I am getting quite worried about letters from home.

One unpleasant sight here is the skeletons of horses and oxen along the roadside; or at times a fresh carcase surrounded by a convocation of parsonic-looking, huge carrion crows, with neat white neck-cloths. The skeletons look like wrecks, and make you feel very lonely on the wide veld.

17 Jan. Again the mail has come and brings me a letter from Tom [Taylor] and Mutter and again not a line from you. It really is cruel of the Col. Office people, for I hardly suppose you would forget to write for two successive months. I must leave this to answer the letters I have received. Sally is in despair at not hearing from home. I only trust no calamity has happened to Janet or any of you, to cause such complete silence from home; but it quite poisons my life here, the feeling that it may be so.

Farewell. Yours ever, LDG.

To Alexander Duff Gordon. Caledon, Sunday.

Dearest Alick,

I have just received both packets, and I therefore believe the fault was at Cape Town. I wrote to Mr Adams there who ferreted them out for me, after the brutes had told Captain Jamieson there was nothing for me. I must send off letters in an hour or two, so I have not time to read all I have received, but your letters are charming.

My dear Alick, you must have fallen into second childhood to think of *printing* such rambling hasty scrawls as I write.* I never could write a good letter; and unless I gallop as hard as I

---

* Alexander suggested in his letter to Lucie that she publish a selection of her letters from South Africa, both on account of their intrinsic interest and also because the book would help defray the expense of her travels. Though Lucie initially demurred, George Meredith was consulted and with his encouragement, Lucie's *Letters from the Cape*, selected and edited by Sarah Austin, were eventually published in 1864. From this point onward in Lucie's correspondence, she was aware of the possibility of a larger audience for her letters: she 'galloped' on just as fearlessly, but also with an eye to the telling incident, and the social, political and moral implications of what she observed. Heretofore she had written to her family and friends; now she begins to write to a larger audience beyond her family circle, including, of course, us.

can and don't stop to think, I can say nothing; so all is confused and unconnected; only I fancy *you* will be amused by some of my impressions.

I have written to Mutter an accurate account of my health. But for the cough and pain in the chest, I should say I was getting well, but that does not mend. At times it is much better, then again it is very troublesome. Last night I coughed continually – not very violently though; and the spitting diminishes a little in quantity, but is thick, sticky and yellow – no blood except now and then – just a tinge. It is better to tell you exactly so as not to cause anxiety or disappointment. You must gather how much stronger I am. The cessation of blood-spitting enables me to eat and drink, and never to lie in bed. I am never up later than six, dressed and out of doors, now the weather makes it possible. Surprising how little sleep one wants; I go to bed at ten, and often am up at four. The cough is the only stubborn fact. Give my love to Tom and H. Reeve, who have written, and to dear Charly, whose letters [about Urania] are a great solace. I am sure she will forgive my not writing to her, and your mother too. I really cannot do more than write you a good yarn, and one to Mutter. I make no comments on any of your news – what's the use at this distance?

Kiss my darlings, and don't try to send Mossey to sea. I love it myself, but the life does not develop much expansion of mind. There seems to be more small gossip on board a man-of-war than in a boarding school for girls.

Dear Rainy! I am glad you take to her so much. I think she is very promising. I received a message from my Malay friends, Abdul Jemaalee and Betsy, anxious to know 'if the Missis had good news of her children – for bad news would make her sick'. Old Betsy and I used to prose about young Abdul Rachman and his studies at Mecca, and about Janet and Mossey and Rainy, with more real heartiness than you can fancy. We were not afraid of boring each other, and pious old Abdul sat and nodded, and said, 'may Allah protect them all!' as a refrain – 'Allah-il-Allah!'

Your most affte Toodie.

To Alexander Duff Gordon. Caledon, 28 January 1862.

Dearest Alick,

Well, I have been to Genadendal and seen the 'blooming parish', and a lovely spot it is. A large village nestled in a deep valley, surrounded by high mountains on three sides, and a lower range in front.

I asked one of the Herrenhut brethren there if there were any real Hottentots, and he said, 'Yes, one,' and next morning, as I sat waiting under the big oak trees in the Plaats (square), he came up, followed by a tiny old man hobbling along with a long stick to support him. 'Here,' said he, 'is the *last* Hottentot; he is a hundred and seven years old, and lives all alone.' I looked on the little, wizened, yellow face, and was shocked that he should be dragged like a wild beast to be stared at. A feeling of pity which felt like remorse fell upon me, and my eyes filled as I rose and stood before him, so tall and like a tyrant and oppressor, while he uncovered his poor little old snow-white head, and peered up in my face. I led him to the seat, and helped him to sit down, and said in Dutch, 'Father, I hope you are not tired; you are old.' He saw and heard as well as ever, and spoke good Dutch in a firm voice. 'Yes, I am above a hundred years old, and alone – quite alone.' I sat beside him, and he put his head on one side, and looked curiously up at me with his faded but still piercing little wild eyes. Perhaps he had a perception of what I felt – yet I hardly think so; perhaps he thought I was in trouble, for he crept close up to me, and put one tiny brown paw into my hand, and stroked me with the other, and asked (like most coloured people) if I had children. I said, 'Yes, at home in England.' And he patted my hand again, and said, 'God bless them!' It was a relief to feel that he was pleased, for I should have felt like a murderer if my curiosity had added a moment's pain to so tragic a fate.

This may sound like sentimentalism, but you cannot conceive the effect of looking on the last of a race once the owners of all this land, and now utterly gone. His look was not quite human, physically speaking; a good head, small wild-beast eyes, piercing and restless; cheek-bones strangely high and prominent, nose quite flat, mouth rather wide; thin, shapeless lips, and an indescribably small, long, pointed chin, with just a very little soft white wool; his head covered with quite close, extremely short white wool. Hands and feet like an English child of seven or eight, and person about the size of a child of eleven. He had all his teeth, and though shrunk to nothing, was very little wrinkled in the face, and not at all in the hands, which were dark brown while his face was yellow. His manner and way of speaking were like those of an old peasant in England, only his voice was clearer and stronger, and his perceptions not blunted by age. He had travelled with one of the missionaries in the year 1790 or thereabouts, and remained with them ever since.

All Genadendal is wonderfully fruitful, being well watered, but it is not healthy for whites — too hot and damp. There are three or four thousand coloured people there, under the control of the missionaries, who allow no canteens at all. The people may have what they please at home, but no public drinking place is allowed, and we had to take our own beer and wine for the three days. The girls are said to be immoral. As to that, there are no so-called 'morals' among the coloured people, and how or why should there be? It is an honour to have a child by a white man and it is a degradation to him to marry a dark girl. An old Dutchman boasted here one day of having had sixteen children born on his farm of his own begetting in one day. A pious, stiff old Dutch woman, who came here for the sacrament the other day which takes place twice a year, had one girl with her big with child by her son (who also came for the sacrament), and two in the straw at home by the other son — this caused her exactly as much emotion as I feel when my cat kittens. No one takes any notice either to blame or to nurse the poor things; they scramble through it as pussy does.

The English are almost as contemptuous; but there is one great difference. My English host always calls a black 'a d–d nigger', but if that 'nigger' is wronged or oppressed he fights for him, or bails him out, and an English jury gives a just verdict; while a Dutch one simply finds for a Dutchman, against anyone else, and *always* against a dark man. I believe this to be true from what I have seen and heard; and certainly the coloured people have a wonderful preference for the English.

19 Feb. The post came in late last night. Again there is none from you, and it is certain that your November letter was never sent till a month later. It is too bad. The post goes out this evening, and the hot wind is blowing, so I really can only write to you, and a line to Mutter. I feel really better now. A clergyman told me that he came here some years ago with one lung gone and the other diseased, and that he went through six months of the process of coughing and spitting exactly as I do, only worse, and at the end of it was quite well. The red mark in my cheek has nearly vanished. I cough much less and have no more pain. I think the constant eating of grapes has done me much good.

Goodbye, dearest Alick. I have no time for more before the post.

Yours ever, LDG.

To Alexander Duff Gordon. Caledon, 21 February 1862.

Dearest Alick,

This morning's post brought your packet. I think you may as well keep my letters [for publication] for a great deal I have seen and told is new to me, and I might turn an honest penny out of them when I get home. Ask Meredith what he thinks.

I feel it is very selfish of me to come and leave you to dullness and discomfort; but if I really do get materially better, it will have been worthwhile – for I could never have survived the winter at home, and even a monthly letter is (I hope) better than a funeral.

God bless you all.

Yours ever, LDG.

To Alexander Duff Gordon. Worcester, Sunday, 2 March 1862.

Dearest Alick,

Oh, such a journey here! Such country! Pearly mountains and deep blue sky, and an impassable pass to walk down, and baboons and secretary birds, and tortoises. I couldn't sleep for it all last night, tired as I was with the unutterably bad road.

To those who think voyages and travels tiresome, my delight in the new birds and beasts and people must seem very stupid. I can't help it if it does, and am not ashamed to confess that I feel the old sort of enchanted wonder with which I used to read Cook's Voyages, and the like, as a child. It is very coarse and unintellectual of me; but I would rather see this now, at my age, than Italy; the fresh, new, beautiful nature is a second youth – or childhood – *si vous voulez*. The only drawback is the thought of you, dull and worried at home. I do wish you were here to try a day of this wild travelling. I really think it would amuse you. Tomorrow we shall cross the highest pass I have yet crossed, and sleep at Paarl – then Stellenbosch, then Cape Town. For anyone out of health and in pocket, I should certainly prescribe South Africa. When I look back upon my dreary, lonely prison at Ventnor, I wonder I survived it at all.

Cape Town, 7 March. Here I am in my old room, looking over the beautiful bay, quite at home again. It blew all day yesterday, and having got rather a sore throat, I stayed in bed, and today is all bright and beautiful. But Cape Town looks quite murky after Caledon and Worcester; there is, to my eye, quite a haze over the mountains, and they look so far off and so indistinct. All is comparative in this world, even African skies.

I hear that two Indiamen [ships], the *Barham* and the *Camperdown* touch here next month. If I don't get a Queen's ship to take me, I shall go in one of these. I am told the *Barham* is the fastest, and the *Camperdown* the most comfortable, but mortal slow. If I find this confirmed, I shall take the *Camperdown* and have all the sea I can for my money. So don't be alarmed if I am three weeks or so after the time that might reasonably be expected. I feel that it would be madness to risk arriving just a little too soon in the Channel after the glorious heat here now, and have a great idea that the voyage will do me more good now than the voyage out did — provided I time it well. To gratify the impatience I now feel and come back to a fresh cold on arriving would be too foolish after so long taking patience.

The Adamses are still here. She is *enceinte*, and her parents have made a sort of half reconciliation, but insist on her stopping here till after her confinement, and torment her incessantly, so that she is really ill with worry.

I have still £25 left out of my second £100, after paying for the cart £12. So if I get my passage home for £70, I shall remit £100 back to you by next mail, and I think the journey will not have cost extravagantly. My living here will be about £30. I hope you think I have been a good child and not squandered your money. If my letters turn out amusing enough, on reconsideration we will make them pay chief part of the expense, and if I remain really better after getting back, you will be glad I came.

15 March. I went to see my old Malay friends and to buy a watermelon. They were in all the misery of Ramadan. Betsy very thin and seedy, and the pious old Abdul sitting on a little barrel waiting for sunset to fall to on the supper which old Betsy was setting out. He was silent, and the corners of his mouth were drawn down just like yours at an evening party. I am all the worse for my return to Cape Town, and its bad

climate, dust, stink, mosquitoes and bugs; my cough has returned, and I shall be glad to get to sea again.

Friday, 21 March. I am just come from prayer at the mosque on the outskirts of town. A most striking sight. A large room, like a county ballroom, with glass chandeliers, carpeted with common carpet, all but a space at the entrance, railed off for shoes; the *Caaba* and pulpit at one end; over the niche, a crescent painted; and over the entrance door a crescent, an Arabic inscription, and the royal arms of England! A fat, jolly Mullah looked amazed as I ascended the steps, but when I touched my forehead and said *Salaam Aleikum* [Peace be upon you], he laughed and said, '*Salaam, salaam*, come in, come in.' The faithful poured in, all neatly dressed in their loose, drab trousers, blue jackets, and red handkerchiefs on their heads; they left their wooden clogs in company with my shoes, and proceeded, as it appeared, to strip. Off went jackets, waistcoats, and trousers, with the dexterity of a pantomime transformation; the red handkerchief was replaced by a white skull-cap, and a long, large white shirt and full white trousers flowed around them. How it had all been stuffed into the trim jacket and trousers, one could not conceive. Gay sashes and scarves were pulled out of a little bundle in a clean silk handkerchief, and a towel served as prayer-carpet. In a moment the whole scene was as oriental as if the Hansom cab I had come in existed no more. Women suckled their children and boys played among the clogs and shoes all the time, and I sat on the floor in a remote corner. The chanting was very fine, and the whole ceremony very decorous and solemn. It lasted an hour; and then the little heaps of garments were put on, and the congregation dispersed. I am quite in a fever to be under weigh for England. Best love to Charly and to your mother. I have written to Mutter. Kiss Mossey and Baby for me, and my dear Janet if she is arrived.★

★ Janet and her husband Henry Ross returned from Alexandria to England in the spring of 1862 because Janet was expecting a child in the late summer.

God bless you, dearest Alick. I do long to be at home again with you and the chicks.

Yr. ever affte. LDG.

To Alexander Duff Gordon. Cape Town, Sunday 23 March 1862

Dearest Alick,

I went on the last evening of Ramadan to the mosque. Priests, men, women, and English crowded in and out. The English behaved *à l'Anglaise* – pushed each other, laughed, sneered, and made beasts of themselves. I asked a handsome stately priest, in a red turban, to explain the affair to me, and in a few minutes found myself supplied by one Mullah with a chair, and by another with a cup of tea, and was, in short, in the midst of a Malay soirée. They spoke English very little, but made up for it by their usual good breeding and intelligence. It was a quaint sensation to sit in a mosque, behaving as if at an evening party, in a little circle of poor Muslim priests.

15 April. Your letters arrived yesterday, to my great delight. I have been worrying about a ship, and was very near sailing today by the *Queen of the South*, at twenty-four hours' notice, but I have resolved to wait for the *Camperdown*.

I am not as well as I was at Caledon, and have very slight threatenings of blood-spitting again, so I am all the more anxious to have a voyage likely to do me good instead of harm. I am persuaded that Cape Town is not healthy; indeed, the town can't be, from its stench and dirt. I feared you would think me dilatory if I waited for a sailing ship, and I felt anxious and nervous about getting home, until I found that you too thought I had better be home after June than before. I am to pay £65 by the *Camperdown* for an upper-deck cabin, next to the stern cabin. I hope you won't think me extravagant if I don't bring home any money. It is so very tempting to bring a few things so unknown in England. I have a glorious blanket of sheepskins for you, sewn and dressed so that moths and fleas won't stay near it. It will make a grand railway rug and outside car covering. I have bought three and a springbok caross for somebody — Janet if she likes. But I have still £115 – £50 over my passage money, and don't owe anything but Dr Chiappini and two days lodgings. I keep always paid up. The staying on here of course costs more. It is so much dearer than Caledon in everything.

Well I must say goodbye. Love to all at home and kisses for my Rainy.

Your own Toodie.

To Alexander Duff Gordon. Cape Town, 8 May 1862.

Dearest Alick,

At last, I shall sail on Saturday the 10th, per ship *Camperdown*, for East India Docks. The mail has come in just now, but brings no letters for me. These weary six weeks [of waiting for the *Camperdown*] have cost money and temper no end. I have been quite eating my heart out at the delay, but it was utterly impossible to go by any of the Indian ships. Sally has just come back from the ship, where she spent the day with the carpenter; and I am to go on board tomorrow, and sail on Saturday, so you may expect us not before the middle of July. We may stop at St Helena for cargo, so if I don't come to hand so soon, lay it to that.

Will you ask Ross to cause inquiries to be made among the Mullahs of Cairo for a Hadji, by name, Abdul Rachman, the son of Abdul Jemaalee, of Cape Town, and if possible, to get the enclosed letter sent to him? The poor people are in sad anxiety for their son, of whom they have not heard for four months, and that an old letter. Henry will thus have a part of all the blessings which were solemnly invoked on me by poor Abdul, who is getting very infirm, but toddled up and cracked his old fingers over my head and invoked the protection of

Allah with all form; besides that Betsy sent me twelve dozen oranges and lemons. Abdul Rachman is about twenty-six, a Malay of Cape Town, speaks Dutch and English, and is supposed to be studying theology at Cairo.

I won't enter upon my longings to be home again, and to see you all. I have really fretted all last month at the loss of time.

God bless you all, and kiss my darlings, all three.

Your own Toodie.

To Alexander Duff Gordon. On board the good ship Camperdown, *500 miles northwest of Table Bay, lat. and long. unknown, 16 May 1862.*

Dearest Alick,

I embarked from Table Bay this day week, and found a good airy cabin, and all very comfortable. We are only twelve first-class passengers. The captain is a delightful fellow, with a very charming young wife. There is only one child (a great comfort), a capital cook, and universal civility and quietness. Compared with the *St Lawrence*, it is like a private house to a railway hotel. Six of the passengers are invalids, more or less: Mr Porter, the Attorney General of the Cape, is over-worked, and going home for health to Ireland; two men, both with delicate chests, and one poor young fellow from Cape Town in a consumption, who, I fear, will not outlive the voyage. The doctor is very civil, and very kind to the sick; but I stick to the cook, and am quite greedy over the good fare, after the atrocious food of the Cape.

One can wander all over the ship here, instead of being a prisoner on the poop; and I even have paid my footing on the forecastle. Sally thinks you would be immensely amused to see her slung up atop of the cabin in a hammock, for there was not room for a bunk.

The little goat was as rejoiced to be afloat again as her mistress, and is a regular pet on board, with the run of the quarter-deck. She still gives milk and is not *enceinte* after all. The butcher, who has the care of her, cockers her up with dainties, and she begs biscuits of the cook. Mossey's tortoises are in my cabin and seem very happy.

The other day we saw a shoal of porpoises amounting to many hundreds, if not thousands, who came frisking round the ship. When we first saw them, they looked like a line of breakers; they made such a splash, and they jumped right out of the water three feet in height, glittering green and bronze in the sun. Such a pretty, merry set of fellows!

We shall touch at St Helena, where I shall leave this letter to go by the mail steamer, that you may know a few weeks before I arrive how comfortably my voyage has begun.

It is very provoking to be so much longer separated from you all than I had hoped, but I really believe that the bad air and discomfort of the other ships would have done me serious injury; while here I have every chance of benefiting to the utmost, and having mild weather the whole way, besides the utmost amount of comfort possible on board ship. There are some cockroaches, indeed, but that is the only drawback. The Camperdown is fourteen years old, and was the crack ship to India in her day. Now she takes cargo and poop-passengers only, and of course only gets invalids and people who care more for comfort than speed.

Monday evening, May 26th. Yesterday a large shark paid us a visit, with his suite of three pretty little pilot fish, striped like zebras, who swam over his back.

My poor goat died suddenly the other day, to the general grief of the ship; also one of the tortoises. The poor consumptive lad is wonderfully better. But all the passengers were very sea sick during the rough weather, except Sally and I, who are quite old salts. Last week we saw a young whale, a baby, about thirty feet long, and had a good view of him as he played round the ship.

I hope you won't expect too much in the way of

improvement in my health. I really don't know quite what to think. The blood-spitting is now next to nothing, but not quite gone, and the cough and spitting is troublesome – not bad, but permanent, i.e., I am never twenty-four hours free from it. Sometimes I think that it looks like consumption – sometimes that it is an improvement. The Cape doctors don't use the stethoscope, and call nothing consumption that does not kill in six weeks. So it is no use speculating till I see English doctors again.

I look forward, oh so eagerly, to being with you again, and with my brats, big and little. God bless you all.

Yours ever. Toodie.

Part III

NOOR ALA NOOR

Chapter Ten

In late July 1862 – almost exactly a year after Lucie sailed for the Cape – the *Camperdown*, with its cargo of invalids, reached the East India Docks in London. Alexander had been keeping an eye on the shipping announcements in the newspapers for days and now was on the pier, waving a white handkerchief, as the boat hove into port. A reunion on the crowded dock, and then a rush for Victoria Station and the express train to Esher where Lucie, after twelve long months, once more embraced her 'brats, big and little': Urania, no longer a baby but a solid little girl of three, Maurice grown tall and thin, and Janet ponderous but still riding (though no longer hunting) in the eighth month of her pregnancy.

A homecoming (the Gordon Arms' lodgers had departed), but, it soon became clear, only a fleeting one. Two days after arriving home, Lucie took the train back to London and saw one of Lady Duff Gordon's retinue of medical specialists – a Dr De Mussy, an expert on lung complaints, who examined Lucie with a stethoscope. De Mussy's verdict was that she showed some improvement, but was not cured. He advised Lucie to depart as soon as possible for a warmer climate: Eaux Bonnes in the Pyrenees for the summer and then on to Egypt when autumn and winter closed in.

Other specialists were also consulted in the hope that they might have a more sanguine opinion. None did. In early August, Sarah Austin wrote to her old friend St Hilaire. 'An hour since I heard the sentence which condemns me to another year's separation from my dear Lucie! Her doctors . . . decided that she must leave England again. When Dr Walsh and De Mussy advised her to go at once to Eaux Bonnes and thence to Cairo, Lucie asked them whether this kind of life was to continue; they declared that if she followed their orders there was . . . hope that her health might be re-established in two years. To this everything must give way, and I shall see her depart with quite different feelings from those of last year. But, my friend, for me, at my age, a year is long; and when I received Alexander's letter announcing the decision, I thought I should die.'

Despite the specialists' opinion that Lucie still might recover in the long run, she and Alexander agreed they must give up the Gordon Arms – a melancholy decision reflecting their doubts that they and the children would ever live together again as a family. Lucie and Sally began packing her trunks again, while all around them Janet supervised the dismantling of the Gordon Arms: the throwing away of old toys, broken crockery, torn linen and outworn clothes, of sheafs of manuscript, letters, papers, theatre and concert programmes. And then the wrapping up and packing away of what remained, to be put into storage. It must have seemed to Lucie the breakdown and dispersal to the winds of her life.

Soon everyone was packing: Maurice to return to Eton, little Urania to go back to her great-aunt Charlotte Austin, Alexander to move in with the Duff Gordons' old friend, the dramatist and journalist Tom Taylor, who had recently married and now lived with his young wife in Clapham. Janet and Henry Ross, too, would soon be off. After the birth of their child in early September, they planned to go to the continent before returning to Alexandria in the new year. With the Rosses' departure, the Gordon Arms would be closed up and advertised for sale.

★

On 20 August, Lucie and Alexander set off for France and travelled by stages through Lisieux, Tours, and Angoulême to Pau, and then finally to Eaux Bonnes on the border of Spain. But here the 'good waters' poured from the sky as well as the spa springs; it was cold and rainy and Lucie fell ill with her old enemies: a sore throat and cough. Then harrowing news from

Esher precipitated a complete relapse with fever and blood-spitting. Just two days after Lucie and Alexander left home, Henry Ross fell ill of typhoid fever and for some weeks it seemed doubtful he would survive. Janet, who was now nine months pregnant, spent day and night at her husband's bedside nursing him, determined that if he must die, he would not do so alone; she would be there to help him out of the world. In a crisis, wayward, selfish Janet was splendid: strong, brave and, most surprising of all, compassionate. As Sarah Austin described it, 'this young woman, apparently so giddy, seemingly caring for no one, only thinking of her own amusement, shows a devotion and a courage which astonishes every one. Never a word of complaint, never an allusion to her own condition.'

At last, in early September, Lucie had a telegram in Eaux Bonnes with the doubly good news that Ross was out of danger and that on 8 September Janet had had a baby boy whom she named, after the most important person in her life, Alexander Gordon Ross. The birth had been a long and difficult ordeal, and almost as soon as it was over, Janet announced that she would never endure another. And to Sarah Austin and close friends she also declared that she had no idea how she had ever got pregnant – she insisted that she must have been drugged. However attentive and self-sacrificing Janet had been at her husband's sickbed, she never had any intention of performing as a mother. As one friend put it, Janet was like a salmon that swims upriver to spawn and then blithely swims out to sea again to get on with her life. Before little Alexander Gordon Ross was many weeks old, he was sent off to a wet nurse named Mrs Walsh in Godalming, and he remained there when Janet and Henry sailed back to Egypt the following January.

When Lucie was well enough to leave Eaux Bonnes, she and Alexander went to Marseilles, where they were able to stay with some of Sarah Austin's Taylor relatives. But by this time Alexander was due back at his Inland Revenue office in London. He and Lucie parted with less hope than they'd felt when Lucie sailed to South Africa the previous year. Now another year-long separation stretched ahead of them, and they no longer had a settled home where they could end it if Lucie somehow recovered in Egypt.

Marseilles was almost as disagreeable, wet and cold as Eaux Bonnes, and Lucie and Sally soon set off on their own for the port of Leghorn to await a steamer with the appropriately eastern name, the *Byzantine*, on which they had booked passage to Alexandria. *En route* to Leghorn they stopped briefly at Genoa and Pisa. Lucie dashed off a note to her mother that the weather was 'delicious', but 'sickness and sightseeing are not compatible, alas!' They cooled their heels at a miserable inn at Leghorn for several days, and then with great relief embarked on the *Byzantine* on 13 October.

As had been the case when she sailed to and from South Africa, Lucie thrived at sea. She put this down now to the warm, tropical air of the Mediterranean, but it must have been the sensation of being unmoored – of liberation – that also gave her a sense of both physical and mental well-being whenever she was on a boat, no matter how stormy the passage. In addition, the *Byzantine* had precisely the sort of dramatis personae and ambiance to delight her. No cargo of invalids on this voyage. Instead, Lucie's fellow travellers included: 'French café *chantant* women, an Italian opera troupe, a Spanish consul the image of Don Quixote, four Levantine ladies with 50 peacock power of voice and the best natured creatures possible, Italians, Algerians, Egyptians, I for England and one poor Parisienne on her way to sing at Cairo. No discipline, no order, but plenty of good nature.'

★

On 26 October the *Byzantine* reached Alexandria, and Lucie's colourful seafaring companions disappeared down the maze of winding, dusty streets, leaving Lucie and Sally to find their own way to the Rosses' apartment, quite deserted except for the Egyptian servants. Even Sally's sister, Ellen Naldrett, who was

Lucie Duff Gordon

An engraving from the Henry Phillips painting of Lucie with her signature. This was the frontispiece for several editions of *Letters from Egypt* published after Lucie's death.

Studio photograph of Lucie's devoted dragoman Omar Abu Halaweh ('Father of the Sweets'). After hiring him, Lucie wrote home, 'He is graceful and pleasing and seems to deserve his name.' Her maid, Sally Naldrett, agreed.

View of Luxor Temple from the Nile. By David Roberts.

The entrance to Luxor Temple in the 1860s when it was still submerged in sand. In between the two colossal heads of Ramesses II are a donkey led by a child, and a water carrier holding his heavy skin of water as he chats with another man. Two more men stand to the left of the entrance, and to the right a guard stands erect before the head of Ramesses.

A photograph by Antonio Beato of the crowded village built inside and on top of Luxor Temple. In the distance is the minaret of the mosque of Abu el-Haggag, where Lucie was fêted. It is the only village structure that survived the clearance of the temple in the 1880s, and it remains within the temple today.

In this view of the southern end of Luxor Temple, Lucie's house is clearly discernible: it is the white box-like building to the left of the flag pole.

Enormous graffiti scratched by Prince Pückler-Muskau into a pillar at the Ramesseum, the mortuary temple of Ramesses II, at Thebes. When Lucie saw his name similarly inscribed at Abu Simbel, she wrote home, 'I wish someone would kick him for his profanity.'

Lucie's favourite place in Egypt, Philae Temple, where the Egyptian goddess Isis found the heart of her dead husband, Osiris.

Alexander Duff Gordon the year after Lucie's death, a photograph pasted into the diary of his mother, Lady Duff Gordon.

Janet Ross in old age, seated at Lucie Duff Gordon's desk. The Henry Phillips portrait of Lucie is just discernible, hung high above the desk. The bust to Janet's right is of Alexander Duff Gordon.

Lucie Duff Gordon's grave in Cairo. The photo was taken by her great-grandson, Gordon Waterfield, in the 1930s.

Janet's maid, was back in England with her mistress. The Rosses' home was spacious and quiet, full of the books Janet had shipped from England, and on the roof Henry Ross, a great gardener, had created a delightful garden from which one could view the entire city.

Initially, there was little other than this roof-top oasis that gave Lucie any pleasure in her new surroundings. She was, in fact, repelled by Alexandria. When she ventured out to shop in the bazaar or merely to take a walk in the evenings, she was assailed by the noise, dirt, congestion and general chaos of the street life: 'everybody bawls as loud as they can . . . [and] I am maddened with the dearness of everything', she wrote to Alexander. 'All is *triste*, nay profoundly melancholy. The peoples' faces, the surface of the country, the dirt, the horrible wretchedness, the whacking of the little boys and girls . . . The children are mostly hideous . . . and cry incessantly.'

During these first few days in Egypt, Lucie fought a rising sense of panic, and the impulse to bolt and take the first ship back to Europe. She confessed to Alexander, 'I regret more than I can say that I ever came here.' The Cape had been a colony and thus in some sense familiar and comprehensible. Egypt was a foreign land. And its foreignness made Lucie feel profoundly dislocated and alone. Her isolation was intensified by the fact that she couldn't communicate with anyone because she didn't know Arabic – to European ears, a verbose and histrionic language which grated on Lucie's nerves. Surrounded by 'bawling' voices she couldn't understand and signs she couldn't read, stared at whenever she ventured out, fearing that she was being cheated and mocked in the bazaar, Lucie felt vulnerable and disoriented.

She was also unwell. The benefits of the sea voyage soon wore off, and she told Alexander that she felt 'very weak and poorly', and had a 'hard, dry and very painful cough'. She found it difficult to sleep at night and it didn't soothe her panicky state of mind when she arose in the morning and threw open the shutters of her bedroom window, and saw directly below a hut in which lived 'a poor woman ... dying of consumption which looks to be very common here, judging from what one sees and the coughs one hears'.

Fortunately, at this juncture two friends of the Rosses called on Lucie and were able to relieve many of her anxieties, help with practical problems, and give her a proper introduction to this strange land in which she felt trapped. The first was Hekekyan Bey, a courtly, English-educated Armenian in his fifties, turned out in dapper western clothes and a tarboosh. Hekekyan was a civil engineer who had been an important adviser to the government until it decreed that all Christians (Hekekyan was a Roman Catholic) be dismissed. In his retirement, he worked on a number of archaeological investigations and became well known to Europeans in Egypt. He had met the Rosses through Nassau Senior, the Austins' old friend who had come out to Egypt in 1855 in a party led by Ferdinand de Lesseps to determine the line of the proposed Suez Canal. Lucie's second visitor was Hekekyan's friend William Thayer, a young American who was Consul-General in Cairo, a bachelor with weak lungs himself.* Hekekyan and Thayer were on the verge of returning to Cairo, where they both lived, and they suggested that Lucie and Sally make the rail journey with them.

But before they departed, Thayer interviewed a number of young Egyptian dragomans for Lucie. Because Lucie and Sally were women and knew no Arabic, they would not be able to manage in Egypt on their own. Most Europeans hired dragomans who were not merely interpreters, but servants, tourist guides and general factotums all rolled into one. Among those who applied for the job of Lucie's dragoman was a slight, handsome young Alexandrian with large, soulful eyes named

---

* In his diary Thayer described Lucie as 'handsome, bright and forty and a capital traveller. She knows the literary people of England but does not gossip about them.'

Omar Abu Halaweh; his wonderful surname, Lucie explained to Alexander, meant 'Father of the Sweets', because Omar came from a family of pastry cooks. He too was a gifted cook (his specialities included lamb stuffed with pistachio nuts and sweetmeats in honey), but even more immediately useful to Lucie was the fact that he spoke fluent English and, according to his glowing references, was absolutely honest. Lucie hired him at a salary of £3 per month plus a greatcoat for the cool Egyptian winter. After her marriage to Alexander, it was the wisest and most important decision of her life.

★

'I write to you out of the real Arabian Nights,' Lucie told her mother in her first letter from Cairo early in November. 'Well may the Prophet (whose name be exalted) smile when he looks on Cairo. It is a golden existence – all sunshine and poetry, and I must add, kindness and civility.'

It had all come right in the end. Even Shepheard's Hotel – 'horribly uncomfortable and damp and monstrously dear' – where Thayer and Hekekyan installed Lucie and Sally until Omar had negotiated for the rent of a boat to take them up the Nile, even 'this horrid Shepheard's Hotel',★ as Lucie called it, couldn't detract from her intoxication with Cairo – and with Egypt. Every morning Omar led Lucie and Sally from the 'Frank' or European quarter of the city into an Egyptian 'golden world' which assailed their English senses – sight,

---

★ I, too, stayed at Shepheard's on my first trip to Egypt. But it wasn't the same 'horrid' Shepheard's in which Lucie and virtually every other European (Anthony Trollope, Amelia Edwards and Edward Lear, among others) quartered in the nineteenth century. The original hotel, built by an Englishman named Samuel Shepheard in the 1840s, stood hard by the lush Ezbekiya Gardens in the European (called 'Frank') quarter of the city. At the turn of the century it was torn down and replaced by a larger, grander, four-storey building with a deep, encircling veranda which became *the* place for expatriates to meet in Cairo. On 'Black Saturday', 26 January 1952, Shepheard's, along with so much else in Cairo, went up in flames. Out of its ashes a new five-star Shepheard's arose: relocated on the Corniche bordering the Nile. With its all-night disco throbbing every night, I often found it horrid enough.

sound, smell and touch. Narrow, winding streets, lined with tall, wooden-latticed houses; minareted mosques with their echoing call to prayer; the date-palms along the river and the white egrets and white-sailed, birdlike feluccas that skimmed along the Nile.

They went to Khan el-Khalili, the labyrinthine, fourteenth-century bazaar in the heart of Old Cairo, to buy pots and pans for Omar to cook with on the boat. 'The transaction lasted an hour. The copper is so much an oka, the workmanship so much, every article is weighed by a sworn weigher and a ticket sent with it. More Arabian Nights. The shopkeeper compares notes with me about [Arabic and European] numerals and is as much amused as I. He treats me to coffee and a pipe from a neighbouring shop while Omar eloquently depreciates the goods and offers half the value. A water seller offers a brass cup of water. I drink and give a huge sum of twopence and he distributes the contents of his skin to the crowd (there always is a crowd) in my honour. It seems I have done a pious action. Finally a boy is called to carry the batterie, the cuisine, while Omar brandishes a gigantic kettle which he has picked up a little bruised for 4 shillings. The boy has a donkey which I mount astride *à l'Arabe* while the boy carries all the copper things on his head. We are a rather grand procession.'

Soon Lucie had picked up 'forty or fifty [Arabic] words ... beside my *Salaam Aleikum* and *baksheesh*'. She went to her first fantasia: 'People feasted all over the house and in the street. Arab music ... women yelled the *zaghareet* [shrill, trilling cries of joy], black servants served sweetmeats, pipes and coffee and behaved as if they belonged to the company and I was strongly under the impression that I was at Nurredin's wedding with the Vizier's daughter.' She was learning very quickly that it was impossible to be lonely or unhappy in Egypt.

Thayer took her to the great Cairo mosques: Ibn Tulun, Sultan Hassan and the Mohammed Ali mosque in the Citadel. They returned home under a full moon 'through endless streets and squares of Moslem tombs – those of the Memlooks among them'. On her donkey, Omar leading it by a rope, Lucie threaded her way through the City of the Dead – that vast graveyard in the desert at the margin of the city.

Hekekyan Bey invited her to dinner at his home in the countryside outside Cairo – 'just their common dinner, a bit of boiled mutton, a dish of vegetable marrow, olives, fruit, bread and water served by a black girl who seemed to have just stepped off the front of a temple'. Lucie didn't mind the plain fare in the least, and she quickly got the hang of eating from a large communal tray with her right hand while sitting cross-legged on the floor. Nothing could have been further away from her dinner parties at the Gordon Arms, the whitebait suppers at the Trafalgar Tavern, the Sunday morning breakfasts at Samuel Rogers's in St James's Place.

After the meal, Hekekyan's wife took her for a walk out in the fields. A solitary Bedouin woman saw them and approached 'to shake hands and look at us. She wore a white sackcloth shift and veil. She asked Mrs Hekekyan a good many questions about me, looked at my face and hands but took no notice of my rather smart gown which the village women admired so much, shook hands again with the air of a princess, wished me health and happiness, and strode off across the graveyard like a stately ghost. She was on a journey all alone, and somehow it looked very solemn and affecting to see her walking towards the desert in the setting sun.'

If her health had improved, Lucie might have been tempted to linger in Cairo indefinitely. The city seemed inexhaustible, and there was much that Lucie had not yet seen, including the Pyramids at Giza and the great Sphinx which, in 1862, was still nearly buried beneath centuries of shifting sands. But before Omar could organize any more expeditions, Lucie's cough got worse; she had also lost a good deal of weight and scarcely slept more than three or four hours a night. She met other invalids at Shepheard's who swore by the curative powers of Upper Egypt, especially if the patient persevered to the Second Cataract beyond Aswan at Wadi Halfa.

After a good deal of protracted, 'Arabian Nights' negotiations at the port of Boulak in north Cairo, Omar found a clean, serviceable boat, the *Zint el-Bachreyn*, with captain, mate, eight men and cabin boy for only £25 a month. Thayer gave Lucie letters of introduction for all the consuls upriver. Lucie had an English flag and American pennant attached to the mast. She wrote to Alexander and her mother, and told them to address letters over the next few months care of the agents' names that Thayer had given her. Omar and Sally carried on board and arranged all their goods, equipment and stores – food, wine, beer, pots and pans, tents, linen, bedding, clothes, an iron, portable bath, medicine box. On 20 November, after pious prayers said by the Muslim crew for the safety and success of their journey, they set sail.

★

In the mind's eye, the map of Egypt hangs like a vast, abstract painting, its large, irregular wedge-like shape tinted an arid yellow, except for the green-fringed, winding blue strip of the Nile which splits it vertically into two uneven halves: the east bounded by the narrow sliver of the Gulf of Suez and the Red Sea and the west by the wastes of the Libyan Desert. Egypt is also split horizontally, though you won't see a river, range of mountains or any other natural feature to mark this division. It is men who have staked out the regions of Lower Egypt (extending, roughly, from Alexandria to Asyut) and Upper Egypt (from Asyut all the way down to Abu Simbel and the Second Cataract at Wadi Halfa in the Nubian desert). And the contrast between Upper and Lower Egypt is not so much geographical as cultural: determined by differences in dialect, customs, religious practices, clothes and even food.

Europeans have always penetrated Egypt from the north and their influence has always been most pronounced in northern or Lower Egypt. Upper Egypt to the south – or the Saeed as it is called by Egyptians – remains less Westernized even today: less 'developed' in some eyes; in others (including, in time, Lucie's), less contaminated or corrupted. And since the days of the Pharaohs, Luxor has been culturally, if not politically, the capital of Upper Egypt.

The very designations of Lower and Upper Egypt are, however, confusing. On the map, Lower Egypt is actually on top, bounded by the scalloped coast of the Mediterranean; while Upper Egypt lies below, merging indistinctly into the Sudan. And if you travel from Alexandria to Luxor, it feels as if you are making a descent – moving from an upper to a lower region rather than the other way round. The further south you move – the lower into the bleached shape of Egypt you penetrate – the further down or deeper do you reach into what Lucie later called its palimpsest reality – shedding accretions and overlayers of European civilization until you find something solid and immutable under it all: a bas-relief of widows wailing on a temple wall; a pitched battle engraved on a lofty column; Osiris, re-membered and whole, reigning in a mirror world beyond this one. It was for Upper Egypt, the Saeed, that Lucie was now bound.

★

But first she was unmoored again, this time on a river rather than the sea – the Nile, the greatest river in the world. In a sense, she already knew the Nile: from Herodotus, whose marvellous accounts of Egypt she had read as a girl, to the Nile's most recent explorers, Burton, Grant and Speke, who several years before Lucie came to Egypt had 'discovered'★ the source of the river: Lake Victoria, some 2,000 miles south of Wadi Halfa.

But as Lucie soon realized, you may read about the Nile for a

---

★ African history is full of momentous 'discoveries' – usually achieved at great loss of life (African as well as European) – of places that had, of course, been known for centuries, if not millennia, to Africans who had travelled their rivers, including the Nile, from their sources to the sea.

lifetime and still not be prepared for its splendour and magic. Small wonder that the ancient Egyptians worshipped it: the Nile blessed their parched land, carving out a ribbon of lush, fertile green soil from the encroaching desert – making life possible. Now Lucie dwelt in this timeless landscape; she recognized it from the Bible, from Herodotus, from the *Arabian Nights*.

Nothing seemed to have changed in the past 500, 1,000, 6,000 years. There was the life-giving river, its banks lined with papyrus and reeds and the bullrushes where Moses had been secreted. Just beyond the river banks lay intensely green fields of beans, clover, maize and sugar-cane. In the distance, farmers followed the tracks of their ploughs; closer at hand, stolid brown oxen trudged round and round, turning the wheels which carried the Nile's water to the fields. Tall, barefoot women in black walked to the river banks, with huge clay water-jars gracefully balanced on their heads. Broad-winged egrets – so large that they looked like children's parchment kites – swooped and flew off, or stood poised, absolutely still, like birds on a Chinese screen, amidst the water reeds on the river's edge.

All this Lucie saw.★ And her heart expanded within her. As the days passed, and Cairo and – more distant still – Europe were left further and further behind, it seemed as if the *Zint el-Bachreyn* was travelling into a heart of light and heat and life. All so familiar yet so fantastic. 'It is all a dream to me,' Lucie wrote to her mother. 'You can't think what an odd effect it is to take up an English book and read it and then to look up and hear the men cry – Yah Mohammed. "Bless thee Bottom, how art thou translated!" [*sic*] It is the reverse of all one's former life when one sat in England and read of the East . . . [I am] in the real, *true* Arabian Nights, and don't know whether "I be I as I suppose I be" or not.'

★ As you will still see it if you go to the Nile today.

Every few days they called in at villages, but these stops did not break the spell of the Nile. At Beni Suef, seventy miles south of Cairo, they halted to buy meat and bread. Dressed in her European clothes, and holding a parasol to protect her from the sun, Lucie 'walked about the streets escorted by Omar in front and two sailors with huge staves behind, and created a sensation accordingly'.

Fleetingly, with Western eyes, she recoiled from what seemed the squalor and dirt of the scene. Then she looked more closely. 'The best houses have neither paint, whitewash, plaster, bricks or windows – nor any visible roofs. They don't give one the notion of human dwellings at all at first, but soon the eye gets used to the absence of all that constitutes a house in Europe, the impression of wretchedness wears off, and one sees how picturesque they are with palm trees and tall pigeon houses and here and there a dome over a saint's tomb.' And then the timelessness of this life struck her again: 'the men at work on the river banks are exactly the same colour as the Nile mud with just the warmer hue of the blood circulating beneath the skin. Prometheus has just formed them out of the universal material at hand and the sun breathed life into them.'

The village women were entranced with Lucie, and grabbed her hands, begging her in Arabic, which Lucie was beginning to understand, to come and eat in their mud houses. 'I have eaten many odd things with odd people in queer places,' she reported home. But if she politely refused to go with the village women, they dashed home and returned with their arms full of bread, sweet butter, milk, dates and eggs. One woman came running with a nondescript, rather threadbare mat which she offered to Lucie with obvious pride. At this point Omar intervened and translated, explaining that the mat was, as Lucie put it, the woman's 'nuptial couch', upon which her marriage had been consummated. It was the most precious gift she could give to Lucie, who told Alexander, 'I treasure it accordingly.'

This present prompted Omar to reminisce about his own

249

marriage the previous year to his young wife Mabrooka, now at home in Alexandria. Certain taboos don't obtain in Egypt. Omar proceeded to give Lucie 'an exact description of his own marriage, the whole ceremony in detail, and did not drop any curtain at all, appealing to my sympathy about the distress of absence from his wife. I intimated that English people were not accustomed to some words and might be shocked.'

Omar in turn was embarrassed when Lucie referred to Alexander by name, or even worse, as 'my husband' – a great indiscretion among Egyptians and other Muslims. Instead, a wife must address her husband and speak of him in the third person as 'the father of' – *Abu* in Arabic – the name of their eldest son or, if there are no sons, the name of their eldest daughter. If there are no children, a good deal of verbal awkwardness and confusion is endured until they come along. If they fail to appear at all, there is almost always a divorce as childlessness is the worst possible tragedy. Alexander, then, became *Abu Maurice* when Lucie spoke of him in Egypt, and in many of her letters to him as well.

The dreamlike days and miles on the Nile unfurled as they moved further and further south. They stopped one day at a village with a Coptic church and Lucie drank coffee with the priest while a crowd 'collected and squatted about . . . and the sheep and cattle pushed in between us, coming home at eve. The venerable old priest looked so like Father Abraham and the whole scene was so pastoral and biblical that I felt quite as if my wish was fulfilled to live a . . . few thousands of years ago. They wanted me to stay many days.'

Lucie was intrigued by the Copts in Egypt, but perhaps because they were not sufficiently foreign, she was never drawn to them as she was to Muslims, and in time she came to share the Muslims' dislike of the Copts, whom they accused of being bigoted, dishonest and harsh to their women. But even Lucie's prejudice against the Copts was another manifestation of her growing identification with what she was coming to feel was the true Egypt, and an indication, too, of her growing alienation from the Europeans whose far grander and larger boats would sometimes pass the *Zint el-Bachreyn*. She was picking up more and more Arabic and could converse in a rudimentary way with her crew and the people she met in the villages where they stopped. She learned to write her name in Arabic and began signing her letters with Arabic flourishes, just as she sometimes dated them by the Islamic calendar.

To Tom Taylor, with whom Alexander was staying in Clapham, Lucie wrote, 'I am in love with Arab ways, and I have contrived to see and know more . . . than many Europeans who have lived here for years . . . I think . . . I must have the "black drop" and that Arabs see it, for I am always told that I am like them, with praises of my former good looks.' By the time she reached Wadi Halfa in February, Lucie felt she had found the key to the structure of this 'golden world' in which she now dwelt: 'This country is a palimpsest in which the Bible is written over Herodotus and the Koran over that. In the towns the Koran is most visible, in the country Herodotus.'

★

'I long to bore you all with travellers' tales,' Lucie wrote home as they began their return journey down the Nile towards Luxor and then on to Cairo. Most of her tales centred on the people she had met rather than the spectacular monuments. Yet these took her breath away too. As they approached Abu Simbel,★ the dry, intense heat was upon them. They rounded a

---

★ Abu Simbel is no longer at the same place as it was when Lucie visited it. In 1964, just over 100 years after she first saw it, the new Aswan Dam threatened to submerge Abu Simbel with the rising waters of Lake Nasser. At a cost of thirty-six million dollars, both the great temple dedicated to Ramesses II and the smaller one dedicated to the goddess Hathor and Ramesses' wife Nefertari were moved to higher ground. This was not a light undertaking. The temples were sawn up into blocks of about twenty tons each (more than 1,000 blocks in all), each carefully numbered. The blocks were then reassembled at the new site, like some vast Lego set. Within the temple an enormous concrete dome was erected to give internal support and also to house an air-conditioned cinema and tea-room where you can watch a film about the elaborate operation while

bend in the river and the four gigantic statues of Ramesses II suddenly leapt into view: vast stone figures which seemed to glow or tremble in the sun, so that one expected them, like some fantastic mirage, to evaporate into the hot desert air. But when Lucie and Omar and Sally left the boat at the river bank and walked up to the great temple and stood before it, feeling like insects in the shadow cast by the gigantic statues, Lucie was incensed at the graffiti which had been carved on them by passing tourists. 'The scribbling of names is quite infamous: beauty defaced by Tomkins and Hobson.' But 'worst of all', she wrote to Alexander, was the work of Sarah Austin's former inamorato: 'Pückler-Muskau has engraved his [name] . . . in huge letters and size on the naked breast of the august and pathetic giant who sits at Abu Simbel. I wish someone would kick him for his profanity.'*

To Sarah Austin, however, Lucie didn't mention Pückler's 'profanity', merely saying of Abu Simbel that it was 'the most imposing thing I ever saw'. She was almost as vague and laconic about the other 'sights' of Upper Egypt, but she nevertheless saw almost everything then visible after centuries of sandstorms had left nearly all the monuments in Egypt deeply buried and some altogether obliterated. 'I have seen all the temples in Nubia,' Lucie wrote to her mother, 'and nine of the tombs at Thebes [Luxor]. Some are wonderfully beautiful. Abu Simbel, Kalabshe, Kom Ombo, a little temple at El Kab – lovely . . . and most of all Abydos. Edfu and Dendera are the most perfect, Edfu *quite* perfect . . . But the most beautiful object my eyes ever saw is the island of Philae. It gives one quite the supernatural feeling of Claude's best landscapes.'

But then, having listed all the temples she had visited, Lucie

---

sipping a cold drink. The whole project of moving Abu Simbel took four years and was a triumph of modern engineering and mass tourism.

* Pückler's graffiti survived the relocation of Abu Simbel and remains clearly visible today on the breast of 'the august and pathetic giant' to the right of the temple entrance.

digressed on what interested her more: the people she had met in Upper Egypt. 'It is quite worth going to Nubia to see the lovely little girls running about in a graceful dress consisting of a leather fringe four inches wide, and the women draped like Greek statues and *more* beautifully shaped.'

★

Life in the villages they passed through, Lucie felt, was 'the true poetical, pastoral life of the Bible . . . where the English have not been and happily they don't land at the little places'. Luxor – or Thebes,★ as Lucie always called it – was another matter. When they reached Luxor on their return journey from Wadi Halfa, Lucie complained that it had 'become an English watering place. There are now nine boats lying here, and the great object is to *do the Nile* as fast as possible.'

Despite the tourists, Lucie lingered in Luxor to visit the tombs, Karnak Temple and Luxor Temple, which until the 1880s was occupied by a congested village of mud houses, shops, stables and chicken coops, with a mosque at one end and a brothel† at the other. And in the midst of the village, here and there, reared up massive statues and pillars and walls carved with hieroglyphic tales and scenes of wars and pageantry. In its strange embrace of the ancient and the modern, Luxor Temple seemed to Lucie quintessentially Egyptian, and the thought occurred to her that if she had to return to Egypt the following year, she could come and settle in Luxor instead of staying in Cairo or leading a wandering life on the Nile.

In Luxor, Lucie was able to collect letters from home from the consular agent for Britain, Belgium and Russia: a prosperous

---

★ Luxor was for centuries the religious capital of ancient Egypt and was then known as 'Waset'. Before the Arab conquest of Egypt, the town bore the Greek name 'Thebes', which means 'the most selected place', and this was the name Lucie preferred. 'Luxor' comes from the Arabic *al-uqsur,* which means 'the palaces', for the conquering Arabs of the seventh century mistook Karnak and Luxor temples for palaces.

† We know about the brothel in the temple village from Flaubert, who visited Luxor in 1849 and recorded his impressions and adventures in his diary.

Egyptian merchant named Mustafa Agha Ayat. Mustafa had
visited Europe and spoke fluent English, French and Italian, and
he easily ingratiated himself with Lucie as he did with all the
Europeans who passed through Luxor.* She dined with him in
his rather grand house built on top of the sand in Luxor Temple
– a sumptuous meal of stewed pigeons, mutton kebabs, lamb,
kidneys, turkey with cucumber sauce and rice, all prepared
by Mustafa's plump wife, who Lucie was amused to see
'henpecked her handsome old husband completely'. Over
dinner, Lucie broached her idea of settling in Luxor the following year, whereupon Mustafa immediately offered her a house
he owned across the river, 'up among the tombs in the finest
air'.

The thought of living daily in the midst of all of Luxor's
splendour delighted Lucie. To awake morning after morning
and see the deep blue Nile and the coral-pink Theban Hills
beyond it; to wander in the temple village; to seek peace and
silence in the shade of Karnak's vast pillars; to see the orange
globe of the Egyptian sun cast a path of fire across the Nile
evening after evening just before it set, and then hear the call to
prayer echoing in the darkness – all this would be Lucie's world
if she returned to live in Luxor.

And here she might thrive. For in addition to being awesome
and beautiful, Luxor was also decidedly healthy. In its dry heat,
Lucie began to feel stronger than she had since returning from
South Africa the year before. She wrote home to her mother, 'I
feel so much better . . . I still have an irritable cough, but it has
begun to have lucid intervals and is far less frequent at all times.
I can walk four or five miles, my digestion is perfect, appetite
good and the blood-spitting almost forgotten.'

She felt so well, in fact, that she went on an expedition to
Abydos, riding a pack donkey, 'without a bridle and only my

* What Lucie and his other European friends didn't know about the hospitable
and genial Mustafa was that he conducted a considerable illicit trade in antiquities
under the cover of diplomatic immunity.

saddle ... through the most beautiful crops ever seen ... the green of Egypt ... would make English green look black. Beautiful cattle, sheep, and camels were eating the delicious clover while their owners camped there in reed huts during the time the crops are growing. Such a lovely scene, all sweetness and plenty. We ate our bread and dates in Osiris' temple and a woman offered us buffalo milk on our way home which we drank warm out of the huge earthen pan it had been milked in.'

★

Soon after the trip to Abydos, the *Zint el-Bachreyn* set sail for Cairo. It was March by now; Lucie planned to meet Janet in Cairo, and then after a few weeks go with her to Alexandria and wait there for a ship back to England. *En route* to Cairo, they stopped in Asyut and Lucie collected letters from the consul, including one from Alexander, telling her that Lord Lansdowne had died and had left Maurice £5,000 in his will. Because of her old friend's death, Lucie cancelled the fantasia the consul wanted to throw for her, and she went to the bazaar to buy black cloth for Sally to sew mourning clothes. Lucie also had an alarming letter from Henry Ross saying that Janet was seriously ill and it was unlikely they would be able to come to Cairo to meet her. Henry's account made Lucie fear that Janet had had a miscarriage,* and she decided that she would go straight on to Alexandria if the Rosses were not waiting for her in Cairo.

But when she arrived in Cairo in early April, Lucie was relieved to find Janet – pale but recovered – and Henry at Shepheard's Hotel. The Rosses departed, however, just a day or two later. Janet, in her usual capricious way, had decided that she 'hated Cairo'. She refused to go anywhere other than the

---

* If Janet had become pregnant again – despite all her resolutions – it is possible that it was an abortion rather than a spontaneous miscarriage which had made her so ill.

bazaar, but this soon bored her, and so she and Henry returned to Alexandria, leaving Lucie alone at the hotel.

The expatriate guests at Shepheard's were disagreeable and the Cairo weather was chilly after Upper Egypt. Lucie caught a cold which then developed into 'a *very* severe attack of bronchitis', with a violent cough that brought on haemorrhage. This soon subsided, but it was followed, as Lucie wrote to her mother, by 'the old, long tedious story of cough, sweats and utter weakness'.

When William Thayer and Hekekyan Bey called and discovered Lucie so ill, Hekekyan summoned the best doctor in Cairo: Dr Leo Bey, the physician of the new Turkish viceroy, Ismail Pasha. For the next few weeks, Dr Leo visited Lucie two or three times a day, and Hekekyan and Thayer called daily. Omar, meanwhile, recited the Koran outside Lucie's door – Islam's best medicine. Soon Lucie was well enough to make plans to go to Alexandria.

But before she was ready to go, Thayer came one day, much perplexed, with a small black child, a girl named Zeynab from Khartoum in the Sudan. She was a slave and had been sent to Thayer as a gift. He explained to Lucie that he had no women servants and that his cook and groom had been treating the child roughly. What should he do?

In her next letter to her mother, Lucie announced, 'I have a black slave – yes, but a *real* one. I looked at her little ears, wondering they had not been bored for rings. She fancied I wished them bored (she was sitting on the floor close at my side), and in a minute she stood up and showed me her ear with a great pin through it. "Is that well, Lady?" The creature is eight years old. The shock nearly made me faint. What extremities of terror had reduced that little mind to such a state? She is very good and gentle and sews quite astoundingly already. When she first came she tells me she thought I should eat her. Now her one dread is that I should leave her behind. She sings a wild song of joy to Mossey's [Maurice's] picture and about the little Sitt [Urania] . . . Sally teaches her and she is very good. But now she has set her whole little black soul upon me. I hope Alexander won't dislike my bringing her [home].'

Zeynab reminded Lucie of her poor servant, Hassan, whom she had taken in that cold winter's night in Queen Square so many years ago, and like Hatty, Zeynab was utterly devoted to Lucie. The girl also helped assuage Lucie's longing for Urania. Though eight, Zeynab was tiny for her age, and Lucie could hold her as she had not held her small daughter for nearly a year. She hoped she wouldn't have to leave the child behind when she sailed for England.

Alexander, however, made it clear in his next letter that he was not enthusiastic about welcoming a slave into the family circle, especially when they now lacked a common roof over their heads. Urania was still with Charlotte Austin, and Maurice, during his school holidays, stayed with Alexander at the Taylors' in Clapham. But where Lucie was to pass the summer was uncertain. Sarah Austin wanted her and Urania to come to Weybridge, but Lucie and Alexander felt that Nutfield Cottage was too cold and damp and unhealthy. Lucie asked Alexander to rent furnished rooms for her near the Taylors. No one suggested that she might stay with Lady Duff Gordon and her daughters in Hertford Street, though this would have been convenient because Alexander dined with or dropped in on his mother and sisters nearly every day. In the end, it was arranged that Lucie would stay with Dr De Mussy, who lived in Mayfair, not far from Lady Duff Gordon. It was De Mussy who would decide Lucie's fate the following year: whether she could remain in England or must return to Egypt. If De Mussy thought it advisable and the weather was warm, Lucie and Alexander planned to take the children to Bournemouth for several weeks in August. In all these plans there was no room for little Zeynab.

When Lucie took the train to Alexandria in late April, Zeynab went along, for Lucie had decided to leave her with

Janet and Janet's maid, Ellen Naldrett — Sally's sister — while she
was gone. She found Janet in top form, and much excited about
her new job as the Alexandria correspondent for the London
Times. Lucie had intended to stay in Alexandria a month or so,
until she sailed for England. But within days of her arrival she
found it oppressive and the climate disagreeable. She was not
impressed by the Rosses' circle of expatriate friends and their
colonial mentality. Alexandria seemed to Lucie, in fact, a
mongrel city. 'The European ideas and customs have
extinguished the Arab altogether and those who remain are not
improved by the contact.' Only the Bedouin were unscathed by
western influence. In the bazaar one day, Lucie bought a long,
white Bedouin cloak for herself and a crowd of admiring
Bedouin gathered to observe the purchase; when the bargain
had been made, they wrapped 'the long cloak round me [in the]
Bedouin fashion . . . and complimented me on having "the face
of the Arab" '.

★

By early May, Lucie had had her fill of Alexandria and its
expatriate community. She returned to Cairo to await the time
to sail for England. But instead of going back to Shepheard's
Hotel, she moved into Thayer's house — well outside the 'Frank'
quarter — which was empty because Thayer had gone on leave
to America. Sally cleaned and Omar cooked and they hired a
laundress and a donkey boy named Hassan who swept the stairs,
ran errands and took Lucie out riding early in the morning and
again at sunset. The shutters and windows were open all day
and from them Lucie could follow the drama of the street life
below. It was noisy except at midday — 'the few hot hours
when nothing is heard but the cool tinkle of the Sakka's brass
cups as he sells water . . . or liquorice water or carob and raisin
sherbet'. As the afternoon waned, the street came alive again.
'There is a quarrel now in the street — how they talk and
gesticulate and everybody puts in a word. A boy has upset a
cake seller's tray. *"Nal abu'k!"* [curse your father!] He claims six

piastres damages, and everybody gives an opinion *pour ou contre*. We all look out of the windows. My opposite neighbour, the pretty Armenian woman, leans out (baby sucking all the time) and her diamond head ornaments and earrings glitter as she laughs like a child. The Christian dyer is also very active in the row, which like all Arab rows ends in nothing – it evaporates in fine theatrical gestures and lots of talk. Curious: in the street they are so noisy, [but] . . . get the same men down in a coffee-shop or anywhere, and they are the quietest of mankind. Only one man ever speaks at a time, the rest listen and never interrupt: twenty men don't make the noise of three Europeans.'

In the evenings Hekekyan often called, and he and Lucie discussed politics and how Ismail Pasha pursued his 'progressive' schemes through the blood and sweat of the Egyptian *fellahin* or peasants. Ismail and his predecessors – Said Pasha, Abbas and the powerful Mohammed Ali – were all khedives of the vast Ottoman Empire, ruling Egypt, as the Mamelukes had before them, as an Ottoman province and Egyptians as a subject people. The industrialization and modernization of Egypt had begun under Mohammed Ali in the early years of the century. Said and Abbas were less forceful, but the lull of their rule was more than made up for by the ambition of Ismail. He built and then expanded the country's canal system to wrest fertile agricultural land from the desert; he extended the railway, built bridges, made and paved roads, enlarged and developed the cotton industry. But his greatest dream – and triumph – was the Suez Canal, which was in the making for all the years Lucie was in Egypt, and finally opened – with undreamt-of pomp and ceremony – in 1869.

All of Ismail's reforms were, of course, expensive and they also required a huge labour force. He borrowed vast sums wherever he could and soon found himself unable to pay even the interest on his loans. To raise revenue he then levied heavy taxes on every conceivable commodity from flour to soap. The labour problem was dealt with just as ruthlessly by the *corvée* or forced labour policy that Lucie and Hekekyan deplored. Whole towns and villages were raided for able-bodied men who were taken away, often for years, to dig canals, build bridges, dams and railways and work like slaves on the Suez Canal.

In the eyes of most Europeans – including the Rosses and their friends – Ismail was a bringer of light and progress to Egypt and thus to be applauded and supported. But as Lucie told her mother, 'mine is another *standpunkt*, and my heart is with the Arabs. I care less about opening up the trade with Sudan and all the new railways – and I should like to see person and property safe which no one's is here (Europeans of course excepted) . . . Food . . . gets dearer and the forced labour inflicts more suffering . . . and the population will decrease yet faster. This appears to me a state of things in which it is no use to say that public works *must* be done at any cost. I daresay the wealth will be increased if meanwhile the people are not exterminated . . . What chokes me is to hear English people talk of the stick being "the only way to manage the Arabs", as if any one could doubt that it is the *easiest* way to manage any people where it can be used with impunity.'

In her letters to Alexander, however, Lucie avoided political issues. Instead, she talked optimistically of her health, and somewhat defensively of her finances, for she feared that he would think that the £250 she had spent since coming to Egypt was extravagant. As the date of her return to England approached, she became apprehensive and also keenly aware of the distance – in every sense – that she had travelled since she had come to Egypt. 'I hope I shall not be very much in the way,' she wrote to Alexander. Increasingly, it became difficult for her to imagine what her life would be when she got home – with her family scattered about in far-flung houses and her own bivouac still up in the air.

And so, rather than dwelling on the approaching summer, Lucie wrote to Alexander proposing that he visit her in Egypt the following winter for, despite her talk of improved health,

Lucie already guessed that the London doctors would tell her she must return to Egypt in the autumn. 'Now that I have pots and pans and all needful for a house but a carpet and a few mattresses,' Lucie told Alexander, 'you could camp with me [here] *à l'Arabe*. How you would revel in the old *Misr el Kahira* [Cairo], peep up at lattice windows, gape like a *Rasheen* (green one) in the bazaar, go wild over the mosques, laugh at portly Turks and dignified sheikhs on their white donkeys, drink sherbet in the street, ride wildly about on a donkey, peer under black veils at beautiful eyes, and feel generally intoxicated. I am quite a good cicerone now of the glorious old city. Omar is in raptures at the idea that the *Sidi el Kebir* [the great master] might come . . . He plans meeting you on the steamboat and bringing you to me that I may kiss your hand first of all. *Mashallah* [oh God], how our hearts would be dilated.'

On a foggy, wet afternoon in London, Alexander read this letter at his club, the Athenaeum, folded it up and put it away in his pocket before going to dine with his mother and sisters in Hertford Street.

★

In early June, Lucie went back to Alexandria to embark on the *Venetian*, bound for England via Malta. She left both Zeynab and Omar in tears, but with many promises to meet in the autumn. The *Venetian* had a smooth passage, and reached the Victoria Dock in London on 28 June. Because of some confusion, Alexander wasn't waiting on the pier so Lucie and Sally had to make their way to his office at Somerset House in the Strand.

Everything else that we know about the following three months Lucie spent in England, lodging with Dr De Mussy in London, and then with Alexander and the children for a month in Bournemouth, comes from fragmentary entries in the diary of her mother-in-law, Lady Duff Gordon. These, and the gaps and silences that surround them, describe an uneasy interlude between two seasons in Egypt.

13 July 1863. Alice and I went out early to Coutts and to see Lucie who is in London at Dr De Mussy's. I forgot to say that she (to my astonishment) came to see us on Saturday. It is two years since I saw her. She is much aged and looks ill and coughs. Her eyes are too bright and her mouth looks dry. Altogether not satisfactory. Dr De Mussy says that she must return to Egypt in September and that there are tubercles on one lung decidedly. I saw little Rainy for a moment.

14 July. Alexander dined with us – low about Lucie. The doctor again examined her and now thinks that both lungs are affected!!!

6 August. Alexander came from Bournemouth to dine and sleep – a very unsatisfactory account of Lucie – always slightly spitting blood.

6 September. Maurice and Rainy came. I saw Alexander. Georgy [Georgina] went to church and the rain stopped her from going to see Lucie who . . . is preparing for going again to Egypt for the winter.

7 September. Georgy went to see Lucie.

12 September. I saw Lucie who goes away tomorrow to Paris (Alexander goes so far with her) on her way to Egypt.

20 September. I heard yesterday from Alexander . . . that Lucie had had a return of spitting blood at Calais and had stopped them proceeding to Paris. He was forced to [leave Lucie and Sally at Calais and] return to his office at Somerset House.

Chapter Eleven

Lucie and Sally were stranded for some days at Calais because Lucie was too ill to travel further. Besides the blood-spitting, she coughed up a hard, chalky substance she realized must be a tubercle. 'It confirms the worst opinion of my case,' she wrote to her mother, and then went on with weary resignation, 'I cannot say I have much idea of ever recovering . . . Painful as [this] separation is . . . it is something at least to spare others the . . . sight of lingering disease and death if it is to come.'

By late September they were able to set off by easy stages for Marseilles, reaching it just in time to sail for Alexandria on 9 October. Unlike the passage the previous year, it was 'a horrid voyage . . . wretched as to ship and odious as to company'. Crossing the Mediterranean felt like navigating the Styx: bound for the land of the dead. What was Egypt, after all, but one vast cemetery, from the City of the Dead in Cairo to the tombs of the pharaohs at Thebes, to the mortuary temples at Abu Simbel, rising like a mirage out of the desert that lay beyond Aswan? Lucie was going to Egypt to die, and to die alone, 'to spare others'. The last thing she expected to find there was life with a vengeance.

But such was the case – almost from the moment of her arrival. As the boat pulled into the harbour, Alexandria shimmered under a cloudless sky, and both Janet and Omar were waving from the pier, Janet 'as fresh and bright as a spring day and much improved in all ways – and the faithful Omar radiant with joy and affection'. The sun poured down like the rain in England and France; the donkey boy danced in ecstasy in the dusty street; the bazaar shopkeepers sang out '*Salaam aleikum*' and told Lucie they had tasted her absence and that it had been bitter. '*Alhamdulillah* [Praise be to God], the *Sitti* has returned.'

During the summer, Omar's young wife, Mabrooka, had given birth to their first child, a daughter, and Lucie and Sally went to see the new mother and baby. Mabrooka, like many Egyptian wives, was kept in strict purdah and had not stirred from the house since the night she had been brought to it as a bride; nor did she expect to leave it until she was carried out in a coffin. She was a beautiful, slender young woman – really a girl, still – but too shy to do more than smile with downcast eyes when she brought tea and some of the family's famous sweetmeats for Lucie and Sally. Lucie was utterly charmed by Mabrooka's loveliness and sweet docility. Even more, she was touched to learn that Omar had turned down several more lucrative offers of employment while she was away, including one from Lady Herbert of Lea. Omar vowed he was Lucie's slave and would never desert her for any amount of money.

The only discordant note in Lucie's warm reception in Alexandria was that little Zeynab had grown strangely bold and sulky over the summer at Janet's, and also, under the influence of several of Janet's Muslim servants, had now a horror of Christians and Europeans. Lucie regretted more than ever that she had not taken the child with her to England. Reluctantly, she saw that only tantrums would follow if she took Zeynab to Luxor, so she made arrangements to place her with a large Egyptian family with children Zeynab's age.

After two weeks with the Rosses in Alexandria, Lucie went to Cairo by boat – an eight-day journey – because floods had washed away the railway. And not only the railway. 'Whole villages,' Lucie wrote to her mother, were 'gone, submerged and melted, mud to mud, and the people with their animals [were] encamped on spits of sand or on the dykes in long rows of ragged makeshift tents while we sailed over where they had lived.' This swollen Nile was a destroyer. In addition, cattle murrain was raging throughout Egypt and both meat and milk – when you could find them – were extremely dear. One day the boat stopped in a village to buy milk, and 'a poor woman exclaimed, "Milk! From where? do you want it out of my breasts?"' Everything had doubled in price, and cotton, which had been saturated by the Nile floods, lay rotting in the fields. In the midst of this 'spectacle of devastation', boatloads of tourists sailed past blighted villages utterly indifferent to the widespread suffering. It was enough to make Lucie's blood boil.

★

When they arrived at Cairo, Lucie went directly to Thayer's house. He was still away on leave in America, his return having been delayed by ill health. Lucie herself 'was seized with violent blood-spitting . . . worse than I ever had – quite haemorrhage [sic]' the day after she reached Cairo. But after a week in bed, attended by Dr Leo Bey and nursed by Omar and Sally, she felt well enough to begin correcting the edited manuscript of her *Letters from the Cape* which Sarah Austin, who was preparing the letters for publication, had sent to Cairo.

Lucie and Sarah also hoped to collaborate on a book of Lucie's Egyptian letters. Over the summer, in fact, an editor at Macmillan's had suggested that Lucie publish some of her long, diary-like letters in *Macmillan's Magazine*. These would then create an audience for a book-length collection, *Letters from Egypt*, which Macmillan's proposed to publish the following spring. Lucie was already, of course, a keen reader (and sometimes a translator) of travel narratives, a form much in vogue and practised by such Duff Gordon friends as Kinglake, Thackeray, Dickens and Eliot Warburton. But although Lucie was already a published writer and the Cape letters were scheduled to come out at the end of the year, *Letters from Egypt* would be a new departure. She would now be writing about herself rather than performing the subsidiary role of translator; her subject would be her own experiences expressed in her own words.

From this point onwards, Lucie's letters were woven of two sometimes distinct, sometimes imperceptibly merged, strands. Carefully crafted, colourful, descriptive or explanatory passages, clearly destined for publication, alternate with long paragraphs of a purely personal sort meant for Alexander's and Sarah Austin's eyes only: bulletins on Lucie's health, requests for goods to be sent out, and a great deal of information on her day-to-day life with Sally and Omar. The two strands ran on – in tandem, braided, divergent – in nearly every letter, for it was left to Sarah Austin, freed at last from the task of editing her husband's works, to extract *Letters from Egypt* from the voluminous letters Lucie sent home.

Alexander, as before, handled the financial side of things – negotiating with Macmillan's, signing contracts and then, in time, receiving Lucie's royalty payments. And these, after all, were the underlying motive of the whole project. *Letters from Egypt* became the great achievement of Lucie's writing career – the culmination of her literary childhood and London years as Lady Duff Gordon – but it was born of financial necessity. It was now clear that Lucie was unlikely ever to regain her health sufficiently to live permanently again with Alexander and the children in England. Although travel in Egypt was relatively cheap, Lucie's exile still put a heavy burden on the Duff Gordon resources. If she published her letters from Egypt, the book stood a good chance of defraying the cost of her wandering life there. Lucie went to Egypt because she was an invalid, but once there her very invalidism forced her to become a far more professional writer than she had been heretofore.

It was with this new sense of professionalism that she worked on the proofs for *Letters from the Cape*. But at the same time, rereading her South African letters made her long for remote places. Cairo was becoming too familiar and predictable, and it was also overrun with Europeans. 'Here are no end of swells,' Lucie wrote to Alexander in a passage clearly *not* intended for publication. The 'Duke of Rutland, Lord and Lady Scarborough, Lady Herbert, etc., etc. Lord Howard and Lady Meux too. The poor old British Consul is in a seventh heaven of toadydom.'

So she began making plans for Luxor. Dr Leo Bey advised her not to live in Mustafa's house or to camp in tents amidst the tombs on the west bank of the Nile, which he considered unhealthy, and urged her instead to settle in Karnak or Luxor. The previous year Lucie had noticed a large, rambling white house at the southern end of the village built inside Luxor Temple, and she now made inquiries about renting the French House, as it was called because it belonged to the French government. This, it turned out, was easily arranged by the French consul in Cairo.

Lucie and Omar then made another expedition to the labyrinthine bazaar in Old Cairo, Khan el-Khalili, to purchase all the things needed for setting up house in Luxor: 'I have bought divans, tables, prayer carpets, blankets, a cupboard, a lovely old copper hand basin and ewer,' she reported to Alexander, 'and shall live Arab style. The tables only are a concession to European infirmity and four chairs.'

In the midst of her preparations, Thayer returned from America. He was still far from well and he asked Lucie if he could accompany her to Luxor in the hope that he, too, might be helped by the hot, dry air of Upper Egypt. It made sense for them to rent a boat and travel together, though Lucie was well aware that such a plan might raise a good number of European eyebrows in Cairo. 'What do you think?' she wrote to Janet, 'will grey hairs on one side, and *mutual* bad lungs guarantee our international virtue? Or will [people] ask the *Pater* [Alexander] when he means to divorce me? Would it be considered that Yankeedoodle had "stuck a feather in his cap" by leading a British matron and grandmother astray?'

It was soon clear, however, that Thayer was too ill to travel, much less run off with a grandmother, and Hekekyan Bey and his wife insisted that he come to stay with them at their home outside Cairo. Lucie was now reluctant to go to the expense of hiring a boat just for herself and Sally and Omar. She decided instead to travel on a government steamer – much to the amazement of other Europeans who couldn't conceive of an Englishwoman going up the Nile in the company of Egyptians. For Lucie, however, the company, in addition to economy, was part of the appeal; she had had quite enough of the Duke of Rutland and the rest of what passed for polite society in Cairo.

They booked passage on the next government steamer and were scheduled to embark on 25 December, but Christmas came and went and the steamer remained moored at Boulak. On the 26th, Lucie wrote to Janet that they expected to sail the next day. And on the 27th, she informed her mother that 'after infinite delays and worries we are at last on board and shall sail tomorrow morning'. In fact, they did not get underway until the 29th. In the interim, however, Lucie was able to settle herself as comfortably as possible on board. She wrote to her mother, 'I have got a good sized cabin with good clean divans round three sides for Sally and myself [to sleep on]. Omar will sleep on deck and cook where he can. A poor Turkish lady is to inhabit a sort of dust hole by the side of my cabin. If she seems decent, I will entertain her hospitably. There is no furniture of any sort but the divan and we cook our own food, bring our own candles, jugs, basins, and everything. There is no door to the cabin so we nail up an old plaid. If Sally and I were not such complete Arabs, we should think it miserable – but as things stand, we say *Alhamdulillah*.'

★

The journey to Luxor took two weeks and it was made in the company of a highly colourful band of travellers: three Greeks, a group of 'dirty Copts', a Turkish Pasha, an Egyptian *effendi*, a French consular agent, three convicts in chains and their guard, and the twelve-year-old Sultan of Darfoor, who was returning from a state visit to Ismail Pasha. It was only HRH of Darfoor 'dressed in a yellow silk kuftan and a scarlet *burnoos* [cloak]' whom Lucie found somewhat trying. He rudely snubbed her because she was a woman, whereupon the Egyptian captain of the steamer expostulated, '*Wallah! Wallah!* [Good God!] What a way to talk to English *Hareem* [lady]!' But Lucie cleverly won over the boy and his retinue of black Dongola slaves with a box of French sweetmeats. She inquired if he had brothers and, instead of snubbing her again, the Sultan replied civilly, 'Who can count them? They are like mice.'

The journey would have been entirely satisfactory if Lucie had had only this heterogeneous assortment of human companions to contend with. But unfortunately, the steamer was also transporting a good number of rats and fleas to Upper Egypt – much to everyone's distraction and discomfort. 'Never till now did I know what fleas could be,' Lucie wrote to Alexander; 'even Omar groaned and tossed in his sleep, and Sally and I woke every ten minutes.'

It was a relief to escape the fleas and scurrying rodents when they called at villages. And here, as she had the previous year, Lucie felt herself succumbing to the magic of rural life in Egypt and its unchanging rhythms of irrigating and tilling the land, grazing goats and cattle, women washing clothes and pots and pans in the Nile and then carrying their laundry and cooking utensils balanced on their heads back to their mud houses. Life seemed to stand still in the villages; Lucie saw scenes she had read of in the Bible, or had seen carved on the walls of Pharaonic temples. A great stillness reigned; the leaves of the Egyptian palimpsest – of history itself – merged into something that felt eternal.

At Asyut – a town rather than a village – Lucie encountered a solitary Bedouin woman who fascinated her. 'She was . . . dressed like a young man, but small and feminine and rather pretty except that one eye was blind. Her [male] dress was handsome and she had a woman's jewels, diamonds, etc., and an European watch and chain. Her manner was excellent and I was told – indeed I could hear – that her language was beautiful, a thing much esteemed among Arabs. She is a virgin and fond of travelling and of men's society being very clever, so she has her dromedary and goes about quite alone. No one seemed surprised, no one stared, and when I asked if it was quite proper, our captain was surprised, "Why not, if she does not wish to marry, she can go alone . . . She is a virgin and free."'

To Lucie this young Bedouin woman, travelling alone in male clothing, was 'far the most curious thing I have yet seen' in Egypt. She made various inquiries about her and learned that she had been leading her strange nomadic existence for nearly ten years; she was rich and was, despite all her eccentricities, welcomed among the best Egyptian families where she sat and talked with the men, but slept at night with the women in the harem. 'She has been in the interior of Africa,' Lucie wrote to her mother, 'and to Mecca, speaks Turkish and . . . [is] full of interesting information about all the countries she [has] visited. As soon as I can talk [Arabic] better, I must try and find her out.'

Lucie was drawn to this solitary traveller: a woman dressed as an Arab man with a European watch and chain, who broke most of the rules of her culture, but was nevertheless respected because she was, among other things, chaste, intelligent and rich. She was also brave and original, curious and cultured – and alone. In some ways, seeing this Bedouin woman must have been for Lucie like looking in a mirror. But after this brief encounter at Asyut, their paths never crossed again, and Lucie never – as she wished – 'found her out'.

★

They reached Luxor – or Thebes, 'the most selected place', as Lucie always called it – on 12 January 1864. Mustafa Agha, the consul who had so hospitably entertained Lucie the previous year, rushed to the river bank, surrounded by a swarm of children, as Lucie wrote home, 'to conduct me up to my palace': the French House,★ built atop the south-west corner of

★ Lucie's white-washed, mud-brick house in Luxor was built in 1815 by the British Consul-General, Henry Salt. Salt carried out a good many excavations in Egypt, including the removal of the colossal bust of Ramesses II from the Ramesseum in Thebes, a project supervised by the famous explorer Giovanni Belzoni, who himself stayed in the house in 1817. In the 1820s, Salt sold the house

Luxor Temple. It was, as Lucie described it, a big, rambling house ... with good thick walls ... and glass windows and doors to some of the rooms. It is a lovely dwelling. Two funny little owls as big as my fist live in the wall under my window and come and peep in, walking on tip toe and looking inquisitive like the owls in hieroglyphics and a splendid Horus (the sacred hawk) frequents my lofty balcony.'

With the exception of Mustafa's house and the mosque of Abu el-Haggag, Lucie's new home was quite the grandest thing in the temple village. Beyond her garden stretched a confusing labyrinth of dirt lanes and passages with mud hovels, mud pigeon-towers, sheds and stables and mud-brick shops built haphazardly among the temple ruins. Human beings, buffaloes, camels, donkeys, cats and dogs all milled about. 'Cocks crew, hens cackled, pigeons cooed, turkeys gobbled, children swarmed', women baked and gossiped, men strode about in long *galabiyas* or sat desultorily smoking in the coffee houses. And all the while the ancient Egyptians – pharaohs and priests, soldiers, workers and slaves – carved into the temple walls and columns, and the massive stone statues of Ramesses II at the temple gates remained eternally locked in their ancient rituals and battles and worship, oblivious of the teeming nineteenth-century Egyptian life going on in their midst.

---

to the French government and it acquired the name Maison de France or the French House. In 1829 Jean François Champollion, the decipherer of hieroglyphics, lived in it while in Luxor, as did the French officers who later came to remove one of the great obelisks from the first pylon of Luxor Temple. (It now stands in the Place de la Concorde in Paris.) But perhaps Lucie's most famous predecessor in the French House was Gustave Flaubert, who stayed there with his friend, the photographer Maxime Du Camp, in 1850. The French officers who carried off the obelisk had planted a garden behind the house and here Flaubert and Du Camp (and later, Lucie) spent hours lounging and smoking and reading among the date palms, mimosas, lemon trees, oleanders and jasmine. After Lucie's death in 1869, the French House became a place of pilgrimage for travellers such as Amelia Edwards who had read Lucie's *Letters from Egypt*. The house was torn down, along with the rest of the temple village, when Luxor Temple was cleared out in 1885 under the supervision of Camille Charles Maspero, Director of the new Egyptian Antiquities Service.

Mustafa's servants swept and cleaned the high-ceilinged, airy rooms of the French House for Lucie, and then helped Omar and Sally arrange the carpets and divans they had brought from Cairo, nail sconces for candles into the walls, unpack the pots and pans and crates of supplies in the kitchen. A carpenter was summoned to build a writing-table for Lucie – the only necessity they had overlooked in Cairo. To European eyes, the general effect of what Lucie called 'my Theban palace' might have seemed 'very bare and comfortless'* but to Lucie the French House grew daily 'more and more beautiful', and she was only melancholy, she wrote to Alexander, that she didn't have 'you and the chicks to fill it'.

In Egypt, where so much of life is conducted in the open air, the boundary between indoors and out is fluid and indeterminate. Some of Lucie's windows lacked glass and her thresholds doors, but it scarcely mattered; the little owls came and went, as did the translucent chameleons. What Lucie loved most about the French House, in fact, was not contained within its walls: it was the magnificent views she had from her front and back balconies, 'over the Nile in front, facing NW and over a splendid range of green and distant orange buff hills to the SE'. As another visitor noted, these vistas 'furnished the [house] . . . and made its poverty splendid'.

The landscape modulated, an endless spectacle throughout the day, with each subtle variation of light. At dawn everything was a delicate, pastel hue – mountains, sky, the chalky-coloured columns of temples and monuments. At midday colours shimmered in the heat, and the sky turned indigo. Just before sunset, the sun burnished the hills of the Valley of the Kings across the river and set fire to the white cliffs beyond before finally setting – a huge, orange-crimson globe – behind the deep blue Nile.

Life in the French House in the early months of 1864 felt too

---

* Such was Amelia Edwards's description of Lucie's home in Luxor when she visited it in 1873. (*A Thousand Miles up the Nile*, p. 454.)

intoxicating to experience alone. 'If only I had you all here!' Lucie wrote again to Alexander. She could imagine them all together in Thebes: 'How Rainy would play in the temple, Mossey fish in the Nile, and you go about with your spectacles on your nose. I think you would discard *Frangi* [European] dress and take to a brown shirt and libdeh and soon be as brown as any *Fellah* [peasant].'

It was, however, Lucie, not Alexander, who was dispensing with English clothes – literally and metaphorically. As the weather got hotter and hotter in February and March, she began to discard gloves, hat, underskirts, stockings – and finally, that last bastion of feminine apparel: stays. Even more, English customs and forms and habits of thought fell away as Lucie became more and more absorbed by the world she inhabited.

It was an almost entirely Egyptian world,* for Lucie tried to avoid the English and European tourists who passed through Luxor. She grew weary of the women wanting to borrow her saddle and the loud and rude manners of the men – their hearty, ho-ho-ho raillery and jokes about dancing girls and Muslim piety. Sally was really the only English person with whom Lucie was in close contact now, and Sally had shed her layers of European clothing too, and was as fascinated by and enamoured of their new surroundings and neighbours as Lucie. And like Lucie, too, Sally was fast picking up Arabic from Omar.

Within two months of her arrival, Lucie could write home to

---

* There was, however, one other European who lived in Luxor at this time: an Italian photographer named Antonio Beato whose house and studio were situated just outside the northern end of Luxor Temple. Between the 1860s and 1880s, Beato took a large series of excellent photographs of the principal temples and monuments in Egypt, and he sold sets of these photos to tourists who visited Luxor. Curiously, Lucie mentions Beato only twice in her letters, neither time by name, and she seems to have had no social commerce with him. Shortly before I went to Egypt, archaeologists from the University of Chicago working in Luxor had acquired a previously unknown collection of Beato's negatives that had turned up in an old cupboard at a Luxor bookseller's. Among these negatives was a rare picture of the French House at the time Lucie inhabited it. (See photographs.)

Alexander, 'I am on visiting terms with all the "country families" resident in Luxor already.' She had in fact gathered round her a coterie or salon just as she had at Queen Square and the Gordon Arms. The *habitués* of the French House included all the prominent men in Luxor: the consul, Mustafa Agha, the magistrate, Saleem Effendi, a handsome young imam, Sheykh Yusuf, who gave Lucie formal Arabic lessons, and the *cadi* or judge, among others.* In the late afternoons, this inner circle and a fluctuating number of associates and friends would congregate in Lucie's sitting-room overlooking the Nile, recline on her divans and drink thick, black, sweet coffee out of cups only slightly larger than an English thimble, smoke the hookah and talk far into the night. In a surprisingly short time, Lucie could follow much of the conversation – local gossip, denunciations of Ismail Pasha's regime, lamentations over the cattle murrain and the year's crops.

Sometimes the talk took a more personal turn. Alexander's absence was, of course, inquired about. Why had he allowed her to travel to Egypt alone? When was he to arrive? Maurice's photograph was passed around, praised and kissed. Lucie's new friends were amazed to hear that her mother was still alive; they had assumed from her grey hair that she was too old to have a living parent. On their side, Lucie's guests weren't reluctant to make their own confidences. One afternoon, the magistrate, Saleem Effendi, arrived with a broad grin on his face and informed the assembled company that he had just purchased two black female slaves for £35: a daughter and her old mother, the first for his bed and the second for his kitchen. This arrangement was a necessity, he explained to Lucie, because his wife did not want to leave Cairo, where she lived with their eight children.

The degree to which Lucie and Sally soon became

* The Coptic bishop also called, but Lucie thought him 'a tipsy and impudent old monk' and didn't encourage him to come again.

'naturalized', as Lucie put it, was reflected by the fact that Lucie was invited to the village mosque of Abu el-Haggag to have the *Fatah*★ said for her health – a great honour, and almost unheard for an 'unbeliever'. More humorously, she and Sally received a number of proposals of marriage. Sally's hand, indeed, was much sought after, but her most flattering offer came from Mustafa Agha, on behalf of his eldest son, Seyd, 'a nice lad of nineteen or twenty at most', whereas Sally was now thirty. 'As Mustafa is the richest and most considerable person here,' Lucie wrote to her mother, 'it shows that the Arabs draw no unfavourable conclusions as to our morals . . . He said . . . she would [be able to] keep her own religion and her own customs. I said she was too old, but they think that no objection at all. She will have to say that her father would not allow it, for of course a handsome offer deserves a civil refusal. Sally's proposals would be quite an ethnological study, I think.'

Even 'more amusing . . . such a joke against my grey hairs', was a proposal Lucie herself received from 'a very handsome' Bedouin sheykh who was passing through Luxor on his way to the Sudan. He inquired of Omar whether Lucie was a widow or divorced, and said he wished to send a marriage brokeress to negotiate for her hand. 'Omar,' Lucie wrote home to Alexander, 'told him that would never do. I had a husband in England, besides I was not young, had a married daughter, my hair was grey, etc. The Sheykh swore he didn't care. I could dye my hair and get a divorce . . . and I was not a stupid modern woman, but like an ancient Arab [noblewoman] . . . and he would pay all he could afford as my dowry.' It was only with great difficulty that Omar managed to put off the handsome sheykh and his marriage brokeress. For her part, Lucie was less surprised by her admirer's perception of her as an Arab *Ameereh* than his indifference to the fact that she was some thirteen or

★The first *sura* of the Koran, which is recited during the five daily prayers, at the beginning of an undertaking, and as a blessing.

fourteen years his senior. She told Alexander, 'the disregard of differences in age here in marriage is very strange. My adorer was not more than thirty I am sure.'

Yet Lucie knew that the romantic scenario her Arab sheykh proffered was not as far-fetched or as unprecedented as it sounded. Her friends in Luxor, and perhaps Lucie's 'adorer' as well, had heard of the case of Lady Ellenborough (*née* Jane Digby) who, after three husbands, half a dozen children and countless lovers (including King Ludwig I of Bavaria), had finally found the great love of her life and happiness at the age of fifty in Syria when she married a Bedouin sheykh named Abdul Medjuel El Mezrab. Lady Herbert, Lord and Lady Scarborough, Lord and Lady Spencer and Sir Norman Lockhart (whom Lucie thought 'a very disagreeable, conceited prig'), and other aristocratic tourists who passed through Luxor, had often come from, or were bound for, Palestine, the Lebanon and Syria, and in the last they kept a wide berth from the former Jane Digby. 'I often hear of Lady Ellenborough who is married to the Sheykh el Arab of Palmyra and lives at Damascus,' Lucie wrote to her mother. 'The Arabs [here] think it inhuman of English ladies to avoid her. [They say] perhaps she had repented, at all events, she is married and lives with her husband.'

From the point of view of Sheykh Yusuf, Saleem Effendi, and Lucie's other Luxor friends, the important thing was not the past and its indiscretions, but a clear marital status in the present. Lucie and Sally were anomalies: Lucie because she was in a kind of marital limbo and Sally because she was unattached (or, at least, appeared to be).

And yet Lucie, Sally and Omar did form a tight-knit, happy household, even family, at the French House. And other members were gradually added. A tall, silent, dignified young man named Mohammed came every morning to do the sweeping. A water carrier – another Omar – carried eight to ten large skins of water from the Nile each day, for a salary of two shillings a month. A small village boy of six or seven named

Achmet appointed himself *bowab* (doorman and factotum) with 'an assumption of dignity that is quite delicious'. Achmet was particularly fond of flourishing 'a huge staff and he behaves like the most tremendous janissary [military escort]. He is about Rainy's size, as sharp as a needle and possesses the remains of a brown shirt and a ragged kitchen duster as a turban.' He also performed admirably as a *sais* or groom when Lucie went out on her small donkey early in the morning and just before sunset: little Achmet would run before her, clearing the road of ragged children, sleeping dogs and chickens, making sure that Lucie could negotiate something approaching a royal progress through the congested temple village to the gates guarded by the massive statues of Ramesses II and then to the open fields beyond.

★

In late March Lucie wrote to Tom Taylor back in Clapham, 'I am living here a very quiet dreamy sort of life in hot Thebes ... The last few travellers' *dahabiehs* are now on their way down the river. After that I shall not see a white face for many months, except Sally's.' Her Arab life was now beginning to seem like second nature, and when the last Europeans departed with the onset of the great heat of April, there were no counter-irritants, no distractions.

Much of the harmony and contentment Lucie now felt, she owed to two people: Omar and Sheykh Yusuf. Omar was her servant, confidant, interpreter, cook, and, when Lucie was unwell, her nurse. He saw to all her physical needs and many of her emotional ones as well, occupying a position that it would have required a maid, butler, cook, close woman friend and spouse to fulfil in England.

Lucie was moved by the depth of Omar's devotion – all the more so because she realized that it was highly unusual for a Muslim man to reverence a woman. But then he viewed English women differently, as a species apart, as Lucie realized one day when she overheard a conversation between Omar and

277

Saleem Effendi. 'Omar described Janet and was of [the] opinion that a man who was married to her could want nothing more. "By my soul, she rides like a Bedouin, she shoots with the gun and pistol and rows the boat, she speaks many languages, works the needle like an *efreet* [demon] and to see her hands run over the teeth of the music box [piano] amazes the mind, while her singing gladdens the soul. How then should her husband ever desire the coffee shop? *Wallahi* [By God], she can always amuse him at home. And as to my Lady [Lucie], the thing is not that she does not know; when . . . I go to the divan and say to her, do you want anything, a pipe or sherbet or so and so . . . she lays down her book and talks to me, and I question her and amuse my mind, and by God if I were a rich man and could marry one English *hareem* like that I would stand before her and serve her like her memlook.* . . . I am only this lady's servant, and I have not once sat in the coffee shop because of the sweetness of her tongue. Is it not true therefore that the man who can marry such *hareem* is rich more than with money?" Saleem seemed disposed to think a little more of beauty, though he quite agreed with all Omar's enthusiasm, and asked if Janet were beautiful. Omar answered with decorous vagueness that she was a "moon", but declined mentioning her hair, eyes, etc. (it is a liberty to describe a woman minutely.)'†

Omar was an intimate – an adoring 'slave'. Sheykh Yusuf, in contrast, was Lucie's mentor, but of a peculiar sort. Lucie wrote to her mother, 'I wish you could see my teacher, Sheykh Yusuf. I never before saw a pious person amiable and good like him. He is intensely devout and not at all bigoted – a difficult combination! And moreover he is lovely to behold and has the

*A slave. The Mamelukes, who ruled Egypt between the thirteenth and sixteenth centuries and remained powerful until the early 1800s, were originally Turkish slaves.
†Lucie was confident that her eavesdropping was undetected. Given Omar's eloquent and wholly uncritical praise of Janet and Lucie, we may wonder whether he suspected Lucie was sitting in the next room, the door ajar.

prettiest and merriest laugh possible. It is quite curious to see the mixture of ... learning with utter ignorance [of European things] and such perfect high breeding and beauty of character.'

Though an *alim* (a learned Islamic scholar), Sheykh Yusuf was only thirty and because he knew nothing of European culture, he seemed in some ways naïve and unworldly. A handsome, ascetic man, who wore the green turban which signified that he was a descendant of the Prophet Mohammed, Sheykh Yusuf had a delightful little daughter named Zeynab, and a twelve-year-old wife – his second, whom he had married after Zeynab's mother died.

At first, he merely gave Lucie Arabic lessons, and he must have been an intelligent man indeed to succeed as he did considering that he didn't know a word of English and they were without a dictionary. Lucie persevered despite finding the vowels 'maddening ... the plurals bewildering and the verbs quite heartbreaking'. Soon, however, they began to have long philosophical and religious discussions. Lucie read the Koran with Sheykh Yusuf (he refused to read secular literature such as the *Arabian Nights* with her), and this inevitably led to spiritual as well as linguistic teaching.* And confidences. In the worldly, literary, political circles in which Lucie had moved in England, there had been little talk of religious beliefs. In Luxor, with Sheykh Yusuf and others members of the *ulama* whom he brought to meet Lucie at the French House, religion permeated daily life. Five times a day, most of Lucie's friends and neighbours prostrated themselves in prayer – for them Allah's presence was continuous, the Prophet Mohammed's name and blessing never far from their lips.

In his simple, good-natured, devout way, Sheykh Yusuf not

---

*Like many Muslim *ulama* (religious leaders; the singular is *alim*), Sheykh Yusuf could recite the entire Koran by heart, a feat that took him twelve hours to perform.

only spoke of Islam, he asked Lucie about her own faith as she had not been questioned since, perhaps, her days at Miss Shepherd's nearly thirty years before. And such questioning must have provoked self-reflection as well. Lucie was no Christian: as she admitted to Sheykh Yusuf, she thought of Christ, not as the son of God, but, she told him, much as the Muslims viewed him: as a wise and good prophet, who had set a moral example for mankind. Beyond dispensing with the divinity of Christ and the Trinity, it is difficult to know just how far Lucie's scepticism went and whether her mother-in-law's later verdict that Lucie was an agnostic, or even worse, an atheist, was accurate or fair. Not only Sheykh Yusuf, but also Lucie's illness, her nearness to death, must have led her to search her own soul, to confront questions of ultimate meanings, suffering, the possibility – or not – of immortality.

Whatever her own unorthodox beliefs may have been, Lucie was deeply drawn to Islam, but for reasons that were probably more aesthetic than spiritual. This distinction, however, her growing circle of friends did not make. One day, when they were discussing the death of an English girl in Luxor some years earlier, an old man told Lucie that wherever she died and was buried – distant though they all hoped this day would be – they knew that she '"would lie in a Muslim grave". "How so?"' asked Lucie. And the old man replied, while the others nodded gravely, '"Why, when a bad Muslim dies the angels take him out of his tomb and put in one of the good from among the Christians in his place."' Lucie's Luxor friends knew that she came from, and in some ways still belonged to, a foreign world, but they had also taken her to their hearts, and insisted that in the next world – as in the present on the banks of the Nile – she would dwell with them.

Ramadan – the holiest month in the Islamic year when Muslims fast from dawn till dusk – arrived: 'a dreadful business, everybody is cross and lazy – no wonder'. Omar, who was far from devout, nevertheless kept the fast and heroically cooked for Lucie during the day as well. But he found it difficult to arise in time for the dawn prayer, and so Sally, who was a light sleeper, performed as his personal muezzin* and, according to Lucie, roused Omar with the traditional 'prayer is sweeter than sleep' in a prose version. Lucie apparently didn't wonder why or how Sally should be aware of whether Omar was awake before sunrise.

Ramadan was a time of intensified religious devotion, but it did not interfere with the fixed seasonal rhythms of Egyptian life. The first harvest of the year – 'the most exquisite pastoral you can conceive' – was brought in, and no sooner had the wheat, barley and lentils been reaped, than the farmers were out in the fields again sowing dourra, maize, sugar-cane and cotton. Despite the heat, Lucie continued to make expeditions outside Luxor: to Karnak, where she became intimate with the two wives of a Turkish merchant, and where, too, there was an uproar when her pocket was picked by two 'swells' who hung about the temple.

She went, as well, to the Valley of the Kings, across the river. As they approached, 'the mountains were red hot and the sun went down ... all on fire'. The tombs she found simply 'ravishing': 'Death was never painted so lovely. The road [from the tombs] is a long and most wild one, truly through the valley of the shadow of death, not an insect nor a bird. Our moonlight ride home was beyond belief beautiful.' The 'amber light' of day gave way to the haunting illumination that prevails through the long Egyptian night – not a dark night at all, for as Lucie said, 'here you see all colours as well by moonlight as by day ... The night ... is a tender, subdued, dreamy sort of enchanted looking day.'

And all this time Lucie's health grew stronger and stronger: 'my cough is almost gone and the pain quite gone. I still

*The person who calls the faithful to prayer at the five fixed daily times from the minaret of a mosque.

expectorate thick yellow matter, but in smaller quantity, and every now and then bits of chalky stuff . . . the horrible feeling of exhaustion has left me. I suppose I must have salamander blood in my body to be made lively by such heat.' Above all, her blood-spitting had almost entirely ceased – a great relief for, of all her symptoms, this was the most distressing. When it was at its worst, she felt she was coughing up her life's blood; and blood-spitting, too, was the surest sign of consumption. Coughing, breathlessness, lethargy, even expectoration could all be ascribed to a bad cold or bronchitis. But the appearance of blood on a handkerchief, however faint, meant only one thing: tuberculosis.

★

It was highly fortunate that Lucie felt so much better, for shortly after the *Eid el-Fitr*, the celebrations which marked the end of Ramadan in April, a terrible epidemic broke out in Luxor, and Lucie, with her medicine box, was the closest thing to a doctor or *hakima* in the town. Weakened by their month of fasting, young and old fell ill with agonizing stomach pain, constipation and fever. The last carried many off. Mustafa Agha and Omar begged Lucie not to go among the villagers; they feared she might catch gastric fever herself and, if she failed to cure those who sought her help, her patients might accuse her of poisoning them with her 'bullets' (pills) and castor oil, or of giving them the evil eye. But Lucie refused to quarantine herself, and not only treated those who came to her at the French House, but also went out to see others who lay feverish and listless in their mud hovels, too ill to seek help. Strangely, Lucie didn't think the disease infectious. And by chance, she had brought along with all her other medical supplies a 'lavement machine' to give enemas, which proved something of a miracle. She dosed her patients with castor oil, and if this failed to end their 'stoppage', administered an enema. If she saw the patient early enough, she was almost always able to save him.

Her success at 'physicking' the epidemic victims prompted

people with all sorts of other ailments to seek Lucie's help as well. Dysentery, malaria, jaundice, bad eyes, toothache and infertility were just some of the conditions she was expected to relieve, and soon her stores of Epsom salts, senna, aloes, rhubarb and castor oil were nearly depleted. But it was probably just as much belief in Lucie as in her drugs and 'lavement machine' which worked so many cures in Luxor in the spring of 1864. The old ladies in particular spent hours complaining to her of their manifold aches and pains. To one of these old women Lucie gave an innocuous powder wrapped up in an old copy of the *Saturday Review*, hoping this would keep her quiet for a while. But the next day the old woman returned − not to complain or to get more medicine, but to say to Lucie, '*Mashalluh!* The charm was a powerful one, for though I have not been able to wash off all the fine writing from the paper, even that little has done me a deal of good.'

It was her services as the *hakima* of Luxor which earned Lucie her Egyptian name. She wrote to Alexander how the mother of an only child, a boy whom Lucie had cured, kissed her feet in gratitude and asked what her name was so that she might pray for her. Lucie explained that her name meant 'light' − *noor* in Arabic − but because this was one of the names of God, she could not be called by it. A man who was standing nearby then pronounced, '"Thy name is Noor ala Noor" which meant 'Light from the light', and Noor ala Noor it remains.' A spontaneous christening or name-giving, and another way of saying − like the claim that Lucie would rest in a Muslim grave − that she now belonged to this world.

★

In late April, when the worst of the epidemic was over, Lucie was sitting dreamily on her divan on the balcony one evening, watching the swallows and the small bats swoop in the waning light above her, when to her amazement her young cousin Arthur Taylor − from Sarah Austin's side of the family − suddenly walked in. He was on his way to Edfu and Aswan, and as soon as Lucie had welcomed him and heard his plans, she impulsively asked if she might join him. It would be such a relief, she said, to get away 'from all the sickness and sorrow in which I have taken part', and she felt she could do so with a clean conscience, as she'd had no new cases in four days and no deaths in ten.

And so they set off – Lucie, Arthur, Omar and Sally – on Arthur's *dahabieh* for Aswan, stopping *en route* at the temples at Esna and Edfu. It was like journeying into an inferno: 'yesterday we had the thermometer at 110; I was the only person awake all day on the boat. Omar after cooking lay panting at my feet on deck. Arthur went fairly to bed in the cabin, ditto Sally, all the crew slept . . . Omar cooked amphibiously, bathing between every meal. The silence of noon with the *white heat* glowing on the river which flowed like liquid tin . . . was magnificent and really awful.' At Esna and Edfu, 'great was the amazement of everyone at seeing Europeans so out of season; we were like swallows in January to them'.

When they reached Aswan, they left the boat and went on by donkey to the temple at Philae – where Isis had found the heart of her slain husband, Osiris, in her quest to re-member him. Here they spent two magical but intensely hot days and nights: 'the basaltic rocks which enclose the river all round the island were burning. Sally and I slept in the Osiris chamber on the roof of the temple on our air beds. Omar lay across the doorway to guard us.'

Lucie could not sleep for the heat and 'threw on an *abbaieh* [cloak] and went and lay on the parapet of the temple. What a night! What a lovely view! The stars gave as much light as the moon in Europe, and all but the cataract was still as death and glowing hot and the palm trees were more graceful and dreamy than ever. Then Omar woke and came and sat at my feet and rubbed them, and sang a song of a Turkish slave . . . Then the day broke deep crimson and I went down and bathed in the Nile and saw the girls on the island opposite in their summer fashions consisting of a leather fringe round their slender hips; divinely graceful bearing huge . . . baskets of corn on their . . . heads, and I went up and sat at the end of the colonnade [of the temple] looking up into Ethiopia and dreamed dreams . . . until the great [sun god] Amun Ra kissed my northern face too hotly and drove me into the temple to breakfast and coffee and pipes.'

The whole expedition to Aswan and Philae was a dreamlike idyll, marred only by two unpleasant incidents. One of Arthur Taylor's Egyptian servants spied on Lucie when she was bathing naked in a tentlike contraption rigged up from the boat, and Omar went into a rage and came close to murdering the man. And one morning Sally fainted dead away – the effect, Lucie said, 'of heat, fatigue and cucumber for supper'. Omar's reaction was strange: 'he cried over Sally bitterly, frightened out of his senses at seeing a faint'. Sally soon regained consciousness, but refused to eat breakfast, and in the following days was queasy and lethargic, while Omar remained uneasy and irritable.

★

They were back in Luxor by the middle of May and greeted as if they'd been absent for two years rather than two weeks. 'Mustafa came with letters for me and Yusuf beaming with smiles, and Mohammed with new bread made of new wheat and Suleyman [the gardener] with flowers, and little Achmet rushing in wildly to kiss hands.' Lucie was particularly eager to read her letters, because she had written to Alexander that she could not face coming back to Europe again for the summer: the memory of her last miserable summer in London, the thought of the expense of returning, and her fear of becoming ill all daunted her. In fact, she didn't even intend to go north to Cairo or Alexandria – both of which would be considerably cooler – but instead to 'bake' through the summer in Luxor and then travel to Cairo in the early autumn when she hoped Alexander would come and meet her, and then return to Luxor with her for an extended visit. Apparently, he agreed to this plan.*

If it is possible to be miserable in Egypt, then misery will probably descend during the brutally hot months of June, July and August. Lucie was almost the first European within living memory to spend the summer in Upper Egypt. It was a stupefying, depressing time of terrific heat and dust storms, and to make things worse, the cattle murrain continued unabated. The farmers in Luxor and the surrounding villages lost nearly all their herds; men had to turn the water-wheels themselves and pull their own ploughs. The price of meat and milk soared. From her balcony, Lucie saw hundreds of dead cows floating upriver.

Her life contracted; it was too hot to go anywhere or do anything. During the day she stayed indoors, the shutters closed against the heat (112 degrees outside, as low as 98 or 96 inside) and dust. After sunset she moved onto the balcony, but without candles which attracted swarms of insects. She remained outside, sleeping fitfully, until about six a.m., when she came indoors once more, and the monotonous cycle began all over again. The Egyptian sun blazed throughout the summer, but Lucie remained in darkness: during the day in the shuttered house, at night outside on the balcony without light to read or write by.

'I am now . . . in the kitchen which is the coolest place,' Lucie wrote to Alexander in June, several days before her forty-third birthday. 'Omar is diligently spelling words of six letters with the wooden spoon in his hand and a cigarette in his mouth, and Sally is lying on her back on the floor. I won't describe our costume. It is now . . . months since I have worn gloves or stockings and I think you would wonder at the *fellah* who "owns [is married to] you", so deep a brown are my face, hands and feet. One of the sailors in Arthur's boat said, "see how the

*Not only this reply but all of Alexander's letters to Lucie have been lost, perhaps in Egypt after Lucie's death.

sun of the Arabs loves her, he has kissed her so hotly that she can't go home among English people."'

It wasn't until the second week of July that Lucie continued: 'It has been so awfully hot that I have not had pluck to go on with my letter or indeed to do anything but lie on a mat in the passage with a minimum of clothes quite indescribable in English ... The worst is not the positive heat ... but the horrible storms of hot wind and dust which are apt to come on at night and prevent one's even lying down till 12 or 1 o'clock.'

By August she had become, she said, 'stupid [and] lazy... having lain on a mat in a dark, stone passage for six weeks or so — but my chest is no worse — better I think and my health has not suffered at all'. Sally, too, was overcome with lethargy, but she had shaken off her attacks of nausea and faintness.

Because Lucie didn't go out and there were few visitors, she had little to report other than the news that Saleem Effendi's black slave mistress was pregnant and had developed a craving for olives. Lucie roused herself to 'rejoice over the possible little mulatto', as Saleem was very pleased, and as Lucie explained, 'the child will be added to the other eight who fill [his] ... quiver in Cairo [with Saleem's wife], and will be exactly as well looked on and have equal rights if he is as black as coal'.

Closer to home, however, there was domestic disharmony as tempers flared in the heat. The eighteen-year-old wife of Mohammed, the sweeper, wanted to go home to have her mother unplait and wash her hair. Mohammed refused permission, whereupon his wife cut off her hair. Mohammed became enraged and told her to take their baby and return to her father's house and she departed in a huff. 'Ever since,' as Lucie described it, Mohammed 'has been mooning about the yard and in and out of the kitchen very glum and silent'. At this juncture Omar took matters into his own hands and sent Achmet to retrieve Mohammed's baby daughter, and then appealed to Mohammed on the child's behalf: did Mohammed wish her to

grow up without a father? The next morning Lucie found a
'pretty scene' in the kitchen: 'Mohammed in his ample, brown
robes and white turban lay asleep on the floor with the baby's
tiny pale face and little eyelids stained with kohl against his
coffee brown cheek, both fast asleep, baby in her father's arm
... Omar ... contemplating them with his great soft eyes.'
Soon the defiant young mother returned as well, and in time
her hair grew back.

★

By late August, Lucie could no longer tolerate the heat and dust
and incarceration in the French House and set sail for Cairo,
even though Alexander, to her consternation, had told her that
he wouldn't arrive until November or possibly as late as
December. On the eve of her departure, Lucie wrote to him, 'I
hoped you would arrive in Cairo earlyish in November and
spend a month there with me and come up the river in the
middle of December when Cairo gets very cold. Can't you
manage that? Pray try ... Unless you can have four full months
it would not be worth the trouble and expense as the journey
would be three weeks out of that and a month at Cairo, and
two on the river is quite little enough.'

When Lucie arrived in Cairo in late September, everything
seemed to go wrong. She went to Thayer's and discovered that
her poor friend had died.★ Omar found another house to rent,
but the noise and dirt and chaos of Cairo jarred terribly after
Lucie's long, still summer months in Luxor. 'I don't like civilization so very much,' she wrote home, 'it keeps me awake at
night in the grog shops and rings horrid bells and fights and
quarrels in the street and disturbs my Muslim nerves.'

A letter waiting for her from Alexander contained only
vague tidings of his movements, and she wrote back immediately, 'I don't make head or tail of your plans. If you don't

★Thayer was buried in the Christian cemetery in Old Cairo and Lucie may have
visited his grave. Five years later she was buried in the plot next to his.

come here till the middle of November, I shall only see you for a week or two as . . . I must go up river again end of November or very early December. I . . . expected you this month and leave this house the last day of November.' Then, not surprisingly, she fell ill with a high fever as well as her old symptoms of cough, pain in the side, expectoration and blood-spitting. Sally cut off Lucie's long hair and wrote an alarmed letter to Alexander which finally spurred him to book passage.

He arrived in Cairo in mid-November. It had been more than a year since Lucie and Alexander had last seen each other and both were much changed, Lucie especially with her cropped hair and brown skin, wearing loose harem trousers and a shift. At first the visit seemed to go well. Alexander wrote to his mother that he was much impressed by Lucie's fluency in Arabic and amused by her friends, especially by a pair of Bedouin chiefs who called dressed in what appeared to him to be large woollen blankets. They visited the Pyramids and the Sphinx and the famous mosques, and rode out on donkeys two or three hours a day. But it was not as Lucie had imagined it: Alexander didn't exchange his waistcoat and gloves for a loose *fellah* shirt or walk about 'enchanted' with his spectacles precariously balanced on his nose.

Quite suddenly, it became unseasonably cold – the thermometer sank from 84 to 64 degrees overnight, and Lucie felt she must return to Luxor before she fell ill again. And then: a bombshell. Alexander announced that he didn't think he would go with her to Luxor after all. Janet was planning to make an expedition with a party led by Ferdinand de Lesseps, the French diplomat who had the concession for the Suez Canal, then under construction, and Alexander proposed to join the party and also hunt gazelle with Janet in the desert. Afterwards, he would spend several weeks with the Rosses in Alexandria before sailing for home.

Despite the cold, Lucie remained in Cairo while Alexander and Janet were off in Port Said, Ismailia, Suez, and the Red Sea Hills. Perhaps she hoped that when he returned he might have changed his mind and go to Luxor after all. But he didn't have a change of heart – or go. Lucie's only explanation to her mother was that Alexander 'felt the Eastern life to be very poor and comfortless . . . I have got so used to having nothing that I had quite forgotten how it would seem to a stranger.' He would be glad, she said, 'to get back to the European ways in Alexandria', and then depart for England. In a postscript Lucie added that she was sending her long plaits of hair, which Sally had cut off, to Sarah with Alexander.

★

They said goodbye in the Cairo railway station, with some brave, face-saving words, no doubt. Lucie, at least, promised to return to Europe in the summer and they tentatively agreed to meet in Germany. The rest we must imagine: how Omar wrestled Alexander's portmanteau into the train carriage. The sea of milling travellers – Europeans, Turks, Egyptians – of soldiers, Bedouins, veiled women, porters, food hawkers, beggars, lepers. Their stiff embrace on the platform. The train hooting and letting off steam. Alexander in the compartment, lowering the window, leaning out to wave as the train pulled away. And Lucie in the crowd, Omar behind her, turning her back when the train was lost to sight, and plunging back into the world of light, noise and life out on the street.

★

Far away, in London and Weybridge, two old ladies wrote their own post-mortems on Alexander's visit to Lucie. From Lady Duff Gordon's diary:

28 December 1864. I heard from Alexander from Dover where he arrived on Monday. He had had a stormy passage . . . but he was not sick but the better for it. He had been ill when in the desert with Janet. I am very glad to know of him back again in England and with his little Rainy at Dover.

29 December. To our immense surprise, Alexander walked in about 6 o'clock from Dover, looking most terribly – so thin, so haggard and worn – ten years older than when we parted, and his hair cut short like a felon's.

30 December. Alexander's family is always the thorn in my side. Lucie's health and mind, her completely Arab character, make one feel that he has no home or his children, and Janet's mode of life is all what one *can't* approve of and can't mend.

And from Sarah Austin:

December 30, 1864

DEAR M. GUIZOT,

Alexander has been to see his poor wife, and has spent five weeks with her at Cairo. He is now on his way home, and she on hers to *her* solitary home at Thebes . . . It is only at Thebes that she is comparatively well. That she can *live*, and live with something like comfort *anywhere*, is a blessing for which I am duly thankful. But enough of sorrow remains. Her husband's broken life and broken home; her children motherless and homeless; her poor mother – how can I write it? – I shall never see that beloved face again; and so vanishes the last ray of earthly hope out of my horizon. Nor with this extinction of hope is there cessation of fear. The anxiety, the corroding anxiety *for her* remains; and after five weary years of that torture, I find myself as far as ever from repose.

Chapter Twelve

There was no time to brood over Alexander's visit, even had Lucie wanted to. Cairo remained unusually cold and Lucie was anxious and unwell. They needed to start for Luxor as soon as possible, but it proved difficult to find any sort of boat. At last Omar negotiated to rent one from an American mission for the outrageous price of £60. Reluctantly, Lucie agreed to be swindled by the Yankee missionaries, and they set sail on 20 December.

Four nights later, on Christmas Eve, they were far upriver, in one of those desolate stretches of the Nile unbordered by towns or villages or any sort of human habitation. A dark, moonless night, and not a soul awake on the boat, or so Lucie thought until around midnight she heard strange, half-stifled noises coming from Sally's cabin next door. Then Sally suddenly called out for Lucie to come to her: she was in labour and needed a midwife. Three hours later, just before dawn on Christmas Day, Sally gave birth to a fair-haired, blue-eyed boy 'without a twinge'. Omar was the father.

It took them another week and a half to reach Luxor. Despite good weather and fair winds, it wasn't an easy journey: ten long days during which Lucie had to live in the closest quarters with Sally, Omar and their 'squalling' infant. Sally had managed to conceal her pregnancy not only from Lucie, but from Lucie's new English doctor, Dr Patterson, in Cairo, from Alexander and Janet Ross, and even from her own sister, Ellen, Janet's maid.* This was one level of deception. A deeper and more

---

* Lucie told Alexander and Janet that Sally also kept her pregnancy a secret from Omar, but this is highly unlikely. In addition, we can see in certain passages of Lucie's letters – for example her description of Omar's distress when Sally fainted at Philae – that Omar must have known.

disturbing one was Sally and Omar's long-standing sexual relationship. This felt perilously close to betrayal – even infidelity – and Lucie, understandably, was enraged: with Sally, above all, and perhaps also with herself for being so unsuspicious. But she wasn't angry with Omar. Her leniency towards him was instinctive, even self-preservative, though in time, in long letters, Lucie came up with numerous reasons to exonerate her faithful, devoted dragoman.

Shortly after they reached Luxor on 2 January, Omar 'did the decent thing'. He and Sally were married by Sheykh Yusuf, who also arranged a naming ceremony for the baby, henceforth to be called Abdullah. Since Omar was a Muslim, he could, of course, marry Sally and still keep his wife Mabrooka back in Alexandria. Lucie bowed to the necessity of the marriage to avert scandal in Luxor, but she hated the whole idea of it, and from the beginning she made it clear that it was to be a marriage in name only. Sally and Abdullah were banished to a room at the other end of the French House while Omar slept in the passage outside Lucie's room, like a sentinel.

Sally's plan seems to have been to persuade Omar to divorce Mabrooka so that she might become his only wife, and thus recognized by English law. But Lucie vehemently declared that this could never be. She summoned Sheykh Yusuf and Saleem Effendi and in their presence laid down the law to Sally and Omar. If, she said, 'such a cruel injustice' of divorcing Mabrooka was 'perpetrated', Lucie would 'discharge' Omar and 'disgrace' Sally. English law, she reiterated, recognized only Mabrooka as Omar's wife; therefore Sally, according to Lucie, was 'a common adulterer'.

But, of course, Lucie was not really concerned with English law or even adultery. She was happy enough to recognize her Karnak friends, the two wives of the Turkish merchant, as legitimate, and she had warmly congratulated Saleem Effendi on the imminent little bastard his black slave mistress would bear him. But English law and Victorian propriety were Lucie's only weapons in this terrible mess. She could never acknowledge – perhaps even to herself – the fact that she was jealous of Omar and Sally's intimacy. And she could not acknowledge, either, that Omar had been anything other than seduced and led astray against his will, because now, more than ever, Lucie needed, relied upon and cared deeply for him.

In order to keep Omar, Lucie had to do two things in the spring of 1865: she had to persuade those at home that her interpretation of the situation was correct and fair, and she had to get rid of Sally, for she would have no peace of mind until Sally was banished from the French House, and even from Egypt itself. In letter after letter to Janet in Alexandria and Alexander and Sarah Austin back in England, Lucie spelled out her case in detail. She wrote to Janet in early February, 'of course, [Sally's] . . . marriage is *simply no marriage* at all . . . As to Omar, he is completely the victim in the business and I shall not dismiss him.' She described Sally's cool calculation and Omar's abject repentance and despair to Alexander: 'The poor boy has been really ill from remorse and shame . . . I find that these disasters are wonderfully common here – is it the climate or the costume I wonder that makes the English maids ravish the Arab men so continually? . . . You would have thought he was the seduced girl, and she a regular old roué.'

But it wasn't enough to portray Omar as the suffering victim. Lucie also hinted that he might actually be innocent. 'The child,' Lucie told Janet, 'is in my opinion hideous, but I daresay the Arabs think it lovely as it has light hair and blue eyes and an extremely white skin. I need not say not a bit like Omar.' To Alexander she went even further and declared that she 'much doubted' the child being Omar's at all. If Lucie really believed this, and if furthermore it were true, then Omar's heroism would have verged on martyrdom. But neither Janet nor Alexander bought this rather fanciful version of events.

Alexander also greatly doubted Omar's blamelessness in the affair, and he told Lucie that he thought she was being far too hard on Sally – a charge she hotly denied. Lucie assured him that she had no wish to injure Sally, and would say nothing of what had happened to anyone back in England. And to Janet she wrote, 'I have a regard of too long a standing for her not to wish to do all I can in her behalf short of travelling about with her and her babies present and future in my train.' Though Lucie was eager to be free of both mother and child, she said, 'in common humanity I cannot send her off alone and without money to seek employment'.

Lucie's plan instead, as she wrote to Sarah Austin, was to allow Sally to remain at the French House until Abdullah was four or five months – old enough to be given to Omar's wife, Mabrooka, in Alexandria. (The idea of handing the baby over to Mabrooka would seem to indicate that Lucie, along with everyone else, now believed that Abdullah belonged in Omar's 'quiver' after all.) Then Sally could return to England – Omar penitentially promised to pay her passage from his wages – where, as Lucie put it, 'if her family keep a quiet tongue, no one . . . need ever know of her escapade here'. She asked Alexander to give Sally one more quarter's salary and also 'a character' or reference to 'enable her to make a fresh start . . . but she has behaved so queerly that I should not be amazed if she were to perform some other strange antic . . . It is no use lecturing a woman of thirty who evidently has no shame at all in her, and I shall be glad to have done with her . . . I only hope I shall have done well in your eyes and that you will agree with me that there is no cause for dismissing Omar. *He* at all events has had a lesson in sorrow that he won't forget.'

But no one was happy with this solution. Alexander and Janet continued to feel that Lucie was being too harsh to Sally and too lenient with Omar. And though Sarah Austin thought that Lucie had taken the best decision under the circumstances, she hated the idea of Lucie being without an English maid after Sally departed. Lady Duff Gordon, for once, proved an ally: Lucie, she said, 'very properly' wanted to 'turn her maid off'.

But she, too, was distressed at the prospect of Lucie being deprived of a maid.

To everyone's amazement, Lucie herself wasn't the least bit anxious about being without a maid. She told Janet that she could manage perfectly well with just Omar to serve her, and she also said that she intended to take him to Europe with her in the summer. If necessary, she would engage a black woman when she returned to Egypt in the autumn. Dismissing and then refusing to replace Sally meant that Lucie would sever herself from her only link with her old life; after Sally left, Lucie would live in a completely Arab world.

★

But this break was still some months off in the early spring of 1865. As soon as Lucie had banished Sally and Abdullah to the far end of the French House, she settled down to producing several Egyptian letters for *Macmillan's Magazine*, which wanted to publish two or three new ones before bringing out those Sarah Austin had selected and edited for *Letters from Egypt* in June. Travel to Egypt had increased greatly since Lucie's friend Kinglake had published *Eothen* twenty years earlier, and Macmillan's hoped that *Letters from Egypt* would become a kind of handbook for a new generation of pilgrims to the East.

Lucie, in fact, found herself surrounded by English and European tourists as she worked on her letters in January and February. These visitors invariably made their way to the French House, and often proved trying. Baroness Kevenbrinck borrowed Lucie's saddle and insisted on making Saleem Effendi dance a polka with her when they all dined at Mustafa Agha's. Lord and Lady Hopetown arrived in two very grand boats, 'living like in Mayfair. I am so used now to our poor shoddy life, that it makes quite a strange impression on me to see all that splendour – splendour which a year or two ago, I should not even have remarked.' When Lord Dudley arrived, Lucie gave him 'an Arab dinner on a grand scale to meet all the notabilities of Luxor', but she told Alexander 'how vulgar the great English Pasha did seem compared with the . . . company of Luxor, and I saw they thought so and were amazed at his haw-haw laughter and boisterous talk'.

Worst of all, though, was the fourteen-year-old heir to the Rothschild fortune who arrived in a steamer like a royal prince with crowds of attendants, servants and hangers-on. His dragoman, one El Rasheedee, had fallen ill and young Rothschild callously turned him out at Luxor with a mere £5 to take the old man back to his home in Cairo. Then the Rothschild boy – 'so selfish and heartless', as Lucie described him – steamed on to Aswan.

Poor El Rasheedee was far too sick to travel home, so Lucie took him in and nursed him in the French House. But ten days later he died of fever, his hand in Lucie's, who closed his eyes while Omar laid his face to the *kiblah* (the direction of Mecca) and chanted the '*La illaha*' – 'There is no God but Allah.' An hour and a half later they led the funeral procession to the village mosque. 'The scene as we turned in between the broken colossi and the pylons of the temple to go to the mosque was overpowering. After the prayer in the mosque we went out to the graveyard, Muslims and Copts helping to carry the dead and my Frankish [European] hat in the midst of the veiled and wailing women. All so familiar and yet so strange.'

Within days, there was another death of a stranger far from home which also affected Lucie deeply. A young Englishman, travelling alone, fell ill during his stay at Luxor. Lucie herself was unwell – the aftermath of nursing and burying El Rasheedee – and could not care for the young man. But a kind visiting Englishwoman, a Mrs Walker, sat up with him for three nights and was with him when he died. He was buried on the first day of Ramadan in the small Christian cemetery for foreigners. 'Omar and I spread my old flag over the bier and Copts and Muslims helped to carry the poor stranger. It was a most impressive sight. The party of Europeans all strangers to the dead but all deeply moved. The group of black-robed and turbaned Copts, the sailors from the boats, the gaily dressed dragomans, several brown-shirted Fellaheen, Omar and the boatmen laid him down in the grave ... While the English prayer was read, the sun went down in a glorious flood of light over the distant bend of the Nile.'*

Several days after the young Englishman was buried, Lucie was at last visited by a European who brought neither annoyance nor illness and sorrow in his wake – the first 'real' visitor she had had since establishing herself at the French House. This was

* A hundred and twenty-four years after this funeral, I searched for the young Englishman's grave in Luxor. The Christian cemetery is located on the back road to Karnak. No one had visited it in years, and the old man who was the caretaker was reluctant to let me in until I produced some *baksheesh*. This graveyard was for foreigners – passers through – who had succumbed to fevers or malaria or cholera or had drowned in the Nile. (Copts and other Egyptian Christians are buried in a much larger burial ground out near Luxor Airport, on the margin of the desert.) And no one had died thus in forty or fifty years. The graves were choked with weeds, the flat, slab-like tombstones coated with a layer of thick sand and dust. I used my notebook as a shovel to scrape it off. The old gatekeeper impatiently rattled his keys as I copied down inscriptions. 'In loving memory of Henry Robert Harrison of Merton College, Oxford, second son of Charles A. Harrison who died at Luxor March 3rd, 1905, aged 24 years.' 'In loving memory of our dear daughter, Nessie Carrick, who was drowned in the Nile at Luxor, on March 29th, 1916, in her nineteenth year.' And many others. They all seemed to have died *in medias res*, suddenly, in the fullness of their years, like Lucie's young Englishman: 'Anthony Butler died Luxor February 1865 *Requiescat in Pace*.' Probably no one had visited his grave since the day of his funeral. A message had been sent to Cairo, and then a telegram to somewhere in Lincolnshire or Sussex or Norfolk and two middle-aged parents and possibly a fiancée had grieved. Then life had gone on, and they too in time died, and Anthony Butler had disappeared from memory until I found his grave. To the irritation of the caretaker, I lingered in the graveyard, tearing away weeds and vines from tombstones, scraping off dust to reveal inscriptions. Half a mile down the road in either direction lay Luxor and Karnak temples with their vast funereal monuments raised by and for people dead thousands of years. How much more lost and forgotten seemed Henry Robert Harrison and Nessie Carrick and Anthony Butler. I put off leaving because I knew that the chances of anyone else visiting this forgotten cemetery were slim. The old man would lose the key in time; he would die and his sons would sell his house and go to seek their fortunes in Cairo or Alexandria. The graveyard would be buried once more in weeds and vines and dust until one day papers were signed and duly stamped and then a bulldozer would burst through the frail wrought iron gate and plough under the graves as if preparing the earth for some future harvest.

a thirty-six-year-old French diplomat and man of letters named
Lucien Prévost-Paradol. He was a protégé of Sarah Austin's old
friend Barthélemy St Hilaire and, though Prévost-Paradol and
Lucie had never met, they got on famously together. Prévost-
Paradol, for his part, charmed Lucie by being so keenly
interested in her Egyptian friends and life in Luxor. Mustafa
Agha threw a grand dinner-party and invited Sheykh Yusuf
and Saleem Effendi, and Prévost-Paradol behaved as civilly and
graciously as did his Arab hosts. Lucie was delighted that
Paradol was 'intoxicated by Egypt'; he stayed with her three
nights on his way to Aswan and two more when he returned
downriver. They sat up late discussing Swift and Shakespeare –
shared passions – 'a very agreeable interlude of . . . good European talk'.

Prévost-Paradol must have also temporarily dispersed the
tension that still reigned in the French House over the Omar
and Sally affair. Certainly he was unaware of it. From his point
of view, Lucie was not only composed, but majestic and adored:
'the Queen of the Arabs' in Luxor, 'the fairy of those ruins and
the providence of the poor people who inhabit them'. Even had
she been well enough to leave, he asked her, 'could you ever
descend to mere European life' again?

★

Shortly after Prévost-Paradol departed, Lucie received the proofs
of Letters from Egypt from Sarah Austin, who had carefully culled
and edited a collection of several hundred pages from the letters
Lucie had written over the past two and a half years. Proofs are
always a chore, and at first Lucie tried to fob off the labour; she
wrote to Sarah, 'do you cut out and correct, dearest Mutter. I
am stupid and have not felt able to work . . . not being quite
well and having had worries and sad events.'

But after several days, Lucie summoned the energy to sit
down at her writing table and began to work in earnest. The
result, however, left her only with a deep sense of frustration
and inadequacy. Sarah had told Lucie that Letters from the Cape,

which had been published the previous autumn, was still selling well. Lucie wrote back, 'I am glad the people like the Cape letters . . . but honestly I don't think the Egyptian good – [they are] not what I saw and felt and comprehended. You know I don't pretend if I think I have done something well and I was generally content with my translations, but I feel it all to be poor and what Mossey calls *dry* when I know how curious and interesting and poetical the country really is.'

Lucie working on her letters was like an artist standing at an easel before a sublime landscape, full of subtle variations of light, colour, depth, texture. When she looked up from her writing-table to the Valley of the Kings and the Theban Hills, or came back from the bazaar and sat down to her letters again, she felt like the painter does when he compares his small, imperfect representation to the real thing which surrounds him. Art is defeated by life. It would have been easier for Lucie to edit her letters on a cold, grey, wet day in Esher, where they would have sprung to life and delighted her rather than seemed such a meagre and imperfect approximation of her rich, golden world in Luxor.

She persisted, however, and finished. 'If I can manage to write one, I'll send a Preface,' she told Sarah, but she didn't have the heart or energy to introduce or provide a background to the letters, and in the end Sarah herself wrote the preface. To Alexander, Lucie confided, 'I am dreadfully disappointed in my letters. I *really* don't think them good – you know I don't [boast] about my own performances. I have not the slightest inspiration for a novel – but if I get to feel a little stronger I will see if I can't do *something* and get some money.'

Despite Lucie's misgivings about the book, when *Letters from Egypt* was published by Macmillan later in the spring, it did remarkably well. In June, Alexander was paid £100 for the first edition of 1,500 copies, which quickly sold out. It was reprinted twice before the end of the year. The book also received excellent reviews though neither Alexander nor Sarah Austin bothered to send Lucie cuttings of her notices. Thus she probably never read the praise in *Fraser's Magazine* of her 'graphic power' and 'heart full of benevolence' nor the appreciation in the *Edinburgh Review* of her 'singularly captivating and vigorous style'. Even more importantly, nearly every one of the reviewers recognized that Lucie had penetrated the colourful, exotic surface of Egyptian life. As the *Westminster Review* put it, 'we much doubt whether any European . . . has . . . seen more thoroughly into the . . . mind of modern Egypt or caught its tone more truthfully. Lady Gordon differs . . . from the generality of modern travellers. She does not, like them, look upon the people as mere accessories to a strange Eastern scene.' And like her other reviewers, the *Westminster Review* celebrated Lucie's 'true liberality of mind, the generous appreciation of alien races and the genuine admiration of goodness and intelligence' which informed *Letters from Egypt*.

Both commercially and critically, then, *Letters from Egypt* became a great success. But for a long time Lucie was unaware of this, and when she did grasp how well the book had done she was almost indifferent to the fame it brought her. Everything in her past – her childhood as the daughter of a scribbling mother, her years as a London literary hostess, her small but secure reputation as a translator – seemed to prepare for the achievement of *Letters from Egypt*. But by the time success came, Lucie had left the past behind. Her life now was Egypt – a world where books other than the Koran were few and far between, and where publishers, monthly reviews and magazines, literary gatherings and gossip were all unknown. And there is no indication that Lucie missed any of these things in the least.

★

But the success of *Letters from Egypt* and Lucie's indifference to it were still some months ahead. By the time Lucie had finished with the proofs in March, the great heat had set in. In the past she had always found it restorative, but now she felt unwell, both mentally and physically. She wrote to Alexander, 'I am [still] a good bit shaken in nerves, and sleep . . . badly since the fright of Sally's lying-in, and my cough is harassing.' The combination of Ramadan and the heat also made for a good deal of illness among Lucie's friends and neighbours, and her services as a *hakima* were again much in demand. After the epidemic of the previous year, Lucie's medical skills had become famous throughout the district. Parties of sick Bedouins now travelled forty miles or more out of the desert and camped in tents outside the French House, lured there by wandering bards who had sung Lucie's praises: 'the daughter of the English is a flower on the heads of the Arabs, and those who are sick should go and smell the perfume of the flower and rejoice in the brightness of the light [Noor].' Women patients, as before, outnumbered the men, and often requested charms to make them fertile and love potions as well as medicines. By this time, too, legend had invested Lucie with 'a lucky eye'. She told her mother how 'I am asked to go and look at young brides, visit houses that are building, inspect cattle, etc. as a bringer of good luck – which gives me many a curious sight.'

Casting a benign eye on her neighbours' enterprises led to some diverting adventures, but for the most part a season of discontent still reigned in the French House, and also in Luxor and Egypt as a whole as summer approached. The situation with Sally and Omar didn't become any less fraught with the passage of time, and Lucie found Abdullah's 'incessant bawling' as nerve-racking as ever. She had asked Ross to buy a boat for her and send it to Luxor, and she planned to sail down to Cairo in it in late May. But Lucie felt now that having Sally and the baby on her hands until then would be unendurable, and so announced that she wished them to leave on the first government steamer as soon as Abdullah was four months old at the end of April.

In early April, Lucie wrote to Alexander, 'altogether this year is miserable in Egypt. Everyone is anxious and depressed and . . . hungry; the land is parched from the low Nile, the heat has set in six weeks earlier than usual, the animals are scarecrows for want of food, and now [we have] . . . horrid stories of bloodshed and cruelty and robbery for the Pasha [Ismail] takes the lands of whole villages for his own.'

Ismail, indeed, seemed to be bleeding the country dry with his modernization schemes. To subsidize the Suez Canal and his other ventures, extortionate taxes had spread now to cover nearly all crops and animals, charcoal, butter and salt and every other conceivable commodity; fertile land was confiscated by the government and 'replaced' by worthless acreage in the desert. Even worse, *fellahin* were rounded up in villages and sent off to labour on public works such as canals without food or pay.

By the spring of 1865 all this injustice and suffering had reached Luxor. When Lucie looked down from her balcony she could see men limping among the camels, waiting for government boats to take them off. Periodically the sound of the *kurbash* or whip could be heard as ignorant *fellahin* were herded together – disoriented and distraught at being taken away from their villages and homes for the first time. Many, of course, would not survive to return. 'These are not sentimental grievances,' Lucie wrote home, 'hunger and pain and labour without hope and without reward . . . The system of wholesale extortion and spoliation has reached a point beyond which it would be difficult to go . . . Egypt is one vast plantation where the master works his slaves without even feeding them.'

'It is curious,' she said with seething understatement, 'to see the . . . gay *dahabiehs* [of the season's last tourists] just as usual and the Europeans as far removed from all care or knowledge of these distresses as if they were home. When I go [now] and sit with the English I feel almost as if they were foreigners to me, too, so completely am I now *Bint el-Beled* – daughter of the country – here.'

The English at a distance were indifferent too. Lucie filled letter after letter with heart-rending and bitter descriptions of all the suffering she was witnessing, but in their replies Alexander and Sarah Austin and even Janet in Alexandria scarcely mentioned her constant theme. Only Ismail Pasha himself really listened. After *Letters from Egypt* (which contained passages criticizing his regime) came out, Ismail gave orders that Lucie be watched when she was in Cairo, and that her letters from Luxor be intercepted. Lucie, however, soon realized that a good many letters were going astray, suspected why, and began to ask foreign travellers to carry her letters rather than trust them to the post.

Lucie also wrote home of how a mad dervish in Qena proclaimed himself the *Mahdi* – the expected messiah of Muslim tradition who would convert all mankind to Islam. Discontented *fellahin* in Gow and other villages near Luxor rallied to his call to rise against Ismail, and killed hundreds. There were fears that the uprising would spread to Luxor with disastrous loss of life, and Lucie lived for some days with the prospect of evacuation. But Ismail's soldiers ruthlessly put down the revolt before it reached Luxor. More than two thousand men, women and children were killed by government soldiers and thousands more were taken prisoner.

★

In the midst of widespread hardship, Lucie still had her own private problems and plans to resolve. She wrote Alexander yet another long letter devoted to a restatement of what she called 'the grievous history of Sally's misdemeanour', and she also reiterated her intention of sending Sally and Abdullah off at the end of the month and bringing Omar with her to Europe in June. She raised other issues too: whether Maurice might visit her in Egypt the following year and learn Arabic and Turkish to prepare for a career in diplomacy. And she told Alexander that the British Consul in Cairo, a Mr Colquhoun, had retired; Alexander was well qualified to apply for the post, but Lucie had little hope he would do so. 'I wish I could persuade myself honestly to think it would suit you to live in dear old Cairo with me,' she wrote to him. Alexander must have ignored or swiftly vetoed this opportunity, however, for Lucie never referred to it again.

In her letter, Lucie also mooted plans for the summer. When they parted in Cairo at Christmas, they had agreed to meet in Germany, but then Alexander seems to have changed his mind and pushed for a holiday in England instead. Lucie replied, 'I shall be so glad when the time comes to join you. I don't wish to go to Bournemouth again, please. Somewhere nearer London or not in England. Bournemouth disagreed so with Rainy, and I spit blood all the time I was there . . . Janet wishes for . . . Soden [in Germany]. Really, I care but little provided I see you and my chicks. I well recollect that our silver wedding approaches.' In the end, they settled on Soden, near Frankfurt. They would celebrate their twenty-fifth anniversary where they had been so happy on their honeymoon.

In late April, Lucie heard from Ross that he had bought her a fine boat for £200, that it was about to set sail and, all being well, should reach Luxor in late May. Several days later a government steamer bound for Alexandria arrived, and Lucie booked passage for Sally and Abdullah. There must have been some sort of strained farewell and perhaps some misgivings on Lucie's part, but she was enormously relieved when they went on 2 May.

With the departure of Sally and Abdullah, all the tension and bad feeling that had plagued the French House for months evaporated. Lucie was again in entire possession, and the house was blessedly silent and still once more. And the awkward and uneasy triangle of Lucie, Omar and Sally was now replaced by the old, close companionship of just Lucie and Omar. So successfully had Lucie persuaded herself of Sally's guilt and Omar's innocence that she and Omar were actually closer now than ever before.

An idyllic and peaceful month then passed in the growing heat of late spring until Lucie's new boat arrived at the end of

May. She had decided to buy a boat in part because it was clear that despite her plan to go to Europe over the summer, her home now was Egypt, and she didn't want to have to rent boats at increasingly exorbitant rates to go up and down the Nile. In addition, her tenure at the French House was uncertain; the house itself was in disrepair and the French government could at any time ask Lucie to leave if they had other tenants they wanted to house there.

Lucie was charmed with her *dahabieh* and decided to name it the *Urania* after her much-missed Rainy. And to Urania, the following year, she described the boat in some detail. 'My boat is quite a nice little house; there is first a bedroom and a pantry for Omar, then a little drawing-room with divans and a writing table in one corner and your picture and Janet's and Maurice's on the walls; then two little bedrooms, then a bath-place, etc., and quite at the end under the steersman is my bedroom which is very comfortable. All the sailors and the boys sleep outside on the decks ... When we travel there are eight or ten men, the *reis* [captain], a steersman and a boy. Up the river we sail with such a big sail, and if there is no wind, the men tow the boat with a rope, which is hard work against the stream. When we come down the river the great big sail is taken down and we float down or the men row singing very prettily all the while.'

Lucie and Omar sailed from Luxor on 15 May. From the beginning it was 'a tedious voyage of violent, adverse winds', and they were twenty-eight days *en route* to Cairo. At Minya, Lucie fell violently ill with pleurisy – so ill, in fact, that she thought she was dying. Omar sat with her day and night and during her worst hours cupped* her. 'If I had not loved

---

* Cupping was a sophisticated form of blood-letting practised in the nineteenth century. A heated tumbler was applied to the skin; this created suction and pulled up the skin which was then cut with a knife or razor. Like all forms of blood-letting, it was a debilitating procedure, though the counter-irritant effect of cupping may have distracted the patient from his primary discomfort or pain.

Omar before,' Lucie wrote to Alexander, 'I must indeed now. He nursed me as I never was nursed before, and was as handy and clever as he was tender. I believe he saved my life by cupping me Arab fashion with a tumbler and your old razor.'

★

When they finally arrived in Cairo and Lucie saw her English doctor, Dr Patterson, he said that he couldn't imagine how 'I did not die, and that but for Omar's cupping me, I *could not* have fought through. I certainly *never* felt so near death.' Though her crisis had passed by the time she reached Cairo, Lucie was still gravely ill. Dr Patterson told her that her lungs were severely inflamed; she couldn't lie down without feeling suffocated, and she had bad pains in her side. For two weeks Dr Patterson visited twice a day and Omar, in addition to nursing her round the clock, got an imam from the mosque of Al-Azhar to come and recite the Koran outside her door.

Meanwhile, the date when Lucie hoped to depart for Europe arrived and she was still far too ill to travel. Janet Ross, however, who had planned to accompany Lucie, kept to their schedule and sailed from Alexandria without her — extraordinary behaviour, but not untypical of Janet. Shortly after Lucie received news of Janet's departure, she had a letter from Alexander telling her that she was not to bring Omar with her to Europe. It had been written before he had received Lucie's letter describing her illness and Omar's devoted nursing of her but, even after Alexander learned of all this, he didn't change his mind. And then as if she didn't have enough trouble on her hands, Sally (who seems to have still been in Cairo) wrote to Lucie 'full of complaints and wanting money'. Lucie refused to see her or to give her money. She told Omar 'to go once and settle about the child and refuse to go again'. Apparently, he complied, fetched Abdullah and took him to Mabrooka, and then arranged Sally's passage to

307

England. Such, at any rate, was what Lucie understood to have happened.*

Because of her illness, and because of the embargo against bringing Omar to Europe, Lucie had to delay her departure until she was strong enough to travel alone. In mid-June she wrote to Alexander, 'I will let you know when I am able to undertake the voyage, but of course without a servant it will be longer as I now cannot rise from my bed or chair without help. I am much reduced by the frightful cold sweats of suffocation. Dr P. is blistering ... and physicking me.' Then in a postscript she added, 'If I *don't* come round, I beg you won't ever forget Omar's truly filial care and affection for me.'

At last, in early July, Lucie was well enough to travel to Alexandria where she stayed at the Rosses', for Henry Ross had not gone to Europe with Janet. But Alexandria was in a terrible state; cholera had broken out and hundreds of people were dying daily. Panic gripped the city. Virtually all business was suspended. Houses were shuttered up and the bazaar empty. Ismail Pasha had fled abroad, and so too had most of the expatriates. Those who remained were all attempting to get on the next boat bound for Europe, which meant that Lucie had a very difficult time booking passage for herself. Finally, Henry Ross managed to get her a berth on a steamer, the *Poonah*, and she sailed on 7 July.

*

Crossing the Mediterranean took only a week, but the overcrowded conditions on the boat made it uncomfortable and noisy, and then, when they got to Marseilles harbour on 14 July, the *Poonah* was quarantined for forty hours in terrific heat because of the cholera raging back in Alexandria. By the time

---

* I was unable to find any trace of Sally after she parted from Lucie. There are no marriage or death certificates under her name in England. In one of Lucie's letters she mentions the possibility that Sally might take a position in one of the new hotels in Cairo, so perhaps she remained in Egypt and did not entirely relinquish her son – or Omar.

Lucie disembarked, she was too weak and exhausted to travel on to Paris where she had planned to meet Alexander, Janet and Urania. Instead, she went to her Taylor relatives in Marseilles and telegraphed Alexander, who came to meet her while Janet and Rainy travelled on to Soden to await them.

Lucie did not mend quickly, but she was impatient to see her family and so, on the 21st, she and Alexander left Marseilles and travelled by easy stages through Lyons, Geneva, Lausanne, Strasbourg and finally to Soden. In addition to Janet and Rainy, Sarah Austin – looking much aged and crippled with gout – was waiting for her. Everyone, of course, looked older: Lucie, with her prematurely grey hair, perhaps most of all. But it was a joyful reunion, and Lucie was ecstatic to be with Urania, now nearly seven – a tall little girl with large eyes and straight, fair hair.

No sooner had they arrived, however, than Alexander set off once again for England, to collect Maurice from school. In early August they returned together to Soden. At last, the entire family was reunited. For the whole of August they were together as they had not been since Lucie left for the Cape. A precious, happy interlude, and Lucie felt better than she had in months. But they were bivouacked in rented rooms, in a foreign country: this was a snatched holiday, enjoyed on borrowed time, soon to end.

Sooner even than they planned. In late August, Lucie caught a bad cold and her cough and blood-spitting returned. She remained in bed for two weeks, and then, on the night of 15 September, her symptoms suddenly got worse. For some reason, she and Alexander were not sharing the same room – perhaps merely on account of her cold, though their separate rooms may also have reflected an estrangement between them now. In any event, Lucie was too weak to call out to Alexander, but she had a whistle by her bed which she used when she needed something. In the middle of the night, Alexander was roused by it and, when he rushed to Lucie's room, he found her lying in a pool of blood. She had burst a blood vessel and had a major haemorrhage.

The German doctor they called in told Lucie that she mustn't travel until she fully recovered and the danger of haemorrhaging was past. But Lucie was anxious to leave before the cold weather set in in Europe, and argued that she could only recover once she was safely back in Egypt. For years now, she had placed a great deal more faith in climate than doctors or medicine and, after protracted discussion, she persuaded both the doctor and Alexander that it was best for her to return to Egypt as soon as possible. Alexander, of course, had to take the children and Sarah Austin back to England, so they said their farewells in Soden. This leave-taking was heart-breaking for Sarah, who felt certain that she would never see her daughter again.

Everyone now had their own destination. Sarah would return to Weybridge, Maurice to Eton, Urania to Charlotte Austin. Janet was going for a holiday in Hamburg before sailing back to Alexandria. Alexander would resume his bachelor's London life at the Taylors' in Clapham, his office at Somerset House and his mother's house in Hertford Street. Lucie, with a new Belgian maid whom Lady Duff Gordon had engaged for her, was bound for Marseilles, Alexandria, Cairo, and finally her Arab home in Luxor.

The family now seemed irreparably splintered, and Lucie permanently exiled. She was leaving behind not merely her husband, children and old mother, but a whole world and way of life. Whatever brave words were said when they parted, she probably knew in her heart that she would not see Europe, perhaps never see any of them, again.

She sailed from Marseilles one grey autumn day in early October to another home, different ties and loves. Momentarily she was again untethered – suspended between two worlds – crossing the Mediterranean. But painful as it was to look back at all that she was losing, Lucie could still look forward. Her old friend Tennyson had written in the midst of his own great loss, 'Tho' much is taken, much abides', and imagined Ulysses in old age (Lucie was fond of the poem) on the verge of his last voyage. 'Death closes all.' There are many deaths in a human life. Lucie Duff Gordon must have died on that last crossing of the Mediterranean. But there were people in Luxor waiting for Noor ala Noor.

Chapter Thirteen

While crossing the Mediterranean, Lucie decided to set off for the Saeed and Luxor almost immediately upon disembarking at Alexandria. But when she and her new Belgian maid Marie arrived on 26 October, they found Omar overseeing repairs to the *Urania* which detained them for some days. Even so, they had to bail the whole way to Cairo, where they moored at Boulak and Omar orchestrated another course of repairs.

In Cairo, Lucie caught a bad cold and was confined to the boat with a sore throat, cough and chest pain. In late November she suffered another full-blown attack of haemorrhage that left her 'very poorly' and weak. She also lost a good deal of weight despite Omar's production of every delicacy and sweetmeat in his repertoire. Fortunately, Marie was turning out an asset rather than the burden Lucie had feared. 'She is truly attentive,' Lucie wrote reassuringly to her mother, 'without being officious and in no way troublesome – she also seems very efficient and has good sense.' Sarah Austin and Lady Duff Gordon were vindicated – for the time at least – in their insistence on the virtues of European maids.

By early December, the *Urania* was once again seaworthy and Lucie sufficiently recovered to travel, and on the 5th they set sail from Cairo. But there was next to no wind and it took them a full week to get to Beni Suef. Six more days of contrary winds brought them only to Minya, and then they made equally sluggish progress to Asyut. Here they crossed the invisible line separating Lower and Upper Egypt. And here, too, the wind utterly deserted them. The crew had to get out and tow the boat with a rope. Lucie was on deck watching them when suddenly something rose to the surface next to the boat. 'It was a woman: the silver bracelets glittered on the arms raised and stiffened in the agony of death, the knees drawn up and the beautiful Egyptian breasts floated above the water.' The men were stunned and in unison called on Allah to have mercy on the woman. The *reis* who was supervising the towing from the deck next to Lucie told her, 'We are in the Saeed now, and most likely she has blackened her father's face,* and he has been forced to strangle her, poor man.' Some time later Lucie learned that the woman had actually drowned, but even so she was haunted by the memory of the body floating in the river, and wrote home, 'I shall never forget the horrid sight.'

They finally reached Luxor at sunset on 23 December to the usual jubilant welcome: the better part of the temple village rushed to the river as soon as the *Urania* was in sight, and Lucie was swept off her feet and carried in the centre of a lantern-lit, noisy procession to the mosque of Abu el-Haggag, where numerous *Fatahs* were said for her and her family, and fulsome thanks rendered to Allah for returning *Sitti el-Kebir* – the great lady – to her home and people in Thebes.

On the morrow, however, Lucie learned that the suffering under Ismail Pasha's regime had intensified and spread during her absence, and that her friends and neighbours had scant cause for any jubilation – even at her return. Nearly one-third of the male population of Luxor had been carried off to labour on public works; many of them, she knew, would die of exposure and disease. Camels and other livestock had been seized, food was scarce and, when it could be found, exorbitantly priced. In addition, Lucie wrote home, 'we are eaten up by taxes ... every day some new tax. Now every beast, camel, cow, sheep, donkey, horse, is made to pay ... the taxation makes life almost impossible ... I saw one of the poor dancing girls the other day

* Dishonoured him, usually by committing some sort of sexual transgression such as losing her virginity before marriage, or adultery.

313

(there are three in Luxor) and she told me how cruel the new tax on them is.'

'I wish you to publish these facts,' Lucie told Alexander, 'it is no secret to any but to those Europeans whose interests keep their eyes tightly shut and they will soon have them opened. The blind rapacity of the present ruler will make him astonish the Franks some day.' But of course, Alexander didn't publish Lucie's account of the sufferings of a few thousand Egyptians in a remote Egyptian town of no interest to Europeans apart from its ancient monuments. On New Year's Eve, Lucie wrote in a quite different vein to him, 'I felt very dreary on Christmas day away from you all, and Omar's plum pudding did not cheer me at all, as he hoped it would . . . everyone sends you salaam, and all lament that you are not the new consul.'

★

But low and gloomy as Lucie felt, inexorably Luxor began to work its magic on her. And gradually, her health improved; her cough quietened, the blood-spitting tailed off, her night sweats subsided. All this she ascribed to Omar's tender nursing and a new regimen of drinking camel's milk every day: 'To my great surprise it is delicious. I expected it to have a twang, but it is more delicate than cow's milk.' It was also rich, and she began to put on weight.

One morning in late January, Lucie was discussing various matters with Sheykh Yusuf on her balcony when two figures from her English past walked in, appearing it seemed out of nowhere, like genies from a bottle. The first was thirty-six-year-old Marianne North, the younger half-sister of Lucie's girlhood friend Janet Shuttleworth, and behind Marianne, or Pop as she was familiarly called, was her father, Frederick North, who had lost his seat as MP for Hastings the previous year and his wife the year before that. Father and daughter were at the beginning of an extended tour of Egypt and Syria and this was the start, too, of Marianne's worldwide travels, in the course of which she painted hundreds of rare and exotic species of plants and flowers.* She and her father were a rather odd couple: Frederick North morose and nearly deaf, Marianne the quintessential dutiful, self-sacrificing Victorian spinster daughter who booked them into hotels, including the Hotel du Nile in Cairo, as Mr and Mrs North.

Lucie said she would have recognized the Norths anywhere, though she had not seen either in nearly thirty years. She called for pipes and coffee while word spread through the village of the Norths' visit. Soon the French House sitting-room was full of the Luxor élite – an alarming band for Mr North who, Lucie said, 'looked rather horrified at the turbaned society in which he found himself. I suppose it did look odd to English eyes.' The Norths were on their way to Aswan and only paused at Luxor to collect their mail, but before setting off further south they promised to stay with Lucie for a week or more on their return.

True to their word, they reappeared in early February, considerably weighed down by luggage and Marianne's canvases and easels. Marianne had worshipped Lucie as a child, but she was even more intrigued by her now. She thought Lucie at forty-five looked 'old and gray, but ... still handsome ... in spite of having burst two blood vessels that year, and she said the air at Luxor did wonders for her. The natives all worshipped her, and she doctored them, amused them, and even smoked with them.' What struck Marianne most of all was the power Lucie effortlessly wielded, and the enormous respect in which she was held – all the more striking because of Lucie's greatly weakened physical state. Lucie's ill health became painfully clear when they made an expedition to Medinet Habu – the great

* Marianne North (1830–1890) gained considerable fame in her lifetime as a botanical artist and intrepid traveller. In 1882, she built and endowed a large gallery at the Royal Botanical Gardens at Kew which houses hundreds of her paintings and may still be visited today. Her younger sister, Catherine North, with whom Lucie was baptized in 1837, had a very different fate At the age of twenty-seven she married the scholar, critic and art historian John Addington Symonds, who had been urged by his doctor to take a wife as a cure for his homosexuality. The 'cure', however, didn't work, and Symonds in later life campaigned for legal reform and tolerant recognition of homosexuality.

mortuary temple of Ramesses III on the west bank of the Nile – which Marianne wanted to paint. Lucie came and sat with Marianne as she worked, and 'talked in her old clever way and smoked, but soon got so tired I thought she would have fainted as Omar and I helped her over the stones back to her donkey'.

And yet for all of Marianne North's awe of Lucie and her admiration of her courage and awareness of how greatly she was loved in Luxor, she didn't at all grasp the beauty and solace that Lucie found in this world. 'She was idolized by her faithful Omar,' Marianne wrote in her memoirs years later, 'and by all the natives in Thebes, whom she doctored and treated as friends; yet it must have been a dreary existence for a thinking person to live thus among people so little removed from animals.'

It wasn't the least bit dreary, of course, for Lucie, but she was beginning to realize with mounting exasperation that it was for her maid Marie. Marie's jewel-like qualities were in fact fast fading in the sun of the Saeed. In mid-February, after they had been in Luxor only a month and a half, Lucie wrote to her mother, 'I am sorry to say that Marie has become so excessively bored, dissatisfied and she says, ill, that I am going to send her back rather than be worried so ... Of course, an ignorant girl must be bored to death here – a land of no amusements and no flirtation [will be] unbearable.' Marie, unlike Sally, was not the least bit interested in Egypt, never picked up a word of Arabic and, if she did fancy Omar or anyone else, found them impervious to her charms. In short order, she was packed off to Alexandria where she boarded the next ship home, and Lucie, with a great sigh of relief, returned to the old dispensation of Omar and little Achmet.

This, however, was not quite the end of the matter. A month or so later, a letter arrived in Luxor for Marie which was addressed to Lucie, who naturally enough opened it. It was from Marie's irate mother, demanding money that was owed her and funds, too, for the support of Marie's illegitimate child, whom Marie had utterly neglected for the past two years. Lucie's

verdict – that 'Marie was a regular prostitute' – was probably
an overstatement, but she was vindicated in the matter of maids
and vowed, 'I will import no more.' Sarah Austin and Lady
Duff Gordon seem to have bowed to Lucie's refusal to take on
another maid. She assured them, at any rate, that she had found
a capable village woman to do her laundry and that Omar was
not only a gifted cook but had 'developed a very creditable
talent for ironing and turns out collars and cuffs quite in style'.
Not that there were many of either left in Lucie's Arabized
wardrobe to wilt in the Luxor heat.

Shortly after Marie was dispatched back to Europe, Lucie had
a young French architect named Emmanuel Brune 'quartered'
on her by the French government. At first, she was annoyed at
the intrusion and found Brune a prickly character: proud, poor
and shy. But he was scarcely in the way since he spent ten or
twelve hours a day in the temples drawing, and when he came
home in the evening, he forgot his reserve and talked late into
the night with Lucie about his work and ambitions. Lucie's
resentment quickly vanished and shortly before Brune left two
months later, she wrote home, 'I am [now] as much obliged to
the French consul for sending me such an intelligent man as I
was vexed at first. An *homme sérieux* with an absorbing pursuit
is always good company.'

She wasn't nearly as pleased with an Englishman named
William Gifford Palgrave who arrived in Luxor in early April
on a government steamer. Not that it was immediately apparent
that he was English. For like Edward Lane, Palgrave dressed as
an Arab and spoke Arabic so fluently that even Egyptians
couldn't tell that he was really a European. He was a strange,
gifted man of forty, a convert to Roman Catholicism, who had
spent most of his adult life in India, Syria and Arabia as a Jesuit
priest and missionary. In 1865, the same year that *Letters from
Egypt* came out, he published a book which Lucie had read and
admired: *A Narrative of a Year's Journey through Central and
Eastern Arabia*. Now, in the flesh, she found Palgrave a

charismatic, ascetic man, and gathered that he had broken with the Jesuits. He had, in fact, joined the diplomatic service and had come to Luxor as a representative of the British government, to inquire into a quarrel between Lucie's old friend Mustafa Agha and François Mariette, the French founder of the Egyptian Antiquities Service.

It was an unpleasant affair. The previous summer, when Lucie was in Soden, Mariette had accused Mustafa (probably with justification) of stealing and selling antiquities from some of the Luxor tombs and temples. One thing led to another in the 110 degree heat, and they had come to blows and traded insults of 'liar' and 'son of a dog'. Lucie, when she heard of the matter, wrote to the British Consul to protest against Mariette's treatment of Mustafa, and the Consul sent Palgrave to inquire into the affair. Depositions were taken and numerous people interviewed, and in the end Mustafa seems to have been exonerated, but not without tarnishing his reputation. Marianne North, for example, while accepting Mustafa's hospitality in Luxor, called him a thief.

Lucie, of course, was loath to believe any accusation levelled at her old friend. And even if she did think him guilty of pilfering and selling antiquities, she wouldn't have considered this a serious crime. Tourists habitually carried off anything they found in the temples and tombs. Lucie herself sent home scarabs, small statues and antique jewellery which she or her friends had discovered in the rubble in the village or in the Valley of the Kings across the river. At about this time, in fact, she wrote to Janet, 'A man has stolen a very nice silver antique ring for me out of the last excavations – don't tell Mariette. See how we get demoralized. My *fellah* friend said, "Better thou have it than Mariette sell it to the French and pocket the money; if I didn't steal it he would." So I received the stolen property calmly.'*

* In Lucie's defence, it should be said that at this time there was no government policy regarding antiquities and no museums to house them. In addition, their age and value were not properly understood. Today temples and tombs are

Palgrave, however, didn't share this casual view of the dispersal of artefacts. He was a connoisseur and also a bit of a pedant. This Lucie sensed, and though she told Alexander that Palgrave was 'a clever fellow . . . very amusing of course and his knowledge of language . . . wonderful,' she also added, '*entre nous*, I did not much like him'. She found him particularly annoying when they attended the *Eid* celebrations for the great festival marking Abraham's sacrifice, one of the holiest days in the Islamic year. Palgrave later wrote it up for *Macmillan's Magazine* and found it a shoddy and chaotic affair compared to what he'd seen in Syria and Arabia. 'In company with Lady Gordon, I attended the feast,' Palgrave wrote in *Macmillan's*, 'there to witness a scene very imposing when well gone through, which in this case it decidedly was not.' He was unimpressed by the men jousting on horseback and found the prayers poorly performed. But most of all, he objected to the great crowd of women and children 'chattering, scolding, quarrelling and screeching . . . with utter contempt of stillness, reverence, or order, while the men were some too quick at their prayers and prostrations, others too slow: an Irish scene altogether.' Arabist as he was, Palgrave also had something of the English schoolmaster in him and yearned to muzzle the screeching women and cane the children. Fortunately, he left shortly after the *Eid*.

A month later, at the end of May, Lucie decided to take the *Urania* to Cairo and pass the summer there rather than spend the next four sweltering months in Luxor. But the day before they were to leave, Sheykh Yusuf's thirteen-year-old pregnant wife went into labour. She was a slight girl – scarcely more than a child herself – and from the start was clearly in for a hard time. Lucie, as *hakima* and friend, attended (she was also, of

---

swarming with crafty traders selling 'genuine antique' statues, scarabs, wall-paintings, jewellery and other treasures, the provenance of which may be traced back ten or twelve months to a workshop in Cairo or sometimes to a factory in Taiwan.

course, an experienced midwife, having presided at Sally's lying-in). For three days the poor girl struggled to give birth, but in the end she died and the next day the baby did too. Lucie stayed on in Luxor another three days for the funeral ceremonies and the reading of the Koran, and then finally set sail for Cairo with a heavy heart.

★

A long, lonely summer, moored at Boulak, followed. Hekekyan Bey was abroad and Thayer of course dead. Janet was in England and Henry Ross in Alexandria, though he came to Cairo several times on business, when he seemed preoccupied and worried. The only person Lucie saw was Palgrave, who was about to leave Egypt and bequeathed to her his black slave, Mabrook, 'a stout, lubberly boy with infinite good humour'.

Lucie, herself, sank into what she called 'a nervous depression', which made her feel 'unable and ashamed to write'. When she did summon the energy to write a letter, she complained to Alexander of 'blue devils', and confessed she was 'very unwell and above all, horribly nervous and depressed'. She was certain now that she was being watched by government spies. Even worse, she found out that Ismail Pasha had tried to bribe her boatmen to drown her. Lucie trusted her men and was as sure as ever of their loyalty and protection, but at the same time she felt persecuted and vulnerable.

The world beyond the boat, then, had turned into a dangerous and sinister place, with the result that she now rarely left it. She wasn't strong or energetic enough to go out, in any event, and spent her days leafing through books and magazines that Janet had sent in a big trunk from England. A new, fashionable magazine, she found 'far too high falutin for a savage like me. I don't want to improve mankind at all or to assist in the advance of civilization. Quite the other way.'

Lucie had planned to spend the summer writing more Egyptian letters for *Macmillan's Magazine* and starting on a book on religious festivals and folklore in Egypt, but she felt too 'seedy' to put much down on paper. The heat – 110 degrees in her cabin by day, 96 or 98 degrees at night – was debilitating. And then there was the constant din of workmen which made any sort of sustained writing impossible, for they discovered in August that the entire stern of the boat was rotten. It had to be rebuilt, caulked and pitched, the stern cabin enlarged and the whole boat repainted, all of which cost a staggering £260.

In order to pay for these repairs and cover their living expenses, Lucie had to borrow nearly £400 from Henry Ross. Ross could ill afford the loan for, as he told Lucie, the Egyptian Trading Company (which had bought Briggs Bank, his original employer) was on the brink of bankruptcy. All of the Rosses' savings had gone into buying shares in the company, and they were now faced with the prospect of ruin. So much for Janet's 'click' plan of saving £4,000 a year and retiring after five or six years in Egypt immensely rich.

In her letters to Alexander over the summer, Lucie waxed hot and cold over the suggestion (just whose it was is unclear) that he might come out to Egypt again in the winter. In August she wrote, 'how pleasant it would be if you could come – but don't run any risk of fatigue'. Several weeks later, she closed a letter with, 'farewell, dearest old boy. I can hardly say how your hint of possibly coming has made me wish it, and yet I dread to persuade you.' In September she wrote, 'If you do not come (and I do not like to press you, I fear the fatigue for you and the return to the cold winter as well as the expense), I shall go to Luxor in a month or so and send the boat back . . . to let.' Her hope of his coming ebbed away with the summer and she also despaired of ever being well enough to meet him again in Europe: 'I fear that breakdown at Soden sent me down a great terrace. I have never lost the pain and cough for a day since.'

In late September, Omar's wife, with a second baby daughter (the fruit of the previous summer), came to visit. Mabrooka had to travel to Cairo because, as Lucie explained, Omar 'will not leave me for a day on account of my constantly being so ailing

321

and weak'. Lucie didn't mention Abdullah or Sally in her letters home, so there is no way of knowing whether one or both were back in Alexandria or had left Egypt, or even whether Lucie knew what had become of them. What is clear, however, is that she now felt absolutely secure in Omar's devotion and affection. Mabrooka was no threat, and Omar saw her only two or three months out of twelve anyway. Shortly before they departed for Luxor in late October, Lucie wrote to Alexander, 'I hope if I die away from you all, you will do something for Omar for my sake, for I cannot conceive what I should do without his faithful and loving care of me.'

★

They reached Luxor, after a swift journey of only fourteen days, on 11 November, and Lucie immediately sent the *Urania* back to Cairo to let to tourists for £80 a month. Part of the French House had collapsed in the summer, but Lucie's rooms were still habitable. In its dilapidated state, however, the house was a haven for scorpions, snakes and rodents. Lucie stalwartly learned to kill the first two, but rats were more devious, and one morning she woke up to find that her thumb had been chewed and injured in the night by one.

In December, tourists began to descend on Luxor, and Lucie realized more fully than she had before that the success of *Letters from Egypt* had made her a celebrity.★ In the past, she had been pestered by thoughtless travellers for saddles, campstools, blankets, scissors and so forth. Now, curious Englishmen and brazen Americans came to the French House with copies of

---

★ In 1865–66 and for some years after, *Letters from Egypt* enjoyed *A Year in Provence* sort of popularity. A pirated American edition (for which Lucie received no payment) proved even more successful than Macmillan's English edition. Today, the green paperback Virago edition of the *Letters* is sold in almost every bookshop up and down the Nile, and in luxury hotel shops and newsagents as well, so that Lucie Duff Gordon is almost as much of a name to reckon with in contemporary Egypt as she was when besieged by officious tourists 128 years ago. She is also one of the few European writers on Egypt to be read widely by Egyptians.

Letters from Egypt they wanted her to sign. And not only Lucie was famous; her fans also sought out Omar, Sheykh Yusuf, Saleem Effendi and Mustafa Agha. Her friends may have basked in all this attention, but it tried Lucie's nerves sorely and she was often hard put to be civil. She finally resolved 'to bolt the doors when I see a steamer coming'.

For one traveller, however, she made an exception, and not only unbolted the door but gave him one of Omar's best dinners and a bottle of her best wine. But he was no gawking Englishman or Yankee. Lucie's intriguing guest was a penniless German man of about fifty who had spent the past four years in the Sudan, and then walked and begged his way through Nubia and Upper Egypt. He had traversed all this territory, amidst some notoriously hostile peoples, completely unarmed and unmolested. Indeed, as he told Lucie, wherever he stopped the Nubians killed an ox or sheep for him, gave him his own hut, enough drink to make him merry and a comely serving girl. As Lucie wrote to Alexander, 'if you had heard him, you would have started for the interior at once'.

Soon after the German departed, the artist and writer Edward Lear arrived with his Greek valet Giorgio and an American cousin named Archie Jones. They were an odd trio – Lear rather shy and gloomy, Giorgio volatile, and Archie breathtakingly philistine – but Lucie was kind and hospitable to the three. They stayed several days, Lear sketching and painting while Archie 'rushed in and out of temples declaring they had "an affle bad smell"'. Lucie could have dispensed with the American cousin, but she was drawn to Lear and sensed, perhaps, his underlying melancholy. She told Alexander that Lear was 'a pleasant man, and I was glad to see him', and she was touched when he gave her a charming drawing of the French House when he left.

But all this entertaining and unaccustomed English talk was exhausting, and left Lucie far from well. 'My chest does not come right at all,' she wrote to Janet in January, 'and I have a good deal of hectic fever . . . It is some weeks since I have been out as I can't walk and my donkey has grown old and unsafe and I am nervous about his falling.' When she dined with the visiting British Consul on his steamer, she 'was carried to the boat in state in an armchair on the shoulders of four men like one of the Pharaohs in a bas relief; my procession was quite regal. You would have "roared", as Mossey says, to see me "chaired" like the successful candidate in an old fashioned election.' A month later, however, Lucie could no longer joke about her condition. 'I continue very poorly and weak,' she confessed to Janet, '. . . and I think I am getting near the end of the lease: my blood seems to go slower.'

This feeling of the nearness of death came and went, intensifying always, of course, when her symptoms worsened and when she was exhausted and depressed. The weather, visitors, local troubles all took their toll. She also tended to feel particularly low and weak just before what she called 'the crisis of the monthly time', and her blood-spitting often returned just before her period too. The very fact that she was still menstruating, however, indicated that she was not yet mortally ill. But she felt decidedly unwell throughout the spring of 1867, and the prospect of 'the end of the lease' made her worry.

Above all, she was uneasy about Maurice, who was now eighteen and studying with a tutor in Brussels, a city Lucie considered 'a most dangerous place with all the French and English vices'. She had been opposed to sending him there after he left Eton, but Alexander chose it as a cosmopolitan milieu where Maurice could study languages and prepare for a diplomatic career. Lucie had apparently had some reports of Maurice's goings-on in Belgium from Janet and wrote him a stiff letter or 'jobation setting forth that if [Alexander] were to die, he was at present very unfit to have the care of me and Rainy'. She urged Alexander to recall Maurice from Brussels and send him to Paris instead, where they had friends to keep an eye on him and curb his spending and weakness for women.

But Alexander thought Paris would hold out even more temptations and be more expensive. Lucie then changed her tack and
suggested that Maurice spend the following year with her in
Egypt, and she urged Alexander to come with Maurice for a
holiday of several months, unless, she said, Janet has 'too
thoroughly possessed you with the idea that the Nile is a bore?
Ask Mr Lear . . . he was in raptures.'

As it turned out, it was actually Janet herself, along with
Henry Ross, who first visited Lucie in early March 1867. In the
wake of the collapse of the Egyptian Trading Company, the
Rosses had decided to cut their losses and leave Egypt for good,
but before departing they came up the Nile to say goodbye to
Lucie. It was their first trip to Luxor and Upper Egypt; during
their six years in Egypt they had never stirred south of Cairo.

Lucie, of course, was delighted when the Rosses wrote to say
they were coming. But she was apprehensive as well. Janet was
immune to the poetry and charm of Egypt and impatient with
the prevailing customs. Several days before they were expected,
Lucie wrote to Alexander, 'I am afraid Janet will be bored by
all the people's civility; they will insist on making great dinners
and fantasias for her . . . and she won't like it, I fear.' The
morning they were to arrive, Lucie woke up to find that the
French House had been decked with palm branches and lemon
blossoms and that the holy flags of the mosque of Abu el-
Haggag were waving from her balcony. Her faithful water-
carrier had been up since dawn sprinkling a path for the Rosses
from the river bank to the French House.

The Rosses began to grasp Lucie's stature in Luxor miles
before they reached it. They came on a government steamer
and at first when they landed at villages and tried to buy food,
they were told there was none. Then one of the crew announced
that the daughter of *Sitti el-Kebir* was on board. 'The effect was
magical.' Suddenly milk, chickens, lambs and bread appeared
out of nowhere and any sort of payment for them was refused.
By the time they reached Luxor on the morning of 9 March,

the news of their arrival had preceded them. A crowd of people was waiting at the landing place, loaded down with food and gifts, and they swarmed about the Rosses as they made their way up the cool watered path to the French House.

Two days later Janet wrote to Alexander:

DEAR OLD BOY,

Here we are enjoying Mamma's wonderful talk; all we wish for is that you were here too. The little village is bubbling with excitement. *Eid Keteer* (great festival) . . . the heat [is] tremendous . . . However, my mother enjoys it and declares that this burning sun does her good. I can't say she looks well, and I find her a good deal aged. You have no idea what a power she is in the land. Henry, who knows the East, is astonished . . . We had not been long in the house before the notables came to have a look at us, and more coffee was consumed than Omar's frugal mind approved of. In the afternoon the Bedouin, such rough-looking fellows . . . came and did fantasia under the balcony. Such shouting and sticking of spears in the ground to gallop round! Next morning they lent us two horses and some of them accompanied us to the tombs of the Kings on the opposite bank of the river. The ferryman would not let us pay for being taken across; as usual he had received some kindness from the *Sitti el Kebir*, and how could he take money from her daughter whose coming had dilated her heart? . . . In the evening we dined with Saleem Effendi, the . . . magistrate of Luxor, a pleasant jovial man . . . Our procession to dinner was quite Biblical. Mamma on her donkey, which I led, while Henry walked by her side. Two boys in front had lanterns, and Omar in his best clothes walked behind carrying some sweet dish for which he is famous, followed by more lantern bearers. As we went through the village the people came out of their mud huts and called on Allah to bless us, the men throwing down their poor cloaks for my mother to ride over and the women kissing the hem of her dress. The dinner was an elaborate one of many courses, during which we made no end of pretty speeches to each other, and then we had pipes and coffee . . . Yesterday we went to the ruins of Karnak close by, which are magnificent. But I long to tunnel under this [French] house. It is built on the top of a big temple, and our floor is composed of the huge slabs of the roof. Where there are cracks one looks down into seemingly bottomless darkness. I don't think part of it is quite safe, indeed three or four rooms fell in last year, but not where Mamma lives. That side looks all right. Her balcony, looking over the river, is enchanting, and the sunsets are glorious. Tomorrow we go up to Aswan as Mamma thinks a change will do her good . . .

EVER YOUR LOVING JANET.

They spent a week on their Aswan excursion, and the trip did seem to benefit Lucie. Janet wrote to Alexander, 'Mother is ever so much better; I think having a good talk has done her good. And how she talks!' Janet, for once, was herself left speechless by Philae: 'what words can describe Philae. I can't even attempt to speak of its loveliness. There is a colonnade from whence one looks far, far up river towards Ethiopia . . . it made one long to go on and on up the mighty river.' Janet had successfully resisted going up the Nile ever since she came to Egypt, but at this late date she seems to have succumbed to its magic, and this must have brought her closer to Lucie than she had been in many years.

The day after they returned to Luxor, the Rosses departed on their steamer for Cairo again, laden down with chickens, eggs, butter, fresh bread and other gifts from Lucie's friends. Lucie went as far as Qena with them, where they dined with the magistrate – a three-hour banquet, ending with a performance by the two most famous dancing-girls in Upper Egypt, Zeynab and Lateefeh. In Qena, too, Lucie inherited another black slave, named Darfoor, who had been left behind by the previous consul – a tiny eight-year-old boy who didn't yet have all his adult teeth.

And in Qena, finally, Lucie and Janet and Henry said their farewells. No doubt they felt like final ones, but they probably didn't say so. Lucie and Janet were as unlike as it is possible for two people to be. But in their own individual ways they loved and valued each other, and this parting must have been a heart-breaking one. The morning after the magistrate's dinner, the Rosses steamed off to Alexandria, from whence they would sail to Italy, while Lucie and little Darfoor headed south again for Luxor.

Lucie's household now consisted of Omar, Mabrook and the new addition, Darfoor. Achmet, 'who was always hankering after the fleshpots of Alexandria', had found a new position with some Europeans doing the Nile and sailed back north with them. In a remarkably short period of time, Lucie was able to teach Darfoor to perform Achmet's chores: making beds, cleaning and washing up, running errands and so on. Mabrook, older and much larger than Darfoor, was slower, but he never forgot what he was told to do or how to do something once he was shown. His only failing was that he was 'hopelessly dirty as to his clothes . . . and takes a roll in the dust or leans against a dirty mud wall, oblivious of his clean-washed blue shirt'.

Overseeing Darfoor and Mabrook, of course, was Omar: 'Uncle Omar is the form of address, though he scolds them pretty severely if they misbehave, and I observe that the high jinks take place chiefly when only I am in the way, and Omar gone to market or to the mosque. The little rogues have found out that their laughing does not affect my nerves and I am often treated to a share in the joke.' At night Omar slept in the room next to Lucie's, and Mabrook, Darfoor and the guard Mohammed in the hall next to him. If Lucie felt ill or needed something, she summoned Omar by blowing her whistle. He was a heavy sleeper, but if she failed to rouse him, Mabrook or Darfoor would hear the whistle and wake him so that 'I never had to wait one half minute.'

★

In May the *Urania*, which had been rented out to tourists for the past six months, returned to Luxor and Lucie prepared to go to Cairo, where she planned to spend the summer as she had the previous year. There was a vague understanding that Alexander and Maurice would meet her there in the autumn, Alexander for a two- or three-month holiday and Maurice for a longer stay. But nothing was certain, in part because as Lucie wrote to Alexander, 'I never know whether you get my letters, as you never answer my questions or acknowledge them.' She both yearned for and feared their coming and told Alexander, 'I don't like to think too much about seeing you and Mossey . . . for fear I should be disappointed. If I am too sick and wretched I can hardly wish you to come because I know what a nuisance it is to be with one always coughing and panting and unable to do like other people.'

She sailed for Cairo in late May, still unsure of whether they were coming. It was a protracted, 'thirty-eight days' voyage 'of ceaseless, furious wind', which left Lucie feeling 'like the much-travelled Odysseus,' though 'unlike him . . . my companions . . . neither grumbled nor deserted'. When they reached Cairo, Lucie found a letter from Alexander telling her that Sarah Austin had had a heart attack at the end of May, news which threw Lucie into a state of acute anxiety until she had a letter from Sarah herself saying that she continued to feel weak and unwell but was out of danger.

They moored the *Urania* at Boulak, as they had the year before, and Lucie's life – contracted again to the boat – was monotonous and lonely. With the exception of Dr Patterson, she had no visitors. She was somewhat cheered when Dr Patterson told her that her lungs showed no further deterioration and that the consumption seemed arrested for the time being. But the issue of whether or not Maurice and Alexander were coming remained unsettled and dominated Lucie's letters throughout July, August and September. Alexander clearly had misgivings about the proposed trip for Lucie wrote to Sarah in late July, 'Alexander seems to doubt whether he will come, and to fear that Mossey will be bored. Was I different to other children and young people, or has the race changed? When I was that age I should have thought anyone mad who talked of a

Nile voyage as possibly a bore, and would have embarked in a washing tub . . . with rapture. All romance and all curiosity too seems dead and gone. Even old and sick and not very happily placed, I still cannot understand the idea of not being amused and interested. Janet says she thinks her father very unwell . . . Of course, I fancy the voyage must do him good, but "one man's meat is another's poison"! and the dread of ennui is really an illness in itself to Alexander and to Janet.'

But Sarah Austin never read this letter. Before it reached Weybridge, she died of heart and kidney failure at the age of seventy-four on 8 August 1867. Ever since John Austin's death eight years earlier, her life had been a sad, dreary posthumous existence – the main thing that had kept her going was her 'sacred work' of editing and reissuing her husband's works. Once this was accomplished, and once, too, she had brought out Lucie's *Letters* from the Cape and Egypt and seen her dying daughter for the last time, Sarah had no reason to linger.

Lucie's immediate reaction to the news of Sarah's death was relief – above all, relief that Sarah had been spared the blow of Lucie's own death. In her reply to Alexander, Lucie dwelt on practical issues: she thought that Alexander should now establish a home for himself and the children, either at Weybridge or somewhere else, with Sarah's furniture. Lucie herself asked him to keep for her Sarah's old watch (the one that Sarah's spurned suitor had tossed into the carriage after the Austins were married all those years ago), and a locket that her mother had always worn with a lock of John Austin's hair in it. Lucie was also worried about £100 that Sarah had promised to give to Omar. Sarah had told Lucie that she would send the money to Egypt, but it had never arrived. Now Lucie wondered if there was any provision for Omar in Sarah's will.* As she sat writing this

---

* Sarah didn't leave Omar anything in her will. She named Alexander as her executor and bequeathed all her possessions to Lucie (who, curiously, is called Janet Lucy in the will) and all her money – about £4,000 – to Maurice. Nothing was left to either Janet or Urania.

letter on the *Urania*, Lucie could hear the Koran being recited outside her cabin, for Omar had summoned two imams to do this for Sarah's soul. Lucie herself had 'a bad sick headache, quite a new ailment for me. I think it is because I can't cry like other people.'

She may not have been able to cry, but soon enough she felt a leaden grief for her mother, who filled all her waking thoughts and often her dreams at night. 'Poor Mutter weighs on my mind,' she wrote to Alexander in late August. Lucie knew that she should be glad that Sarah's struggle was over, but there was 'something inexpressibly painful to me in the very sense of relief ... I can only feel as the people here say for an affliction *Alhamdulillah*, and yet that very feeling is distressing.' What probably distressed Lucie most about her mother's life was her awareness that all Sarah's gifts and talents and dreams had been repeatedly thwarted and unfulfilled despite her brave exertions. Sarah had married the wrong man and then fallen in love with an even worse one. Both attachments had brought her disappointment, sorrow and despair. She had somehow survived Austin's many failures, Pückler's evasions and defection, and then Austin's death, only to endure yet more anguish because of Lucie's illness, exile and the threat of losing her too. This may well have seemed unbearable; for throughout Sarah's sad life, Lucie had been her one source of consolation – her 'one ray of light' as Sarah herself had put it. Perhaps Lucie realized this and felt that in some way she had let her mother down. She must have felt, at the least, the bitterness and desolation of her mother's last years, and now it was too late to do anything for her.

In her bereavement, Lucie's feelings about Alexander's and Maurice's proposed visit seem to have changed, or at least, she was loath now to press them to come. Instead, she urged Alexander to go to Hamburg with the Rosses or 'anywhere to do you good and never mind about me'. As for Maurice, she wrote, 'if he wishes to see the Nile let him come because it is worth seeing, but if he is only to be sent because of me, let it alone . . . I know I am oppressive company now and am apt, like Mr Woodhouse in *Emma*, to say "let us all have some gruel", and so I am best alone.'

Meanwhile, Omar's wife Mabrooka visited with yet another baby girl (their third – the production of a daughter was becoming an annual event) and Lucie gave them £100 out of her dwindling resources to help them buy a house in Alexandria.

Finally, in late September, Lucie heard from Alexander: 'You may imagine how glad I was yesterday to receive your . . . letter . . . from which I conclude Maurice is coming here, though you say nothing of yourself.' She assumed, correctly, that Alexander's silence about his own movements meant that he would not be coming. In her reply she asked Alexander to send at least £300 with Maurice which she needed for repairs to the boat, to pay Omar's wages (the £100 for his house was to replace the gift that Sarah Austin had promised and forgotten) and Dr Patterson's bill. She also needed cash to buy food and drink for Maurice and his Belgian tutor, Joseph Soubre, who was coming to Egypt with him. In addition to money, Lucie had a long shopping-list of things she wanted Maurice to bring: cod-liver oil, opium pills, calico and flannel for Darfoor's and Mabrook's clothes, a folding armchair, wine, beer, cheese, bacon and ham, and she told Alexander that Maurice should also bring his own fishing-rod, tackle and gun.

She exerted herself to prepare for their arrival, but at the same time Lucie was preoccupied with how the family could be reunited without her back in England. 'My great wish,' she wrote to Alexander, 'is to see you comfortable in a house of your own with Maurice and Rainy, but I feel that I have no business to interfere. I only wish I were not the expense and trouble I am to you. Do just as you like and think best, dearest, and I shall be pleased.' But there was one thing that Lucie did not want to leave up to Alexander. She told him that if she died, she wanted Rainy to stay with Charlotte Austin, and *not* go to either Janet (whose son Alick was also being raised by Charlotte Austin, even though Janet and Ross were now back in Europe) or Lady Duff Gordon and her daughters. In the event, Alexander arranged things to Lucie's complete satisfaction. He moved into the Austins' cottage in Weybridge and brought Charlotte Austin and Rainy and perhaps also little Alexander Ross* to live there with him.

★

On the evening of 5 October, Lady Duff Gordon in Hertford Street wrote with satisfaction in her diary, 'Miss Austin and Rainy came to luncheon and staid [*sic*] till 4:15. Rainy very happy and well and full of *her* garden and *her* pony and carriage, and her *own* Papa at Weybridge. I am most glad to say that it all seems to answer perfectly.' Two days later, Alexander brought Maurice and Joseph Soubre to tea. Lady Duff Gordon was impressed with Soubre and thought him an amiable and 'mild-spoken youth'.

On 10 October, Maurice and his prepossessing tutor sailed from Southampton, and at just about the same time Lucie received a letter from Alexander telling her to expect them to reach Alexandria around the 22nd. Lucie had been in bed since early October with a bad cold and cough, and wasn't well enough to make the rail journey to Alexandria, so she sent Omar to meet them. She had not seen her son for more than two years and scarcely recognized him when they arrived in Cairo and came directly to the boat in Boulak on the night of the 25th. Maurice, at eighteen, was a strikingly handsome

---

* Alexander Gordon Ross's life remains a mystery. He never lived with his parents, and indeed only infrequently saw them. For a number of years he was raised by Charlotte Austin along with Urania, and Lucie treasured a photograph (now lost) of the two sent to her in Egypt. What became of him when Charlotte and Urania moved with Alexander to Weybridge is unclear. As an adult he seems to have visited Janet Ross in Italy, but when she died in 1927 she left him nothing in her will, which he unsuccessfully contested. In her autobiography, *The Fourth Generation* (1912), Janet made no mention of her son at all.

young man: tall like his father, but with Lucie's thick dark hair and large eyes, his own high colour and the most winning of smiles.

Chapter Fourteen

Maurice was a charmer and for Lucie his arrival was the best medicine she'd had in many months. 'I feel it like a new life to me to have the dear boy with me,' she wrote to Alexander, 'he is as considerate and kind as it is possible to conceive.' Maurice was not merely handsome and lively, he was also a fond, caring son, and his warmth and high spirits enchanted Lucie and even reconciled her to his aversion to any sort of intellectual effort. 'I wish he had more brains and a little industry,' she confessed, 'but I am too happy in his pleasant kindly ways and too sick and weary to find fault with anyone who is so affectionate to me. You must not grudge him to me this winter.'

Maurice made other conquests as well. Little Darfoor soon worshipped him and followed him about everywhere like a slave. Omar, too, was enamoured, but he cast himself into the role of Maurice's protector. 'I shall hold the child by his neck,' he told Lucie, 'and not let him go near the bad women' – the prostitutes that Joseph Soubre soon showed a penchant for in Cairo.

It was, however, unfortunately too late for Omar to keep Maurice out of harm's way. Lucie had been right about the temptations of Brussels, for Maurice arrived in Cairo with a bad case of the clap. When she realized how ill he was and the nature of his illness, Lucie summoned Dr Patterson, who probably prescribed mercury.* The treatment at any rate was effective and by late November Lucie was able to write to Alexander,

---

* Janet Ross effaced with black ink and then pasted blank pieces of paper over the passages in Lucie's letters which describe Maurice's illness and also his sexual activities in Egypt. By the time I read the letters in 1989 the glued-on sheets of paper had fallen off. Some of the offending passages are decipherable, but others remain permanently obliterated.

'Maurice is I am glad to say nearly cured, but he has had a narrow escape of a serious ailment. It seems he had been ill for four months and had doctored himself with some remedy got at a chemist's which had made him much worse. I tell you this that if such a thing should happen again you may find him a doctor in time.'

Maurice's illness prevented them from setting off for Luxor, but it wasn't the only reason for the delay. He had arrived in Egypt with exactly £8 in his pocket. Alexander had sent the £300 that Lucie requested by other channels and it hadn't, to her consternation, turned up. After paying Dr Patterson for Maurice's treatment and buying the vast quantities of food that Maurice and Soubre consumed, Lucie was nearly broke. In the end she was forced to borrow from a money-lender – 'a great nuisance and [it] . . . cost me a deal'.

And then, on top of everything else and worse by far, there was Joseph Soubre. To Janet, Lucie described Maurice's tutor as an 'illiterate, vulgar, impudent little beast . . . always wanting to drag Maurice out to the sixpenny women who frequent the places for the sailors and servants'. With Alexander, she was a bit more temperate, but no less chagrined. 'I suppose he must have been wonderfully on his good behaviour with you or you never would have sent such a vulgar, ill-educated man.'

Soubre behaved as if he were on holiday in Egypt rather than employed to teach Maurice. He spent much of his time patronizing the smart expatriate haunts such as Shepheard's Hotel or frequenting the brothels of Cairo – usually on his own, though he tried his best to persuade Maurice to accompany him. On more than one occasion, Lucie overheard Soubre luring Maurice to go out on the town. This so alarmed her that she 'told Maurice plainly that I dreaded the worst diseases and [said] that if he *must* have an outbreak, I would give him a pound or two to have a good dancing girl rather than a lot of four-penny women. I fear it was not moral,' she told Alexander, 'but it has worked.'

When Soubre went out alone, his absence from the boat was a great relief. But inevitably he returned at odd hours 'to eat, sleep and ride rough shod over us'. He would lounge in a chair reading a Dumas novel and order Lucie about as if she were his employee rather than the other way round. If he happened to be there when Lucie and Maurice were reading French together, he would come and sneer at their accents. So much for Lady Duff Gordon's amiable, 'mild-spoken youth'.

The situation became even worse when they finally set off for Luxor in late November. Now perforce Soubre was on the boat and in their midst twenty-four hours a day, and they realized that in addition to being insolent, thoughtless, greedy and selfish, he was also decidedly malodorous: 'As you may suppose, a man who never washed for two months and shut up every door and window was not agreeable in this climate.' The strain of being cooped up on the boat with Soubre and her constant anxiety over his influence on Maurice further undermined Lucie's fragile health, and below Asyut she had a bad attack of haemorrhage which confined her to bed for the last ten days of the journey.

They reached Luxor on 17 December, only to find that half of the French House – including Lucie's rooms – had collapsed and fallen into the temple beneath. Fortunately, her furniture had been moved out in her absence and was safe but, as she wrote to Janet, 'there is the end of the Maison de France'. The French government had no interest in rebuilding the house, and to do so was far beyond Lucie's means.* Henceforward, the *Urania* was her floating and only home.

The next day – after the general jubilation at their return, and after all of Lucie's friends had come to greet and marvel at Maurice – the inevitable 'blow-up' with Soubre – the climax of the storm that had been brewing all the way up the Nile – took place. A vociferous argument mushroomed out of some trivial

* At some point, however, the house was rebuilt, for in 1873 Amelia Edwards visited it and saw some of Lucie's belongings there.

difference and Soubre stamped his foot and threatened to leave. Lucie seized her chance and said then he had better go. She gave him 1,500 francs and paid for a room for him in the first and only hotel in Luxor, which had just opened. Soubre accepted her terms, and removed himself and his belongings from the *Urania*, but the next day he sent Lucie 'a pert note asking for a testimonial that he had never given me offence'. She wrote to him that 'I was sorry I had not been able to show him as much attention as I had hoped, but he had from the first reduced me to the position of an hotel keeper by the tone of command and rudeness he had taken towards me.' She did not enclose a testimonial with her letter. On 22 December Soubre departed for Cairo on the first boat heading north.

Maurice's libido did not depart with Soubre – much as the tutor had catered to its needs – but it was now under Lucie's and Omar's control. It says a good deal for the candour and trust in their relationship that when Maurice felt compelled to have sex, Lucie gave him sufficient money and directed Omar to take him to 'clean' dancing-girls rather than the squalid brothel at the other end of the village. After the first such excursion, Maurice returned and told Lucie his dancing girl had been 'a darling, but he was comically disconcerted by the way in which [the girl] told him that Omar and Mohammed [one of the crew on the *Urania*] . . . were good men and never went to her house'. Later, when Maurice asked Omar himself why he stopped at the threshold and never entered to enjoy himself, Omar replied, 'No, my feet don't know that road; if I *fall* in, God is merciful, but I won't *walk* into it, nor would I sit at the door for any man in the world but you who are like my brother.' The upshot of all this was, as Lucie told Alexander, that Maurice 'is getting a little shy of telling Omar that he *must* go to the woman . . . the old adage of examples better than precepts is not bad'.*

---

* These passages from Lucie's letters were censored by Janet Ross.

Divested of his evil genius, Soubre, Maurice now thrived in Luxor. Lucie wrote to Alexander, 'Mossey . . . has got back his old, round, boyish face; he eats like an ogre, walks all day, sleeps like a top, bathes in the morning and has laid on flesh so that his clothes won't button.' He was also rapidly picking up Arabic – not through study, for intellectual application didn't figure in his rejuvenation – but simply from being with Omar and the crew and Lucie's friends in Luxor day in and day out. Like his mother – and in marked contrast to Alexander and Janet – Maurice had a natural gift for getting on with people from a wholly different culture, speaking an alien tongue, worshipping a foreign god. Though he lacked Lucie's intellect and wit, he responded almost as intensely to her 'golden world' in Egypt, and this, of course, forged a bond of great intimacy between them.

★

In late January, they left Luxor for a leisurely two-month trip through Nubia, stopping at all of Lucie's favourite spots: Esna, Edfu, Kom Ombo, Aswan, Philae and Abu Simbel. Maurice, alas, had no appreciation of temples nor any interest in the peoples who had built them thousands of years ago. But he was in his element shooting wild geese, quails and sand grouse. The fishing was excellent too. Little Darfoor accompanied him on all his hunts in distant swamps and called him 'son of a crocodile' because of Maurice's love of the river and its wildlife. While Maurice hunted or fished, Lucie stayed on the boat and read or wrote letters or dozed in the sun on the deck. These were slow, dreamy days. Lucie and Maurice felt entirely cut off and unmoored – unhitched from both the past and the future. For Lucie it was a healing, idyllic time.

But of course it couldn't last. In late March, they headed north again, and they were back in Luxor by the middle of April. 'I was best in Nubia,' Lucie wrote home soon after they reached Luxor, 'but I got a cold at Esna . . . which made me very seedy. I cannot go about at all for want of breath and palpitation.' Her health, in fact, had taken a sudden turn for the worse. She asked Alexander if he could send her a special invalid's chair which two men could carry her about in because 'a common chair is rather awkward for the men where the banks are steep, and I am nervous so I never go out'. She'd seen the sort of chair she needed advertised in a magazine, and hoped he could buy one. Otherwise, she would become a recluse, confined to the boat and her bed.

Before Lucie heard from Alexander, the 'great broil' of the Upper Egyptian summer descended on Luxor and she and Maurice set sail on the *Urania* for Cairo, where they planned to pass the next few months. The journey down the Nile was not difficult, but Lucie's health continued to deteriorate alarmingly. She was now 'very feeble and very short of breath', and also 'so bent as to be almost deformed . . . quite like an old hag'. On her worse days, she could scarcely walk from one end of the boat to the other. She tried her best to tutor Maurice in French, but sometimes 'my breath is so bad I cannot read or correct reading, still less dictate'. She had stopped spitting blood, but her cough was very bad and she brought up thick, yellow expectoration.

As soon as they reached Cairo and were moored at Boulak, Lucie was examined by Dr Patterson, who confirmed that she was worse. There was no more quibbling now over whether Lucie's was a bronchial or tubercular complaint. No one could doubt now that she was consumptive. Still, it was believed then that consumptives – even advanced cases like Lucie's – were sometimes cured by a change of climate. Dr Patterson urged Lucie to go to Beirut or Istanbul, both of which, he said, were salubrious. Patterson himself was about to move to Istanbul and set up practice, and so could continue to treat Lucie there. But Lucie recoiled at the great distance; Lebanon or Syria felt much closer than Turkey. She opted for Beirut.

Writing to Alexander of her plans, she tried to put a cheerful face on things: 'Don't think I am going to die directly. Dr P. says my first bad place in the right lung is in fact cured, but the left which got a damage at Soden is a good deal worse and my heart is hindered and bothered.'

But most of Lucie's letter to Alexander was devoted to Maurice and his future. Lucie was trying to find a tutor for him in Cairo who could go with them to Lebanon, and if she found a good one, she thought that Maurice might as well finish his education in Egypt as anywhere else. He had no intellectual interests whatsoever, but was clever with languages and Lucie hoped he might carve out some sort of career in the Foreign Office. 'If you think M. would be better elsewhere,' she wrote to Alexander, 'I am not so selfish as to wish to keep him. Here he is well in health, steady in conduct and very happy. Would he be less idle and might he not be dissipated if you again sent him to such places as Brussels? He knows nothing and the education he has had is such as effectually to prevent his ever learning. He is so deeply embued with the idea that it is "snobbish" to read and to know, and that nothing on earth is worth living for but animal pleasures . . . He says he likes being with me, but is rather ashamed of my being supposed to be "blue" [a bluestocking]; he says "why, you know, even the governor [Alexander] says you talk like a governess." However, he is a dear, good boy and you must make the best of him as he is. I observe all the "Eton fellows" of his age have exactly the same *baronial* views of life and hate the "cads" who are base enough to read books. The living among Arab *canaille* has greatly improved M.'s manners which were terribly strong of the billiard room and brandy. He has all my faculty for getting on capitally [here] . . . and likes Upper Egypt and its rude ways far better than Cairo.'

Finding a suitable tutor in Cairo proved difficult and, by late August, Lucie felt they must embark for Lebanon without one. They booked passage on a Russian steamer. Just before they left, the invalid's chair from Alexander arrived: 'My men are delighted with the chair . . . and say they can carry me like a Sultan.' But they had so much other luggage that Lucie left the chair behind in Cairo to use on her return.

★

They were in Lebanon for less than two months, since Lucie realized soon after their arrival in Beirut that its 'climate is absolute poison to consumptive people'. It was a cold, damp, unwelcoming city where Lucie and Maurice knew absolutely no one. All Lucie's symptoms rapidly worsened and she needed immediate medical attention. But 'the Sisters of Charity wouldn't nurse a Protestant, nor the Prussians a non-Lutheran'. Finally, she found a European doctor who 'told me to settle my affairs, for I had probably only a few days to live, and certainly should never recover'.

But Lucie, sick as she was, had no intention of dying in this inimical place. Instead of winding up her affairs, she insisted they go back to Egypt immediately on the Russian steamer that had brought them hither. She had to be carried on board, 'too weak for anything', and then 'we were nearly shipwrecked coming back, owing to the Russian captain having his bride on board and not minding his ship'. Lucie lay in her cabin the whole way as 'we bumped and scraped and rolled very unpleasantly'.

The only benefit of this ill-starred journey to Beirut was that Lucie had found there a tutor – or more accurately, a governess – for Maurice: an Englishwoman of an uncertain age named Emma Matthews who could also double as a maid to Lucie. For, despite her aversion to European maids, Lucie was now so weak that on her worst days she needed assistance to wash and for other intimate acts that Omar and Darfoor couldn't help her with.

'I have got M. to take a French lesson every morning from Miss Matthews,' Lucie wrote to Alexander from Cairo, 'and when we go up the river I will get a sheykh for his Arabic.' Lucie was still worried about Maurice's future and what would happen to him when he returned to England. He had told her that after he left Egypt he wanted to go to Germany or France and study languages in 'some sort of out of the way place', if

Alexander would give him 'a moderate allowance'. And Lucie thought this a reasonable plan, in part because she felt Maurice would 'not relapse into his bad ways with regard to women. He tells me that he finds the craving after that greatly lessened owing to my prevailing on him to restrain himself, and that he sees I was right when I told him he was in a quite morbid state of mind and body . . . when he came here. Another six months in Brussels would most certainly have killed him.'

Women, however, were not the only worry. Money was also a source of anxiety in Maurice's future. It wasn't so much that he was extravagant as 'careless and helpless . . . and the money . . . slips through his fingers'. In addition, he had 'the wildest ideas of making impossible percentages' from investments. Thus Lucie entreated Alexander not to hand over Lord Lansdowne's bequest of £5,000 when Maurice came of age. 'My mother's money is quite enough [for him] to play ducks and drakes with.'

★

Once she was safely back in Cairo, the Egyptian sun and heat repaired some of the damage Beirut had done to Lucie's health. 'I now feel so much like living on a bit longer,' she wrote to Alexander in early November, 'that I will ask you to send me a cargo of medicines . . . I didn't think it worthwhile before to ask for anything to be sent to me that could not be forwarded to Hades, but my old carcass seems very tough and I fancy I have still one or two of my nine lives left.' But she wanted to live these remaining lives out in Upper Egypt, not Cairo, and so they – Lucie, Maurice, Emma Matthews, Omar, and Darfoor – sailed southwards on the *Urania* in late November.

They paused at Luxor for several days, where, as usual, there was much rejoicing at their safe return. Then they carried on to Nubia, spending Christmas Day 1868 at Esna, where a fantasia was staged in their honour: 'How I did long to transport the whole scene before your eyes – Ramadan warbling intense love songs and beating a tiny tambourine, while Zeynab danced before him and gave the pantomime to his song; and the sailors and girls and respectable merchants sat pele-mele all round the deck, and the player on the *rabab* drew from it a wail like that of Isis for dead Osiris. I never quite know whether it is now or four thousand years ago, or even ten thousand years, when I am in the dreamy intoxication of a real Egyptian fantasia.' It was an evening unsnared from the net of time – and thus it comes down undimmed to us as Lucie dreamily lived it.

By the time they reached Aswan in January 1869, however, the dream had dissolved. Lucie again was very ill, 'more ill, I believe,' she told Janet, 'than you quite suppose. I do not like your father to be worried, but I may say that I think it hardly probable I can last much longer.' Nothing specific, no list of symptoms or medicines: just the flat statement that the end was bearing down on her.

Meanwhile, Emma Matthews had turned out 'an utter fool, full of airs and graces . . . a hideous woman of thirty with false teeth [who] wants more waiting on than I do . . . I shall get rid of her as soon as I can without being unkind . . . she is a grievous trouble and a fatigue to me.' Emma Matthews, in fact, had gone the way of all of Lucie's other maids – whether or not she was indeed 'an utter fool', or because Lucie had simply lost touch with how conventional Englishwomen of Miss Matthews's station behaved. But Emma Matthews was not as easy to dislodge as Sally or Marie. Lucie could scarcely ask her to leave the boat in Nubia and make her own way back to Cairo and Beirut. And so Miss Matthews remained, a 'fearful aggravation . . . always cackling and screeching and calling Omar and Darfoor to find her worsted needle or lace her boots and very sulky because I can't chaperone her about and give her gaieties'.

They were still in Aswan and Lucie very ill when the Prince and Princess of Wales, who were in Egypt in connection with the opening of the Suez Canel later in the year, came up the Nile. The Prince and Princess had read *Letters from Egypt* or at least heard about the book and Lucie and her life in Egypt, and they were eager to meet her. Before they actually reached Upper Egypt, they sent her an invitation to visit their *dahabieh* when they arrived in Aswan. Ismail Pasha, however, got wind of the proposed meeting, which he feared because he knew Lucie would denounce him to the Prince and Princess, and so Ismail threatened to arrest all of Lucie's Arab boatmen if she visited them. It was a needless threat: Lucie was too ill to visit anybody, and sent the Prince and Princess a letter explaining why she very reluctantly must refuse their kind invitation. When the royal visitors reached Aswan, however, they called on Lucie on the *Urania* and were profoundly moved by her plight. The Prince of Wales offered any help that might be needed, and Lucie asked him to employ Omar as his dragoman after her death, to which the Prince readily agreed.

'Can you thank the Prince of Wales for Omar,' Lucie asked in her next letter to Alexander, and then went on to describe how 'my sailors were so proud at having the honour of rowing him in our own boat and of singing to him'. For her part, Lucie was almost as struck with her guests as they were with her. She found Princess Alexandra 'the most perfectly simple-mannered girl I ever saw . . . she looks at one so heartily with her clear, honest eyes, that she must win all hearts – but she is not pretty . . . the Prince . . . was well bred and pleasant. I wish he didn't drink so much and were more dignified, but he too has the honest eyes . . . and I am sure he has a kind heart.' Lucie was not one to be intimidated by royalty but, as always, she had an eye that penetrated to the heart of things: the Princess was plain and the Prince tippled but they were honest, kind people.

★

Lucie lingered in Nubia until the great heat was upon them once again, and then returned to Luxor in early May for a brief stay. As usual, she planned to spend the summer in Cairo, but she feared she might not live to return to Luxor in the autumn and so felt she must dispose of most of her possessions and say goodbye to everyone. They didn't want her to leave, and the *cadi* or judge tried to persuade her that if she must die she should do so in Luxor and 'he made ready my tomb among his own family'. Lucie promised that she would come back and lie with her people in the Saeed.

On the morning in late May when they set sail for Cairo, hundreds of people thronged the banks of the Nile in front of Luxor Temple where the *Urania* was moored. Mustafa Agha, Saleem Effendi, Sheykh Yusuf, Maurice's dancing-girls, sheykhs, imams, the *cadi* who had prepared Lucie's tomb, black-shrouded widows, the carpenter and stonemason, the bazaar sellers, water carriers, donkey boys, *fellahin* and Bedouin all came to say farewell to Noor ala Noor. The women were loaded down with gifts for Lucie: loaves of bread they had stayed up all night baking, fresh butter, cheese and eggs; others had fish and geese, quail and even a whole ram to load down the *Urania*.

At last, with Omar's assistance, Lucie was able to extricate herself from the crowd and was carried back onto the boat. As the sails of the *Urania* filled with wind and the boat got underway, she stood on the deck and watched the crowd of people and the temple behind them, and then the columns of Karnak, grow smaller and smaller until the boat negotiated a bend in the river and it was all lost to sight.

★

When they reached Cairo in early June, they moored at Helwan, to the south of the city, rather than at Boulak. A letter from Alexander, who had been told by Janet that Lucie felt close to the end, was waiting for her: he wanted to come out to Egypt immediately.

On 15 June 1869, nine days before her forty-eighth birthday, Lucie wrote back to him:

DEAREST ALEXANDER,

Do not think of coming here ... it would be almost too painful to me to part from you again; and, as it is, I can patiently wait for the end among people who are kind and loving enough to be comfortable without too much feeling of the pain of parting. The leaving Luxor was rather a distressing scene, as they did not think to see me again. The kindness of the people was really touching . . .

Omar sends you most heartfelt thanks, and begs the boat may remain registered at the Consulate in your name for his use and benefit. The Prince has appointed him dragoman. But he is sad enough, poor fellow; all his prosperity does not console him for the loss of 'the mother he found in the world'. Mohammed at Luxor wept bitterly, and said, 'poor I, my poor children, poor all the people!' and kissed my hand passionately, and the people at Esna asked leave to touch me 'for a blessing', and everyone sent delicate bread and their best butter and vegetables and lambs. They are kinder than ever now that I can no longer be of any use to them.

If I live till September I will go up to Esna, where the air is softest and I cough less, and live in a house there, and send down the boat to be let. I would rather die among my own people in the Saeed than here.

You must forgive this scrawl, dearest . . .

Goodbye for the present, dearest love. I can't say more.

YOUR OWN L.D.G.

Over the next few weeks, Lucie was preoccupied with what would become of those she was leaving behind. She had provided for Omar by arranging his post with the Prince of Wales and by asking Alexander to leave the *Urania* for him to let. She also begged Alexander to do something for little Darfoor. Then she decided that it was time for Maurice to go home. Lucie was now far too ill to pursue the plan of educating him in Egypt. Even more, she wanted to spare him the pain of watching her die. Thus Maurice's passage was quickly arranged. In late June, Lucie bade him farewell – knowing in her heart that she would never see her handsome, loving boy again – and Maurice sailed for home.

After Maurice's departure, Lucie spent the days in her cabin, where she had photographs of him, Janet, Rainy and Alexander on the wall. She now had almost continual pain in her side, her coughing exhausted her, and her breathing remained very bad, especially when she lay down. This made it almost impossible for her to get any rest. But her kind old friend Hekekyan Bey found a dentist who gave Lucie a reclining chair which supported her and enabled her to sleep a few fitful hours at night.

For a time she was wracked with regrets. She passed through a dark phase when her life didn't seem to add up to much. She wished she had written of all that she'd learned in her seven years in Egypt. She had told Alexander some months earlier, 'now that I am too ill to write I feel sorry that I did not persist and write on the beliefs of Egypt in spite of your fear that the learned would cut me up, for I honestly believe that knowledge will die with me which few others possess. You must recollect that the learned know books, and I know men, and what is more difficult, women.'

But most of Lucie's regrets and worries now must have been more personal: why had Janet turned out such an indifferent mother and devil-may-care wife? What damage had been done to Rainy, growing up almost entirely without Lucie? What would become of Maurice, and was she somehow to blame that he wasn't more serious and responsible? And then, like any married woman, she knew that there had been times when she was uncaring and wilful and hard on her husband – a husband whose family and life, Lucie may well have felt, she had wrecked. These were bitter, painful thoughts to live with as her time ebbed away.

On 9 July, Lucie wrote to Alexander again – a short letter, which, however, was long in the writing because she was continually interrupted by fits of coughing. She now realized there was no point in dismissing Emma Matthews and she wanted to reassure Alexander that the woman was no longer a burden. Then, with whatever words she could summon, she felt she must say goodbye.

DEAREST ALEXANDER,

Don't make yourself unhappy, and don't send out a nurse. Miss M. has come out excellent and I am nursed as well as possible. My two *reises* [boat captains] Ramadan and Yusuf are strong and tender, and Omar is as ever. I am too absorbed in mere bodily suffering to wish anyone else to witness it. The worst is I am so strong. I rehearsed my death two days ago and came back again after being a whole night insensible.

I repeat I could not be better cared for anywhere than by my good loving crew. Tell Maurice how they all cried [when he left] and how Abdel Haleem forswore drink and hasheesh. He is very good too. But the *reises* are incomparable.

God bless you, my dearest of all loves. How sad that your Nile project [to come and visit Lucie] was too late.

Kiss my darlings all, and dear Charly ... I don't write very well, I suppose, being worn out with want of sleep and incessant suffocation. Forgive me all my faults towards you. I wish I had seen your dear face once more – but not now. I would not have you here now on any account.

YOUR OWN L.D.G.

Four days later, on 13 July, Lucie wrote a telegram to Alexander, informing him of her death, leaving blanks for the time and date to be filled in later. She continued to fight for breath throughout the afternoon and evening, but she was growing progressively weaker. At midnight, despite the 96 degree heat in her shuttered cabin, she said she was cold. Emma Matthews and Omar wrapped her in blankets, but she still shivered. Emma brought her a hot cup of *café au lait* which Lucie gratefully drank and said warmed her. Then she said to Emma and Omar, 'You know what is coming,' and seeing their faces contorted with grief, told them not to be afraid and reassured them that she was not in pain.

Eight days before, she had taken off her wedding ring and asked that it be sent to Alexander. Now she told Omar that she wished to be buried in a white linen Asyut shift and wrapped in

349

a white sheet. She knew that he would understand, because that is what Muslims wear to the grave. Then Darfoor and Ramadan and Yusuf and her other crew came in and she thanked and reassured them too. And finally, she turned to Emma Matthews and, finding genuine sympathy for this woman who, after all, through some strange concatenation of events, was going to see Lucie out of the world, said, 'My dear child . . . I did not know how much you could do. Receive my dying thanks and best love.'

Those were Lucie's last words, though she remained fully conscious. Slowly night dissolved above the still river and intimations of sunrise – a faint haze of light – rimmed the horizon. Dawn – another dawn, at the other end of this human life from the dawn that had broken on Queen Square all those years ago – emerged from the cusp of the night. And when the sun began to cast golden stripes of light across the cabin wall, Lucie had another, violent fit of coughing which she was too weak to withstand – she suffocated and died.

★

An hour later, the Koran was recited by two imams outside her cabin as she was prepared for burial. Omar insisted they obey the Muslim injunction that the dead must find their final home before nightfall on the day of death. Thus a carpenter was quickly summoned from the bazaar to construct a coffin while Hekekyan Bey went to an American missionary of his acquaintance, a Dr Garnett, to ask him to perform the funeral ceremony that very afternoon.

At sunset, Lucie's coffin was borne on the shoulders of her crew across the narrow, fertile belt of land bordering the Nile to the Christian cemetery where Europeans were then buried. Dr Garnett spoke his pious words, and Emma Matthews threw the first clod of earth onto the coffin after it was lowered into the ground. Later a large, granite monument with an engraved epitaph would be raised over the grave: a memorial. Lucie would not, perhaps, have liked this one, but she would have understood why those who loved her – back in England – had it erected.

Lucie lies far away from them: in Cairo – in Egypt – though not, as she had hoped, 'with my people', in the Saeed, where Isis found the heart of Osiris and, in her anguish and love, re-membered him.

Epilogue

THE FIELDS OF OFFERING

As a married woman, Lucie left no will.* Not that she had much to bequeath anyway. For the past seven years, she had led a pared-down, unfreighted existence, making do quite happily with a small shelf of books, some saucepans and wooden spoons, a bit of crockery and next to no cutlery, a handful of cotton shifts plus a few survivals from her European wardrobe, and her wedding ring, which she had told Emma Matthews to send back to Alexander. Her only possession of value was the *Urania*, which she had asked Alexander to allow Omar to rent out while it remained registered in Alexander's name in Cairo.

With Lucie's death, Omar and Emma Matthews and little Darfoor disappear from view. Omar undoubtedly prospered in the employ of the Prince of Wales and with the *Urania* at his disposal. Lucie's *Letters* had made him a minor celebrity in expatriate circles, so he won't have lacked attractive opportunities. Emma Matthews – single, faded, genteel and poor – one imagines had a far from brilliant life after leaving Egypt, and little Darfoor no doubt was simply absorbed into the crowded, noisy, street life of Cairo; with luck, he may have found a kind master.

Hekekyan Bey we know lived on until 1875, of great service to the last to the many European visitors to Egypt. His journals, drawings and letters are now in the British Library in London. In Luxor, Mustafa Agha continued as consular agent – and continued his illicit trade in antiquities and, latterly, in mummies

---

* Until the Married Women's Property Act was passed in 1870, all the possessions, assets, and earnings of married women automatically belonged to their husbands. Hence, unlike spinsters or widows, they did not leave wills.

as well — until his death, as a very old man, in 1887. By that time the congested village in Luxor Temple had been completely demolished and cleared out by Gaston Maspero of the Egyptian Antiquities Service. Only the mosque of Abu el-Haggag, where Lucie was so often fêted, survived the clearance of the temple in 1885.* Mustafa, crafty as ever, demanded £3,000 as compensation for the demolition of his house and then built an even grander one just outside the temple walls.

★

Back in England, a year or so after Lucie's death, Alexander, who was now nearly sixty, proposed to a wealthy twenty-eight-year-old widow named Fanny Ball Hughes. She turned him down, but fell in love at first sight with Maurice, then just twenty-two. Her feelings were reciprocated, but Fanny and Maurice didn't act on them for some time because Alexander developed cancer of the tongue.

It was a terrible illness which in its last stages made eating and talking nearly impossible. But Maurice proved just as fond and caring a son to his father as he had been to Lucie during the last year of her life. He took Alexander to the United States, and for more than a year they visited various spas in Michigan, Vermont and New York where Alexander took the waters. Unfortunately with scant result, for after their return to England in the spring of 1872, Alexander was bedridden and in great pain.

As his father lay on his deathbed, Maurice astonished everyone by announcing his intention of marrying Fanny Ball Hughes. Old Lady Duff Gordon was aghast and Janet Ross, when she heard of the engagement, furious: Fanny, Janet said, was old, plain and a Roman Catholic. Lady Duff Gordon called her 'an egregious goose'. Undeterred, Maurice and Fanny took 'the matrimonial plunge', as Lady Duff Gordon put it in her diary,

---

* This small, beautiful mosque survives intact today, perched on top of the Great Court of Ramesses II at the northern end of Luxor Temple.

on 18 June 1872 in Geneva. No one in Maurice's family attended the ceremony; the bride and groom honeymooned in Paris.

Alexander finally died, with Janet by his side, on 27 October 1872. He was buried in Cheam in Surrey, next to his baby son, who had died in 1845. Janet and Lady Duff Gordon were prostrated with grief. Alexander had, after all, been the greatest love of both their lives. But Lady Duff Gordon – who was now eighty-three – was more than just heart-broken. She was also haunted by what she felt was the great tragedy of Alexander's marriage to Lucie. For years she had criticized her daughter-in-law; now at last the fundamental reason for her disapproval was articulated, albeit in the privacy of her own diary.

Several months after Alexander's death, Lady Duff Gordon wrote a long, hagiographical diary entry on her first-born, cherished son, extolling his many virtues, but also lamenting the bad fortune she felt had darkened his life. And she clearly implicated Lucie as the source of Alexander's unhappiness: because Lucie was ill so much of the time and then away from home. But even more, Lady Duff Gordon condemned Lucie for not subscribing to orthodox religious beliefs: Alexander 'had a great admiration for Lucie's cleverness and [her] power (more like a man's than a woman's) of clearly discussing subjects. She had been almost self-educated . . . and all religious instruction was entirely unknown to her, but she felt . . . that she was not a Christian (having *never been christened*), and when she was a big girl of 12 or 13 years . . . she was christened . . . But when I first knew her about 30 years ago, all trace of such a good deed was washed away! She was an excellent German scholar and trans-lator . . . and German materialism and living with men of cleverness and no Christian humility and they flattering her vanity (which was *very great*) . . . made her lose all Christian feelings – no adoration, no humility. And she took great hold of Alexander's mind and his admiration for her wonderful intellect made him forget *from whom* all such blessings spring!'

★

Lady Duff Gordon died three years after her son, in 1875, at the age of eighty-six; still *compos mentis*, though very deaf, till the last. The year before her death, in 1874, Maurice and Fanny's only child was born and they named her Caroline Lucie after her great-grandmother and grandmother, though from the time she was a baby she was always called Lina. Lady Duff Gordon duly noted Lina's arrival in her diary, but never saw her. Lina's sixteen-year-old aunt, Urania, however, was enchanted with her niece. But in 1877, when Lina was only three, Urania died of tuberculosis, aged nineteen, at Weybridge, where she still lived with Charlotte Austin. She had probably contracted the disease years before from Lucie, and it had lain dormant within her until a time when her mother was beyond the heart-break of losing her last and most beloved child.

In 1884, Maurice – or Sir Maurice as he had been since his father's death – was further enriched when he inherited Fyvie Castle in Scotland from his father's cousin, Captain Alexander Gordon, who died without issue. It was a splendid edifice with towers and turrets, winding staircases and a spectral 'Green Ladye' who appeared to the lords of Fyvie when they were about to die. For Lina, now ten, it was an exhilarating as well as terrifying place to live.

But she did not remain there long. Maurice fell in love with another woman, and Fanny left Fyvie, taking Lina with her. In 1889, Fanny died and Maurice married Sophie Marie Steer. By this time, he was burdened with numerous debts and, in the end, he lost Fyvie and most of his money, including his legacies from Lord Lansdowne and Sarah Austin, and the considerable fortunes of both Fanny and Sophie Marie Steer.

Maurice's health broke down after he and Sophie moved back to London in the early nineties. The syphilis which he had contracted nearly thirty years before – and which Lucie thought Dr Patterson had cured in Cairo – now went into its last debilitating phase. By 1894 it had affected his brain, producing a mental disorder then called 'general paralysis of the insane'.

Maurice suffered all the classic symptoms: memory loss, delusions, and finally dementia. On 21 January 1896 his wife committed him to Holloway Sanatorium in Virginia Water, Surrey. Maurice died there on 5 May; the causes of death were certified as pneumonia and 'general paralysis of the insane' of two years duration. Maurice was just forty-six.

*

All this time, Janet and Henry Ross had been living in a beautiful villa near Florence called Poggio Gherardo. In 1875 Janet edited Lucie's *Last Letters from Egypt*, culled from those Lucie had written between 1866 and her death in 1869, and to them Janet added a selection of the Cape letters which by then were out of print. At Poggio, Henry cultivated rare orchids, Janet painted them, wrote numerous books,★ and entertained nearly all the rich, famous and artistic people who lived in and passed through Florence.

When Lina's mother, Fanny, died, Janet persuaded Maurice to let Lina come to Italy and live with the Rosses. Unexpectedly, Lina thrived with her formidable aunt and elderly uncle. When she was invited to a fancy-dress ball, but had no suitable dress to wear, Janet drew out of a tin box from under her bed 'the most beautiful cloth' Lina had ever seen: the deep rose silk woven with real gold thread that had been given to Lucie by Nana Sahib half a century earlier. (Nana Sahib's necklace of pearls, emeralds and rubies had belonged to Lina since she was a child.) Lina had a gown made out of it modelled on one in a Leonardo da Vinci painting. And Lucie's old friend George Frederic

---

★ Janet wrote non-fiction: history, art history, translations, memoirs and even a cookery book, *Leaves from Our Tuscan Kitchen*, though the cooking in 'our kitchen' at Poggio Gherardo was actually done by Janet's gifted chef Guiseppe Volpi, who dictated his recipes to her. *Leaves from Our Tuscan Kitchen* has been reissued in a revised edition by Janet's great-great-nephew Michael Waterfield. One of Janet's finest books is *Three Generations of Englishwomen*, a biographical study of Susannah Taylor, Sarah Austin and Lucie Duff Gordon, published in 1888. In writing it, Janet drew upon a mass of family papers, many of which were later lost.

Watts – who had painted Caroline Duff Gordon, and Janet as a child – did a magnificent oil-portrait of Lina in the gown made of Nana Sahib's rare rose silk.

But Lina's happy life with her aunt and uncle came to an end when she fell in love with and became engaged to the painter Aubrey Waterfield, whom Janet thought too poor to marry her niece. Both Rosses strongly opposed the marriage, and did all they could to make Lina break off her 'miserable engagement'. But Lina went ahead and married Aubrey Waterfield on 1 July 1902. Soon afterwards, Henry Ross died at the age of eighty-two. The following year, 1903, Gordon Waterfield, the first of Lina and Aubrey's three children, was born. Though the Waterfields spent a good deal of time in Italy and eventually settled there, they and Janet remained partially estranged.

Janet's life after Henry's death and Lina's marriage was a desolate and lonely one. For many months, she was felled by grief. She managed, however, to bring out a new collection of *Letters from Egypt* which included letters from both the 1865 and 1875 editions. Janet asked her old friend George Meredith to write an introduction and she herself added a long memoir of her mother.

The following year, in November 1903, Janet returned to Egypt, which she had not seen since she had visited Lucie in Luxor in 1867. When she arrived in Alexandria, she learned that Omar had died just a few months earlier. Cairo was 'so altered', Janet wrote, that 'I recognized nothing' and she doesn't seem to have visited her mother's grave. She took the overnight train to Luxor (a journey that used to take ten days to a month or more on a steamer or *dahabieh*), and found it too almost unrecognizable now that the temple was cleared. Mustafa Agha and Saleem Effendi had long since died, and Sheykh Yusuf and his family had moved away – no one knew where. But despite the absence of all of Lucie's friends, she was not forgotten. Even if they couldn't remember her, everyone knew about Noor ala

Noor, and when they understood that this white-haired old lady questioning them was her daughter, they crowded round Janet, all talking at once and kissing her hands.

From Luxor, Janet went on to Aswan and Lucie's beloved Philae, and here her sense of the death of the past was at its most painful. The first Aswan Dam had harnessed the Nile, stopping 'its rushing, tearing course, and instead of dangerous foaming cataracts there was a large placid lake up which we rowed to Philae'. The island palm trees were dead and the bushes a tangle of withered branches and weeds. The temple's foundations 'had been carefully strengthened with cement and all that was possible had been done to save them from destruction – but Philae, beautiful, wonderful Philae, was no more'.★

After her return from Egypt, Janet lived on in Italy, at Poggio Gherardo, for many years, until she died at the age of eighty-five in 1927.

During the Second World War, Lina and Aubrey Waterfield

★ Philae today, as it has been reconstructed, more closely resembles Lucie's temple than what Janet Ross saw in 1904. In the early 1960s, the new High Dam at Aswan threatened to submerge Philae completely. In a UNESCO operation second only to the removal of Abu Simbel, the temple complex was disassembled and moved, block by block, from the island of Philae to nearby Agilka Island, which was laid out and landscaped to look exactly like the original Philae.

In the spring of 1991, I made my third visit to Philae under peculiar circumstances. When the Gulf War broke out in January 1991, tourism in Egypt came to a standstill and all the monuments were closed. By the time I returned to Egypt in late March they had just reopened, but the country was still almost completely devoid of tourists. I was living in Luxor, but I went down to Aswan for several days and decided to go to the evening 'sound and light' show at Philae. The technicians and workmen took me to the island in their boat because there were none operating for tourists yet. And then, when we reached the island, they put on a command performance for me – an audience of one. Spotlights bathed the engraved temple walls (to the annoyance of bats hanging upside-down in dark corners), unearthly music boomed from concealed loud-speakers; the voices of Egyptian gods and goddesses were heard as if from on high. Because I was alone in the temple, it seemed utterly believable and profoundly moving. It was, in fact, a night not unlike the one Lucie spent with her cousin Arthur Taylor, Omar and Sally at Philae, when Lucie couldn't sleep for the heat and lay awake and entranced under the stars.

had to flee Italy for England. After they left, Poggio Gherardo was badly damaged by shells and ransacked by troops. Not only furniture and other household goods were carried off: a mass of papers and letters – including a good many of Lucie's – also disappeared. Watts's painting of Lina in the gown made of Lucie's material from Nana Sahib miraculously survived, and belongs now to Lina's daughter, Kinta Beevor. Aubrey Waterfield died in 1944. Lina lived on another twenty years and died at ninety in 1964. When she was well into her eighties, she wrote a remarkable book about her family – Lucie, Maurice, Janet and herself and Aubrey – called *Castle in Italy*. It is a book coloured by two world wars and thus inevitably elegiac, but it is also a moving evocation of another world that resonates in unexpected ways with her grandmother's *Letters from Egypt*.

Lina and Aubrey Waterfield's eldest son, Gordon Waterfield, first went to Egypt as a young man in 1926, and worked as a journalist and foreign correspondent there for a number of years. At some point he searched for, found and photographed Lucie's grave in Cairo. In 1937 he published a biography of his great-grandmother: *Lucie Duff Gordon in England, South Africa and Egypt*. And in 1969, a hundred years after Lucie's death, he brought out a new edition of her *Letters from Egypt* which contains a great deal of material that had been omitted in earlier editions.

★

When I met Gordon Waterfield at his home in Kent in July 1987, he gave me a copy of his life of Lucie, which by then was long out of print. Janet Ross's 1902 edition of *Letters from Egypt* had recently been reprinted by Virago and there was talk of reissuing the biography too. But Gordon Waterfield generously told me he wouldn't pursue bringing it out again if I wanted to do a new life. After our meeting, I returned to West Africa where I then lived, but we corresponded over the next five months until he died, at the age of eighty-four, the following December. A year later, in the winter of 1988, after I had been to Egypt for the first time, just a month after my husband's death, I found the photograph of Lucie's grave among Gordon Waterfield's papers in Kent. But it was too late to ask him where it was.

I returned to Egypt in 1989 and spent days combing the cemeteries of Cairo for Lucie's grave. I knew from documents that her grave was number 482, next to that of her friend William Thayer, in what was variously called in the records the English, European, Christian or Protestant Cemetery in Old Cairo. So I began my search in Old Cairo, in the British, Commonwealth and American cemeteries there. When I failed to find Lucie's large granite monument in any of these (none had graves dating before the 1890s), I searched every other Christian cemetery in the city – Coptic, Greek Orthodox, Protestant, Roman Catholic, in areas far from Old Cairo, which Europeans seldom visited. Inevitably, I came upon many funerals and many widows. Eventually I appealed to the Bishop of Cairo and the Cairo British Council for help, and later still I wrote to historians of Cairo and urban geographers about Lucie's grave. I even put author's queries in various newspapers and magazines. All to no avail. Though I found so many other graves in Egypt – a country that with all its mortuary monuments seems one vast cemetery – I never found Lucie's.

But for a long time, I kept looking. Each time I returned to Cairo, I visited and revisited the cemeteries of the city. The search became for me a kind of metaphor of writing biography: a tenacious and intermittently inspired pursuit of the dead. But it was more than that too. I was driven, like Isis, by something beyond my control. I ached for the past – for those I could no longer touch or see. I longed for some tangible proof of their death – and life – something beyond absence and desire.

Only when I was close to finishing the book did I abandon the search. Not because it was fruitless, though it did become pointless after I exhausted all the possibilities and discovered what churches and likely cemeteries had been destroyed to build flyovers and office blocks in Cairo. In the end, I realized that it was better not to find Lucie's grave, for, if I did, it would signal some sort of completion – a death, in fact – and the end of my re-membering.

I understood now that however much we yearn to possess the past, it is not of our creation. Our re-memberings are partial – versions crafted of collected fragments – and this means the pursuit is never finished. Yet the past is real and true, however fragmentarily we recover it. Above all, it is not over. It is down there in the pool of time, and we sit on the shore and cast our lines, sometimes catching rare moments – epiphanies – sometimes reeling back only the hook of desire. Sometimes glimpsing, in shadowy depths, the faint but iridescent light of resurrection.

Notes

The most important sources for this book have been unpublished letters, manuscripts and documents, many of them still in private hands, and also my own travels in Egypt. Lucie Duff Gordon's letters from the Cape and from Egypt have been published in numerous editions from 1864 to the present, but none of these is complete, and they do not include any of the letters that she wrote before she went to South Africa in 1861. My references to her letters are not to published editions, but to the originals when these have survived and to handwritten transcripts of the originals. Lucie's daughter, Janet Ross, had all her mother's letters transcribed when she began work in the 1880s on *Three Generations of Englishwomen*, a biographical study of Susannah Taylor, Sarah Austin and Lucie Duff Gordon which was published in 1888. In addition to Lucie Duff Gordon's own correspondence, *Three Generations of Englishwomen* contains a mass of letters written by and to Susannah Taylor and Sarah Austin, and a few of John Austin's letters. After Janet Ross's death in 1927, most of the original Austin letters and a good many of Lucie's disappeared, probably when Janet's home in Italy was occupied during World War II. Fortunately, the transcripts of Lucie's letters survived, though it becomes clear when comparing them with surviving manuscript letters that Janet Ross sometimes censored and omitted passages when the letters were transcribed. She also effaced passages in the originals with black ink and glued pieces of paper over other sections. Some, but not all, of these passages I've been able to decipher. The Austin letters published in *Three Generations of Englishwomen* are also probably bowdlerized. Both the surviving original letters and the handwritten transcripts now belong to Lucie Duff Gordon's great-granddaughter, Kinta Beevor.

In the following notes I refer to unpublished material, but place a greater emphasis on books and articles that the interested reader can more easily pursue. Full publication information for these, including that for Lucie Duff Gordon's own books, is given in the Bibliography. The following abbreviations are used for frequently cited names and works in the Notes:

ADG	Alexander Duff Gordon
Beevor	Papers belonging to Kinta Beevor
Bowood	The archives of the Earl of Shelburne, Bowood House
CA	Lotte and Joseph Hamburger, *Contemplating Adultery*
DH	Papers belonging to Sir Andrew Duff Gordon, Downton House
FG	Janet Ross, *The Fourth Generation*
GW	Gordon Waterfield, *Lucie Duff Gordon in England, South Africa and Egypt*
JA	John Austin
JM	The John Murray Archives
JR	Janet Ross
Laughton	John Knox Laughton, *Memoirs of the Life and Correspondence of Henry Reeve*
LDG	Lucie Duff Gordon
PJD	Sarah Austin, Preface to *The Province of Jurisprudence Determined*
SA	Sarah Austin
TG	Janet Ross, *Three Generations of Englishwomen*
TL	Lotte and Joseph Hamburger, *Troubled Lives*

Chapter One

The day and circumstances of Lucie's birth are described in an unpublished letter written by Henry Reeve in 1873 to Janet Ross (Beevor) and also in Volume I of Laughton. For many years, JA's Malta diary and his written proposal of marriage to Sarah Taylor belonged to their descendants, but the location of both is now unknown. Gordon Waterfield had access to them when he wrote his 1937 biography of LDG and quotes liberally from both. The Austins' marriage settlement is at DH. *TG* is the major source of information for the Taylor family, the Austins, and SA and JA. Lotte and Joseph Hamburger have written two biographical studies of John and Sarah Austin: *TL* and *CA*, which contain a great deal of information about the families, courtship, marriage, and judicial and writing careers of the Austins. George and Harriet Grote both have long entries in the *Dictionary of National Biography*. Elizabeth Eastlake published a memoir of Harriet Grote in 1880.

Chapter Two

Susannah Taylor's letter to SA is in *TG*. The information on John Stuart Mill comes from *TG*, *The Earlier Letters of John Stuart Mill*, Michael St John Packe's biography of John Stuart Mill and Bruce Mazlish's *James and John Stuart Mill*. SA's letter to her mother is published in *TG*, as are all subsequent letters written by SA, unless otherwise indicated. Most of the information on Lucie's childhood in this and the following chapters comes from *TG*. Lucie's friendship with Bentham is described in GW. SA's description of JA's working habits comes from her biographical preface to his *PJD* which SA edited and published after his death. The Austins' decision to have only one child is discussed in *CA*. JA's December 1827 letter to George Grote is quoted in *TG*. Henry Crabb Robinson's account of JA's inaugural lecture at London University is quoted in *TL*. JA's letter to SA written during his solo holiday in Sussex is quoted in GW. Phyllis Rose's *Parallel Lives* contains an illuminating chapter on the relationship of Harriet Taylor and John Stuart Mill. Most of the information on JA's chequered professional career and his writing is drawn from *TL*. The description of Lucie as 'really remarkable' and 'excessively odd' is quoted in Una Taylor's *Guests and Memories*. The letters exchanged between SA and Pückler-Muskau and Lucie's letters to Pückler are now at the Jagiellonian University Library in Cracow, Poland. My quotations are from the originals. SA's reflections on JA's academic career come from *PJD*. Information on the Carlyles comes from *The Collected Letters of Thomas and Jane Welsh Carlyle* and Fred Kaplan's biography of Carlyle.

Chapter Three

Bentham's letter to SA is in *TG*. Sydney Smith's reflections on the Reform Bill are in an unpublished letter to SA. Photocopies of Sydney Smith's letters to SA are in the Beevor papers. Lucie's letters to Alice Spring-Rice are among Henry Taylor's papers in the Bodleian Library, Oxford. Alice Spring-Rice's diary is quoted in GW. Both the Heine episode and the wreck of the *Amphitrite* come from *TG*. SA's letter to *The Times* about the *Amphitrite* wreck is quoted in *CA*. Carlyle's instructions for house-hunting come from Volume 5 of *The Collected Letters of Thomas and Jane Welsh Carlyle*, as does Carlyle's description of JA as acidified. Marianne North describes Lucie as a girl in *Recollections of a Happy Life*. SA describes JA's panic attacks in *PJD*. SA's breakdown in the spring of 1835 is discussed in *CA*; her letter to John Murray is in the JM Archives, London. Lucie's description of her departure from Boulogne and the stormy crossing to England comes from a letter she wrote to Janet Shuttleworth dated 12.10.36. The original is lost; this is one of the first transcribed letters that JR had made when she was about to start writing *TG*. All subsequent quotations from Lucie's letters, unless otherwise indicated, are either from the original manuscripts or from the transcribed copies (Beevor).

Chapter Four

The educational programme at Miss Shepherd's school is discussed in GW. Janet Shuttleworth's diary entry on Lucie at Miss Shepherd's is quoted in *TG*. Henry Reeve's impressions of Lucie's 'improvement' at Miss Shepherd's come from Laughton.

The description of Lucie at the Seniors' comes from M. C. M. Simpson's *Many Memories of Many People*. Henry Reeve's letter to his mother describing Bowood is quoted in Laughton. The most recent biography of Caroline Norton is Alan Chedzoy's *A Scandalous Woman*. Unfortunately, though Lucie and Caroline Norton were intimate friends over a number of years, very few of their letters have survived. In *Castle in Italy*, Lina Waterfield tells of Georgina and Alice Duff Gordon's lifelong habit of sharing a single egg for breakfast. Lady Duff Gordon's voluminous diaries are now partly at Sir Andrew Duff Gordon's home, Downton House, in Wales, and partly at the National Library of Wales, Aberystwyth. ADG's proposal to Lucie is described in *TG*. Lucie's and ADG's manuscript letters to JA when he was so dismayed by their wish to marry have not before been published, nor did Janet Ross have them transcribed (Beevor). Lucie and ADG's visit to the Norths in Lancashire is described in Marianne North's *Recollections of a Happy Life*. The Richmond fire episode comes from Henry Reeve's diary in Laughton. Lucie and ADG's wedding is described in Henry Reeve's unpublished 1873 letter to Janet Ross (Beevor).

Chapter Five

Tennyson's offer to be a footstool for LDG comes from Ralph Waldo Emerson's *Journals*. His outburst to ADG is quoted in GW. The information on Samuel Rogers and his Sunday morning breakfasts comes from Alethea Hayter's *A Sultry Month* and GW. LDG on children comes from an unpublished biography of JR by Gordon Waterfield (Beevor). SA's description of herself as the most foolish of grandmothers is quoted in *TG*. Kinglake's description of LDG comes from a letter he wrote to JR and is quoted in *FG*. LDG's letters to her publisher John Murray are in the JM Archives. The information on the Nubian boy, Hassan, comes from *FG*. The American writer's and the maid's hostility to him are recounted in GW.

LDG's letter to Lord Lansdowne about her baby's death and all LDG's subsequent letters to Lord Lansdowne are in the archives of the Earl of Shelburne at Bowood. LDG's letter to Kinglake is quoted in Gordon Waterfield's unpublished biography of JR.

Chapter Six

All the information on the Brookfields in this chapter comes from Charles and Frances Brookfield's *Mrs Brookfield and Her Circle* and from Ann Monsarrat's *Thackeray*. Details of LDG's negotiations with John Murray, her earnings and sales figures are in the JM Archives. Melbourne's behaviour at Dickens's production of *Everyman in His Humour* is described in Laughton. Young Janet Duff Gordon's exasperation with Peel and the Corn Laws comes from FG. The heat-wave of the summer of 1846 and Gräfin Hahn-Hahn and Baron von Bystram's colourful visit to London are wonderfully described in Alethea Hayter's *A Sultry Month*. ADG's nearly fatal bout of cholera comes from FG. Janet's fifth birthday party, her refusal to believe that Mrs Grote was ever beautiful and her run-ins with Carlyle and Tennyson all come from FG. The threatened duel between John Forster and Thackeray is recounted in Ann Monsarrat's *Thackeray*. LDG's resemblance to Prince Pierre Buonaparte is described in FG. The account of Tennyson's dinner party for the Duff Gordons and the Brookfields comes from Volume I of Tennyson's *Letters*. Emily Eden's description of LDG at Bowood comes from Emily Eden's *Letters*. Guizot's flight to England and welcome at Queen Square and Ranke's visit are both described in FG. LDG's letter to Alice Taylor is at the Bodleian Library, Oxford.

Chapter Seven

Thackeray's description of LDG's 'tawdry rainbow gown' comes from his *Letters*. The information on Mary Ellen and

George Meredith comes from Diane Johnson's *The True History of the First Mrs Meredith and Other Lesser Lives*. The account of LDG's illness in 1851 is drawn from *TG* and unpublished letters. The idea that illness is 'the nightside of life' is explored in Susan Sontag's *Illness as Metaphor*. Thackeray's verse directive to LDG is quoted in GW. ADG's letters to his mother are among the Beevor papers. The account of the christening of the Tennysons' first child comes from Emily Tennyson's *Journal* and Robert Bernard Martin's biography of Tennyson. The information on Janet's education (or lack thereof) comes from *FG*. SA's letters to Lord Lansdowne are, like LDG's, at Bowood. The quotation about 'lesser lives' comes from Diane Johnson's life of Mary Ellen Meredith.

Chapter Eight

Emily Eden recorded her distaste for India in her book, *Up the Country*, published in 1866. The information on Azimullah Khan, Nana Sahib and events at Cawnpore in 1857 comes from a variety of sources: LDG's letters, Lady Duff Gordon's diary, contemporary newspaper accounts, books by the handful of survivors of the siege such as Mowbray Thomson's *The Story of Cawnpore*, and more recent studies such as P. C. Gupta's *Nana Sahib and the Rising at Cawnpore*. Lady Duff Gordon's criticism of her granddaughter was recorded in her diary. LDG's reunion with the dying Heine comes from *TG*. The Christmas houseparty at The Grange, Jane Carlyle's discontent and Tennyson's recitation of *Maud* are described in Martin's biography of Tennyson. The details of ADG's career as a Commissioner of the Inland Revenue come from Inland Revenue records, Lady Duff Gordon's diary and *FG*. LDG's letter to Henry Layard is in the British Library. JR tells of how George Meredith re-entered the Duff Gordons' lives in 1858 in *FG*. Janet's visit to the Tennysons at Freshwater also comes from *FG*. Urania Duff Gordon's birth is described in detail in Lady

Duff Gordon's diary. Janet's presentation at court and the Great Marlow inn episode are both described in *FG*, which is also the source for LDG's vigil at JA's deathbed. LDG's speech to the 6th Surrey Rifles is described in *GW*. Janet's courtship and marriage to Henry Ross comes from *FG* and Gordon Waterfield's unpublished biography of JR. Lady Duff Gordon's agitation over Janet's approaching marriage was recorded in her diary. JR's description of her wedding comes from *FG*. George Meredith's account of LDG to JR comes from Volume I of his *Letters*. The days before LDG sailed for the Cape and her departure are described in Lady Duff Gordon's diary.

Chapter Nine

This chapter consists of excerpts from LDG's letters to ADG written between July 1861 and May 1862, covering her voyage to, stay in and return from the Cape. There have been three published editions of LDG's letters from the Cape: the first, edited by Sarah Austin, was published by F. Galton in 1864 in a 'Vacation Tourists' series. In 1875, Macmillan published LDG's *Last Letters from Egypt*, to which are added *Letters from the Cape*, edited by Janet Ross. In 1927, Oxford University Press published *Letters from the Cape*, edited and annotated by Dorothea Fairbridge. None of these editions contains all the Cape letters and they are now out of print. The various editors of *Letters from the Cape* have all to some degree omitted personal passages in the letters and virtually all references to LDG's health. In fashioning this chapter, I have drawn upon the manuscript and transcribed letters rather than printed editions. But I, too, of course have cut the letters drastically: first by excluding LDG's letters to her mother and to her close friends, and more importantly by giving her illness the central place it has in her original letters. I have also chosen passages which seem to foreshadow her experience in Egypt – in particular her growing interest in and sympathy for Islam.

Chapter Ten

All of LDG's letters from Egypt in this and the following chapters are taken from the originals or the transcribed copies (Beevor). The most complete edition of *Letters from Egypt* is Gordon Waterfield's, published in 1969, which has a long, informative introduction and useful explanatory footnotes. It, however, still omits a good deal of material and often runs together letters written on different dates in order to create the effect of a continuous travelogue. Michael Bird's *Samuel Shepheard of Cairo* provides an interesting history of Cairo's most famous hotel and its colourful gallery of guests in the nineteenth century. Afaf Lufti Al-Sayyid Marsot's *A Short History of Modern Egypt* discusses Mohammed Ali's and Ismail Pasha's strenuous efforts to modernize Egypt.

Chapter Eleven

The description of the congested village inside Luxor Temple comes from Amelia Edwards's *A Thousand Miles up the Nile*, as does the observation that the magnificent views from LDG's house made its poverty splendid. LDG says very little in her letters about ADG's visit to Egypt in late 1864. ADG himself wrote an article for *Macmillan's Magazine*, 'A Trip to the Isthmus of Suez' (May 1865), about his excursion with JR to the Red Sea. Lady Duff Gordon's diary and FG contain more information about his brief and apparently not very enjoyable sojourn in Egypt.

Chapter Twelve

In her diary, Lady Duff Gordon approved of LDG's desire to 'turn her maid off'. Between 1865 and 1868, LDG published seven letters from Egypt in *Macmillan's Magazine*: 'Masr-el-Kahira', January 1865; 'Extracts from Lady Duff Gordon's

Letters from Egypt', March 1865; 'Letter from Egypt', December 1865; 'On the Nile', May 1866; 'Longshore Life at Boulak', March 1867; 'Life at Thebes', August 1867; 'Life at Thebes', June 1868. Prévost-Paradol's fulsome description of LDG in Egypt is taken from *TG*. After *Letters from Egypt* was published in June 1865, it was widely reviewed both in newspapers and weekly, fortnightly and monthly magazines and reviews. The three most interesting notices appeared in *Fraser's Magazine*, the *Edinburgh Review* and the *Westminster Review*, all of which praised the depth of LDG's understanding of contemporary Egyptian life. LDG's reunion with ADG and the children in Soden in the summer of 1865 and her burst blood-vessel and severe haemorrhage were all recorded in Lady Duff Gordon's diary.

Chapter Thirteen

The account of the Norths' stay with LDG in Luxor comes from Marianne North's *Recollections of a Happy Life*. Palgrave published 'A Visit to Upper Egypt in the Hot Season' in the November 1866 issue of *Macmillan's Magazine*. Years after LDG's death, JR wrote in a letter to a friend that Ismail Pasha had tried to bribe LDG's crew to drown her (Beevor). Edward Lear's visit to Luxor is described in Vivien Noakes's *Edward Lear*. JR published her letter to ADG describing the Rosses' visit to Luxor in *FG*.

Chapter Fourteen

All the information about Maurice's bout of venereal disease, his womanizing and Joseph Soubre comes from the surviving manuscript letters LDG wrote from Egypt. JR did not have the passages of the letters dealing with these things transcribed and, as indicated in the footnotes, she effaced some of them with black ink and glued on slips of paper. All of the information about Lucie's last few days, death and funeral comes from a long letter that Emma Matthews wrote a month after LDG's death to Charlotte Austin (Beevor). Hekekyan Bey sent a briefer account of the funeral to ADG, which is now in the British Library.

Epilogue

Information on Mustafa Agha comes from *Who Was Who in Egyptology*. ADG's terminal illness and Maurice Duff Gordon's courtship and marriage to Fanny Ball Hughes are described in Lady Duff Gordon's diary and Lina Waterfield's *Castle in Italy*. Holloway Sanatorium was closed in 1979; the details of Maurice Duff Gordon's admission to and treatment at the sanatorium and his death there in 1896 are now in the archives of the Surrey Record Office. Lina Duff Gordon's childhood is described in *Castle in Italy*. JR wrote at length of her return to Egypt in 1903 in *FG*.

Bibliography

The Bibliography includes only published works. Details of manuscript sources, upon which the book is largely based, are given in the chapter reference notes.

Primary Sources

Austin, John, *The Province of Jurisprudence Determined*, edited and with a preface by Sarah Austin; London: John Murray, 1861.

Duff Gordon, Alexander, 'A Trip to the Isthmus of Suez'; *Macmillan's Magazine*, March 1865.

Duff Gordon, Lucie (trans.), *Ferdinand I and Maximilian II of Austria or A View of the Religion and Political State of Germany after the Reformation* by Leopold von Ranke; London: Longman, Brown, Green and Longmans, 1853.

(trans.), *The French in Algiers* by M. de France and Clemens Lamping; London: John Murray, 1845.

(trans.), *The History and Literature of the Crusades* by H. C. L. von Sybel; London: Chapman & Hall, 1861.

Last Letters from Egypt to which are added *Letters from the Cape*, ed. Janet Ross; London: Macmillan, 1875.

Letters from the Cape; London: F. Galton, 1864.

Letters from the Cape, annotated by Dorothea Fairbridge with an introduction by Janet Ross; London: Oxford University Press, 1927.

Letters from Egypt, 1863–1865, ed. Sarah Austin; London: Macmillan, 1865.

Letters from Egypt, revised and with a memoir by Janet Ross and a new introduction by George Meredith; London: R. Brimley Johnson, 1902.

Letters from Egypt, ed. Gordon Waterfield; London: Routledge and Kegan Paul, 1969.

Letters from Egypt; London: Virago, 1983. (Reprint of 1902 edition.)

(trans.), *Mary Schweidler: The Amber Witch* by W. Meinhold; London: John Murray, 1844.

(trans. with Alexander Duff Gordon), *Memoirs of the House of Brandenburg and History of Prussia* by Leopold Ranke; London: John Murray, 1849.

(trans.), *Narratives of Remarkable Criminal Trials* by Anselm Ritter Von Feuerbach; London: John Murray, 1846.

(trans.), *The Russians in Bulgaria and Rumelia* by Count Helmuth von Moltke; London: John Murray, 1854.

(trans.), *Stella and Vanessa: A Romance from the French* by Leon de Wailly; London: Richard Bentley, 1850.

(trans.), *Stories of the Gods and Heroes of Greece* by Berthold Niebuhr; London: John W. Parker, 1843.

(trans.), *The Village Doctor* by Countess Sophie D'Arbouville; London: Chapman and Hall, 1853.

Ross, Janet, *Early Days Recalled*; London: Chapman and Hall, 1891.

The Fourth Generation; London: Constable, 1912.

Three Generations of Englishwomen; London: John Murray, 1888.

Waterfield, Gordon, *Lucie Duff Gordon in England, South Africa and Egypt*; London: John Murray, 1937.

Waterfield, Lina, *Castle in Italy*; London: John Murray, 1961.

Secondary Sources

Acland, Alice, *Caroline Norton*; London: Constable, 1948.

Ahmed, Leila, *Edward W. Lane*; London: Longman, 1978.

Bird, Michael, *Samuel Shepheard of Cairo*; London: Michael Joseph, 1957.

Blanch, Lesley, *The Wilder Shores of Love*; 1954; reprinted London: Abacus, 1987.

Brookfield, Charles and Frances, *Mrs Brookfield and Her Circle*; London: Sir Isaac Pitman and Sons, 1905.

Butler, E. M., *The Tempestuous Prince: Hermann Pückler-Muskau*; London: Longmans, Green and Co., 1929.

Carlyle, Thomas and Jane Welsh, *The Collected Letters of Thomas and*

Jane Welsh Carlyle, ed. Charles Richard Sanders and Kenneth J. Fielding; Durham, North Carolina: Duke University Press, 1977.

Chedzoy, Alan, *A Scandalous Woman: The Story of Caroline Norton*; London: Allison and Busby, 1992.

Dawson, Warren and Eric P. Uphill, *Who Was Who in Egyptology*; London: The Egypt Exploration Society, 1972.

De Gaury, Gerald, *Travelling Gent: The Life of Alexander Kinglake*; London: Routledge and Kegan Paul, 1972.

Eastlake, Elizabeth, *Mrs Grote*; London: John Murray, 1880.

Eden, Emily, *Miss Eden's Letters*, ed. Violet Dickinson; London: Macmillan, 1919.

Edwards, Amelia, *A Thousand Miles up the Nile*; 1877; reprinted London: Century, 1982.

Emerson, Ralph Waldo, *The Journals and Miscellaneous Notebooks of Ralph Waldo Emerson*, ed. Merton M. Sealts; Cambridge, Massachusetts: Harvard University Press, 1973.

Festing, Sally, *Gertrude Jekyll*; London: Viking, 1991.

Flaubert, Gustave, *Flaubert in Egypt: A Sensibility on Tour*, ed. Francis Steegmuller; Boston: Little Brown, 1972.

Foster, Shirley, *Across New Worlds: Nineteenth-Century Women Travellers and Their Writings*; Hemel Hempstead: Harvester Wheatsheaf, 1990.

Gupta, Pratul Chandra, *Nana Sahib and the Rising at Cawnpore*; Oxford: Clarendon Press, 1963.

Hamburger, Lotte and Joseph, *Contemplating Adultery: The Secret Life of a Victorian Woman*; New York: Fawcett Columbine, 1991.

 Troubled Lives: John and Sarah Austin; Toronto: University of Toronto Press, 1985.

Hanson, Lawrence and Elizabeth, *Necessary Evil: The Life of Jane Welsh Carlyle*; London: Constable, 1952.

Hayter, Alethea, *A Sultry Month: Scenes of London Literary Life in 1846*; 1965; reprinted London: Robin Clark, 1992.

James, T. G. H., *The British Museum and Ancient Egypt*; London: British Museum Publications, 1981.

Johnson, Diane, *The True History of the First Mrs Meredith and Other Lesser Lives*; London: Heinemann, 1973.

Kaplan, Fred, *Thomas Carlyle: A Biography*; Ithaca, New York: Cornell University Press, 1983.

Kinglake, Alexander, *Eothen: Traces of Travel Brought Home from the East*, 1844; reprinted Oxford: Oxford University Press, 1982.

'The Rights of Women'; *Quarterly Review*, December 1844.

Lane, Edward, *Manners and Customs of Modern Egyptians*, 1836; reprinted London: East-West Publications, 1981.

Laughton, John Knox, *Memoirs of the Life and Correspondence of Henry Reeve*; London: Longmans, Green and Co., 1898.

Lott, Emmeline, *The English Governess in Egypt: Harem Life in Egypt and Constantinople*; London: Richard Bentley, 1866.

The Grand Pacha's Cruise on the Nile in the Viceroy of Egypt's Yacht; London: T. Cautley Newby, 1869.

Nights in the Harem: Or the Mohaddetyn in the Palace of Ghezire; London: Chapman and Hall, 1867.

Manniche, Lise, *City of the Dead: Thebes in Egypt*; London: British Museum Publications, 1987.

Marsot, Afaf Lufti Al-Sayyid, *A Short History of Modern Egypt*; Cambridge: Cambridge University Press, 1985.

Martin, Robert Bernard, *Tennyson: The Unquiet Heart*; Oxford: Clarendon Press, 1983.

Mazlish, Bruce, *James and John Stuart Mill: Father and Son in the Nineteenth Century*; London: Hutchinson, 1975.

Melman, Billie, *Women's Orients: English Women and the Middle East, 1718–1918*; London: Macmillan, 1992.

Meredith, George, *Diana of the Crossways*, 1885; reprinted London: Virago, 1980.

Evan Harrington, 1861; reprinted London: The Boydell Press, 1983.

The Letters of George Meredith, ed. C. L. Cline, Oxford: Clarendon Press, 1970.

Mill, John Stuart, *The Earlier Letters of John Stuart Mill*, ed. Francis E. Mineka; London: Routledge and Kegan Paul, 1963.

Mills, Sara, *Discourses of Difference: An Analysis of Women's Travel Writing and Colonialism*; London: Routledge, 1991.

Monsarrat, Ann, *Thackeray: An Uneasy Victorian*; London: Cassell, 1980.

Nightingale, Florence, *Letters from Egypt: A Journey on the Nile*; London: Barrie and Jenkins, 1987.

Noakes, Vivien, *Edward Lear*; London: Fontana, 1979.

North, Marianne, *Recollections of a Happy Life*, ed. Mrs John Addington Symonds; London: Macmillan, 1892.

Some Further Recollections of a Happy Life, ed. Mrs John Addington Symonds; London: Macmillan, 1893.

Norton, Caroline, 'Lady Duff Gordon and Her Works'; *Macmillan's Magazine*, September 1869.

The Letters of Caroline Norton to Lord Melbourne, ed. James O. Hoge and Clarke Olney; Columbus, Ohio: Ohio State University Press, 1974.

Packe, Michael St John, *The Life of John Stuart Mill*; London: Secker and Warburg, 1954.

Palgrave, William Gifford, 'A Visit to Upper Egypt in the Hot Season'; *Macmillan's Magazine*, November 1866.

Poole, Sophia, *The Englishwoman in Egypt: Letters from Cairo*; London: Charles Knight and Co., 1844.

Pratt, Mary Louise, *Imperial Eyes: Travel Writing and Transculturation*; London: Routledge, 1992.

Ray, Gordon, *Thackeray: The Age of Wisdom*; Oxford: Oxford University Press, 1958.

Rose, Phyllis, *Parallel Lives: Five Victorian Marriages*; London: Chatto and Windus, 1984.

Sattin, Anthony, *Lifting the Veil: British Society in Egypt 1768–1956*; London: Dent, 1988.

Simpson, M. C. M., *Many Memories of Many People*; London: Edward Arnold, 1898.

Sontag, Susan, *Illness as Metaphor*; Harmondsworth: Penguin, 1983.

Spencer, A. J., *Death in Ancient Egypt*; Harmondsworth: Penguin, 1982.

Stevenson, Lionel, *The Ordeal of George Meredith*; London: Peter Owen, 1954.

Taylor, Una, *Guests and Memories*; Oxford: Oxford University Press, 1924.

Tennyson, Emily, *Lady Tennyson's Journal*, ed. James O. Hoge; Charlottesville: University Press of Virginia, 1981.

Thackeray, William Makepeace, *The Letters of William Makepeace Thackeray*, ed. Gordon Ray; Cambridge, Massachusetts: Harvard University Press, 1946.

Thomson, Mowbray, *The Story of Cawnpore*; London: Richard Bentley, 1859.

Trevelyan, George, *Cawnpore*; London: Macmillan, 1899.

Yalland, Zoë, *Traders and Nabobs: The British in Cawnpore 1765–1857;* Salisbury: Michael Russell, 1877.

Index